THE SPACIOUS WORD

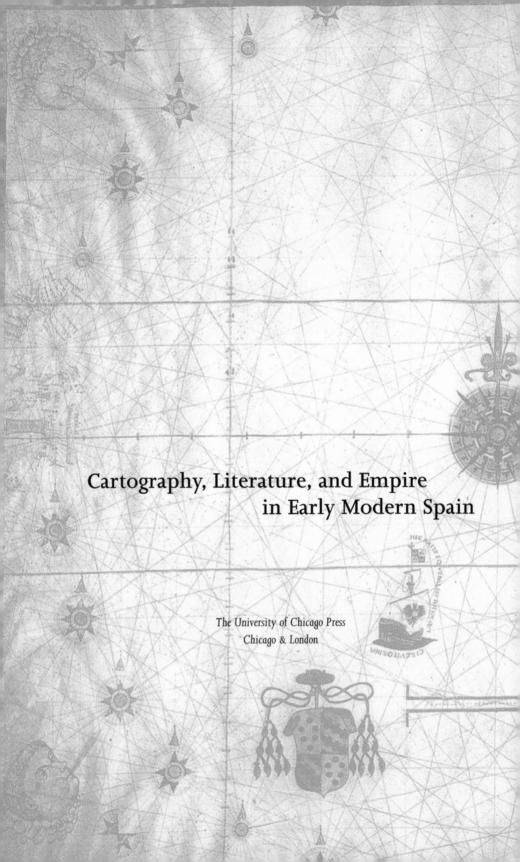

Cartography, Literature, and Empire
in Early Modern Spain

The University of Chicago Press
Chicago & London

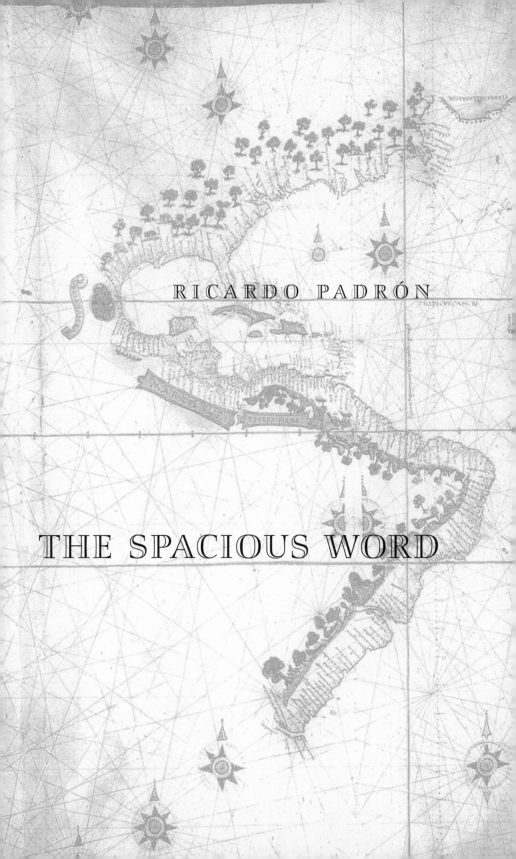

RICARDO PADRÓN

THE SPACIOUS WORD

Ricardo Padrón is assistant professor of Spanish at the University of Virginia.

The University of Chicago Press, Chicago 60637
The University of Chicago Press, Ltd., London
© 2004 by The University of Chicago
All rights reserved. Published 2004
Printed in the United States of America
13 12 11 10 09 08 07 06 05 04   1 2 3 4 5
ISBN: 0-226-64433-2 (cloth)

The University of Chicago Press gratefully acknowledges the generous support of the Program for Cultural Cooperation Between Spain's Ministry of Education, Culture and Sports and United States Universities toward the publication of this book.

Title page illustration: Nuno Garcia de Toreno, detail from Planisphere (1525). For complete source information, please see the caption to figure 27 on page 133 below.

Library of Congress Cataloging-in-Publication Data

Padrón, Ricardo, 1946–
    The spacious word : cartography, literature, and empire in early modern Spain / Ricardo Padrón.
    p. cm.
    Includes bibliographical references and index.
    ISBN 0-226-64433-2 (cloth : alk. paper)
    1. Cartography—Spain—History—To 1500.   2. Cartography—Spain—History—16th century.
3. Spain—History—711-1516.   4. Spain—History—House of Austria, 1516–1700.   I. Title.
GA1003.3 .P33 2004
526'.0946—dc22   2003015707

♾ The paper used in this publication meets the minimum requirements of the American National Standard for Information Sciences—Permanence of Paper for Printed Library Materials, ANSI Z39.48-1992.

FOR ZOË

CONTENTS

ILLUSTRATIONS

ACKNOWLEDGMENTS

The reading and writing that went into this book unfolded in a variety of places, on both sides of the Atlantic and of the Mason-Dixon Line, where I benefited from the generosity and expertise of numerous individuals. I would like to express my gratitude for their assistance. The project has its roots in a graduate seminar at Harvard University, in which Doris Sommer encouraged me to pursue my nascent interest in cartography and literature. This book would not have happened had she not supported my pursuit of what may have seemed like an oddball idea. My work on cartography and literature continued as a dissertation written under the kind but rigorous guidance of Mary Gaylord and Tom Conley, who have continued to provide inspiration and friendship. The dissertation was transformed into a very different book while I served on the Spanish faculty of my undergraduate alma mater, the University of Virginia. I want to thank all of my ever amiable colleagues in the Department of Spanish, Italian, and Portuguese for their unfaltering advice and support. Thanks in particular to Javier Herrero, Ruth Hill, Gustavo Pellón, Randolph Pope, and Alison Weber, all of whom commented upon earlier versions of the material here. Thanks, too, to Michael Gerli and David Gies, for their sage advice and moral support. My gratitude extends beyond the grounds of the University of Virginia as well, particularly to David Buisseret, Margaret Greer, John Hebert, Richard Kagan, Walter Mignolo, Ignacio Navarrete, Francisco Ortega, and Alison Sandman, all of whom provided valuable insights and assistance at different points in the development of the project. I would also like to thank those who participated in the various conference panels at which some of this material has appeared for their attention, their questions, and their suggestions.

This book could not have been written without drawing upon the resources of many institutions, in particular, the expertise of their staff. The early work was carried out within the walls of Widener, Pusey, and Houghton Libraries at Harvard University as well as at the John Carter Brown Library in Providence, Rhode Island. I continued my work at the University of Virginia Library, particularly at the Albert and Shirley Small Special Collections Library there. Along the way, I had the opportunity to travel twice to Spain. Through the generosity of the Real Colegio Complutense of Cambridge, Massachusetts, and the Department of Romance Languages and Literatures at Harvard, I had the opportunity to visit the Archivo General de Indias in Seville, Spain, where I made what I consider to be some of the most important insights of my entire argument. Later, through a summer-study grant from the University of Virginia and a travel grant from the Program for Cultural Cooperation between Spain's Ministry of Culture and United States Universities, I was able to spend some time at the Biblioteca Nacional in Madrid. Finally, I had the time I needed to assemble the final manuscript thanks to sabbatical-year funding from the University of Virginia, particularly the dean of Arts and Sciences, and from the American Council of Learned Societies, who made it possible for me to spend several months as a Library of Congress Fellow in International Studies. I have also drawn upon the resources and expertise of the Artists' Rights Society, the Biblioteca Medicea Laurenziana, the British Library, and the University of Texas Library. I would like to express my sincere gratitude to the staffs of all of these institutions, particularly those who helped me identify difficult-to-find materials, and those who eased the onerous task of assembling the illustrations. Thanks especially to the John Carter Brown Library; the University of Virginia Library; the Spanish Ministry of Education, Culture, and Sport; the Nettie Lee Benson Latin American Collection of the University of Texas Library; the Saul Steinberg Foundation; the British Library; and the Italian Ministry of Cultural Treasures and Activities. Special thanks go to Susan Danforth of the John Carter Brown Library, Prosser Giffford and Les Vogel of the John W. Kluge Center of the Library of Congress, John Hebert and Anthony Mullan of the Geography and Map Division of the Library of Congress, and Michael Plunkett of the Albert and Shirley Small Special Collections Library.

Portions of chapter 2 appeared previously as "Mapping Plus Ultra: Cartography, Space, and Hispanic Modernity," *Representations* 79 (2002): 28–60. Portions of chapter 4 appeared in "Charting Empire, Charting Difference: Gómara's *Historia general de las Indias* and Spanish Maritime Cartography," *Colonial*

Latin American Review 11, no. 1 (2002): 47–69 (http://www.tandf.co.uk). Portions of chapter 5 appeared in "Love American Style: The Virgin Land and the Sodomitic Body in Ercilla's *Araucana*," *Revista de Estudios Hispánicos* 34 (2000): 563–86. My thanks to the University of California Press, Francis Taylor Publishing, and the *Revista de Estudios Hispánicos* for permission to reprint these materials. Thanks to the John Carter Brown Library, the University of Virginia Library, the Spanish Ministry of Education, Culture, and Sport, the Nettie Lee Benson Latin American Collection of the University of Texas Library, the Saul Steinberg Foundation, the British Library, and the Italian Ministry of Cultural Treasures and Activities for permission to reproduce illustrations in their collections.

Special thanks go to my editor at the University of Chicago Press, Randolph Petilos, whose advice and unflagging enthusiasm have helped a great deal to see me through the process of publication. Thanks also to Laura A. Leavitt, who indexed the book.

Finally, I am forever indebted to my family, and particularly to my wife and friend Zoë and my son Santiago, who have patiently endured living with *The Spacious Word* for much too long. Thanks to Santiago for letting me cover the walls of his playroom with maps, and to Zoë for turning a critical eye toward my ideas and my prose, for putting up with my half-baked rantings about maps and books, particularly when they came after a long day at work, and for supporting me in my efforts, in countless ways, from beginning to end.

NOTE ON SPANISH USAGE AND TRANSLATION

All translations from Spanish are my own unless otherwise noted. No attempt has been made to mimic antiquated spelling, capitalization, or punctuation with English equivalents. Original Spanish text is provided only for long citations of poetry, since I have translated these passages into the poor substitute of prose. References to Hispanic authors by surname alone follow conventions standard in the Spanish-speaking world. When an author's first surname is exceedingly common, I have dropped it and used the second surname alone. Thus, "Francisco López de Gómara" becomes "Gómara," not "López." In some cases, where reference to an author by a single surname has not become commonplace, I have preserved both surnames. Thus "Juan López de Velasco" appears as "López de Velasco." In every case, however, the author's work appears in the bibliography according the place determined by the first surname. Thus, Gómara's *Historia general de las Indias* appears under "López de Gómara," not "Gómara." In-text citations use both surnames as well, regardless of how the author is referred to in the text. When "Monarchy" appears capitalized, it refers to what was known in the early modern period as the *Monarquía Hispánica*, the dynastic empire ruled by the Spanish Hapsburgs.

THE INVENTION OF AMERICA AND THE INVENTION OF THE MAP

1

The Collusion of Empires and Maps

In part 2 of Cervantes's *Don Quixote*, the world's most famous knight-errant and his trusty squire take an extraordinary journey on the back of a magical creature belonging to the enchanter Malambruno. Or, so they believe. The opportunity comes courtesy of a duke and duchess who amuse themselves by perpetrating a series of pranks upon the would-be heroes. In this one, Don Quixote and Sancho Panza are invited to sit on the back of a wooden hobbyhorse of sorts, which they have been told is none other than the legendary beast Clavileño. They are then blindfolded, so that they will not notice that the motions of their mount and the wind that whistles past their ears are nothing more than crude special effects generated by the pranksters' henchmen. The ruse, of course, works perfectly. Don Quixote is certain that Clavileño has taken them up into the celestial spheres, leaving the earth far below, reduced to a speck in the distance. Sancho, in turn, clings to his master's body, dreadfully afraid of falling all the way back down.

Their misadventure serves to cast barbs at numerous targets, both literary and historical. The names in the story—Malambruno, Clavileño—single out some Spanish chivalric romances that are now remembered only because they served as the source for this parody, but the general contours of the story—a magical beast that takes a hero on a ride through the cosmos—suggest that this is a piece of parodic buckshot meant to hit other, better-known targets as well. Among them we might spot a number of Renaissance epics in which a ride on a magical creature or a glimpse into a magical device serves as the vehicle for inscribing a vision of the world or even of the cosmos, a vision, moreover, that serves to flatter a powerful prince. In the Clavileño episode, therefore, Cervantes does not just mock the fanciful extravagance of romance: he takes aim at the panoptic ambitions of panegyrical literature cast in a cosmographical register. And if the general contours of the tale are not enough to make us suspect this, then Sancho Panza provides us a telling malapropism. The squire complains about the toll the ride is taking on his ample posterior: "All I can say is that if that lady Magellan or Magalona was happy with this crupper, her flesh can't have been all that delicate" (Cervantes Saavedra 2001, 2. 41). "Magalona" is a character from one of the chivalric romances that takes the brunt of the parodic attack. Sancho, however, slips from the register of romance into that of history, converting "Magalona" into "Lady Magellan," hypothetical wife of the famed explorer, and imagines her unladylike endurance in the face of the discomforts of travel. At issue here are numerous attempts to encompass the world, both in word and deed, including those of the Spanish Hapsburgs, who had sponsored Magellan's expedition and had enjoyed the praise of both Spanish and Italian epic poets.

By the time Cervantes wrote these words, the Spanish Hapsburgs had built upon the successes of their predecessors, Ferdinand of Aragon and Isabella of Castile, to transform their domains into major players on the stages of Europe, the Mediterranean, and the Atlantic. In the space of a few generations, the Catholic Kings and their Hapsburg successors had completed the centuries-old project of expelling Islam from the Iberian Peninsula, had asserted Iberian sovereignty over much of the Low Countries and much of Italy, had frustrated the ambitions of the French and the Ottomans, and had extended themselves into the New World. Much of this occurred during the reign of Charles V, king of Castile and Aragon and Holy Roman Emperor, the grandson of Ferdinand and Isabella. His ascendancy was resented by many, but it was also celebrated by others, both in Spain and beyond, who saw in him the return of imperial glories not seen since the days of Rome. During Cervantes's lifetime, Charles's son, Philip II, managed to add the kingdom of Portugal, with its colonies in Africa and Asia, to the vast inheritance left him by his father, making him monarch of the first-ever empire upon which the sun never set.

In the light of this preponderance of power, an exquisite atlas drawn more than a half-century before the publication of Don Quixote reads like a herald of things to come.[1] The atlas includes a map of the world that reflects the changes in Europe's view of the world by the previous seventy or so years (see fig. 1). It speaks, furthermore, of the wonder of this new view of the world and of the Iberian achievements that have made it possible. A guilt frame, a mass of clouds, and the heads of the various winds surround the cartographic image, setting it in a three-dimensional space and referring it to an onlooker who enjoys the prospect from a godlike point of view.[2] Curved lines of longitude suggest a curved surface, reminding us that the world is round and that, therefore, our ability to view the whole of it in a single glance is indeed a wondrous thing. They also attest to the modernity of the map, its maker, and its owner, by associating the image with the emerging science of scale cartography. A red line—a hallmark of this particular mapmaker—cuts across the map, tracing the route of Magellan's *Victoria* around the earth. As we follow its course, we realize not only that the earth can be circumnavigated, but that it has indeed been circumnavigated. The daring of Iberian explorers has reduced the terraqueous globe to an apprehensible object. It has realized the promise inherent in Renaissance cartography by making the world in its entirety available for the sort of spectacularization accomplished by this map.

But it is the power and not just the daring of early modern Iberians that marks the surface of this map. Gilt lines cross the Atlantic, tracing the routes of Spanish treasure fleets, attesting to Spain's conquest of the sea in the creation of a trans-Atlantic empire. Their presence reminds us of the imperialistic motives behind Magellan's expedition, one meant to add Asian spices to the American precious metals that were then sailing from the New World into Seville. The frontispiece of the atlas affirms this joint celebration of power and knowledge. The atlas was prepared for the emperor Charles V by the Italian mapmaker Battista Agnese, apparently as a gift for the emperor's son, Philip II, upon the occasion of the heir's accession to the crown midcentury. It opens with an image of God handing the world to Alexander the Great, and surrounds this image with emblems of Charles and Philip as his imperial successors (see fig. 2). The frontispiece determines the reception of the world map, converting the endless circle of Magellan's route into an emblem of the Hapsburg *imperium sine fine*. The map and the opening image together speak not only of comprehension but of apprehension, at once both intellectual and political. They speak of a worldwide monarchy that was still an ambition in Agnese's time but that had apparently been realized by the time that Don Quixote left La Mancha in search of glory, honor, and empire. They provide a cartographic analogue to those visions of the world that appear time and again in Renaissance epic and, in particular, in such Iberian masterpieces as Luiz vaz de Camões's *Lusíadas*, Alonso de Ercilla's *Araucana*, and Bernardo de Balbuena's *Bernardo*. Just as the warriors in these tales view the world through the magical devices of romance, so does the Hapsburg monarch view the world in Agnese's map through the wondrous intervention of a new cartography.

Certainly, Don Quixote's ride on Clavileño must have something to do with a satire of Spanish imperialism during the first decades of the seventeenth

1 Battista Agnese (c. 1542), map of the world. The gilt frame, the clouds, and the heads of the various winds function to set the map in a three-dimensional space and to place the implied viewer in an ideal position from which to view the Earth in its totality. The John Carter Brown Library at Brown University.

2 Battista Agnese (c. 1542), frontispiece to the Charles V portolan atlas. On the left, God hands the globe to the young Alexander the Great. On the right, the Hapsburg coat of arms. The John Carter Brown Library at Brown University.

century or, at least, of the sort of imperial cartographies in verse that we find in the texts I have mentioned. But mine is not a book about *Don Quixote*, nor about the troubled times during which Cervantes wrote his masterpiece. Rather, it is about the century prior to the first sally of the mad knight, the century during which that empire was first forged on the ground and first imagined on the page. From early on in the history of Iberian territorial expansion, cartography and empire were inseparable. In 1494, the Treaty of Tordesillas divided the world into Portuguese and Castilian spheres of influence by drawing a line through a map of the world. Thenceforth, both crowns recognized the importance of cartography to their expansionist ambitions, as a practical tool of empire and as a means of monumentalizing their achievements. Castile was soon to copy Portuguese efforts to regulate its mercantile empire through the establishment of the Casa de la Contratación in Seville, an official institution modeled after Lisbon's Casa da India. The Casa de la Contratación was soon charged with regulating the production and distribution of maritime charts, as well as the maintenance of a master chart of the world, the *padrón general*. The process of official institutionalization of cartography that began with this charge reached its apex in the reign of one of the dominant figures of the sixteenth century, Philip II, a king who understood the importance of maps both as instruments and as symbols of power.[3] Under his rule, a survey of the Iberian Peninsula was completed, producing the most accurate atlas of Spain to date. New initiatives were begun in the geographical mapping of the Americas, and nautical cartography was further regulated. An international contingent of all kinds of technical specialists were brought together in Madrid under the auspices of an academy meant to employ the applied sciences in the service of the crown.[4] Like their king, these technical experts were aware that imperial power and cultural sophistication had become intertwined with technical disciplines of various kinds, including cartography.

Many readers, I suspect, would be entirely unsurprised by this collusion of cartography with empire in the early modern Hispanic world. "As much as guns and warships," it has been said, "maps have been the weapons of imperialism" (Harley and Laxton 2001, 57).[5] In countless ways, J. B. Harley argues, maps directly supported the execution of territorial power both at home and overseas. They assisted in the planning of military operations, the construction of fortifications, and the exploitation of trade routes, particularly maritime ones. In Latin America, maps even supported efforts to distribute the human resources of ecclesiastics eager to proselytize indigenous peoples by mapping the territories of the faithful and the idolatrous. But maps have also worked in ways better understood as ideological rather than practical. Over time, they became associated with the emerging science of geography, and their scientific authority served to naturalize the territorial claims of both empires and nation-states and to claim authority and grandeur on behalf of both (Harley and Laxton 2001, 57–60). Who can doubt the ideological force of a nineteenth-century map of the British Empire that offers a clear contrast between the bright red bits of the Empire and the dull tones of the rest of the world (fig. 3)? In our own day, that form of collective self-fashioning that we know as the nation-state, like the empires that have so recently fallen apart, is inseparable from a clear image of a territory that inspires our affection, demands our loyalty, calls us home. Images of national territories are even lifted off paper maps to make earrings, paperweights, auto decals, and all sorts of bric-a-brac attesting to our topophilia as citizens of modern states (Anderson 1991, 170–78; see also Thongchai 1994). In this light, Agnese's map of Philip's world, like other early modern maps intended to flatter a monarch, seems to represent nothing more than an early manifestation of a durable tendency to ground the authority, even the identity, of nations and empires alike in maps of their territories or of their territorial ambitions, serving purposes both practical and ideological.

But to understand Agnese's and other similar maps of the world as nothing more than an early manifestation of modern habits of practice and thought is to appreciate, at best, only half the story of the collusion between cartography and early modern empire. For while it is true that many of those involved in the business of colonialism—from the crown on down—often appreciated the power of maps, such appreciation was not universal. This may have been especially true in Spain, where the Hapsburgs guarded their advanced geographical knowledge from international rivals by prohibiting their maps from appearing in print, thereby encumbering their dissemination among people who were not actively involved in the business of empire and perhaps facilitating the persistence of cultural trends that the full dissemination of modern maps would later displace. But even those who had access to the manuscripts did not necessarily view those maps in precisely the same way that later generations did. Only a few generations before Columbus, maps seem to have been rare things in Europe, found only in certain social contexts, and varying widely in composition and function from one context to the next. There are relatively few extant medieval maps, and most of these take the form of dreamlike ecclesiastical *mappaemundi* or nautical charts that would have been all but unknown outside the world of traders and mariners. Certainly, many medieval maps have been lost to the ravages of time, but it is difficult to imagine that this corpus of lost maps would have been very large, since medieval vernaculars barely possessed a word for them. The various modern derivatives of the Latin word *mappa* did not enter into general circulation until well into the

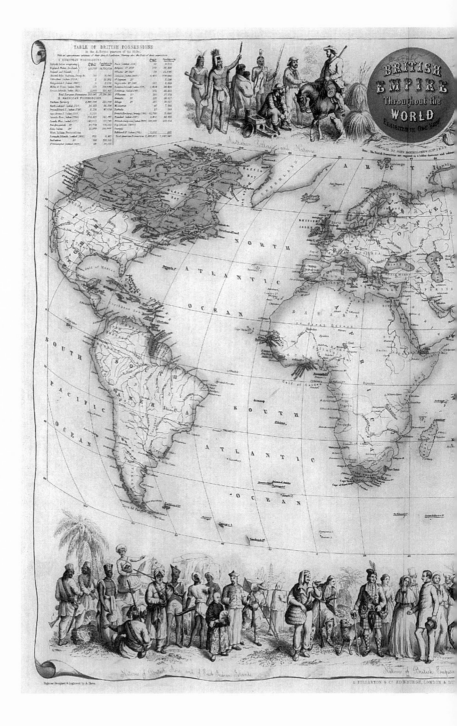

3 John Bartholomew, *British Empire throughout the World Exhibited in One View* (ca. 1850). The Geography and Map Division of the Library of Congress.

sixteenth century. Likewise, vernacular derivatives of the Latin *spatium* meant something quite different in the European Middle Ages (Zumthor 1993, 51). "Space," for medieval Europeans, was not what it would become for the cartographically literate generations of later centuries, a geometric, abstract, isotropic expanse. It was, instead, something quite different, something that held sway over the European imagination well after Renaissance humanists issued in the so-called "cartographic revolution" on the heels of their rediscovery of Ptolemy's *Geographia* and, with it, of the gridded scale map. And so, the Iberian cultures that first planted European banners on non-European shores were—like the French, the English, and the others—cultures only beginning to make and use maps. More important, they were cultures that were only beginning to think cartographically. They were only beginning to learn how to imagine their world, relate to it, and transform it in ways that depended upon the unique conceptualization of space that lay at the heart of the modern map.

In this book, I explore the cartographic literature—iconographic and discursive—produced by this culture, which built its empire at a time when it was only first learning how to picture the world. Specifically, I explore cartographic literature from the vast corpus of Spanish Americana, texts written by and for people of Hispanic extraction having something to do with the New World. As we shall see, the story I tell about these pieces of cartographic literature is neither one of triumphant conquests, military or intellectual, nor one of sudden cultural transformations. Instead, it is a story of how the old lingers long after the initial emergence of the new, of how hybrid cultural products only gradually shed themselves of an outmoded past, of how a central aspect of modernity slinks into existence.

The Invention of America [6]

Some readers may be surprised to learn that Spanish Americana is not necessarily an obvious place to look for the modern collusion between empire and cartography. There is, first and foremost, the stumbling block posed by the scarcity of cartographic sources. The corpus of sixteenth-century Spanish Americana provides us with relatively few maps of the New World, particularly in comparison with the cartographic output of other European countries later in the sixteenth century and into the seventeenth. Although maps were important to the crown and its collaborators, precious few sixteenth-century Spanish maps made it into print, and so therefore relatively few have survived.[7] Should we not then turn away from the Hispanic world, suspecting that the scarcity of sources—or even the very practice of *not* printing maps—

suggests that empire was not in cahoots with cartography in the world of the Spanish Hapsburgs, or at least that the conspiracy was not sufficiently established to merit study? Should we not then turn to more promising objects of investigation, such as the early modern Netherlands or nineteenth-century Britain, with their rich treasure-troves of beautiful printed maps and their vast cartographic surveys?

My response to such questions is that the relative scarcity of sixteenth-century Spanish maps and the Spanish practice of keeping them in manuscript form are precisely what makes the Hispanic context so interesting. Maps were by no means absent from Spain's imperial efforts, ambitions, and self-representations, as I have mentioned, but neither were they ubiquitous. Spain's attempt to map itself as an Atlantic empire, or even a global empire, thus has the look of an emergent phenomenon and as such promises insights that may be more difficult to come by in the cartographic efforts of later empires.[8]

This emergent phenomenon will be discussed further in the following section, but first I would like to address another problem with Spanish Americana as a site for the study of imperial cartography, one having to do with the novelty of the New World and its place in the ways early modern Spaniards understood themselves. For many Spaniards, their country's experience in extending itself into the New World and, in particular, in acquiring its gold and silver represented nothing less than the downfall of their national culture, its disastrous surrender to monstrous avarice. The texts penned by these individuals tend therefore to condemn empire rather than celebrate it, justify it, or otherwise underwrite its objectives. Although their texts sometimes "map" empire, their critical stance toward empire assures that such maps are anything but the precursors of later, manifestly imperialistic cartographies. More will be said below about some of these critical mappings, but, overall, I emphasize the work of Spaniards for whom the experience of sailing the oceans, reaching the Indies, and rounding the world provided the central touchstone of their nation's coming of age. Among them is the humanist-historian Francisco López de Gómara, who famously asserted in 1552 that "[t]he most important event in the history of the world, save for the Incarnation and Death of Him who created it, is the discovery of the Indies" (1979, 7). Among them is also Pedro de Medina, a widely recognized sixteenth-century authority on the art of oceanic navigation. His words, which date to the year 1548, anticipate those of Gómara:

> In our own times, we have seen how the whole universe has been circumnavigated by Spanish navigation . . . This is a deed so great that since the creation

of the World by God nothing comparable has ever been accomplished, nor has been imagined, nor has even been believed to have been possible. This accomplishment requires not only industry and spirit but the skill of finding one's way on water where nature has denied it to us . . . and with this navigation new seas never before sailed have been discovered, and unknown lands never before known, nor heard of . . . [W]ith good reason they are called the New World. (Medina 1944, 42–44)[9]

Shrill hyperbole characterizes these and other generalizations about the importance of the discovery of the New World, the circumnavigation of the earth by Magellan's *Victoria*, and other episodes from the Age of Discovery. It had to, since the mid-sixteenth-century culture to which these words were addressed knew little of the Americas, and valued them even less. Here we come upon another reason why Spanish Americana does not necessarily present itself as an obvious site upon which to explore the emergence of imperial cartography. Various historians have noted that the Americas seem to have mattered little to sixteenth-century Europeans, particularly during the first three quarters of the century. After an initial wave of excitement attending published versions of letters by Columbus and Vespucci, European interest in the new discoveries seems to have tapered off. It was not until the last quarter of the century that any serious attempt was made to integrate things American into accepted notions of the world's geography or of the origins of the human family.[10] Thus, in the first quarter of the sixteenth century, when a Tyrolese mapmaker by the name of Johannes Bucius sought to give iconographic form to the vision of universal empire that had become associated with the emperor Charles V, he depicted a European empire with Spain as its head and the Holy Roman Empire as its heart, but with no place for the Americas (see fig. 4).[11]

Even in the work of someone like Pedro de Medina, an emphatic proponent of the importance of Spain's experience abroad, the New World occupied a surprisingly marginal position. Medina was born only one year after Ferdinand of Aragon and Isabella of Castile had successfully conquered the kingdom of Granada, and he lived to witness the discovery and conquest of Mexico and Peru. Eventually, he secured a position as a cosmographer at Seville's Casa de la Contratación, where he trained pilots in the art of oceanic navigation, produced maritime charts for their voyages across the sea, and contributed to maintaining the crown's *padrón general*, its master chart of the known world. The passage quoted above about the importance of Spain's journeys of exploration comes from a text meant to advance Medina's career as a humanist, the *Libro de grandezas y cosas memorables de España* (1548). The text constitutes nothing less than the first historical geography of Spain widely available in the vernacular. It begins with a brief summary of Spanish history, followed by a survey of the historical, cultural, and economic riches of Spain, listed king-dom by kingdom, province by province, city by city, town by town. Medina joins various classical and medieval authors in praising Spain as the "head" of a geography whose body is Europe, in this way reiterating the vision of the Monarchy that we find in the Bucius woodcut. But Medina's ambitions for Spain are even grander. "The region of Spain," Medina writes, "is the begin-ning and the head of *all the other regions of the world*" (7; emphasis added). Medina, the author of a universal cosmography (now lost) and of a world map, clearly understood his country's destiny as the head of a truly universal monarchy, one that would eventually dominate, not just Europe, but the whole world. Signifi-cantly, although his description of the places that together make up Spain does not extend into the New World, the book does come include a chart of the Atlantic world (fig. 5) that silently witnesses to Spain's imperial grandeur by displaying the vast reaches of its newly won possessions in the Indies.

Yet Medina's relative silence about the Indies in the *Libro de grandezas* speaks more loudly about his times than do his various brief and breathless references to the New World. Descriptions of the Caribbean and parts of Mesoamerica were already available in the published accounts of Christopher Columbus (1493), Amerigo Vespucci (1503), Martín Fernández de Enciso (1519), An-tonio Pigafetta (1525), Hernán Cortés (1522), Gonzalo Fernández de Oviedo (1526 and 1535), Pietro Martire d'Anghiera[12] (1530), Alvar Nuñez Cabeza de Vaca (1542), and Bartolomé de las Casas (1542).[13] Add to these the numerous other works that circulated in manuscript form, as well as the official reports to which Medina would have had access by virtue of his ties to the Casa de la Contratación, and it becomes readily apparent that Medina had at his disposal ample information about the New World. He could have easily extended his *Libro de grandezas* into a companion volume dedicated to the *grandezas y cosas mem-orables* (grandeurs and memorable things) of what we might call "España Ultra-mar" or "Overseas Spain." But he does not. Instead, before the New World, his pen falters. Rather than enumerate its wonders, Medina reduces America—in its vast geographical expanse, in its acknowledged cultural diversity—to the status of a single *grandeza* figured in his book through bits of rhetorical bom-bast and a mute map. It is clear that even for this Spaniard, so actively involved in Spain's American enterprise, so enthusiastic about the significance of the New World for his country's reputation, America has only begun to dawn on the intellectual horizon. Although the New World has been drawn on the map, it has not yet been entirely assimilated into the body politic of Castile.

In this way, Medina's *Libro de grandezas* reflects the larger pattern of European culture in the mid-sixteenth century. Although Medina has mapped what he knew of America into his chart of the emerging Atlantic world, he has still not

4 Johannes Bucius, *Europa Regina* (1537). An allegory of Hapsburg rule over Europe by a Tyrolese cartographer. The Geography and Map Division of the Library of Congress.

5 Atlantic World. From Pedro de
Medina, *Arte de navegar* (Seville, 1545).
The same chart was printed with
his *Libro de grandezas y cosas memorables
de España*. The Rare Books Division of
the Library of Congress.

found a place for it in his conception of what he clearly considers to be his
"nation," Spain. Medina represents only one link in a series of texts that, col-
lectively, created a place for America in European discourse. I say "create" because I agree with the Mexican historian Edmundo O'Gorman that "America"
is something that was invented rather than discovered. Since the publication
of O'Gorman's *The Invention of America* almost half a century ago, many contemporary scholars have come to accept one of its central contentions, that America—like the Orient in Edward Said's famous account—cannot be understood

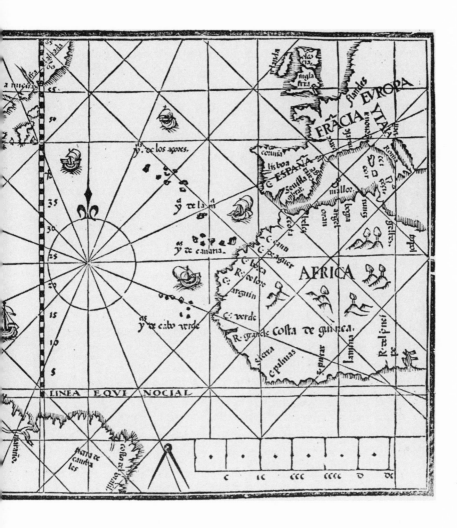

as a purely natural object, available to knowledge through simple inspection.[14] Instead, it must be understood as something produced historically, through the complex interaction of culturally contingent expectations and interests with observed geographical phenomena. "America" is indeed a slice of the natural world, but it is one that has been cut from the globe by a particular people, at a particular time, interested for particular reasons in carving the world up in the first place. Its invention, moreover, represented the culmination of years of exploration in the New World and reflection in the Old. As we shall see, this process of "inventing America" can be understood as the process or "remapping" the European imagination in ways that bring to light the connections between the early modern cartographic revolution, a larger process of cultural "mapping," and deep changes in Europe's conception of itself and its world. In this way, Spanish Americana, whatever its limitations, becomes an *ideal* site for examining the emergence of the map in the imagination of empire.

The early modern invention of America involved many actors, both explorers and intellectuals. According to O'Gorman, it culminated in the 1507 publication of Martin Waldseemüller's brief introduction to the science of cosmography, the *Cosmographiae introductio*, as well as the massive wall map of the world that accompanied it (fig. 6). Columbus had thought the lands he discovered were part of Asia. Vespucci thought that they were a New World not only distinct but fundamentally different from the Old. Waldseemüller, by contrast, asserted the geographical independence of America from Asia while at the same time denying the alterity assigned to it by Vespucci. He depicted the lands discovered by Spanish and Portuguese exploration on the far side of the Atlantic as a fourth part of the *orbis terrarum* geographically independent of Asia and gave them a name—"America"—that signaled it was commensurate with the traditional three (fig. 7; O'Gorman 1986, 134–36).

Since O'Gorman, scholarship about the invention of America—or, as J. H. Elliott puts it, the assimilation of America by the European consciousness—has tended to emphasize the protracted nature of the project. It has emphasized the long delay that separated early innovations like that of Waldseemüller from later intellectual projects that fully included America and all things American in their considerations of universal geography, natural history, politics, theology, and the like. Their work demonstrates that the invention of America was a process neither linear nor monolithic. It took place as a series of fits and starts that unfolded in different historical moments, in different places, and in different sectors of early modern culture, sometimes drawing widespread attention to themselves and sometimes remaining all but ignored.[15] Over time, these fits and starts gathered momentum, consolidated, and eventually produced new intellectual frameworks that synthesized the new with pieces of the old. Almost invariably, these various inventions of America figured the New World in language that often suppressed or distorted all that was alien about them.[16] As Michael Ryan puts it, to assimilate America in early modern Europe was "to locate exotics within the context of familiar discourse." "The assimilation of new worlds," he adds, "involved their domestication" (1981, 523). And so, in 1570, when Abraham Ortelius finally discarded the *Geographia* of Ptolemy in favor of a new atlas of the world drawn on the basis of what had been learned since Columbus, da Gama, and others, he introduced his collection with an illustration that left no doubt as to how the newly discovered fourth part of the world fit into this world conceived by and for European culture (fig. 8).

This process, moreover, involved many different types of discourse, not just maps. This is clear from the start, in O'Gorman's own work, despite the prominent role he assigns to Waldseemüller's map. When it is not obsessed with maps, O'Gorman's case is built upon early modern attempts to synthesize what was then known about America and its inhabitants in the register of humanistic historiography. These include the *Historia general y natural de las Indias*, written by Gonzalo Fernández de Oviedo during the second quarter of the sixteenth century, the *Apologética historia sumaria*, written by Bartolomé de las Casas halfway through the century, and the *Historia natural y moral de las Indias*, written by José de Acosta during its last decade. This use of historiography as well as maps anticipates later efforts to understand the process of invention as a complex operation involving many sectors of the culture and many kinds of texts. Maps—in the invention of America, the Orient, Australia, or any other such entity—join history, literature, painting, architecture, and many other kinds of cultural endeavor to create a mutually reinforcing, albeit partially fictional, geography, one that locates and characterizes both self and other.

But how, precisely, do these other forms of cultural endeavor, particularly discursive texts, engage in this sort of work? Much of this book is dedicated to examining how historical narrative from sixteenth-century Spain does so and why it cannot be ignored in any discussion of the invention of America. Historical narratives make their contribution not only by characterizing the other or by emplotting the historical relationship between self and other but, more fundamentally, by mapping the regions in which their stories unfold. They do so, among other ways, by *describing* them. "Description" would seem to be the most mundane of discursive modes, the most innocent, most purely referential way of utilizing language. But "description," like "emplotment," entails the encounter between data and expectations, between observations and culturally contingent assumptions about the production of meaning.[17] While "emplotment" shapes time into narratives, "description" likewise draws boundaries, making places out of disparate locations. It does so, moreover, under the cover provided by its putatively ancillary function. As Paul Carter (1988) argues, the invention of space and territory in historical discourse fails to attract suspicion, even from those quite suspicious about how historiography emplots time, precisely because it constitutes nothing more than a mise en scène for the real work of historiography, which is narrative. But by the time the story gets going, the stage has been set, and in its construction much

6 Map of the world. From Martin Waldseemüller, *Universalis cosmographia secundum Ptholomaei traditionem et Americi Vespucii aliorumque lustrationes* (1507). America appears as a single continent, separate from Asia, and stretching from north to south. Facsimile. The Geography and Map Division of the Library of Congress.

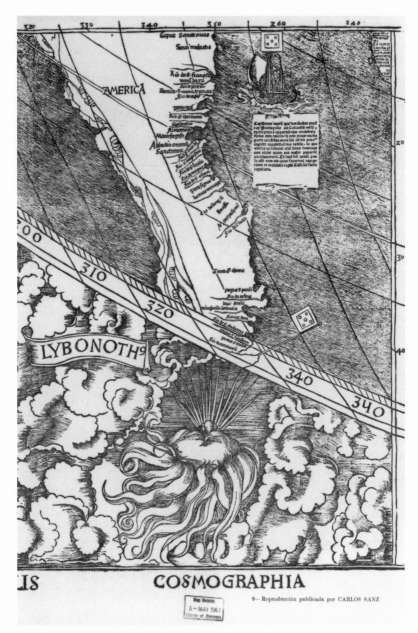

7 Detail from Martin Waldseemüller, *Universalis cosmographia secundum Ptholomaei traditionem et Americi Vespucii aliorumque lustrationes* (1507). The name "America" appears on the southern half of the continent. Facsimile. The Geography and Map Division of the Library of Congress.

8 Title page from Abraham Ortelius, *Theatrum orbis terrarum* (1570). The Albert and
Shirley Small Special Collections Library, University of Virginia.

of the ideological work has already been done. This, then, is a book about cartography—or, to put it a better way, a book about "mapping"—but it is a book that defines cartography in a very broad sense, as a form of cultural work that is carried out by maps, yes, but also by other kinds of texts in which we can identify a crucial cartographic dimension.

Together, early modern maps and histories—not to mention lyric poems, plays, paintings, and countless other types of texts that I will not have the opportunity to examine—reforge what O'Gorman calls the *metageography* of European culture. Neologisms—particularly academic ones beginning with the prefix "meta"—are often loathsome concoctions that beg for justification and apology if they are to be used at all. In its defense, I suggest that the term "metageography" is neither all that new nor terribly odious. O'Gorman himself uses the term very sparingly and never defines it explicitly, so I turn to a recent definition advanced by Martin Lewis and Kärin Wigen (1997), one consistent with O'Gorman's use of the term:

> By *metageography* we mean the set of spatial structures through which people order their knowledge of the world: the often unconscious frameworks that organize studies of history, sociology, anthropology, economics, political science, or even natural history. (ix)

Lewis and Wigen assert, in other words, that much if not all discourse is predicated upon a set of logically prior assumptions about space and geography. These assumptions establish the parameters of discourse in ways that are both enabling and disabling, but their importance and their arbitrariness often go unrecognized. In *The Invention of America*, we follow the adventures of European culture as its encounter with the New World forces it to reconfigure its basic notions about the world it inhabits, its boundaries, its very nature. Briefly put, O'Gorman argues that the invention of America tears down the medieval notion of the *orbis terrarum*, the inhabitable world, as an insular entity closely bounded by a menacing ocean, and replaces it with an image of the world as a fully masterable terraqueous globe. This change, in turn, supports a transformation in Europe's image of itself. Capable now of domesticating the once ominous seas, the European subject discovers his own, Adamic authority over the world and finds in America an object that he can recreate in his own image (139–52).

The argument leaves ample room for disagreement and debate. Most important, O'Gorman never once acknowledges that the native inhabitants of the lands that came to be understood as "America" had metageographies of their own, as well as cartographies with which to represent them. Blind to what was there before the European invention, O'Gorman then cannot attend to the

many ways in which indigenous Americans resisted European efforts at territorialization and sometimes even appropriated the cartography of Europe for
their own ends. Guaman Poma de Ayala, a Peruvian-born chronicler of mixed
European and Amerindian extraction whose own Nueva corónica y buen gobierno,
finished around 1615, constitutes an important counterpoint to early modern
histories of the Americas penned by Spaniards and other Europeans, drew a
map of the world that adapted metropolitan cartography to his own, anti-
imperialists ends. His map has no place in O'Gorman's account. That account
nonetheless serves as a useful point of departure for scholarship—like this
book—that addresses itself to texts that reflect little of the cultural mestizaje
(hybridity) present in the work of the Andean chronicler and others like him.
It has even been argued that O'Gorman's work makes it possible for all such
scholarship to assume a truly critical stance in that it relativizes European
knowledge about the New World, strips it of the aura that often attends to putatively scientific enterprise (Mignolo 1995, 264). It is only when we recognize America—indeed, the whole system of "continents"—as an invention of
European culture that we can begin to read cartographic literature as a creative
enterprise rather than as a simply descriptive one. It is a creative enterprise,
moreover, that colonizes not just the Amerindian imagination, but, as we shall
see later on, the European one as well.

For now, however, I would like to put some distance between the way
O'Gorman uses these discursive cartographies and the use I make of them.
Each of the histories that O'Gorman uses makes prominent mention of Waldseemüller's hypothesis, even though they do not mention his name. As syn-
theses of knowledge about "the Indies," each of them takes for granted something that the indigenous inhabitants of what we now know as "the Americas"
had never imagined. They assume that the lands opposite Europe and Africa
on the Atlantic constitute a single, coherent geographical entity, and that its
inhabitants therefore comprise a coherent group of human beings. To put it
another way, the invention of America constitutes their condition of possibility. Their assertions about American geography, in turn, bear directly upon
the ways that these texts figure both the availability of those human beings
for conquest and rule by Europeans (i.e., Spaniards), as well as the nature of
those imperialistic efforts. In this way, they provide lucid examples of what
O'Gorman means by a "metageography." Their assumptions about space and
territory ground what they have to say about the other that inhabits America
and about the sort of relationship that the self has, can have, or should have
with that other.

None of these books, however, names Waldseemüller's invention, "America," as its subject matter. Instead, they address themselves, as their titles

suggest, to the moral and natural history of "the Indies." The difference in terminology is crucial. "America" is an invented entity understood as a natural one. "The Indies," by contrast, is a political entity. "The Indies" were all the lands beyond the Atlantic that belonged to the crown of Castile. Eventually, they included not only the Americas but the Philippines as well, and by some accounts, the Spice Islands. When they needed to be distinguished from the colonial possessions of the Portuguese, they were called "las Indias occidentales," as opposed to "las Indias orientales" of Castile's neighbor and rival. Fittingly, then, each of these texts understands the history of the Indies and of its inhabitants in ways that subordinate them to the imperial destiny of Catholic Castile. Whatever else they may be, the Indies are for all of these texts the arena in which that destiny plays out, the place where, sometimes heroically and sometimes tyrannically, Spain extends itself as the sword of orthodox Christianity. In effect, they extend the metageography gestating in the *Libro de grandezas*. Medina's book lies caught between a traditional metageography still dominant in the culture and another emerging from the work of the cartographic avant-garde. Its chart of the Atlantic world ties the traditional homeland to its new Atlantic possessions, while the text continues to operate under long-established assumptions about the limits of "Spanish" geography. Those assumptions, in turn, determine what peoples, places, and events are to be held up as the *grandezas* of the nation—Iberian ones—and consign the New World to a problematic position, at once at the heart and beyond the pale of things properly Spanish. The work of Oviedo, las Casas, Acosta, and others, meanwhile, take the leap that Medina himself does not take. They inhabit the blank map of the New World with discourse, thereby assimilating it within a new metageography of Spain as a trans-Atlantic empire.

Significantly, however, Oviedo, las Casas, and Acosta each reject Waldseemüller's assertion that the Americas are not physically connected to Asia. Like other sixteenth-century writers and mapmakers—most famously, Giacomo Gastaldi (fig. 9)—they bring together those components of the world's geography that Waldseemüller separates, producing a single supercontinent out of Waldseemüller's two island-continents.[18] At one point, Oviedo insists upon the geographical unity of the Eastern and Western Hemispheres, by way of a land bridge in the extreme North Atlantic (2: 39). Las Casas simply asserts that the West Indies are part of the East Indies, without further specifying the way in which the two are joined (1967, 1: 22). Acosta argues that a land bridge must connect America to Asia in the North Pacific (1986, 1: 21). None of these texts advances its alternative geography as a matter of empirical necessity. For each of them, the resultant singular supercontinent—like Waldseemüller's paired continents—is built upon speculation and serves to ground central ideological postures.[19] So, while the invention of America constitutes the condition of possibility of all of these texts, it is the larger universal geography into which they insert America—a geography that reconnects the New World to the Old—that becomes the ground of their specific historical and imperial ideologies. That universal geography, I reiterate, represents an instance of backsliding from Waldseemüller's hypothesis. Each of these texts in its own way holds on to that old, insular *orbis terrarum* bounded by ocean on all sides that Waldseemüller had rejected when he made the *orbis terrarum* coextensive with the whole of the globe.[20]

In this way, these texts exemplify the sorts of fits and starts that I have mentioned and that I will examine in the chapters that follow. In their variety, no one of these texts can be equated with a monolithic European consciousness that "invents" America once and for all. Their metageographies represent more localized affairs, the sort of unexamined spatial structures that ground what they can and cannot say about the Indies. They draw and redraw continents as needed, often grafting geographical speculations onto empirical data to make their contours conform with the exigencies of more localized historical contingencies. Although they all aspire to invent America as a component of empire, as a Spanish *grandeza*, they disagree among themselves on the precise geography of that empire and, concurrently, about the nature of the Americans and of the justifiability of their conquest by Spain. Likewise, the historical narratives that I examine in the chapters that follow each draws its own metageography of empire and thereby grounds different postures toward America, the Americans, and the Encounter. Like the larger project of invention that reaches one of its milestones in Ortelius's *Theatrum*, all of these narratives domesticate much of what is alien about the Americas for the purpose of drawing those metageographies.

The story of this domestication, this figurative colonization that played so important a role in the larger process of reducing America to the status of a colonial periphery, is not the story that I tell. That story is an important one, but it is also one that has been examined time and again. My story concerns not all that is lost of American identity in the process of figuring the New World but some of the resources that Europeans had at their disposal for the job. It is not just the process of invention that cannot be understood in monolithic terms: it is also the "European consciousness" doing the inventing. Europe, we cannot forget, was in the process of transforming itself at the same time that it began to transform the rest of the world. One of the things that was changing was the way Europe imagined space and drew maps. "America," therefore, was not only invented and reinvented over the course of the early modern period. It was redrawn on the surface of maps that were themselves

9 Paolo Forlani, *Universale descrittione de tutta la terra conosciuta fin qui* (1565). Based upon an earlier map by Giacomo Gastaldi. What we now know as North America is depicted as a landmass contiguous with Asia. The Geography and Map Division of the Library of Congress.

changing, and changing in ways that could have profound impact on the inherent possibilities of each individual invention.

Maps and Mapping

The changes experienced by European cartography during the period when Spain explored, colonized, and mapped so much of the New World were not limited to matters of geographical content. The very medium of cartographic representation was itself undergoing significant transformations in its form, its availability, and its significance. At the center of these transformations lay the *Geographia* of Ptolemy, a treatise on mapmaking originally written during the second century and rediscovered by Italian humanists during the fifteenth century. In the *Geographia*, Renaissance humanists, who were becoming increasingly interested in the accurate depiction of the way the world looked, found a prestigious, classical authority to place at the center of their emerging science. Divided into a treatise on cartographic projections, tables of geographical coordinates for numerous places in the greater Mediterranean world, and, often, a collection of maps derived from both, the *Geographia* circulated widely, first in manuscript and then in printed editions. Together, its three parts carried out a project that had only been sketched out by medieval cosmography: it rationalized the known world according to the principles of Euclidean geometry. In this way it spoke of a new order of things, one in which mathematical abstraction promised to make the world apprehensible in ways that it had never been before. This novel, intellectual apprehensibility, in turn, supported an emerging culture of commercial, military, and political expansionism—or so it has been argued.

The cultural and cartographic historians who have argued this point often turn to a contrast between the new, Ptolemaic maps of the Renaissance and the *mappaemundi* of the Middle Ages. For the sake of readers unfamiliar with the history of cartography, I shall do the same, at the risk of oversimplifying many issues.[21] The *mappaemundi* of the European Middle Ages were rare and extraordinary documents that graced the walls of cathedrals and the pages of illuminated manuscripts. Once considered the inaccurate geographical representations of an ignorant medieval mind, they are now better understood as the cartography of ecclesiastical mapmakers more interested in orienting the soul toward heaven than in directing the body through the physical world. As such, they depict the world largely as it was imagined by a long-established geographical tradition heavily informed by the classics, the Bible, and traditional lore. The two most famous examples, the *mappaemundi* of Hereford Cathedral and of Ebstorf Cathedral, offer on their surfaces a rich jumble of texts and im-

10 *Mappamundi* on display in Hereford Cathedral, England. (1290). Asia appears at the top of
the map and includes a circular island, the Garden of Eden. Europe is found on the lower
left, and Africa on the lower right. Outside the frame, at the top of the image, God sits in
judgment.

ages, both geographical and historical, drawn from such sources (fig. 10). On
these maps, Adam and Eve, the Garden of Eden, Gogg and Magog, the River of
Gold, Prester John, and the Mountains of the Moon share cartographic space
with images of cities and the names of geographic regions both near and far:
Jerusalem, Rome, Cádiz, Gallia, Macedonia, Ethiopia, and India.

The pictorial jumble of *mappaemundi* like these is only apparent. Underlying

europa & affrica   De Aſia & eius partib

giones·quarū breuiter nomina et ſitus expediam·ſu
a paradiſo   Paradiſus eſt locus in orientis partibɪ
tus·cuius vocabulum ex greco in latinum vertitur ɛ
hebraice eden dicitur·quod in noſtra lingua delicie
quod vtrumq̃ iunctum facit ortum deliciarum·eſt

pellata· qu(
quos imp(
tenuit. He(
bis parte c
oriente ort
ridie·oceào
noſtro ma
ſeptentrion
lacu & tan;
minatur.
prouincias

11   Mappamundi from a 1472 edition of the *Etymologia* of Saint Isidore of Seville. This represents the first European printed map. The Prints and Photographs Division of the Library of Congress.

their seemingly chaotic assemblage of places and peoples is a clear spatial structure best glimpsed by looking at an older, more schematic map from the same tradition.[22] In the *mappamundi* that accompanied a printed 1472 edition of the *Etymologia* of Saint Isidore of Seville, we can readily appreciate that basic spatial structure that is common to many medieval *mappaemundi*, the T-O form (fig. 11). The inhabited (and by some accounts, inhabitable) world, the *orbis terrarum*, appears as a tripartite disk surrounded by a circumfluent ocean. Asia forms the top half of the disk, while Europe and Africa constitute, respectively, the lower left and lower right quadrants. These three parts of the world are separated from each other by three bodies of water arranged in a "T" shape, the Mediterranean Sea, the Tanais River, and the Nile River. On this particular map, each of the three parts of the world has been labeled with the name of the son of Noah responsible for repopulating it after the Biblical Flood. Other symbolic and theological aspects of this map are less obvious. The T-O form allows the map to function not just as a representation of the *orbis terrarum* but also as its anagrammatical emblem. Its cruciform, meanwhile, lends itself to Christological renderings. In the Ebstorf map, the *orbis terrarum* becomes the mystical body of Christ. The head of Jesus appears at the top, his hands at each end of the "T," and his feet at its bottom. Jerusalem, placed at the center of this and other medieval *mappaemundi*, becomes Christ's navel, the omphalos of the world. Space, to borrow a distinction from Walter Mignolo, has been rationalized by these maps, but this rationalization has been carried out on the basis of cultural priorities unique to medieval Christendom rather than on the universal principles of Euclidean geometry (Mignolo 1995, 221–43).

By 1500, the old *mappaemundi* had been replaced, among learned people at least, by a new type of map derived from Ptolemy. The map of the world from a 1513 edition of the *Geographia* can serve to summarize some of the most relevant changes (fig. 12). We might be most struck at first by the dramatic transformation that has taken place in the geographical content of this map when compared with that of its medieval predecessors. Historical, mythological, and theological materials have been excised, while the shapes and relative locations of many seas and landmasses have come to better reflect empirical realities. Clearly, the circulation of this map and others like it indicates a renewed interest in geographical empiricism as well as in knowledge of what lay beyond the known world. Gone is the circumfluent ocean that converted the *orbis terrarum* into a bounded entity. In its place is an arbitrary frame that cuts the map off at the point, presumably, where knowledge ends and ignorance begins. The map's grid of latitude and longitude clearly acknowledges that the geographical area it depicts is but one part of a larger whole. The map adopts the parallels at 64° N and 14° S as its northern and southern boundaries and wraps around only 180° of the earth's surface from east to west.

For our purposes, this grid is the map's most salient characteristic. Here is the geometric armature that is entirely absent from the medieval *mappaemundi*. Geometry, not a pseudosymbolic form, provides the basic spatial armature of this map. It speaks to the mapmaker's interest in using mathematics to correctly model the relative positions of different places on the spherical earth as locations on his two-dimensional map. It also inscribes something that we cannot readily identify on the medieval *mappaemundi*: an empty space that is entirely distinct from a "blank spot" on a map indicating an unknown or unpopulated land or sea. That space is not the blankness produced by ignorance of an undiscovered geographical or hydrographical feature—a "negative" emptiness"—but the abstract space into which geographies and hydrographies are plotted—a "positive" emptiness. That space subtends the entire

12 *Mappamundi* from a 1513 edition of Ptolemy's *Geographia*. The Albert
and Shirley Small Special Collections Library, University of Virginia.

surface of the map, but its "positive emptiness"—its substantial independence from the objects and locations it serves to plot—only becomes visible when we realize that it logically extends far beyond the borders of the image. It extends into that vast part of the spherical earth that is not represented here but whose existence is presupposed by the geometry of the grid.

Moreover, the grid allows us to take issue with one of O'Gorman's fundamental contentions that the globalization of the *orbis terrarum* came only with the invention of America, not earlier. The Mexican historian refers constantly to maps of this kind in *La invención de América*, but he finds little ideological significance in the novelties of their form. For him, it is the invention of America—a geographical innovation—that renders the *orbis terrarum* coextensive with the terraqueous globe, not the earlier adoption of the cartographic grid. But when America was invented, a global space of a kind—if not a global geography—was already deployed in European culture. By then, serious maps came equipped with grids, and these grids provided a new global space into which could be set all sorts of geographies—those known, those dreamt of, and those yet to be imagined. They provided the armature within which could be assembled what Frank Lestringant calls a bricolage of the known and the unknown (1993a, 262). It was within the global grid of the new cartography that Waldseemüller cast the landmass that he christened America (figs. 6 and 7 above) and that Pedro de Medina figured his country as a trans-Atlantic empire (fig. 5 above). It was that grid, perhaps, that allowed him to imagine a global *orbis terrarum*. It was this grid, perhaps, and not the invention of America, that broke through the oceanic boundary that had circumscribed the medieval world and domesticated the ocean for imaginative appropriation. If this is the case, then the cultural transformation that O'Gorman describes as a consequence of the invention of America—the transformation of the European subject into a new Adam—becomes the consequence of something else: the Renaissance cartographic revolution.

In effect, what American geography is for O'Gorman, this grid is for other students of the nexus that links modernity, imperialism, geography, and space. In his seminal work, *The Production of Space*, Henri Lefebvre describes a period spanning from the sixteenth to the nineteenth centuries in which a common spatial code served to organize Western European culture. "Space," for Lefebvre, is not a natural given of any kind but something that each and every society produces as a fundamental part of its existence and particularly a part of the ways it distributes power among its members. It is made up of various conceptual, perceptual, and practical components. Individual societies are distinguished, among other things, by the way they favor one or another component in their "production of space." The modern West, according to

Lefebvre, gives disproportionate emphasis to what he calls "representations of space," space as it is conceived rather than as it is perceived or lived. It is a particular representation of space, moreover, that acquires a determinative power over many aspects of life. Modernity naturalizes geometric, optical, isotropic space as a fundamental epistemological category and thereby gives undue authority to the abstractions of the mapmaker, the surveyor, the planner, the architect, and the like. Traditional "representational spaces"—spaces as they are perceived—such as the hearth or the geography of the sacred are correspondingly stripped of their authority. In the order of abstraction, everything comes to be understood as either a location or an object within this space, and thereby becomes amenable to systematic understanding, commodification, appropriation, or subordination by a viewing subject.

Lefebvre's examples of the particular representations of space that embody this new, powerful order of abstraction privilege the perspectival space of Renaissance painting and urban design. They dwell upon cartography only long enough to consign it to the category of those representations of space that are to be held suspect for their complicity in abstraction (Lefebvre 1991, 229–91). Other scholars writing after Lefebvre, by contrast, put the cartographic revolution front and center. For them maps are no longer to be considered the transparent representations of a purely scientific enterprise but instead "thick" texts laden with cultural baggage and complicit with dominant powers.[23] Even the apparently innocent grid is found to be complicit in the operation of power. As David Woodward argues, its advent constitutes a revolution in the kind of "spatial understanding" that serves to organize geographical knowledge. With it, geometric space—abstract and homogeneous—comes to be deployed for the first time in Western culture (Woodward 1991, 84–87).[24] Like Lefebvre, Woodward emphasizes that this new spatiality makes universalist claims that empower modern, Western European culture at the expense of premodern others. He places the emphasis, however, on the territorialization of the non-European world for European purposes. The cartographic rationalization of space, he writes, allowed for the idea of a world "over which systematic dominance was possible, and provided a powerful framework for political expansion and control" (87).

This geometric rationalization of space thus has everything to do with the history of the encounter between Europe and America. According to Mignolo, the Ptolemaic revolution provided Europeans with a powerful cartography, "powerful" in that it combined the appearance of ideological transparency with an unacknowledged political function. Between 1570 and 1630, Spain brought this powerful cartography to bear upon the rationalization of its sprawling American empire. The gridded spaces of Renaissance maps had established themselves in the eyes of Europeans as the only true and accurate way of representing territory. Now, their authority would be used to strip Amerindian territorial imaginations of their ability to do likewise, and would contribute in significant ways to the deterritorialization of Amerindians (Mignolo 1995, 219–58). A modernity at once scientific and imperialistic thus finds one of its origins in the twin phenomena of Renaissance cartography and the European invention of America.

We would do well, however, to refrain from believing that this revolution in cartography and spatiality was sudden, quick, or universal. As Richard Kagan has recently noted, the cartography of this period—and he is referring specifically to Spanish mapmaking—was not a unified, homogeneous enterprise. The geometrically rationalized cartography introduced by the cartographic revolution was labor-intensive and intellectually demanding. It required suitably trained experts and considerable material support, both of which were in limited supply in early modern Spain. What resources were available were primarily concentrated in Seville, where the cosmographers of the Casa de la Contratación supervised the official cartography of the crown. Eager to keep its up-to-date geographical knowledge from international rivals, the crown prohibited the printing of these maps. As a result, the vast majority of Spanish maps produced during this period were those developed on the margins, or even entirely outside the methods, assumptions, and institutions of the cartographic revolution (Kagan 2000, 55–63). This was especially true of the period before 1570, when Philip II began to aggressively institutionalize the geographical (as opposed to the nautical and maritime) cartography of Hispanic imperialism. Outside of the efforts of the Casa de la Contratación, the mapping of empire before 1570 was a haphazard affair, often carried out by people with little technical training.

But while we should not mistake the elite culture of the cartographic revolution for the whole of Spanish mapmaking, neither should we be too hasty about generalizations regarding the cartography of nonelite mapmakers. Some cultural historians have opposed the new cartography of the Renaissance to a monolithic alternative, a "symbolic cartography" or a "poetic cartography" that has its roots in some very old habits of mind and that persists well into the early modern period, sometimes alongside and sometimes even within the new gridded maps.[25] One of the problems with these concepts is that all maps are in some sense "symbolic" or "poetic" in that they all inscribe and support notions of space and world that are logically prior to their specific content. What these concepts seem to distinguish, then, is a type of cartography in which the symbolic and/or poetic dimensions inherent in all maps are not camouflaged by the overt presence of claims to strict empiricism. The trouble is that not all of the alternative cartographies of the early modern period—the sorts of maps that the early modern period inherited from the late Middle Ages and that persisted alongside the new cartography—are of this kind. The *mappaemundi* of medieval ecclesiastics represent only one kind of medieval map. Other communities made and used very different sorts of maps, even maps just as "empirical"—that is, not as overtly symbolic as a medieval *mappamundi*—as any map of the European Renaissance. These maps, however, were built upon a notion of space that was quite different from that of the new Renaissance cartography, a notion of space that responded to the scarcity of maps of any kind in the medieval world, that suited a world in which the words "map" and "space" hardly circulated at all.

The sixteenth century sometimes clung to the old as a site of resistance to the newly hegemonic gridded map. Thus, in the Hispanic world, we find that a variety of past trends continue to hold a strong lease on life, remaining uninformed by Ptolemy and his grid.[26] The century opens with earliest extant map depicting the coastlines of the Caribbean, a nautical chart drawn by Juan de la Cosa sometime around 1500. It is a so-called portolan chart, a type of nautical chart developed in the late Middle Ages, and exhibits none of the innovations favored by contemporary humanists enthusiastically thumbing through Ptolemy (fig. 13). At century's close, maps like this one were still being used and produced not only in Spain but throughout the Mediterranean. Along the way, we also find hybrids of the old and the new, like the chart that accompanies the *Libro de grandezas y cosas memorables de España*. Its grid, like any grid, speaks of the era's newfound mastery of the sea and stretches across the old boundaries of the *orbis terrarum* to include a world much wider than the geography of old. But it also exhibits a compass rose, like that of Juan de la Cosa's chart, as well as images of ships crossing its seas. These elements, as we shall see in the next chapter, are the hallmarks of an old spatiality that persists even here, in this chart drawn by a well-known member of Spain's cartographic elite. In that chapter, I survey the cartographic culture of the early modern Hispanic world, in search not of its monumental achievements but of its pockets of resistance, its tendency to produce hybrids of the old and the new, its reluctant assimilation of the new cartography and its new, geometricized space. As we shall see, this search entails the interrogation of some commonplace assumptions, including the very definition of the words "map" and "space," as well as the reassessment of texts that, for many readers, probably seem only "maplike."

In the three chapters that follow, I turn to discursive, rather than iconographic, cartography, as it unfolds in three monuments from Spain's attempt to write about the Americas. The move from iconographic to discursive maps,

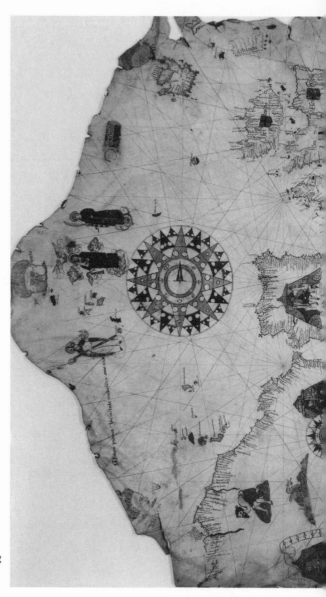

13 Mateo Prunes, maritime chart on vellum of the Mediterranean and Western Europe (Majorca, 1559). Catalonia was one of the major centers of chart production in the late Middle Ages and continued to produce charts in the traditional style well into the sixteenth century and beyond. Note the rhumb lines emanating from elaborate compass roses, and the densely packed rows of place names along the coastlines. The lavish illustration of this chart was typical of the Catalan style. The Geography and Map Division of the Library of Congress.

as I argue at the beginning of chapter 3, responds to the discussion of space and cartography that I carry out in chapter 2. The balance of the chapter is devoted to Hernán Cortés's "Second Letter from Mexico." I examine some of the ways in which Cortés's famous account of the conquest of Mexico depends upon the traditional notion of space outlined in chapter 2. In chapter 4, I turn to Francisco López de Gómara's *Historia general de las Indias*, an early-modern bestseller that adapted Cortés's account and combined it with a general history, as the name implies, of the entire Spanish experience in the Americas. My analysis focuses on the first of its two volumes, the general history, as an attempt to map the Americas as a whole into European consciousness and into Spanish imperialism. Here we see medieval conceptions of space gradually yield to modern ones. Finally, in chapter 5, I turn to the masterpiece of Spanish cartographic literature, the epic poem *La Araucana* by Alonso de Ercilla y Zúñiga. This verse narrative of the conquest of Chile was also a bestseller in Spain, if not elsewhere. It was praised by Cervantes on two occasions and may even have influenced the composition of *Don Quixote*. At one point, the knightly protagonist in the *Araucana* enjoys a magical vision of the whole world that the mad knight only imagines, but, anticipating Cervantes's satire of imperial ambition, the *Araucana* only appears to marshal cartography in the service of empire. On its pages, the old and the new mingle in what ultimately becomes an acerbic attack on Spanish imperial ambitions and even on the very possibility of imperial cartography. A brief conclusion returns to the problematic emergence of the collusion between empire and map as I have traced it in these contributions to Hispanic cartographic literature.

2

I have been using "map" and related words as if they required no definition, although I have hinted at some, and have acknowledged that it is possible to approach a map in a variety of ways. Of course, I cannot remain silent about the meaning of these words, especially since they have become pervasive in many intellectual disciplines and as a result have come to mean many and varied things.[1] What, then, do I mean by a map? We might begin with an old-fashioned but quite respectable definition of a map as "[a] representation, usually on a plane surface, of all or part of the earth or some other body showing a group of features in terms of their relative size and position" (Thrower 1996, 254).[2] This definition certainly describes many, if not all, of the images reproduced in this book, but it is difficult to understand how it could be applied to the texts that I discuss in chapters 3 through 5, texts that I have referred to as pieces of "cartographic literature." Although some of these texts carry out lengthy descriptions of the Indies, in part or in whole, in no case is "the representation" of "all or part of the earth" the primary objective. All are historical narratives of some kind, not primarily geographical ones. As such, moreover, none of them can be categorized as a representation on a "plane surface," if by this we mean some sort of image. How then, can I claim that these texts constitute pieces of "cartographic literature"? Obviously, I have an alternative definition of a map, or of cartography, waiting somewhere in the wings.

In order to bring this new definition center stage in the clearest possible manner, I dedicate most of this chapter to discussing what a map is and what it has been. In doing so, I hope to tease out some of the diversity inherent in the culture of early modern Spain. First, I locate the gridded map and the abstract spatiality it supports in a particular sector of Spanish culture, a cartographic elite that worked, primarily, in the interests of the crown. Then, I turn to certain kinds of maps produced in Europe during the late Middle Ages before the advent of the gridded map and the particular kind of technical specialists that worked with it. These maps, I argue, are predicated upon a notion of space quite different from the abstract, isotropic expanse of the gridded map. I then return from the Middle Ages to the sixteenth-century Hispanic world, to see how these kinds of maps—and, with them, the notion of space they embody—persisted well beyond the fifteenth-century rediscovery of Ptolemy. Finally, I turn to an innovative piece of Spanish geographical writing in order to explore an important nuance to this history of maps and spatiality. In the *Suma de geografía* of Martín Fernández de Enciso (1519), we see how the two notions of space in question—one modern and emergent, the other medieval and dominant—could coexist in a single, hybrid text. In Enciso's *Suma* we find a snapshot of the early modern effort to assimilate the new while remaining rooted in the old. The same text, moreover, provides the point of departure for chapter 3, in which I turn from iconographic to discursive cartography. There, I argue that the history of space in sixteenth-century Spain not only makes it possible to consider discourse as a type of mapping, but actually makes it desirable, even necessary, to do so.

The Location of Abstract Space

To begin, I offer another definition of a "map," one even more restrictive than the one I have just cited. This definition appears in print at a crucial time, during the first third of the eighteenth century. By then, the scale cartography pioneered by the Renaissance had made significant technical strides and, as a result, had become indispensable to all kinds of activities. With this expansion in the quality and quantity of scale maps naturally came the naturalization of words like "map" and "space" in the languages of Western Europe. As I mentioned above, the various modern derivatives of the Latin *mappa* were new to the tongues of most sixteenth-century Europeans, and the derivatives of the Latin *spatium* were only then coming to mean what they mean for later periods (Zumthor 1993, 51). The monumental *Diccionario de autoridades*, composed by the Real Academia Española in an attempt to establish uniform standards for Spain's national language, registers both *mapa* and *espacio* as do other prominent Enlightenment dictionaries.[3] Significantly, the *Diccionario de autoridades* ties the two terms together and links both to modern scale cartography. It defines *espacio* primarily as an abstract expanse, a definition consistent with the sort of space that structures the gridded map. It even makes explicit reference to latitude and longitude: "ESPACIO . . . Capacity, breadth, longitude or latitude of a terrain, a place, or a field. It is taken from the Latin *spatium*, which signifies the same."[4] The *Diccionario de autoridades* defines "Mapa," meanwhile, in terms that also associate it exclusively with the learned cartography of Europe since the Renaissance and the sort of spatiality referred to in its own definition of *espacio*:

> MAPA . . . The geographical description of the earth, usually done on paper
> or canvas, and upon which one puts the places, seas, rivers, mountains, other
> notable things, with proportionate distances, according to the scale one chooses,
> marking the degrees of latitude and longitude of the country one describes, so
> that the location or place of these things on the earth can be known.[5]

If the *Diccionario de autoridades* is any indication, it seems that by the time of its publication (1726–39), the new culture of cartography and abstract spatiality had taken hold in Spain as it had elsewhere, but what about earlier periods? How far back in the history of Spanish culture can we take this link between mapping and abstract space?

An earlier dictionarypaints a very different picture. In the *Tesoro de la lengua castellana o española* (1611),[6] Sebastián de Covarrubias Horozco registers only a vague spatial definition for *espacio*, one that simply reduces it to a synonym of "place": "ESPACIO. From the Latin word SPATIUM, *capedo, intervallum*; meaning place. Much space, little space" (Covarrubias Horozco 1994, 503). *Mapa*, in Covarrubias, also lacks the specificity of the definition in the *Diccionario de autoridades*. Like its academic successor, the *Tesoro* defines "mapa" through reference to a preferred object of representation, the surface of the earth, and to its physical medium, a flat surface, usually made of paper. Unlike the *Diccionario de autoridades*, however, Covarrubias makes no mention of any abstract spatial armature: "MAPA. Is what we call the table, canvas or paper on which one describes the earth, in whole or in part, and might be derived from MAPPA, which means canvas or towel" (Covarrubias Horozco 1994, 735). Lacking any mention of that spatial armature, his definition of *mapa* remains entirely independent of his definition of *espacio*. This lack of precision in Covarrubias's definitions comes as no surprise. His relatively vague treatment of both terms registers the novelty of *mapa* and of at least one sense of *espacio*. It thereby suggests that the twin phenomena of the scale map and an abstract, geometricized notion of space had not yet come to dominate what was meant more generally by these two terms. That modern spatiality that gives pride of place to abstraction was still only gestating.

But the *Tesoro* has even more to reveal. Not only is Covarrubias's definition of *espacio* as "place" rather vague, it shares the entry with another definition that was much more in tune with contemporary linguistic usage. That usage, significantly, had nothing to do with space. For this father of Spanish lexicographers, as for most early modern Spaniards, *espacio* simply did not refer to spatial extension: it referred to an interval of time. "It also abbreviates the interval of time," Covarrubias writes, "and so we say for a *space* of time of so many hours, etc" (1994, 503). The examples of this temporal definition in early modern Spanish usage are legion. It constitutes, for example, the most common meaning of the word in Fernando de Rojas's literary classic, *La Celestina* (1499–1502):

> What a long *space* [time, delay] the old bearded woman takes! (Rojas 1989, 138)
> Give, sir, relief to your heart, for in so short a *space of time* such great good fortune does not fit. (220)
> O *spacious* [slowly moving] clock, how I would like to see you burn in the living fire of love. (292; emphasis added)[7]

The lifespan of this temporal sense of *espacio* stretches well into the eighteenth century, at least. The *Diccionario de autoridades* registers it: "It also means interval of time, and so one says 'For the space of one hour, one day, one month, one year, etc.'" Among the literary authorities cited to illustrate this definition are of Saint Teresa of Ávila's *Libro de la vida* (1565; "One can very well represent it before one's imagination, and remain gazing upon it some *space*"; emphasis added) and the *Historia de España* of Juan de Mariana (1592; "A drought of land and air, which lasted for a *space* of twenty-six years"; emphasis added). We could also mention an example from Pedro Calderón de la Barca's allegorical drama, *El gran teatro del mundo* (ca. 1634). In this instance, Calderón's Spanish clings to the temporal definition of the word even as the speaker invokes an optical regime that should, it seems, play upon its spatial sense: "I look upon my extended empires, / my majesty, my glory, my grandeur, / in whose variety nature / *spaciously* [slowly] perfected its cares" (1987, 961–64).

But while *espacio* had not yet come to be identified with an abstract, two-dimensional expanse either in the work of Spain's first lexicographer or in the culture at large, it nonetheless makes its appearance in the writings of a small minority of technical specialists. In these writings, *espacio* does indeed appear as the term for an abstract, two-dimensional (or sometimes three-dimensional) expanse that is occupied by various objects, that can be measured, and that can be subdivided. We find it, for example, in the definitions given the terms "zone" or "climate" by various cosmographers and geographers:

> Note that climate means the same as region or part of the earth, which, according to Columella, is seventy feet wide, and another seventy long . . . The astrologers

do not understand climate in these terms, but rather say that climate is a *space* of earth, large or small, whose beginnings are toward the equinoctial and whose end is toward the Pole. (Chaves 1545, 81v)

And so a climate can be defined as a space of earth, placed between two parallels. (Girava 1556, 35)

These zones, just as they divide and embrace the heavens, so too they divide and embrace the land in another five parts . . . in this way on the earth (many times smaller than the heavens) another set of *spaces* are represented. (Pérez de Moya 1573, 145)

Climate is the same as sheet, or region, and this is a space of land that is included between two parallels. (Ferrer Maldonado 1626, 198)

These authors occupied a particular location in early modern Hispanic culture. All of them were technical people, actively involved in drawing maps and sea charts or in disseminating the new, mathematically rationalized geography to other practitioners. Many of them might have answered to the name of "cosmographer." Together, they constitute the avant-garde of Hispanic cartography and, with it, of Hispanic spatiality. That sense of *espacio* so noticeably absent from Covarrubias and from the rest of literate Hispanic culture, *espacio* as a two-dimensional expanse—three-dimensional, if we consider that some of these passages refer to climates as portions of a sphere—appears here in their technical writings.

Who were these "cosmographers"? Cosmography was that branch of learning dedicated to understanding the natural world. It endeavored to understand as a unified whole a number of subjects that the West would eventually consider separately, including astronomy, meteorology, chronology, and geography. During the Middle Ages, cosmography was a formal academic affair, studied in universities like the one at Salamanca. During the fifteenth and sixteenth centuries, however, cosmography began to extend itself beyond its traditional, strictly theoretical concerns into novel, more practical matters. Navigation, surveying, and mapmaking were among the new applied sciences that came to live under the cosmographical umbrella. With this change came a change in the social location of cosmography. Although it continued to be studied at the universities, it also attracted practitioners far removed from its cloisters. It became possible for an experienced pilot of ships to decorate his practical experience with a veneer of book learning and thereby call himself a cosmographer. Likewise, it became possible, eventually, for university students to make their book learning pay by asserting their authority over unschooled practitioners such as pilots. As Portugal and Castile came to compete with each other for overseas trade routes, Alison Sandman argues, the activities of these applied cosmographers came to the attention of the powerful.

Both crowns turned to cosmographers for the technical help they needed in negotiating their competing territorial claims, and, in the 1494 Treaty of Tordesillas, dividing the world between them. When Portugal and Castile renegotiated the terms of that treaty in 1524, they once again turned to the cosmographers to settle the necessary cartographic matters and thus sealed the relationship between cosmography and state power (Sandman 2001, 26–91).[8]

Spain, as I mentioned briefly in chapter 1, soon followed the earlier example of Portugal in recruiting skilled technicians to map its expanding Atlantic empire. In 1508, the crown created the position of pilot major at the Casa de la Contratación in Seville. Among the responsibilities of this manager of overseas trade was the maintenance of a *padrón general*, or master pattern chart, which would be used to record the data of incoming expeditions of discovery and to produce up-to-date charts for outgoing expeditions. Other cosmographers residing in Seville and licensed by the crown made their living by fabricating and selling charts based upon the *padrón general*. As the century progressed, the mapmaking activities of the Casa de la Contratación were further professionalized. More academically oriented cosmographers, like Pedro de Medina, asserted their authority over the self-made pilots. Eventually, the chartmaking activities of the Casa de la Contratación came under the supervision of the chronicler-cosmographer of the Indies, a cosmographer more closely associated with the court. Cosmography was no stranger to the court of Charles V, where for many years Alonso de Santa Cruz served as cosmographer-royal. He drew a salary from the crown and provided various scientific services, including the cosmographical education of the king and investigations into crucial problems such as that of measuring longitude. In 1571, the crown's American interests had grown so large and complex that the Council of the Indies, the royal body charged with supervising all American affairs, created the post of chronicler-cosmographer of the Indies. It appointed Juan López de Velasco to the job, and charged him with investigating the history and geography of the Americas. Eventually, it gave him supervisory authority over the cartographic activities of the Casa de la Contratación. Philip II crowned this process of institutional development with the creation of the Academy of Mathematics. Operating from 1582 to 1627, it worked to professionalize a number of technical activities, among them cosmography and navigation.[9]

These institutionalized settings were not the only ones that brought cosmography into the orbit of the state. Many of the period's most notable cartographic achievements were the work of independent favor seekers and professional freelancers. The first geographical description of the Americas in Castilian, for example, appeared in the *Suma de geografía* (Seville, 1519) written independently by the conquistador Martín Fernández de Enciso. The first extensive geographical description of Spain itself, meanwhile, is the unfinished *Descripción y cosmografía de España*, written in 1517 by Fernando Colón at the behest of Ferdinand the Catholic. Pedro Esquivel, a professor of mathematics at the University of Alcalá, was hired by Philip II to execute the first triangulated survey of Spain, while Francisco Domínguez was hired to do the same for New Spain. Finally, a group of royal engineers, often Italians hired on an ad hoc basis, were responsible for maps of individual fortifications and cities, including those in Spain's vital port cities along the coasts of the Caribbean and the Gulf of Mexico.[10]

The cosmographers operating in these various contexts did not work in isolation from each other. Far from it—cosmographers working in the Iberian Peninsula were often brought together by accident or design, in increasingly regularized institutional settings, at exceptional cosmographic juntas organized by the crown, or by virtue of sheer geographical proximity, particularly in Seville. Distrust and mutual recrimination was just as likely to mark their interactions as was a spirit of shared scientific enterprise. Nonetheless, together they formed an identifiable community of intellectuals dedicated to resolving a shared set of problems, albeit in disagreement over how best to do so. The coherence of the group only grew as the century progressed. The university men asserted their authority over unschooled pilots, and the assumption of the Portuguese throne by Philip II made it easier for Seville and Lisbon to share information and expertise.[11] As a group, these cosmographers shared a set of canonical texts, including the *Geographia* of Ptolemy and the *De Sphaera Mundi* of Joannes de Sacro Bosco. Whether or not they held university degrees, all of them shared a commitment to geometric abstraction as the preferred method for mapping the earth and its parts, as well as a commitment to improving scale maps. It is among the members of this community, particularly among those writing after, roughly, the middle of the sixteenth century, that *espacio* comes to refer to planar extension. It is among them that the new spatiality emerges as a cultural phenomenon.

But these technical specialists formed only a portion of those Iberians that dedicated themselves to Spain's imperial enterprise. They were a minority even among those who, for whatever reason, in whatever manner, put pen to paper in an attempt to help Castilians imagine their newfound colonies. Among the authors of all kinds of Spanish Americana, whether historical, geographical, cartographical, we find conquistadors with only rudimentary educations, highly educated humanists, friars, low-level colonial administrators, ambitious courtiers, scribes of mixed Spanish and Amerindian ancestry, and many others who remained uninitiated, entirely or partially, in the science of cosmography. These participants may have seen and handled sophisticated maps at some time or another, but on the whole, they remained unequipped to imagine territory in the geometrically rationalized manner that formed part of the emergence of abstract space in Western culture. Among them is no less important a figure than Hernán Cortés, who clearly understood the value of maps in conquering and exploiting territory but who, in his five letters to the king about the conquest of Mexico, never once uses the word *mapa* and never uses *espacio* to refer to two-dimensional space.[12] Among them, too, is Francisco López de Gómara, author of one of the period's most popular histories of the conquest and a highly educated humanist. Gómara was obviously familiar with maps and had no trouble using the word *mapa*. Nonetheless, when he wants to communicate the notion of a two-dimensional expanse, he does not use *espacio*, but rather its adjectival form, *espacioso*: "The place was *spacious* and level and with fewer rivers, and there they availed themselves of their firearms, which always hit their mark, and their swords, for they finally had to fight hand-to-hand" (López de Gómara 1987, 73). With this oblique invocation of two-dimensional space through the use of the adjective "spacious," Gómara marks his position outside the technical elite ready to use the more substantial *espacio*. He may be familiar with maps, but he has not entirely assimilated their order of abstraction. Neither has Alonso de Ercilla, author of the landmark epic poem about the conquest of Chile, the *Araucana*. As an integral member of the court of Philip II, Ercilla undoubtedly had access to maps, globes, and atlases of all kinds. Yet, never once, in any of his poem's thousands of verses, does he use *espacio* in its emergent sense.

But such observations about what these authors do not do leaves us with an important, as yet unanswered question. If space was not imagined as an abstract two-dimensional expanse, then how was it imagined? Can we even speak of "space" and "maps" in a culture that was then only entering modernity, with its plentiful maps and its habitual abstractions? In order to venture an answer, we will have to heed Jose Antonio Maravall, who reminds us that if history is to identify what is there, rather than merely what is not there, we must take the trouble to "reshape in part the a prioristic, interpretative schemas with which we come prepared" (Maravall 1972, 1: 7). It is not that we can eliminate such a priori schemas—history can never be thought outside of the horizon of our own historicity—but we can replace them with others that promise to provide a more nuanced account of the sources before us. This is what I attempt to do in the pages that follow. I turn to certain strands of medieval cartography, discover in them another way of conceptualizing space, and then trace the persistence of this conceptualization into the sixteenth century. Certainly, it is not the only way, besides geometric abstraction, that space was conceived and represented in early modern Spain, but it is one that is particularly germane to Hispanic attempts to map its Atlantic empire.

Itineraries, Charts, and Medieval Space

Historians of cartography know very well that the *mappaemundi* of the Middle Ages and the Renaissance shared the cultural field with other kinds of maps, ones that tend to be forgotten when the scholarly conversation turns away from the history of cartographic techniques to questions of "space" and its history. Along with the *mappaemundi*, they recognize at least three other strands of medieval mapmaking: local and regional topographical maps; portolan charts; and celestial maps. Each type, the *mappaemundi* included, belonged to a distinct, relatively independent tradition of mapmaking, associated with particular communities outside of which mapmaking and map use were extremely rare (1987b, 283).[13] For reasons that should become readily apparent, the two types most relevant to my argument are local and regional topographical maps and portolan charts. Together they defy the stereotype suggested by privileging ecclesiastical *mappaemundi* as representatives of medieval mapmaking as a whole, that it was exclusively or even primarily concerned with a symbolic or theological conception of space and world. They also provide a preliminary answer to the question I posed above about the possible spatiality of the great majority of early moderns who were not technical specialists.

I begin with the local and regional topographical map, and, in particular, the itinerary map. Some of the extant medieval maps of regions and local topographies, P. D. A. Harvey reminds us, are actually geometrically rationalized maps, obviously drawn on the basis of some kind of survey. These include the ninth-century plan of the Abbey of Saint Gall in Switzerland and the fourteenth-century map of Palestine by Pietro Vesconte. These maps, however, constitute exceptions in a world in which scale mapping was almost entirely unknown (Harvey 1987a, 466–84).[14] That world tended to map regions by means of a kind of map known as an itinerary map. According to Harvey, this kind of map "seems to have been better understood in medieval Europe than other kinds of cartography" (1980, 495). The itinerary map is the clear locus of that alternative spatiality to which I have alluded, a spatiality that is very different from the planar extension of the gridded map and one that the Middle Ages bequeaths to the early modern period.

Like any type of map, an itinerary map represents the result of a variety of choices. The mapmaker, any mapmaker, must decide which of the many and varied aspects of the territory to include, which to exclude, and how to handle the material selected for representation. The maker of an itinerary map selects as his or her chosen objects of representation, privileged travel destinations and the routes that connect them. All other aspects of the territory—its general topography, its predominant kinds of vegetation, its aridity or humidity—are usually excluded. The Middle Ages offer various examples of itinerary maps, many from England, but the most famous of them is the so-called Peutinger Tabula (fig. 14). This is essentially a road map of the Roman Empire dating from no later than the fourth or fifth century, and known to us through a copy from the eleventh or twelfth century. It consists of eleven sheets of parchment (a twelfth is missing) that can be assembled into a strip about twenty-three feet long and fourteen inches wide. It rationalizes territory as a series of destinations along preferred routes of travel, and it does so as clearly as possible, even at the cost of sacrificing other spatial characteristics of the geography depicted. North-south distances have been dramatically abbreviated relative to east-west ones. As O. A. Dilke points out, on the Peutinger Tabula, Rome looks like it is closer to Carthage than Naples is to Pompeii (Dilke 1987, 238).[15] It compensates for this spatial distortion by marking distances from one place to another, thereby allowing a competent user to derive useful travel information from its deformed image. In this way, the Peutinger Tabula resembles a modern subway or road map, or the sort of map that we scribble when we give driving directions to an out-of-town visitor. Like those maps—modern versions of the medieval itinerary map—the Peutinger Tabula abandons any hope of a fixed, uniform scale for the sake of serving the traveler's needs (Harvey 1980, 139). It can be used to get from place to place along one of its marked routes, but it cannot be used to cut across the territory (Harvey 1987a, 495).

In this way, the two-dimensionality of the itinerary map does not mean the same thing as that of the gridded map. The blank spaces of the itinerary map are empty in a way that the blank spaces of the gridded map are not. As we saw earlier, the blank spaces of the gridded map may be bereft of geographical objects, but they nonetheless speak of the plenitude of Euclidean space. They do not represent the parts of the map's surface that are left over once the territory has been drawn, but the portions of the cartographic grid that have yet to be filled. The empty spaces of the itinerary map, by contrast, represent nothing as substantial as this. Like the spaces that separate one letter from another or one word from another in writing, they are simply the portions of the space of representation that are not inscribed upon. They provide the "spacing effects" that are necessary for the inscription to be legible, but lacking any geometric basis, they do not provide a spatial framework into which one can plot new locations. Certainly, one can add a road to the itinerary map, thereby cutting through this space and connecting locations that were not previously attached. In doing so, however, one is merely writing over one of the leftover bits of the original blankness, not plotting locations into an isotropic space.

These characteristics have led historians of cartography to categorize itinerary maps—whether those of the European Middle Ages or of other places and times—as "way-finding maps." They are not "maps," but "drawings," "sketch-maps," or in Spanish, "croquis." [16] Like late medieval and early modern nautical charts, they are pieces of practical cartography meant to serve of the purpose of "getting there," but not to be mistaken for serious representations of space and world. Such maps are very important to anthropologists and historians of cartography. In the study of some non-Western cultures, way-finding maps may be the only kind of map in circulation, and thus become crucial to understanding how those groups conceptualize and use space. In the history of cartography in the West, way-finding maps, particularly nautical charts, constitute an important object of study in their own right. Rarely, however, do they impinge on histories of Western spatiality, where the more theoretical cartography of the learned—whether of medieval ecclesiastics or Renaissance humanists—is left to glitter all on its own. Walter Mignolo, for example, sets aside way-finding maps in his discussion of early modern European spatiality. As he explains, "These maps," referring to the nautical charts of the Casa de la Contratación, "do not conceptualize the Indies so much as the coastlines hitherto unknown to Western Europe" (Mignolo 1995, 286). [17] It seems that one would never confuse practical maps like these—be they sixteenth-century nautical charts, contemporary maps of subway systems, or our own sketched maps of the roads leading to our houses—with maps of a more scientific nature. The scale map and its spatiality serve as synecdoches for the cartography and the spatiality of the culture as a whole, while the way-finding map can be consigned to the category of second-order cartographic products and omitted from further discussion of spatiality. [18] In the pages that follow, I hope to challenge this tendency to marginalize way-finding maps by arguing that they do indeed encode an important way of conceptualizing space.

During the final decades of the twentieth century, definitions of the map like the one in the *Diccionario de autoridades*, or the much more recent one cited at the beginning of the chapter, have been brought into question for their excessive exclusivity. Historians of cartography have come to understand the pitfalls inherent in building a definition of the map on the basis of a particular kind of cartography that is peculiar to the West. A vastly more inclusive definition has been proposed. "Maps," writes J. Brian Harley, "are graphic

PEVTINGERIANA TABVLA ITINERARIA
ex Augusta Bibliotheca Vindobonensi.
cura Francis. Christ. Von Scheyb. 1753.

Segm. I.

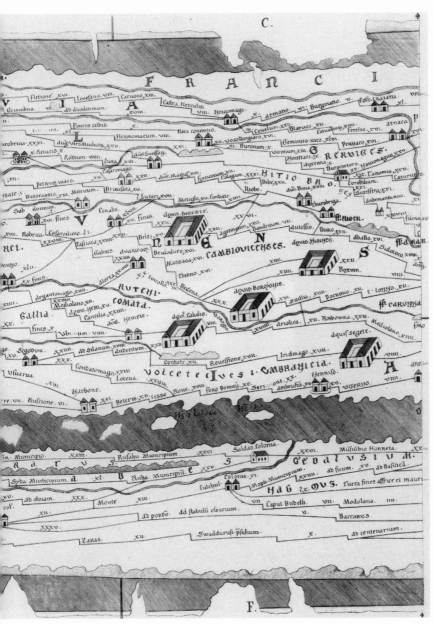

14 A portion of the Peutinger Tabula, which is an eleventh- or twelfth-century copy of a map drawn ca. 400 C.E. This section depicts parts of Britain and Spain near its left edge. Most of the upper landmass is modern France, and the lower landmass is part of North Africa. The Geography and Map Division of the Library of Congress.

representations that facilitate a spatial understanding of things, concepts, conditions, processes, or events in the human world" (Harley and Woodward 1987, xvi).[19] Let us look at some of the ways in which this definition dramatically revises its predecessors. First, it denies "the surface of the earth" the status it once enjoyed as the privileged object of cartographical representation, and replaces it with an extremely ample set of possible referents, "things, concepts, conditions, processes, or events in the human world." Second, it transfers the definitional accent from the map's referent to the cartographical sign and its unique nature. A map, apparently, is not a representation of the earth, but a particular kind of graphical sign, one that provides a "spatial understanding" of all kinds of referents. The definition, furthermore, does not specify what is meant by a "spatial understanding" of the map referent. In this way, it avoids the exclusivity of a definition like that of the *Diccionario de autoridades*, which asserts that maps plot their referent into a particular kind of space, the abstract space of Euclidean geometry. It thereby acknowledges, albeit implicitly, that "space" is a plural, contingent concept that varies over time and across cultures, and that maps can differ in the sort of "spatial understanding" they provide just as much as they can differ in the kinds of referents they represent. It thus becomes possible to recognize all sorts of artifacts quite exotic to the modern Western imagination, not as maplike images, not as drawings, not as paintings, but as *maps*, that are in some meaningful way commensurate with anything published by Rand McNally.

But how can the "spatial understanding" of these itinerary maps, their representation of territory as a network of routes connecting preferred destinations of travel, be understood as anything more than just an attempt to suit the needs of the pilgrim or the merchant? How can their "spatial understanding" be understood as a vision of space and world commensurate with that of a *mappamundi*? Philology provides an important answer. Unlike the various vernacular derivatives of the Latin *mappa*, vernacular descendants of *spatium* did indeed circulate in the Middle Ages, but they meant something very different from what they would come to mean in modern times, something spatial in addition to their temporal use. Medieval European culture, Paul Zumthor tells us, thought primarily in terms of *place* rather than *space*. For the medieval imagination, places were charged with a positive sense of thickness, stability, and indivisibility.[20] Space, by contrast, was nothing but the empty "in between," something that only came into existence as the distance separating two places, two significant points of reference (Zumthor 1994, 52). It was, in effect, the unidimensional distance that one would have to travel to get "there," to go to a distant place, or to return from one. Thus, "space," when it was used to speak of spatial extension rather than of time, did not refer to area but to distance. It was the "chronological or topographical interval that separated two points of reference" (Zumthor 1994, 51). The network of lines connecting significant destinations on medieval and early modern itinerary maps represents, perhaps, its most appropriate medium of iconographic representation. It is the spatiality of a culture for whom the road map, the subway map, exists as an idiom for figuring territory in the absence of a hegemonic notion of the scale map.

According to Zumthor, this usage of *spatium* to refer to a topographical interval appears in French, and then in other European vernaculars, when European culture begins to turn its gaze beyond its borders toward the East. Fittingly, it is the sense of space that underpins one of the most famous travel narratives of the European Middle Ages, the book written by the Venetian merchant Marco Polo in collaboration with the romance writer Rustichello da Pisa. The title often given to editions of this book—*The Travels* or some iteration thereof—responds to the very nature of the text, which concatenates descriptions of significant places through reference to the routes one would travel to get from one to the other,[21] in the following manner:

> After leaving the Province of which I have been speaking, you come to a great Desert. In fact you ride for two days and a half continually down hill. On all this descent there is nothing worthy of mention except only there is a large place there where occasionally a great market is held . . . After you have ridden those two days and a half down hill, you find yourself in a province towards the south which is pretty near to India, and this province is called Amien. (Polo 1993, 2: 106–7)

But one of the original titles of Marco Polo's book suggests that it was meant to be taken as something else. That title, *Le divisament du monde*, or "The Description of the World," suggests a geographic piece rather than a travel narrative.[22] Indeed, Marco Polo's book often disappoints the reader looking for a tale of heroic exploration. "Nothing is more striking here," John Larner points out, "than Marco's silence about the difficulties and dangers he must have faced or about the character of the journeys he made" (Larner 1999, 68). Although the text pays constant attention to the routes of travel, it rarely mentions the travails of the traveler. This silence contributes to Larner's conclusion that the itineraries reproduced by the text "are fantasies . . . an organizational device . . . the route through the Book" (69). Finally, Larner asserts that the text is not really travel narrative at all, but "simply and essentially a work of geography" (77). Its primary purpose is not to narrate Polo's trip to the East but to describe the land he traveled through.

It would be mistaken, however, to conclude that the itinerary that serves to concatenate Polo's descriptions of the cities and wonders of the East represents nothing more than a "mere" organizational device. That skeletal travel narrative, like any skeleton, may be bare bones, but it is not superficial. Consider the following example:

> Now, we will quit this country. I shall not, however, now go on to tell you about India; but when time and place shall suit we shall come round from the north and tell you about it. For the present, let us return by another road to the aforesaid city of Kerman, for we cannot get at those countries that I wish to tell you about except through that city . . . On the road by which we return from Hormos to Kerman you meet with some very fine plains, and you also find many natural hot baths . . . Now, then, I am going to tell you about the countries towards the north, of which you shall hear in regular order. (Polo 1993, 1: 109–10)

Why should the narrator need to backtrack to a city previously described in order to push his description forward? Why not simply describe the next place, whether it be to the north or the south? While Marco Polo's text may not tell of the hazards and impressions of the journey, it does not entirely forget the limitations of the flesh-and-blood traveler. The result is something richer than what Larner identifies. This is not just geography organized as a textual itinerary, but geography organized as a journey, as a linear movement through space, a route of travel, albeit a possibly fictive one. By reminding us, at this point, that we need to backtrack to a particular node in a network if we wish to move in a certain direction, the discourse invites us to relate to the territory from a particular point of view. It apostrophizes the reader, not as an onlooker looking down on the territory from a height, as in a map, but as a traveler, moving through that territory, place by place, along routes.

In this way, Marco Polo's text can be thought of as representing the opposite of a map. Maps can be understood as a technology through which European culture learned to regard its world from an elevated point of view (Hillis 1994, 10; Lestringant 1991, 16). Maps invite the reader to situate him or herself in an Apollonian position from which he or she can gaze down upon a territory. Hence the clouds and personifications of the various winds that often frame Renaissance maps of the world (fig. 1 above). Through them, these maps self-consciously announce a new framework for spatial representation that was only beginning to come into its own, one in which the world—the whole world, that geography only available to the eye through the mediation of the map—was not just figured, but spectacularized for consumption by an ideal reader looking down from a commanding height (fig. 1 above). Marco Polo's itinerary, by contrast, assumes that the reader is earthbound and must, therefore, live and work within the limitations that bodies suffer as they move through territories. His text does not invite the reader to abstract him or herself from the body's limitations, to assume that commanding position from which the eyes can follow any route, not matter how difficult, no matter what the obstacles. While the map apostrophizes a reader who enjoys an abstract, idealized, and static point of view, the itinerary addresses a reader who is embodied, earthbound, and dynamic.

The itinerary map, in turn, does indeed spectacularize the territory for ocular inspection by an Apollonian onlooker, but it only does so to then draw that reader back into its territory and have him trace journeys along its routes. Remember, the distortions inherent in the way itinerary maps figure territory do not allow the reader's eye to wander in any useful or meaningful way off the network of routes. Although the image is two-dimensional, it can only be read and used in ways that are, in a sense, unidimensional. Its spectacularization of the territory is therefore only tentative, illustrative. It is also exceptional. The medieval itinerary map dates from a period before that early modern revolution in mapmaking, from a time when maps of all kinds were rare things, when the vernacular derivatives of *mappa* were not even in general circulation. In the absence of sustained contact with readily available maps, Europeans, it seems, had nothing that could accustom them to making the imaginative leap of picturing territory from an imaginary, Apollonian height. Instead, they imagined territory as a series of stopping places and obstacles on the body's trip through it. "Space," in other words, was the space of the itinerary. The reader could only follow routes, from one place to the next. He or she could not light out across the territory, for there was no "space" in which to wander.

According to the Italian classicist Pietro Janni, this habit of constructing space as something linear, unidimensional, and dynamic, is something that the Middle Ages inherited from Greco-Roman antiquity.[23] It is also something that began to change, not with the itinerary map or with the gridded map, but with that other major strand of medieval mapmaking, the portolan chart (fig. 13 above). It is to this second strand of medieval alternatives to the ecclesiastical *mappaemundi* that I now turn. By the fourteenth century, the portolan chart had established itself as the preferred nautical chart of mariners sailing and trading in the Mediterranean. As I mentioned above, it represents a mapmaking tradition quite distinct from either the *mappaemundi* of medieval ecclesiastics or the itinerary maps used in a variety of contexts. One of the most striking characteristics of the medieval portolan chart is its relatively high degree of geographical accuracy, particularly when compared with the ecclesiastical *mappaemundi*. Clearly, this is the cartography of a community more interested than the monkish ecclesiastics in worldly destinations. The portolan chart, used in conjunction with another technology new to the West, the compass, allowed the Mediterranean merchant to get to places in this world where he could buy and sell goods.

Fitted out with compass and chart, a late medieval sailing vessel no longer needed to hug the safety of the coast but could venture out across open water. Its navigator simply set out on the chart the ship's intended course from point A to point B, and then used the chart's network of rhumb lines and compass roses—that spider web of lines that stretches across the surface of every portolan chart—to translate that course into a compass heading that would take his vessel where he wanted to go.[24] For now, this network of rhumb lines is what matters most about these charts, because they represent the material manifestation of an emerging spatiality crucial to both the construction and the use of the portolan chart. The maker of a portolan chart drew distances to scale and used compass bearings to establish the relative angles among lines connecting different places. The result is a scale map produced without the benefit of a geometric projection or a geographical grid. The user of the chart could then set out, in theory at least, along any of the many routes made possible by the compass and the rhumb lines. As the cartographic space becomes saturated with possible routes, it becomes a surface rather than a network. A space no less two-dimensional than that of the gridded map, and likewise spectacularized for consumption by an abstract observer, thus comes into view. For this reason, in many histories of cartography the portolan chart fittingly plays the role of a transitional style of mapmaking, the harbinger of modern cartography.

Nonetheless, the portolan chart clings in significant ways to the older sense of space as a line of travel. Although the history of its origins is fraught with controversy, it is possible that they were the cartographic successors to discursive predecessors called portolanos, verbal descriptions of the prominent features of the coastline.[25] The linear succession of toponymy in such coastal itineraries seems to have left its mark on the portolan chart, which typically features a closely packed series of place names along the coastline, set at right angles to the outline of the coast itself (fig. 13 above). One historian calls such charts "a list set in space" (Jacob 1992, 171). Whether or not they have their roots in the discursive portolanos of old, it is easy to find in the portolan chart's dense rows of coastal toponymy the linearity of the old lists. What reader can resist the invitation proffered by those rows of names to trace a voyage along the coast? Just like the itinerary map, the portolan chart presents its reader with a two-dimensional space but invites him or her to relate to it in a way that preserves the old unidimensionality of the discursive itinerary. It even does this in and through those rhumb lines that constitute the portolan chart's most significant spatial innovation. Taken as a whole, these lines inscribe an emerging sense of space as surface, but individually they cling to the older sense of space as distance. Like the rows of coastal toponymy, the rhumb lines invite the reader to trace voyages, real or imagined, across the surface of the chart.

The Limitations of Abstraction and the Persistence of the Itinerary

During the fifteenth and sixteenth centuries, both the itinerary map and the portolan chart came to the attention of humanists interested in the practical application of the sort of scale cartography outlined by Ptolemy. Lacking any method for measuring longitude, these humanists brought the compass ashore and used it to rationalize the itinerary map, converting it into the early modern topographical map. Some medieval itinerary maps, Harvey explains, already exhibited a notion of consistent scale. The mid-thirteenth-century itinerary of the route to the Holy Land by the Englishman Matthew Paris, for example, tries to space destinations along routes in ways that consistently reflect the real-life distances between them (Harvey 1987a, 496). The fifteenth century added compass bearings to this kind of itinerary map, thereby fixing the angles of the routes as well as their relative distances. In this way, it became possible to map regions of limited size with surprising accuracy. One of the intellectuals who did so was the Tyrolean theologian and philosopher Nicolas of Cusa, who included his topographical map of Germany in a manuscript version of Ptolemy's *Geographia* prepared by Henricus Martellus in 1490.[26] According to Harvey, Cusa's techniques provide a point of departure for much of the large-scale mapping done in Europe during the sixteenth century, when itineraries would be rationalized in the service of the new scale map (Harvey 1980, 146–47). Cusa's innovations were improved upon by others, notably the sixteenth-century mathematician Gemma Frisius, who provided the most workable means for drawing any scale geographical map, including many of those that came decorated with a Ptolemaic grid. Their techniques were used to produce some of the most sophisticated maps available to the Spanish Hapsburgs. When Pedro de Esquivel set out to map Spain under the sponsorship of Philip II, he too relied upon measures of distance and direction and ended up producing some of the most extensive, most precise maps of any European country then available.[27] Similar efforts were expended in the New World. One of the results was a 1590 map of the route from Veracruz to Mexico City produced under the supervision of the Italian engineer Giovanni Battista

15 Giovanni Battista Antonelli, "Descripción (mapa) del camino, que se pretende hacer empezando de la venta de Butrón hasta la Ciudad de México" (1590). This map of a proposed road from the Gulf of Mexico to Mexico City reveals the mapmaker's reliance upon techniques pioneered for nautical cartography. Ministry of Education, Culture, and Sport, Spain. Archivo General de Indias. MP Mexico, 39.

Antonelli (fig. 15). Its crisscrossing network of rhumb lines emanating from an ornate compass rose, a feature typical of nautical charts, speaks to the engineer's reliance upon measures of distance and direction, rather than geographical coordinates, to map the route.

In the meantime, cosmographers struggled to make these methods obsolete. Although they worked well enough for mapping small regions, they were impracticable across vast territories, like Spain's far-flung empire. To map the Indies, it was necessary to determine the geographical coordinates of distant locations. Juan López de Velasco, the chronicler-cosmographer of the Indies, presented the Council of Indies in 1574–75 with a geography of the Americas that included quite accurate maps of its various portions, as well as the first-ever map of the Indies to stretch as far as the western Pacific (fig. 16; Parker 2002, 107–8). Subsequently, he worked to improve the crown's maps by availing himself of techniques devised by his predecessor, the cosmographer-royal Alonso de Santa Cruz.[28] In 1577, he sent printed questionnaires to local colonial officials, asking them, among other things, to provide the latitude of their localities and to observe and record two predicted lunar eclipses. By comparing their data with that of metropolitan observations, he hoped to determine the longitude of these places and thereby devise even more accurate maps of the far-flung Monarchy.[29] Beginning in 1583, the Academy of Mathematics in Madrid initiated its own efforts to further this work, arranging for the simultaneous observation of a 1584 lunar eclipse in Antwerp, Toledo, Seville, Mexico City, Manila, and possibly Macao (Parker 2002, 108). With this project, the early modern scale map attempted to free itself from its dependence upon rationalized itineraries and to build itself from the astronomical calculations necessary to construct an abstract, geometric space.

Maritime cartography likewise came under the purview of intellectuals who thought of Ptolemy as a crucial authority, particularly in the state-sponsored cosmographical institutions of Portugal and Castile. In Lisbon and Seville, the cosmographers advocated a further transformation in the art of navigation, one that supplemented the compass with the quadrant and the mariner's astrolabe as the crucial instruments of successful pilotage. No longer would pilots determine their position by means of bearing and distance alone: they would make the necessary astronomical observations to determine their latitude. The cosmographers insisted upon astronomical navigation in order to solve some of the problems that presented themselves when European navigation set out from familiar shores and well-traveled routes down the west coast of Africa and into the western Atlantic. They insisted, too, upon modifying nautical charts to serve the needs of the new navigation. During the fifteenth century, scales of latitude began to appear on Portuguese nautical charts. When the crown of Castile recruited the services of Portuguese cosmographers, lines of latitude began to appear on Spanish charts as well. Soon, they came accompanied by a full grid, and the early modern "plane chart" was born. This was the type of chart that the cosmographers associated with the Casa de la Contratación provided to pilots bound for America, and it was the type of chart on which they maintained their cartographic record of new discoveries. All of the extant manuscript planispheres believed to have been derived from the Spanish *padrón general* are small-scale plane charts (fig. 17).[30] Even the sole sixteenth-century printed sheet map of the Americas known to have been constructed from Spanish sources exhibits the rows of coastal

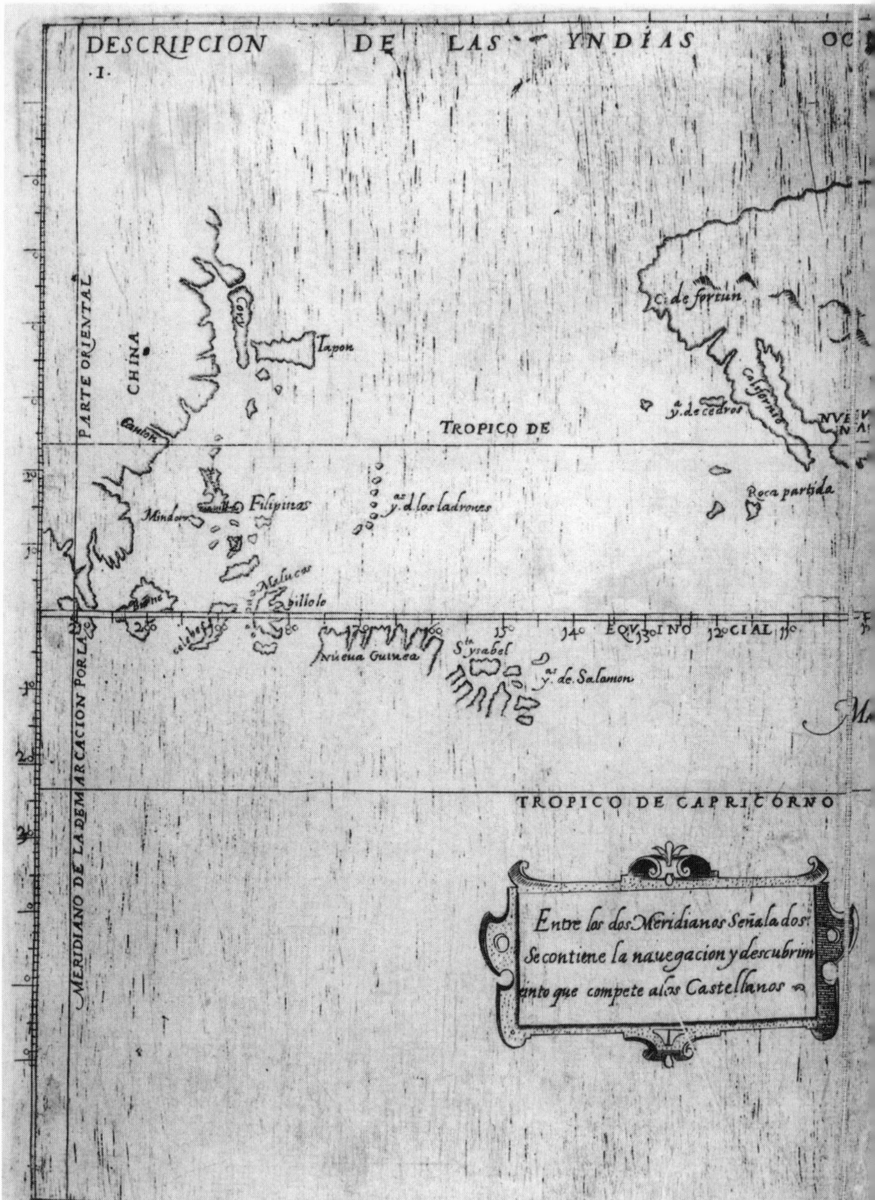

.I.

PARTE ORIENTAL

CHINA

Japon

C. de fortun

Californias

y. de cedros

NVE
VA

TROPICO DE

Mindoro

Filipinas

y. d los ladrones

Roca partida

Maluco
billole

Nueua Guinea

Sta ysabel

y. de Salamon

EQVINOCIAL

MERIDIANO DE LA DEMARCACION POR LA

TROPICO DE CAPRICORNO

Entre los dos Meridianos Señalados
Se contiene la nauegacion y descubrim
into que compete a los Castellanos

16 Juan López de Velasco, map of the Indies (1570). The geography
of the Indies is bounded by the original line of demarcation between Castilian and Portuguese spheres of influence, on the right,
and the extension of that line over the poles into eastern Asia, on the
left. The Geography and Map Division of the Library of Congress.

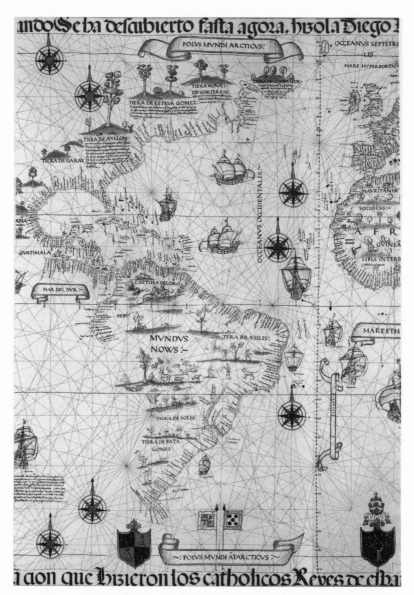

17 Diego Ribeiro, detail from planisphere (Seville, 1529). From a facsimile by W. Griggs,
    1886. Original in the Museum of Propaganda, Rome. Note the densely packed rows of
    coastal toponymy, set perpendicularly to the outline of the coast itself. This treatment
    of the toponymy, along with the wind roses and the rhumb lines, are inherited from the
    tradition of portolan chartmaking. The vertical dotted line to the right of the compass
    roses is the chart's scale of latitude. It, along with a faint graticule, identify Ribeiro's chart
    as a plane chart rather than a pure portolan. The Geography and Map Division of the
    Library of Congress.

toponymy typical of maritime charts and features images of ships sailing across its seas (fig. 18). For Janni, the development of astronomical navigation, and the plane chart that supported it, marked the turning point in the shift from the one-dimensional spatiality of the itinerary to the two-dimensional spatiality of the map. The practice required a cognitive leap on the part of the navigator: it required him to imagine his course as a route, yes, but as a route traced across a *surface*.[31]

It was perhaps inevitable that the new spatiality of abstraction would find many of its original enthusiasts among those interested in charting the seas. The ocean, Lestringant reminds us, is "an abstract place . . . without shape or points of reference" (Lestringant 1994, 15). It was only natural, then, that the line of demarcation separating Spanish and Portuguese spheres of influence established by the Treaty of Tordesillas (1494) "was in the beginning traced across the indefinite space of the seas" (15). Not only did such a space, the ocean, give free play to an imperial imagination, but it also provided a meeting place for the spatial imaginations of the navigator and the cosmographer. There, in the ocean, "devoid of relief or definite colour and without any boundaries or routes . . . cosmographical theory and the concrete experience of the navigator coincided" (15). Pedro de Medina, one of those cosmographers in the business of educating navigators in the new art of astronomical navigation, thus marvels at the emptiness of the ocean, at its vast, trackless expanse. To cross the ocean was a wondrous thing, Medina suggests, because it was to trace a course across "a thing so vague and spacious . . . where there is neither path nor trace" (cited in Lestringant 1994, 15). In Medina's *espacioso*, Euclidean geometry comes down to earth, so to speak, to coincide with its material cousin, the ocean. There, on a surface at once Euclidean and physical, the navigator could effect the leap from a unidimensional conceptualization of space to a two-dimensional one.

In this way, we see that the story of the early modern cartographic revolution is thus not just one of the sudden irruption of gridded maps into European consciousness in the wake of the rediscovery of Ptolemy. It is also the story of a broader convergence among various kinds of mapmaking and various kinds of mapmakers who shared an interest in using emerging technologies to map the world empirically. Under the auspices of new, state-sponsored institutions, or of various forms of ad hoc sponsorship from the rich and powerful, intellectuals in various parts of Europe began to collect some of the bits and pieces of late medieval mapmaking into a more-or-less unified enterprise.[32] That unity was unknown in the Middle Ages, which would never so much as group together as a single class of objects the various kinds of documents that we identify as "medieval mapmaking" (Harvey 1987a, 464).

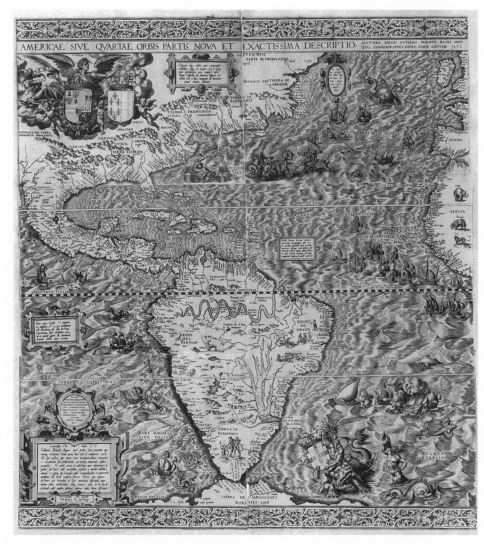

18   Diego Gutierrez, *Americae sive quartae orbis partis nova et exactissima descriptio* (1562). The only sheet map printed during the sixteenth century that is known to have been derived from Spanish sources. Although it lacks compass roses and rhumb lines, it preserves the rows of coastal toponymy typical of the Seville planispheres. The Geography and Map Division of the Library of Congress.

Ptolemy changed this. His grid became the universal idiom that brought the strands together as expressions of a single cartographic enterprise that could chart the sea and that could map the earth, that could depict a single city or the entire globe. With this development, a single type of map, the gridded map, becomes hegemonic in European culture: it establishes itself as the standard by which all other maps should be judged. The cosmographer, in turn, becomes the commanding figure in the production of maps. Others might continue to represent space and territory, but only his product counted as a true map. By the eighteenth century, the *Diccionario de autoridades* blatantly recognized the cosmographer's hegemony. A map, the dictionary tells us, is something produced by a cosmographer, not by some other mapmaker: "When a *cosmographer* comes out with a general map of Spain or of the whole world, he puts upon it all its principal things."

The hegemony of the gridded map is something from which we are only beginning to liberate ourselves, as we gradually shed our old definitions of maps and mapping and look for more inclusive language with which to think about territorial representation. It is also something that was far from complete during the sixteenth century. The prestige enjoyed by both the cosmographer and the gridded map among the educated and the powerful should not be mistaken for a monopoly over sixteenth-century mapmaking or for complete dominance over other mapmakers. Despite the popularization of Ptolemaic cartography, the gridded map represented more of a cartographic ideal than an achievable reality. This can be seen even in Spain's impressive effort to map the far-flung Indies. Sixteenth-century cartography, both geographical and nautical, continued to depend in one way or another upon the measure of distance and direction despite the fact that these methods only proved accurate when used to map relatively small areas, such as the Iberian Peninsula. When they were applied to large ones, particularly ones that involved transoceanic distances, they broke down. Distance at sea was difficult to measure with accuracy, especially since many pilots continued to rely on the traditional method of "dead-reckoning," that is, making an educated guess about distance traveled on the basis of one's experience with sailing one's ship. The method could prove surprisingly accurate on short trips along familiar routes but fell apart as voyages extended themselves over many months and along unfamiliar shores. The measure of direction likewise posed problems for the cosmographer. Most pilots and cosmographers understood that the compass needle did not point toward true north and that its variance from true north became more pronounced in certain parts of the world than in others. No one, however, understood why, and thus no one could systematically correlate compass bearings made in different, distant places in such a way as to plot the data they provided onto a small-scale chart or map. Finally, the cartographic projections described by Ptolemy were inadequate for representing either distance or direction in any consistent way, particularly outside of the middle latitudes, those within eighteen degrees of the equator. The crown repeatedly called for the revision of the flawed *padrón general*, and its cosmographers repeatedly drew it anew and analyzed its problems. But although they understood the nature of the limitations suffered by the projections they favored, they failed to develop new ones that addressed the salient problems. When the Flemish cartographer Gerhard Mercator succeeded in doing so, Iberian cosmographers failed to take advantage of his innovation.[33]

The ability to locate places according to their latitude and longitude promised to ameliorate at least some of these problems. In theory, latitude was easy to measure, but in practice it posed serious problems. On both land and sea, an unobstructed view of the horizon, something essential for making the measurement, was often unavailable due to haze or hills. Longitude, on the other hand, proved to be a nearly intractable problem. The methods developed by Iberian cosmographers and put into practice by López de Velasco, were cumbersome ones, requiring time and astronomical know-how on the part of the cosmographer's collaborators. Both seem to have been in short supply. Few of the responses to López de Velasco's questionnaires made their way back to the cosmographer's desk, and those that did were marred by serious inaccuracies. It seems that the would-be respondents either did not have the skills or the interest necessary to carry out the orders of the starry-eyed cosmographer. López de Velasco's successors nonetheless made their map, using data on distance, direction, and latitude to plot the many locations for which they did not have geographical coordinates determined by the observation of lunar eclipses (García de Céspedes 1606, 140). At sea, the problems were even more acute. No one, it is well known, could devise a method for measuring longitude from the deck of a ship at sea.[34] Ships laden with lives and precious cargo were often lost when they stumbled upon unexpected shoals or headed in the wrong direction after losing their bearings in a storm. It was impossible, moreover, to determine the longitude of any place that ship reached, however desirable it may have been to have included it on a map. Once again, distance and direction—supplemented, whenever possible, by the measure of latitude—continued to provide the stuff from which maps and charts were made.

But it is another limitation of sixteenth-century cartography that matters most to us here. Obviously, the cosmographers could not map the world alone. They relied on the cooperation of various kinds of field agents, we might call them, to make the measurements they needed to assemble their maps and charts. Sometimes these field agents were technical people sent out to the field specifically to execute cartographic projects. Juan Battista Antonelli and his staff were among these, as was Francisco Domínguez, the man sent to map New Spain the way Pedro Esquivel had mapped Castile and Aragon. More often than not, however, these field agents included pilots, military men, petty colonial officials, and others more or less pressed into doing the work needed by the cosmographer, often without the benefit of much or any technical training and often with little personal interest or motivation. As we have seen, the plan of the cosmographers to map the Monarchy according to geographical coordinates determined by astronomical observations were frustrated by the lack of skill or interest exhibited by the would-be field agents. During the same period, other field agents unwittingly frustrated the efforts of the cosmographers to acquire regional maps directly from local officials. They did so in their responses to questionnaires distributed during the reign of Philip II that sought to collect all sorts of information about the natural and moral history of the many localities that, together, made up the crown's American possessions. Among other things, these questionnaires asked for maps of regions and localities. In response, colonial officials often sent maps penned by indigenous artists who imagined space and world in a cartographic idiom of their own. Although these maps have proven fascinating to modern-day scholars interested in the transculturative pressures of colonialism, they must have been quite disappointing for the cosmographers back in Seville and Madrid. Deemed, undoubtedly, incomprehensible or ignorant by the cosmographers, these maps seem to have been filed away and forgotten.[35]

Other field agents produced documents that must have been equally disappointing to the cosmographic powers that be, but for reasons that had nothing to do with the persistence of Amerindian habits of mind. These field agents were of European origin, but they do not seem to have enjoyed the technical training necessary to draw their maps the way their superiors would have liked. We can hear the voice of one of these field agents—his actual identity is lost—in a passage from an early-sixteenth-century manuscript called the *Descripción y cosmografía de España*:

> Toledo is a city of 18,000 heads of household it is at the top of some mountains and valleys . . . and has very good fortresses near the said Tagus River . . . on the way to Burguillos there are a league and a half of mountains and rising slopes, and in coming out of these we pass the Tagus by a bridge that runs along the righthand side and on the way to Xofira there are three leagues and they pass through Burguillos and on the way to Mazambron there are three leagues of large mountains and hills and when we come out of them we pass the said river which runs along the righthand side and on the way to Sonseca there are four leagues. (Colón 1988, 1: 136)

The *Descripción y cosmografía de España* emerged from an early effort to map Spain, one sponsored by Ferdinand the Catholic in 1517 and supervised by Fernando Colón, son of Christopher Columbus. The passage in question is representative of the manuscript as a whole and is not likely to have been written by Colón himself. Not only does the Spanish ramble well outside the syntactic norms of an educated person, but it also fails to include data that he very much needed to complete his project. Elsewhere, Colón states his intention to produce "tables," or maps, of Spain, graduated "by degrees of latitude and longitude" (Colón 1988, 1: 24). Presumably, he planned to build those maps from the data contained in itineraries like this one. Notice, however, that the route from Toledo to Burguillos is described by noting various landmarks, the mountains and a bridge, that one would pass in going from one place to the other. In what direction do these mountains and this bridge lie? How can one use this information to plot the spatial relationship between Toledo and Burguillos if one has not actually made the trip and seen the landmarks? The itinerary lacks the crucial data, the compass bearings, that would allow one to transform this local information into a universal idiom. It is no wonder, then, that we know of no maps that came out of Fernando Colón's project.[36] The mapping of Spain would have to wait almost half a century, until Pedro Esquivel could venture out with more disciplined, knowledgeable field agents at his disposal.

To put this another way, this passage from the *Descripción y cosmografía de España* imagines territory from the perspective of the earthbound traveler, moving from one location to another along a linear route. Like Marco Polo's text, it recalls the earthbound body in its figuration of space. The positions of various topographical features are noted by referring them to the body's spatial attitude and its movement through space: "we pass the Tagus by a bridge that runs along the righthand side . . . we pass the said river which runs along the righthand side." One has difficulty imagining how such references could be translated into the static, optical abstractions of a map, but absolutely none in imagining how they could be used when making the trip. We know that if we are in Toledo and want to go to Burguillos, we should look for the mountains, and head for them. If we need help finding them, we can ask a local. Once on the other side of the hills, we know that we should look toward the right for a bridge over the Tagus River. And so on.

We see, then, that in 1517, among the people working for Fernando Colón, the linear sense of space that was so much a part of the medieval imagination was still very much alive and well. It persisted among many sixteenth-century Europeans as well, and for many decades after Colón's abortive attempt to map the territories of the Catholic king. In Spain, this linear sense of *espacio* does not register in the definitions offered by either Covarrubias or the *Diccionario de autoridades*, but it can nonetheless be identified in countless texts from the period. Again, in *La Celestina* we read, "The natural courses [of the celestial bodies through the sky] do not learn to turn without order, for to all the same path is given, the same *space* for death and life" (292; emphasis added). Here, the space through which bodies celestial and terrestrial move is a course of linear progress from birth to death. It manifests the proximity of meaning between *espacio* as an interval both chronological and topographical.

Other texts offer usages that are more clearly spatial. In Gómara's *Historia general de las Indias* we read, "From the Palmas River to the Pánuco River there are more than thirty leagues. In this *space* lies Almería" (López de Gómara 1979, 23; emphasis added). In Juan de Escalante de Mendoza's *Itinerario de navegación de los mares y tierras occidentales*, we read "why, in so little *space of travel* as this, have I seen so many people disagree?" (26; emphasis added). We find this usage in literary texts. In part 2 of Ercilla's *Araucana* (1578), the two senses of *espacio* as "a length of time" and "a distance in space" are made to coincide in a fascinating rhetorical figure: "Returning to our story, I say that our ordered ranks marched *a great space in a brief one*, away from the border constituted by the Talcaguano riverbank" (Ercilla 1993, 22.6; emphasis added). In part 1 of *Don Quixote* (1605), we read how one character rides to meet his companion, "Who was waiting for him a good *space* away" (Cervantes Saavedra 1998, 1: 8; emphasis added).[37] Curiously, even the examples that the *Diccionario de autoridades* uses to support its spatial definition of *espacio* refer to this linear imagination rather than to the planar one that it pretends to identify in them. The dictionary cites Herrera's *Anotaciones a la poesía de Garcilaso* (1580; "The Pyrenees divide France from Spain, cutting it for a *space* of almost eighty leagues, from the Mediterranean Sea to the Gallic Ocean"; emphasis added) and Pedro de Espinel's *Vida del escudero Marcos de Obregón* (1618; "The space was small, and in an instant of running we fell upon their houses"; emphasis added). The examples multiply.

Thus, even during the last quarter of the sixteenth century, we continue to find cartographic products that reflect the linear sense of space embodied in the passage from Colón's manuscript. Among these are various maps produced in response to questionnaires sent to Mesoamerica by the authorities in Spain during the reign of Philip II. Although many of these maps, as I mentioned above, were drawn by indigenous artists who drew upon their own notions of space and world, some were penned by colonists of European extraction. Among these, there are some that suggest their makers enjoyed considerable skill at making navigational charts.[38] Others, however, take the form of itinerary maps (Mundy 1996, 35).[39] These include the maps that accompanied the *Relación geográfica de Cuahuitlan, Pinotecpa, Potutla, y Icatepeuque* (1577), that of Los

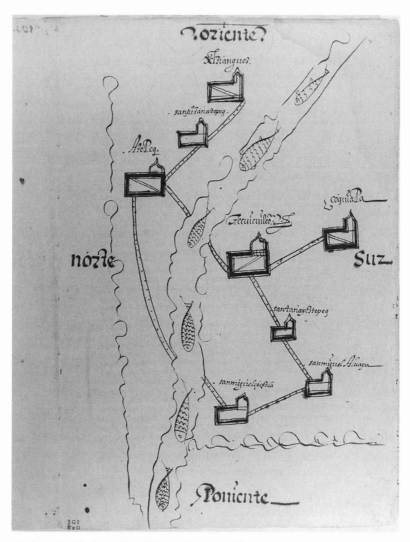

19 Map from the *Relación geográfica* of Tecuicuilco, 1580. The Nettie Lee Benson Latin American Collection, University of Texas Library.

Peñoles (1579), that of Tecuicuilco (1580; fig. 19), and that of Altatlauca-Malinaltepec (1580; fig. 20).[40] All of these maps figure the locality under consideration as a series of stopping places along a route of travel. With one exception—the *pintura* of Tecuicuilco—the maps themselves do not indicate the distances from one location to the next. Nor do they specify the angles of the routes they depict, going only so far as to mark the four cardinal direc-

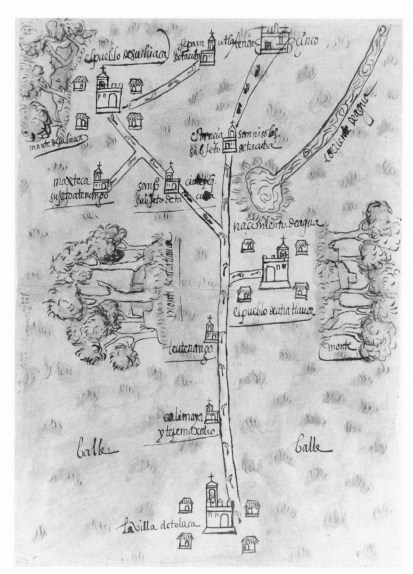

20 Map from the *Relación geográfica* of Altatlauca-Malinaltepec, 1580. The Nettie Lee Benson
    Latin American Collection, University of Texas Library.

tions to orient the map. The spatial information they provide, in other words,
is more impressionistic than precise.

The texts that accompany these maps provide some of the information they
lack—directions and distances—but they do so in ways that leave no doubt
that the maps give visual form to territories constructed, in their author's

minds, out of the itineraries of travel. As a whole, their descriptions resemble the following passage from the *Relacion geográfica de Tecuicuilco*:

> The town of Tecuicuilco . . . Is seven great leagues from the said city [Oaxaca], where the mayor always resides, going through very high mountains, toward the north of the city. This town has another village subject to it—what is known here as an "estancia"—which is called Santa Inés Tepeque; it is one league from here . . . So is the town of Atepeque . . . It is four leagues from the said town of Tecuicuilco, on the northeast side, along rough, mountainous, twisting paths. (Acuña 1982, 3: 87–88)

Note the limitations of the information here. Although the author has provided distances in leagues from one place to the next, he has provided directions only in fairly vague terms, "the northeast side," rather than precise compass bearings. Note, too, the traces of the author's embodied experience. The description registers the perpetual absence of the mayor. It acknowledges the site of enunciation: "one league from here." It complains about the difficulty of the route from Tecuicuilco to one of its subordinate villages. Other *relaciones* are even less precise in their indications of direction, making use only of the four cardinal directions. In the *Relación geográfica de los Peñoles*, for example, we read: "The first Peñol, called Itzcuintepec, is six leagues away from the city of Antequera, the bishopric of Oaxaca, where the cathedral is, leaving the said city toward the east; this is true of the other Peñoles, for they run, as it was mentioned, one after the other from north to south" (Acuña 1982, 3: 45). Here, again, we find traces of the author's embodied experience of space. He redundantly mentions that Antequera is the seat of the bishop and the place where the cathedral is, for reasons that may well be entirely his own. He expresses the spatial relationship between Antequera and Itzcuintepec as the direction in which one travels from one to the other. And he locates the series of towns known as "Los Peñoles" as a chain of stopping places along a linear route. In another case, information about routes takes a form that is surprisingly local, considering the trans-Atlantic destination of the document in which it appears: "Quauxoloticpac is two leagues, more or less, from Extitla, atop a very high hill. In order to go up to the said town, leaving from Eztitla, one goes up a great mountain range and there, at the peak, is the town" (Acuña 1982, 3: 49).

It has been argued that the recourse to itinerary maps—and, we might add, to discursive itineraries—responds to the central role played by travel in the lives of colonial administrators. These petty officials of Spain's empire were required to perform regular tours of inspection that involved extensive travel throughout the region they governed. They were also required, on occasion, to relocate to other areas in order to prevent them from forming local attachments that could vie for their loyalty to the crown. Travel thus formed an important part of their experience, and itinerary maps may have given cartographic form to this way of relating to the landscape (Mundy 1996, 35–38). But behind this explanation, I argue, lies the hegemony that the cosmographer's map enjoys in our own historiography. We are told, in effect, that the colonists have figured the territories they governed with way-finding maps, and that they have done so because of the prominent role played by way-finding in their own lives. It is assumed, in other words, that the documents they have provided are not really "maps," and therefore are not indicative of any notion of "space" or "territory" other than that formed by their unique experience of travel as officials of colonialism. One assumes that if they had been allowed to stay put—if they had not been required to make inspection tours or to move from one charge to another—they would have imagined and figured space and territory in some other way. One assumes that they would have drawn some other kind of map.

But notice how strange is the decision of the colonists to map their *corregimientos*—administrative localities—in this way. The questionnaire asks them to provide a "painting" of the *corregimiento* that would illustrate its "setting and location." It also asks them to describe routes of travel in the province, noting distances and directions from one town to the next, as well as from the *corregimiento* to its *audiencia*, the major administrative center to which it responded (Acuña 1982, 2: 21). It asks all these things, however, in *separate questions*. The colonists, in effect, conflate them, providing a map of the routes as if it were the general "painting" that the cosmographer requested. They treat matters that are clearly separate in the minds of the cosmographers as if they were synonymous. And they do not apologize for this choice. They readily refer their descriptions of routes to their maps, without ever alluding to that other map or view—that general painting—that they have not drawn. Other mapmakers working outside the context of the *Relaciones geográficas* project, moreover, do the same thing. A 1550 map of New Spain figures the colony's most important centers of population between Mexico City and New Galicia as stopping places on a route of travel extending northwestwards from the city (fig. 21). A 1610 map of Chile replaces the road with a powerfully linear, schematic depiction of the Andes Mountains, that ties the theater of war, at the extreme right of the image, to colonial administrative centers at its extreme left (fig. 22). Why should they present themselves in this way? Is it simply because their authors, like those of the *Relaciones* maps, traveled a great deal?

No, I argue. It is because these mapmakers understand space itself in terms inherited from the Middle Ages. They do not see "space" as an expanse.

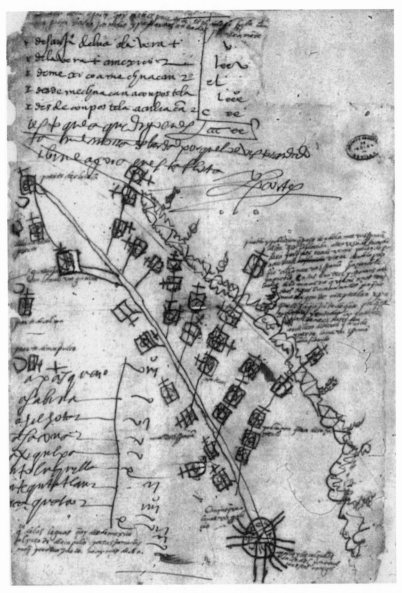

21 Pedro Cortés, Diseño o apunte de parte de la Nueva España, desde Mexico hacia la Nueva Galicia (ca. 1550–60). Note the construction of space as an itinerary from Mexico City toward the northwest, in this map of a part of New Spain. Ministry of Education, Culture, and Sport, Spain. Archivo General de Indias. MP México, 8. 1550–1560.

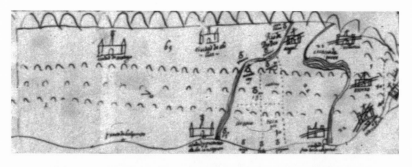

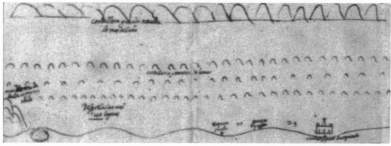

22 Mapa del reino de Chile (1610). This map of Chile was produced as part of a report on
the state of the Spanish attempt to suppress an indigenous rebellion in Chile. The theater
of war is in the extreme south of the country, at the right of the top image. The bottom
image depicts Chile north of the theater of war. The Pacific Ocean runs along the bottom
edge of both images. Note hatch marks that indicate destroyed settlements. The linearity of
a road has been replaced by the linearity of the signs used to indicate the two ranges of the
Andes Mountains. The lowlands between them and those between the mountains and the
sea thus become the itinerary from the more peaceful north to the theater of war. Ministry
of Education, Culture, and Sport, Spain. Archivo General de Indias. MP Perú y Chile, 172.

Instead, they perceive "place" and "nonplace," and they understand "space"
as the route one takes to get from one place to another.[41] Thus, when they are
asked to make a "painting" of the territory they administer, they do not appreciate any difference between this request and a separate one that refers to
routes and distances. And when they draw that painting, they produce itinerary maps that, like any such map, invite the reader to come back down to
earth, so to speak, and relate to these territories as an armchair traveler rather
than a drawing room Olympian. The invitation becomes all the more com-
pelling when the maps are read alongside the texts that accompany them, with
their references to the ruggedness of the mountains that one must cross or the
need to ascend a hill in order to reach a particular town. Despite their inevitable two-dimensionality, then, these itinerary maps cling to the unidimensional spatiality still so common in Hispanic culture. Like any transitional

product, they anticipate emergent trends, but they also drag the past along with them.

That older sense of *space* as interval rather than area subsists on the maritime charts of the period as well. I mentioned above that Iberian cosmographers adapted the medieval portolan chart to the exigencies of long-range voyages along unfamiliar shores and across empty oceans by equipping it with a Ptolemaic grid meant to support the chart's use as an instrument of astronomical navigation. Yet, in the absence of any method for measuring longitude at sea, of any way to account for the variation of the compass needle, of any way to draw a nautical chart that efficiently corrected for the convergence of meridians at the poles, that grid must be understood as an embodiment of a technological aspiration—the aspiration, furthermore, of the educated and well-placed few. Mariners disliked the new charts and saw little need for the astronomical methods favored by their makers. Pilots, after all, only needed to find their way: it was the cosmographer who was interested in plotting locations.[42] Those locations, furthermore, could only be plotted by correlating latitude—if it was available—with distance and direction from a known location. The fabrication and use of the plane chart was thus intimately connected, like its portolan predecessor, to travel, and to its dyanamic, linear sense of space. And this was so despite the efforts of the cosmographers to impose astronomical navigation and the gridded map upon the pilots. Rhumb lines therefore continued to appear on nautical charts, even when the inadequacies of the projections used severely limited their usefulness. In this way, the plane chart hangs suspended, Janus-like, between the two different senses of space, one dominant and the other just emerging. While its grid points toward a modern future, its rhumb lines and its rows of coastal toponymy recall a medieval past.

This coincidence of the old and the new appears even in the writing of some of the technical specialists who occupied the vanguard of the cartographic revolution in Spain. Alonso de Santa Cruz's *Libro de las longitudines*, for example, uses *espacio* only in the linear, not the planar sense. For him, as for other cosmographers, latitude and longitude are not primarily the axes of a planar expanse, but alternative, hopefully more accurate, measures of distance.[43] Pedro de Medina's *Arte de navegar* does something similar. As we have seen earlier, this work has been cited for the way it wonders at the spaciousness of the sea, "a thing so vague and spacious as the sea, where there is neither path nor trace" (cited in Lestringant 1994, 15). We are to believe that Medina identifies in this spaciousness a physical analogue to the empty expanse of the new gridded map. This, indeed, is what we would expect from Medina, one of the cosmographers involved in asserting the authority of theory over traditional practice in the training of pilots and the production of maritime charts in Seville. It is what we would expect, moreover, from his *Arte de navegar*, a well-known manual on the art of astronomical navigation. The pilots, however, would have known from experience that the oceans are not the trackless expanses that appear in this piece of cosmographical hyperbole. They are structured by such things as prevailing currents and winds that favor the passage of sailing vessels one way rather than another. Medina must have known this, too, since his duties in Seville would have certainly acquainted him not only with the *padrón general* but also with the *derroteros*, the verbal sailing directions that were maintained by the Casa de la Contratación.[44] These directions for sailing along the maritime routes most important to Spanish commerce spoke of a practice of navigation that, despite the efforts of the cosmographers to impose their culture of geometrized space, continued to think of the sea in terms of unidimensional *espacios*.

And so, despite Medina's manifest commitment to an emerging culture of abstract space, both his *Arte de navegar* and his printed chart of the Atlantic world betray his debts to the dominant culture of linear space. Although Medina may wonder at the spaciousness of the sea, he does so only to praise the art of navigation, which makes it possible to domesticate this spaciousness, to find routes where there are apparently none. Here is his remark again, placed back into its context:

> Who is capable of putting words to so subtle a thing as the ability of a man with a compass and some lines marked on a chart to know how to round the World, and to know day and night where he is to head, and from where he is to depart, and how long he should travel from one place to another, and to know how to travel along a thing so vague and spacious as the sea, where there is neither path nor trace? Certainly this is a subtle and difficult thing, and it was so considered by Solomon, who said that one of the most difficult things to find is the way of a ship at sea, for it neither follows a marked track nor leaves a trace of its passing. (Cuesta Domingo 1998, 329)

The reference to Solomon—the Book of Wisdom—leaves little doubt that the spaciousness and tracklessness of the sea is an object of dread. In the Biblical text, the traceless passing of a ship at sea becomes a figure for the oblivion to which human vanity is destined.[45] Navigation, remarkably, conquers this powerful figure of oblivion by finding the routes that it does not seem to have. It renders the spacious seas useable by reducing their expanse to a network of routes of sail. Medina's chart of the Atlantic world, included in his *Arte de navegar* as well as in his *Libro de grandezas*, gives iconographic form to this task of tracking space (fig. 5 above). While its grid inscribes the spaciousness of the seas, the images of ships sailing the Atlantic along established routes of navigation demonstrate its domestication. They mark a Hispanic *mare nostrum* by indicating how the seas have been converted into useable space, a repeatable route of travel, an itinerary there and back again.

These examples taken from Santa Cruz and Medina are crucial to everything that follows in this book. In geographical mapping, the opposition between unidimensional and two-dimensional space is a matter of the relationship between two different cartographic forms—professional gridded maps and amateur itineraries—that can be located, more or less, in different social spaces. Its history suggests that, despite the continued presence of the itinerary on the cultural stage, the map must eventually triumph over it, consigning the itinerary to the diminished status of a derivative, secondary, "merely" way-finding cartographic product. The plane chart and the discourse surrounding it, by contrast, suggest a different approach. As a highly rationalized cartographic product that retains its connection with way-finding, the plane chart seems to internalize the opposition between plane and line. There, our two senses of space coexist on a single cartographic surface, a single chart, that comes to be produced and used by both highly literate mapmakers and the most illiterate mariners. As the hybrid product of a transitional historical moment, the nautical chart reminds us that the social groups and spatialities that we have traced so far were not always so neatly compartmentalized. The cosmographers who championed production and development of the plane chart in the Hispanic world could sometimes cling to the old unidimensional *espacio* even when they investigated or advocated the new cartography's most "modern" characteristics. The history of spatiality in this period must be understood, then, neither in terms of an opposition between two spatialities located in different texts written by different authors in different social locations nor in terms of the gradual replacement of one spatiality with another, first in a vanguard class and then among everyone else. Rather, it should be understood in terms of the give-and-take between two tendencies, a give-and-take that can manifest itself within the writings of a single author and even within the confines of a single chart or a single text.

The Janus-Like Space of Empire: Enciso's *Suma de geografía*

The Janus-like hybridity of space is perhaps best glimpsed in the *Suma de geografía* of Martín Fernández de Enciso (1519).[46] Enciso was a conquistador who had made two trips to the Caribbean, but he was exceptional in that he possessed a university education. This equipped him better than most for the task of reconciling the novelties of the discoveries in America with the bookish cosmography of the European Renaissance. During at least one stint in Seville, he spent time in conversation with writers who were working on precisely this project, including Pietro Martire d'Anghiera and, possibly, Gonzalo Fernández de Oviedo (Taylor 1932, xiv–xv). From his efforts issued his Suma, the first printed text to provide a description of the Americas in Spanish. It is composed of two principal sections. The first combines a treatise on the sphere—a standard piece of learned cosmography ultimately derived from the work of Joannes de Sacro Bosco—with a manual on the art of navigation, the first of its kind published in Spanish. The second part offers a descriptive geography of the known world, largely culled from established sources as well as from eyewitness accounts and Enciso's own experience in the Caribbean. The Suma de geografía also seems to have come outfitted with a "figura en plano," or plane chart, specifically drawn for inclusion in Enciso's book. The map, sadly, survives in none of the extant editions of the text.

Enciso dedicates his Suma de geografía to the new king and Holy Roman Emperor Charles V, in terms that leave little doubt that his project represents science in the service of empire. The preface explains that so young a monarch could not possibly have had the time to learn about the wider world and therefore needs a summary of geography, like Enciso's, to familiarize him with the subject. Such geographical learning becomes, in Enciso's argument, a crucial building block in the education of the prince. The conquistador reminds Charles that, at his age, Alexander the Great had already set out on his career as a conqueror. On Enciso's map and in his description of the world, the young king could appreciate the extent of Alexander's achievements, as well as those of other illustrious predecessors in empire-building, both Greek and Roman. From them, Charles could learn to aspire to great things. Specifically, he would be moved to "conquer and take those provinces and lands that are possessed by those peoples who are not Christians" (Fernández de Enciso 1948, 7). From the treatise on the sphere and on navigation, in turn, Charles could learn where and how to direct his conquistadorial efforts.

Typically, a treatise on the sphere dealt with the whole Ptolemaic cosmos, beginning with the celestial spheres and moving inward toward the terraqueous globe, describing it in the same universal, quantitative language of cosmography used to describe the heavens. In other words, lines and geometry (the equator, the tropics, the ecliptic, parallels, meridians) mattered more than the particularities of physical topography. In Enciso's hands, this standard piece of cosmographic literature becomes a stunning example of the way the geometrical abstractions favored by Renaissance cosmography could be recruited in the service of empire. Following the usual procedure, Enciso explains how the terraqueous globe is divided into quadrants by the intersection of the equator and a prime meridian, but then he departs from precedent by choosing as his meridian an extended version of the line of demarcation established by the Treaty of Tordesillas (1494). The treaty defined this line as a half-meridian extending from one pole to the other through the Atlantic, it but did not specify where that line would fall if it were to be extended into a full meridian encompassing the whole globe.[47] This approach sorted out the immediate conflicts facing Portugal and Castile in 1494, but it only deferred a question that would come to a head later. As the Portuguese extended themselves into the Pacific Ocean from the east and the Castilians did the same from the west, it became necessary to figure out where in that unknown expanse between the East and West Indies lay the rest of the line of demarcation, the other half-meridian that was left unspecified at Tordesillas. Cosmography had no better answer to this question in 1519 than it had in 1494. Enciso nonetheless provides one. He assigns arbitrary values to certain key, debatable variables in order to draw a full meridian, one that cuts through Asia as well as the Atlantic and, unsurprisingly, maximizes the extent of Castile's territorial claims. To Castile he assigns all the riches of Asia and the Pacific east of the Ganges River, including the coveted Spice Islands (Fernández de Enciso 1948, 25). At the same time, Enciso's choices have the effect of inflating the empty space that lies between what was then known of the East and West Indies. He calls upon Charles to send his ships into that blank expanse in search of new worlds to conquer. The fabulous East Indies and the recently discovered West Indies have become the bookends of a more alluring geography to be discovered, of fabulous terrae incognitae to be found in the blank expanse of the sphere.

In this way, Enciso's text apostrophizes the young monarch as that ideal, other-worldly cartographic observer who looks down upon the terraqueous globe from Apollonian heights. But it does not leave him there. Instead, the text incites the monarch's desire for conquest by enumerating the wealthy Oriental provinces that fall within Charles's half of the world. Cipangu, Java, Solomon's Ophir—not to mention the Spice Islands—are among them. The momentum of the catalog then presses against the empty space beyond it, and the tone becomes exhortative: "And so all of the one thousand six hundred fifty leagues of the universe that are yet to be discovered fall within the part belonging to Your Highness, and so Your Highness . . . should command the discovery of all that is left of your part, for the king of Portugal, although he is younger than you, has discovered so much" (Fernández de Enciso 1948, 26). Enciso inscribes an itinerary of sorts, a metonymic chain of rich provinces that encroaches upon that emptiness, that invites continuation through vigorous exploration and conquest. In this way, the globe ceases to be an object to be contemplated from a distance and becomes a surface to be traversed by an itinerant eye. Even here, in the portion of the *Suma de geografía* most thoroughly saturated with the new culture of abstraction, it is movement through space, however figurative, that sparks imperial desire.

The second half of Enciso's text, his universal geography, begins by once again dividing the globe into hemispheres along a prime meridian. This time, it is a more conventional one, the line going through the island of Hierro in the Canaries. In this way, Enciso attempts to ground his descriptive geography in the geometry of the quantitative treatise that precedes it. He even extends these efforts by providing coordinates of latitude for many of the places he mentions.[48] But, in this latter half of Enciso's book, geometric abstraction no longer provides the dominant register. Instead, it yields its command over Enciso's material to a narrative itinerary. The reader learns that the text will describe the known world by means of a narrative itinerary along its coastlines and major rivers. The description will begin in Spain, the westernmost part of the Old World, and will trace its way northward along the European coast toward Scandinavia. Afterward, it will return to the Strait of Gibraltar and will trace a course around the Mediterranean, Africa, and then eastward into Asia and the East Indies. Along the way, it will mention all the major places it passes, including those inland, and will tell of their most interesting characteristics (Fernández de Enciso 1948, 62). Like a plane chart, then, Enciso's *Suma de geografía* rationalizes space geometrically, only to then draw its reader into that space. It spectacularizes the world for an Apollonian observer only to then address that observer as a traveler along shores and streams.

We can understand this hybrid spatiality with more precision by comparing a passage from Enciso with descriptions drawn from other geographies, written both before and after his own. It has been argued that Enciso's use of the itinerary as his principal organizing device recalls the *peripli* of classical geography, and particularly the first-century *Chorographia* of Pomponius Mela (Melón 1950). Here is how Mela describes the south of Spain, known in his day as Baetica:

> The Atlantic and the line of Baetica's oceanfront receive those who travel this way
> and follow the righthand coast. This coastline is virtually straight as far as the
> Anas River, except where it draws back gradually once or twice. The Turduli and
> Bastuli are its inhabitants . . . In the nearest bay is the port of Gades and a woods
> they call Wild-Olive Grove; then a fort, Ebora, on the coast; and far from the
> coast, the colony of Hasta [Mesa de Asta]. On the coast again there is an altar and
> a temple of Juno, and on the sea itself, the monument of Caepio, which is set
> on a cliff rather than an island . . . The Baetis [Guadalquivir] River, coming from
> the Tarraconensis region more or less through the middle of this one, runs down
> for a long time in a single stream. (Romer 1998, 104)

Like Mela, Enciso clings to coastlines and rivers as much as possible in his own description of the same region. Here, the city of Gades is referred to by its modern name, Cádiz:

> Tarifa is in the Strait of Gibraltar, at thirty-six degrees. From Tarifa to Cádiz there are thirteen leagues; the coast lies toward the north. In this province are the fields of Tarifa, which are among the most abundant in grass of all of Spain, and where the best and largest cattle are raised. The country is hot and abounds in grain and wine and all other victuals. Cádiz is a little island where Hercules set his pillars. It stands hard by the mainland and on the south side has many shoals and banks, and on the north side has a bay that provides a very good harbor with an entrance from the west. The ships that pass from west to east and from east to west repair to this bay, which is one of the great stopping places of Christendom. Within this bay is Port Saint Mary, which is a good port. In this bay is the mouth of the Guadalete River, and here took place the battle in which King Don Rodrigo was lost, and with him, Spain. From Port Saint Mary to Sanlúcar there are five leagues. In Sanlúcar we find the mouth of the Guadalquivir, which is a great river. Ships sail up this river to reach Seville, which is sixteen leagues away. The two heads of this river are in the mountains of Granada and Segura. The two streams meet between Seville and Córdoba, near Palma del Río. Along its banks are three cities that are among the greatest and largest of Spain, Granada, Córdoba, and Seville, which was reconquered by the king Don Ferdinand III. Córdoba has been very well known in science and chivalry . . . From Seville to Sanlúcar the river forms two large islands that divide the river into three parts, but in Sanlúcar they come back together to empty out into the sea through one mouth. Sanlúcar lies at thirty-six degrees, Cádiz at thirty-six and a half. From Sanlúcar to the Bay of Lepe there are thirteen leagues. The coast stretches toward the northeast then quarters west. (Fernández de Enciso 1948, 65–67)

Immediately, however, it is the differences between Mela and Enciso that stand out rather than the similarities. To begin with, Enciso's description is not only more modern but also more detailed with regard to topography, climate, history, and economy. It is the product of a conquistador with university training, aware of the needs of navigators but also attentive to the possibilities of commerce and the historical significance of places.

It is also the work of someone accustomed to the use of the plane chart and the practice of astronomical navigation. Mela's description clearly takes the form of an itinerary of travel, albeit an imaginary one, since the journey that starts here eventually circumnavigates the whole *orbis terrarum*. It refers "to those who travel this way," out of the Mediterranean through the Strait of Gibraltar, "and follow the righthand coast," that is, the coast of Spain rather than that of Africa. It is the bodily orientation of a hypothetical traveler that serves to identify the coast in question, not a cardinal direction. Mela, furthermore, locates places along the coast exclusively in terms of their sequence along the route of travel, providing neither the distances nor the cardinal directions that would allow us to plot their relative locations onto any cartographic surface other than a schematic itinerary map.[49] Unlike Mela, Enciso does not personalize the description by making references to the movement of a traveler or by using the orientation of the traveling body to identify the location of the coastline. Instead, he provides the latitudes of major stopping places along his route, as well as distances from one major place to the next. While Mela's itinerary, like that of Marco Polo or the ones in Fernando Colón's *Descripción y cosmografía de España*, describes space from a point of view that is truly local and embodied, Enciso's text takes an important step toward depersonalized abstraction. Like Mela's, it constitutes a geographical description, but, unlike Mela's, it can also be classified as what one scholar has called a "prose cartography" (Cuesta Domingo 1992, 299).

Nonetheless, it does not go too far in that direction. Compare Enciso's description of the south of Spain with the following one, from Gerónimo Girava's *Dos libros de cosmografía* (1556):

> Baetica is separated from Lusitania by the Guadiana River, or the Aná, as it is called, which passes near Extremadura: from the Tarraconensis it is separated by the Cape of Gata, which is a promontory called Charidemo by the ancients. In this way, all that lies between the Guadiana River and the Cape of Gata is that part of Spain that the ancients called Baetica. Lusitania is separated from the Tarraconensis by the Duero River . . . The kingdom of Portugal begins south of the city of Leppe, and ends in the north in Galician Bayona . . . Let us turn now to the parts . . . The three kingdoms of Tarraconensian Spain are . . . Those of Lusitania are . . . The three of Baetica are the kingdoms of Granada, of Andalusia, and of Extremadura. Each of these kingdoms has its principal city, which is the head of the kingdom . . . and they are sixty in all, counting the fourteen already named: thirty in Tarraconensian Spain, nine in Lusitania, and seven in Baetica, as can be seen in the table that follows. (Girava 1556, 64–65)

Girava was a Spanish cosmographer who lived in Milan during the mid- to late sixteenth century, where he translated and synthesized the work of other European cosmographers. His description of Spain—taken, like Enciso's, from a description of the whole world—is more like Mela's than Enciso's in its relative poverty of topographical, historical, nautical, and economic detail. Such things are not absent from Girava's text, but neither are they abundant. In its method, however, Girava's description is unlike that of either of his predecessors. Girava has begun by delineating the whole, Europe, and then enumerating its parts, the various "provinces" of the continent. He then takes each of these parts and once again dissects them into their constituent kingdoms. He then enumerates the cities, rivers, and other particularities of each kingdom. At each level, he draws the boundaries of each province or kingdom without regard to routes of travel. The tables to which he refers, which follow the prose descriptions of each and every part of Europe, of Africa, of Asia, and of America, provide the names and geographical coordinates for the cities, islands, rivers, mountains, and ports of each part. Brief prose descriptions account separately for their climate and their natural resources (i.e., Girava 1556, 66–78). While Mela and Enciso move through space, Girava analyzes it into its constituent parts. While Mela and Enciso handle places as integral wholes, with histories, unique inhabitants, and the like, Girava dissects places into parts and assigns each part a place in his geographical taxonomy.

In light of these comparisons with Mela and Girava, we can appreciate how the spatiality of Enciso's *Suma de geografía* looks back toward the linearity of Mela just as much as it looks forward to an emergent planarity. Although the space inscribed by Enciso's description is more "cartographic," more planar, than that of Mela's, it is not the fully abstract space of the geometric grid, but rather a relative one, with a built-in temporality. Lacking any way to measure longitude, Enciso cannot locate a place by simply providing its full geographical coordinates. He can only do so by assigning its proper place in a discourse that unfolds in time just as it moves through space, tracing routes from a known point of origin, from one location to the next. Although he makes no reference, at least in this passage, to a hypothetical traveler and his or her perception of the coast being described, travel of a kind is nonetheless fundamental to his descriptive method. It is a fitting commentary to his map, which must have resembled the great planispheres of his day. The movement of his text activates those itineraries implicit in the chart's rhumb lines and long rows of toponyms, placing the map in motion. Like the chart, it achieves the spatial fix common to all maps, at least insofar as it allows its reader to imaginatively reconstruct the layout of the territory, but also like the chart, it does not allow this spatial fix to become immobile. The proliferation of places and their riches that appears on its pages are never anything other than stopping places along an itinerary that ultimately pushes up to the boundary between the known and the unknown. The known world thus becomes a sign of what is to come, a metonymic chain extending to the end of the known world. Enciso promises to follow those toponyms all the way eastward to "Gatigara, which is the utmost place of which there is memory in these times" (Fernández de Enciso 1948, 62).

The end the road in the *Suma de geografía* is populated with enticements. Having reached the farthest east, Enciso dwells upon the land of Cathay described by Marco Polo as something of a social and political utopia. "May it please God," Enciso prays, "that in our Spain there should be such good order." But just before reaching this melancholy conclusion, his itinerary arrives in Gatigara, where Enciso remarks that from there on "there is no more notice of lands, for no one has sailed further on." He nonetheless speculates that beyond the boundary of the known lies nothing less than the terrestrial paradise (Fernández de Enciso 1948, 200). Something analogous happens when Enciso turns then to the New World. Like the Indies of Medina's *Libro de grandezas*, Enciso's New World seems unpopulated by historical memory.[50] Except for a few references to anonymous indigenous groups, to their poor diets, and to their cannibalism, much of the description reads like the following passage:

> And from this freshwater sea up toward Paria the coast travels along the line between west and northwest; and it is all shallow, so that ships cannot reach land. From this river to Paria there are two hundred fifty leagues. In this freshwater sea the tides rise and fall as much as in Brittany, and it is at six-and-a-half degrees. (Fernández de Enciso 1948, 205)

Near the end of the itinerary, however, Enciso shares the rumors that explorers have heard from the indigenous people of the Caribbean that just beyond the boundary of the known lie islands "where there is much gold and many pearls" and "a land where the Indians say there are people who have books and who read and write like we do" (Fernández de Enciso 1948, 228). Having speculated about what lies beyond, Enciso provides his itinerary with a coda, a brief description of the coastline of Labrador. The brief itinerary that, in the treatise on the sphere, had impinged upon the sphere's empty space has been amplified in the descriptive geography into a tour of the known world equally directed toward framing and penetrating the unknown. Its forward momentum impels the reader onward toward Utopia, Paradise, gold, pearls, and most importantly, a land with people like us, people who share our literate culture. These are the rewards that await a king willing to send his ships to the boundaries of the known and beyond. In the next chapter, we shall take a look at one of the most important texts from the history of those voyages into the beyond, one that returns with news of the very people to whom Enciso unknowingly alludes.

3

With this chapter, I turn my attention away from the sort of document that we readily identify as a map and toward the sort of cartographic historiography that I have alluded to above. Specifically, I turn to the "Segunda carta de relación" or "Second Letter from Mexico" written in 1520 by Hernán Cortés (1485–1547) and first published in Seville two years later (Cortés 1993 [2001]).[1] With this move, it becomes necessary to address one of the questions I posed at the beginning of chapter 2, that of how a discursive text can be thought of as a map. Enciso has already provided us with one answer. In his Suma de geografía, we find a minute description of the world that includes the data necessary for us to derive a cartographic image, however crude, from the text: compass bearings, distances, and latitudes. Enciso's description, in other words, constitutes a "prose cartography," a specific type of geographical writing designed to assist its reader in forming a cartographic image, whether on paper or in his or her imagination. More will be said about this kind of writing in chapter 4, where I take up the work of several historians who adopted Enciso's methods in their own texts. Here, I look at Cortés's "Second Letter," a text that provides us with a very different answer to our question about how discourse can be cartographic.

Cortés was well aware of the usefulness of maps. Upon establishing himself in the Mexica capital of Tenochtitlán, he availed himself of indigenous maps of Mesoamerica to search for ports, mines, and other resources (Cortés 1993, 223 [2001, 94]). When he reported on this city to his king in the "Second Letter," he seems to have included a map of some kind—now lost, although perhaps the source for a map that later appeared in some print editions of the letter—that depicted the city in some detail. When Cortés lost his way in the forests of the Yucatán while on an expedition in 1526 into modern-day Honduras, he used a compass and a chart to set a crosscountry course (e.g., Cortés 1993, 530, 50 [2001, 340, 55]). Nonetheless, we cannot conclude that Cortés's grasp of maps and mapping, their uses and their potential meanings, was fully commensurate with that of later decades. Never in his correspondence does he use the word *mapa*, preferring either *figura* or *pintura* in reference to Mexica territorial representations, and *carta* to refer to the nautical chart he takes with him to Honduras.[2] More to the point, however, his "Second Letter" maps New Spain in ways that speak of the persistence of the older spatiality of the voyage. While the *Suma de geografía* inscribes the hybrid spatiality of that sector of the culture that was attempting to assimilate emerging cartographic and spatial trends, the "Second Letter" is built upon that linear spatiality that continued to dominate the spatial imagination of the vast majority of Europeans. This does not mean that it was a "primitive" spatiality inadequate to the task of forging empire—far from it. As we shall see, the "Second Letter" provides a keen example of how the linear spatiality inherited from the late Middle Ages could be forged into a robust rhetorical weapon that could indeed map Mesoamerica into a novel, trans-Atlantic, imperial space. It also demonstrates the close relationship that exists between that linear spatiality and narrative. The "Second Letter" constitutes, in effect, a narrative of space.

On August 16, 1519, Cortés and his small band of sailors and adventurers, financed by private speculation and operating under a dubious cloud of legality,[3] set out from the newly founded city of Veracruz in pursuit of a fabled city deep in the interior of a land unknown to them. There—they were certain—could be found those "people like us" rumored in the geography of Enciso, as well as in other period texts. The expedition would later become the stuff of legend, in no small measure due to Cortés's own considerable effectiveness in telling its tale. The so-called "Second Letter from Mexico"—there are five, including a "First Letter" whose attribution to Cortés has been a matter of debate—was written in the newly founded colonial town of Segura de la Frontera on October 30, 1520. There, Cortés and his men licked the wounds they had suffered during their narrow escape from the Mexica capital of Tenochtitlán, a city that had originally received the Spaniards peacefully but that turned against them after the conquistadors asserted themselves as its new rulers. Cortés writes to Charles V in order to win the material and legal support that he needs to succeed in his imminent attempt to retake the city by force. He attempts to persuade his monarch by recapitulating the narrative of events between his initial departure from the coast, through his stay in Tenochtitlán, and up to a time just after his subsequent flight from the city. Along the way, he constructs an image of himself as an uncompromisingly loyal and consummately skillful servant of the king. He also describes the world of the Mexica in ways that are clearly meant to incite the monarch's interest in its conquest. The rhetorical strategy worked. Not only did Cortés receive the support he was looking for, but he managed to monumentalize himself and his conquest in the eyes of an even wider audience.[4] In 1522, shortly after the conquest (and destruction) of Tenochtitlán was completed, the "Second Letter" appeared in print in Seville. This and subsequent letters were soon translated into several other languages, including Latin, and circulated widely throughout Western Europe. At the time, they fed other monumentalizing accounts of Cortés's conquest that joined the conqueror's own letters on European bookshelves. They continue to be read, to be studied, and to seduce even to this day.[5]

The fortunes of the "Second Letter" as a piece of official correspondence that was eventually printed and widely distributed create two distinct layers of analysis that, for clarity's sake, I keep separate in this chapter. I dedicate most of this chapter to the first layer, the one that involves the text authored by Cortés himself as it has been established by modern editors. There, Cortés invents—out of the disparate city-states and settlements through which he marched, fought, and schemed—a place that he calls "New Spain." I examine how Cortés invents this place by combining an itinerary structure much like that of Marco Polo with other traditions of geographical and historiographical writing inherited from medieval Spain. Then, in the final section of the chapter, I turn to the second layer of analysis, which involves the "Second Letter" as it was adapted for publication in Seville and, shortly afterward, in Nuremburg and Venice. Publication necessarily involved the addition of a number of paratexts meant to package the letter for consumption by the European reading audience. These include a brief but telling prologue, a woodcut image from the first edition, and, most important, two woodcut maps from the 1524 Nuremburg edition. I argue that these paratexts can be understood as commentaries on the Cortés correspondence that extend our understanding of its particular spatiality. Specifically, they address the question of how to map the place invented by Cortés into a larger imperial space. I conclude this chapter with a discussion of a manuscript map drawn in the mid-1520s that most fully demonstrates how the "Second Letter" fits within my larger narrative about the invention of America and the history of spatiality.

Maps and Discourse

Harley and Woodward define "maps" as "graphic representations that facilitate a spatial understanding of things, concepts, conditions, processes, or events in the human world" (1987, xvi). As we saw in chapter 2, this definition dramatically expands the range covered by older definitions of the map: it does not specify the surface of the Earth as a privileged object of representation, nor does it specify the assumptions and techniques of modern Western cartography as the sole locus of what is meant by a "spatial understanding." This expanded definition thereby makes the study of maps and mapping a much more inclusive enterprise than it has been in the past, one open to the study of decidedly exotic objects that we might not, at first glance, even recognize as maps. In one sense, however, it continues to be excessively restrictive, at least for those of us interested in discussing the relationship of maps or mapping to verbal discourse. "Maps," the definition tells us, are "graphic representations," and by "graphic" it means "iconographic." Writing, or *graphos*, is excluded from the semantic field.[6] Although written texts—especially such things as cosmographies, geographies, and histories that engage in geographical or topographical description—may very well inform the study of maps, it is not because these texts themselves are to be thought of as maps. Whatever "spatial understanding" they might provide of "things, concepts, conditions, processes, or events in the human world," if any, is clearly not of the same order as that provided by an image of some kind. The image counts as a map, while the verbal description does not.

Immediately, then, the definition of the map that I have adopted in this book places writing on the margins of the discussion. In order to move writing to the center, to discuss how it can be considered to be a "map" or to engage in "mapping," we must address the hoary question of how writing can be like an image. We must take a look, in other words, at the problem of ekphrasis, the verbal depiction of space or of an object in space. Debates over ekphrasis have produced adamant defenders and detractors of the capacity of the word to figure spatial things, such as pieces of plastic art. One of the fundamental problems is that language produces meaning and figures objects by unfolding in time—quite appropriately—as *discourse*, the "onward course; process or succession of time, events, actions, etc."[7] In Murray Krieger's extraordinary analysis of ekphrasis, this intrinsic temporality of language works at cross-purposes with any attempt to use it to figure objects in space, a project that is inherently visual and synchronic.[8] Ekphrasis, in Krieger's analysis, represents a paradoxical activity, one that suspends language between a craving for "the spatial fix" and its intrinsic yearning "for the freedom of the temporal flow." Ultimately, in Krieger's view, language inevitably falls short of the spatial fix it craves because "words cannot have capacity, cannot be capacious, because they have, literally, no space." The temporality of discourse always wins out in the end (Krieger 1992, 31–64). If—for now at least—we assume that what makes a map a map is much like what makes an image an image, then maps must count among the images that words can only aspire to imitate. If the cartographic dimension of language involves its capacity to make places visible to the eye of the reader, then it is a dimension of language that is inevitably doomed to failure.

Others disagree with Krieger about whether or not language in general, or a given text in particular, achieves the spatial fix it craves and whether such an achievement is to be considered good, proper, or desirable. Of particular interest are those arguments that find in the print revolution of the fifteenth and sixteenth centuries a decided shift in favor of the visibility and spatiality of language against its inherent temporality. Whether or not language is inherently spatial or inherently capable of figuring spatiality, the early modern print revolution makes it so. Walter Ong summarizes this argument: "Print replaced the lingering hearing-dominance in the world of thought and expression with the sight-dominance which had its beginnings with writing but could not flourish with the support of writing alone. Print situates words in space more relentlessly than writing ever did" (Ong 1988, 121). In the wake of Gutenberg, in other words, language acquires precisely what Krieger says it lacks—spaciousness. More than ever before, language becomes a plastic entity that occupies a specific space, that of the printed page, and its typographic arrangement acquires meaning. For Tom Conley, this development has a specifically cartographic dimension:

> As soon as we realize that the discursive or vocal order of printed literature happens in no small way to be a product of our imagination . . . it becomes clear that rhetorical orders are not unrelated to diagrammatic processes. Meaning is produced through both printed and diagrammatic means. Speech is relayed, but it is also rendered visible . . . In incunabular and sixteenth-century literature, we behold works that betray the touch of the architect, the stage designer, the painter, and, no less, the cartographer. By virtue of spatial modes of composition, the writer tends to "map out" the discourse of the work before our eyes and to invite us to see the self-constituting of its being in patterns that move into space by means of diagrammatic articulations. (1996, 4)

In Conley's account of French cartographic writing, the early modern revolution in cartography and spatiality becomes a cultural earthquake whose repercussions are felt far from the world of iconographic maps and geographical and topographical description. Any text, it turns out, can be understood as "cartographic," no matter what its subject matter, as long as it appears in print and arranges its typographic space in ways that have something to do with the space of the map.

I propose a third alternative, one that responds to my discussion in the preceding chapter of cartography and spatiality in the early modern Hispanic world. Behind both Krieger's and Conley's analyses lie notions of map and space rooted in modernity.[9] For both, the identification of a spatiality in literature involves the delineation of an optical regime—one in which objects become available, in synchronous manner, to the gaze of the reader—that exists over and above, or perhaps despite, the temporal unfolding of language. In this way, both Conley and Krieger seek in language what the history of cartography looks for, but cannot find, in the culture of medieval and much of early modern Europe: the space of the image. Conley finds it, while Krieger does not. Neither, however, gives much attention to the possibility that the spatiality of language can be understood in other ways, ones that correspond to differing conceptualizations of space.[10] When "space" is understood not as a surface but as a distance, the opposition between spatiality and temporality that exists at the heart of both arguments begins to dissolve. The itinerary interweaves time and topography as two kinds of intervals: "space" becomes inseparable from the action of moving through it. It is at once discourse and course.

Recall the passage from Ercilla cited in the previous chapter, "Returning to our story, I say that our ordered ranks marched *a great space in a brief one*, away from the border constituted by the Talcaguano riverbank" (Ercilla 1993, 22.6). The culture that produced these verses is not one for whom "space" is something to be appreciated synchronically: it is something to be taken in diachronically. This culture instead holds the business of mapping, of figuring "things, concepts, conditions, processes, or events in the human world" in such a way as to provide a "spatial understanding" of them does not necessarily entail their reduction to an optical regime. It entails, instead, a discursive movement through such objects, a tour rather than a map. As such, space becomes inseparable from a rudimentary notion of narrative as a meaningful concatenation of events. In the space of the voyage, places stand in for actions: the route becomes the narrative thread leading from one to the next. The culture that wrote these verses, to put it another way, is a culture for whom *discourse* is the primary means of figuring space, because it is discourse that, in its very linearity, best approximates the shape of space itself.[11] It is this sense of space that becomes crucial to understanding the mapping of empire in

Cortés's "Second Letter" as well as in the other examples of Spanish carto-graphic literature examined in this book.

Inventing New Spain

Renaissance cosmography distinguished between "cosmography," the de-scription of the universe, "geography," the description of the terraqueous globe, and "chorography," the description of a particular part of the globe, such as an individual region or a city. Strictly speaking, Cortés's "Second Let-ter" is none of these things. It is a historical narrative in epistolary form and follows the rhetorical conventions of the period established for a text of this kind. Nevertheless, the "Second Letter" can easily be described as a historical narrative with chorographic ambitions, so to speak. Cortés addresses his letter to Charles V, claiming that it is a product of the conqueror's desire to inform the monarch of "[a]ll the things of this land." These "things" include events as well as places and their inhabitants, but it is clearly the latter kind of detail that matters most, for they "are so many and of such a kind that one might call oneself emperor of this kingdom with no less glory than of Germany, which, by the Grace of God, Your Sacred Majesty already possesses" (Cortés 2001, 48 [1993, 161]). This very famous assertion does something unprecedented in Spain's discourse on the New World: it hypostatizes it not as a marginal land of wonders or as a stopping place on the way to the East, but as a political en-tity in its own right and, moreover, as a polity commensurate with a European one.[12] It also marks the "things of this land," its people and places, as central to Cortés's discourse about himself and about the world that he conquers on the king's behalf. They are what make New Spain an "empire."

Although the description of New Spain is thereby identified as one of the principal objectives of the "Second Letter," the hinge upon which its imperial discourse swings, Cortés cannot be said to "describe" very much at all, if by "description" we mean the sort of ekphrastic discourse that struggles against the temporality of language in order to reduce its object to the synchronous mastery of an optical regime. To begin with, Cortés never surveys New Spain as a whole. There is never a moment, by way of preface or conclusion, in which the narrative voice pretends to command New Spain in its entirety by delineating its boundaries, tracing its rivers, or outlining its topography.[13] Cortés alludes to "[a]ll the things of this land," and then shortly afterward tells of his departure for the interior from the coastal city of Cempoala. Descrip-tions of localities punctuate the narrative of the journey from Veracruz to Te-nochtitlán. New Spain appears piecemeal, a series of isolated passages dedi-cated to particular places spread out along the story of Cortés's journey from its periphery to its heart. With few exceptions, these passages pay little atten-tion to landscape.[14] They reduce the natural world to a collection of conven-tional epithets, like the "beautiful valleys and plains" (68) surrounding the city of Tlaxcala or the "high and rugged mountains" (153) that flank Guaca-chulla (Huaquechula). Like Marco Polo, Cortés is more interested in the built and social world of the land he passes through than in its natural wonders. It is the city-states of Mesoamerica that provide Cortés's discursive cartogra-phy with its "things, concepts, conditions, processes, or events in the human world."[15] We learn of their temples, their palaces, their markets, and on one occasion, even of the presence of beggars (75). When his tale reaches the Mex-ica capital, it gives way to a lengthy account of the city's location in the midst of a lake, its physical layout, its spectacular marketplace, and its many temples and fine houses, among other things.

But like the conquistador's treatment of the kingdom as a whole, his ac-counts of the cities also resist understanding in terms of an optical regime. Some of the passages dedicated to the cities of Mesoamerica, like the follow-ing one, provide enough of the right kind of detail so that the reader can form a visual image of the city's geographical setting, however rudimentary or approximate:

> The city of Guacachulla [sic] is situated in a plain bounded on the one side by some high and rugged mountains and on the others by two rivers about two crossbows apart which run through large and deep ravines . . . The whole city is surrounded by a very strong wall built of stone and mortar which is as high as twenty-four feet on the outside and almost level with the ground on the inside. All along the top of this wall runs a battlement three feet high. (Cortés 2001, 153 [1993, 301])

Needless to say, even a description like this one falls far short of providing an "accurate" visual image of what the city was like. It is left to the readers to fill in many crucial details, something that they will only be able to do by drawing upon their repertoire of familiar, and therefore inappropriate, images of what a "city" looks like. Many of Cortés's other descriptions require even greater leaps of imagination for the reader interested in visualizing the cities in question. These descriptions enumerate the city's principal attributes—its impressive palaces, its marketplace, its temples—but do so in ways that do not lend themselves to visualization of any kind. About Tlaxcala we read:

> The city is so big and remarkable that, although there is much I could say of it which I shall omit, the little I will say is, I think, almost unbelievable, for the city is much larger than Granada and very much stronger, with as good buildings and many more people than Granada had when it was taken, and very much better

supplied with the produce of the land . . . There is in this city a market where each and every day upward of thirty thousand people come to buy and sell . . . There are establishments like barbers' where they have their hair washed and are shaved, and there are baths. Lastly, there is amongst them every consequence of good order and courtesy, and they are such an orderly and intelligent people that the best in Africa cannot equal them. (Cortés 2001, 67–68 [1993, 184–85])

Although Tlaxcala is infinitely larger than Guacachulla—and, as the home of his staunchest indigenous allies, much more important to Cortés—the conquistador actually describes it less. His description allows us to picture a bigger and better Granada, but it does nothing to situate the city or describe its physical layout. We know that the city has an impressive market, barbershops, and baths but have no idea where these are located.

These limits present themselves even in Cortés's extensive description of Tenochtitlán. We know more about the physical layout of Tenochtitlán than we do of any other city in Mexico. The initial description of Tenochtitlán takes the form of a point-by-point account of Cortés's route into it, an account that tells of the cities along the shores of Lake Texcoco through which the expedition passes, then of the causeway it crosses into the island capital, then of the fortifications that guard the causeway, and so forth (1993, 205–8 [2001, 80–84]). Later, however, Cortés describes the city and its environs in a register that is heard in no other description. He generalizes about topography and spatial relations as if from a commanding height. He begins by telling that the province of "Mesyco" is

[c]ircular and encompassed by very high and very steep mountains, and the plain is some seventy leagues in circumference: in this plain there are two lakes which cover almost all of it . . . One of these lakes is of fresh water and the other, which is the larger, is of salt water . . . The great city of Temixtitan is built on the salt lake, and no matter by what road you travel there are two leagues from the main body of the city to the mainland. There are four artificial causeways leading to it . . . The city is as big as Seville or Córdoba. The main streets are very wide and straight; some of these are on land, but the rest and all the smaller ones are half on land, half canals where they paddle their canoes . . . The city has many squares where trading is done and markets are held continuously. There is also one square twice as big as that of Salamanca, with arcades all around. (Cortés 2001, 102–3 [1993, 232–34])

There are many things we learn about the city's physical layout, but there are also limitations to what we are told, particularly following this description of the city's overall layout. For instance, Cortés's description of the main market square does nothing to locate it in the physical layout of the city. His descriptions of the city's temples and palaces likewise do little to place them in the urban topography he has outlined. Clearly, as Jorge Checa points out, it is not so much the cities themselves that interest Cortés but instead their civility, their *policía* (1996, 187). Cortés's "descriptions" direct themselves not to the eye of the reader but to his or her mind. They work to make the cities intelligible rather than visible.

It is in this way, ironically, that the descriptions come closest to the language of cartography. A map differs from other kinds of images—such as a landscape painting—in the unique limits it imposes upon the question of visibility. Although it renders visible the spatial relationship among the components of the territory, the map does so by reducing those components to a series of what are acknowledged to be abstract signs, such as lines, colors, and various kinds of pictorial symbols. No one assumes that the icon for a "city" on a map is meant to depict what the city looks like. On that level, the map communicates something intelligible rather than sensible about the territory it figures. It identifies certain features of the territory to be figured as members of a particular class and then assigns to that class a more or less uniform mark. The particularity of places is thus sacrificed in favor of their shared pertinence within a single class. These marks tend to distinguish among members of the class only in quantitative terms, such as size or political importance, rather than in qualitative terms. Likewise, Cortés's cityscapes emphasize intelligibility over visibility. They identify important Mesoamerican settlements as "cibdades," and figure each through a series of "civility markers." The length and content of the list vary with the size and importance of the city. All of them, however, are submitted to the same system of figuration, one that emphasizes their commonalities and converts their differences into matters of quantity rather than quality. The "Second Letter" organizes these city markers into a space of sorts. Mesoamerican geography, as others have noted, appears as a series of city-states whose degree of *policía* increases with altitude above sea level and proximity to Tenochtitlán (Checa 1996, 187; Rabasa 1993, 100–1). To put it another way, that geography is charted as an itinerary along Cortés's route of travel from Veracruz to Tenochtitlán, stopping at the most significant places along the way.

By contrast with Cortés's account of his 1526 journey to Honduras in the "Fifth Letter from Mexico," the "Second Letter" makes no reference to charts or compass bearings that could be used to rationalize the route. We know that Cortés had his pilots along with him when he fled Tenochtitlán in 1520, but he never once mentions their compasses. As far as we know, he did not call upon them in any way to chart the expedition's route from Veracruz to Tenochtitlán. As a result, the route appears in the "Second Letter" as a schematic one, a linear movement "inward" from coast to capital. If it can be said to resemble a map at all, it would be one of the itinerary maps that the Spanish colonists drew to accompany their responses to the questionnaires sent by the cosmographers in Spain. The chronological unfolding of the letter could be said to coincide with the shape of the space it figures. The "Second Letter from Mexico" would become cartographic without needing to overcome its discursive flow. It would find its spatial fix in and through its temporal unfolding. It would render visible not a place, or a series of places, but a territory organized within the confines of a particular spatial modality, that of the linear route taken to conquer it.[16]

Still, the "Second Letter" does not explicitly work to render much of anything "visible" at all, at least not anything larger than a city and its surrounding countryside. As a narrative text, it does not even render visible its unidimensional space in the manner of an itinerary map. As I mentioned above, Cortés did not preface his account with a description of New Spain as did the humanist Cervantes de Salazar, nor did he append one to his narrative in the manner of his fellow soldier Fray Francisco de Aguilar (Aguilar 1977; Cervantes de Salazar 1971). Neither—as far as we know—did Cortés draw an itinerary map to accompany his text. At no point, in other words, does he consolidate what he knows about Mexican geography in a way that would invite the reader to picture it in a manner independent of his narrative. On the contrary, Cortés's narrative often works to bring the reader down to earth, to follow the itinerary on the ground rather than imagine it from above. Space, in the "Second Letter," is not only described in and through the movement of a journey, it is also marked by the frontiers that the invaders transgress in their efforts to conquer. While Marco Polo's itinerant narrator avoids potentially hostile territory and excessively rough terrain, Cortés marches right into it. He marks his passage over difficult mountain passes (1993, 169–70 [2001, 55]) and dwells upon his decision to penetrate the wall that the fiercely independent Tlaxcalans have erected to keep would-be conquerors out (1993, 173–74 [2001, 57]). With each such crossing of a New World Rubicon, the reader accompanies Cortés in his attempts to pick his way through the labyrinth of Mesoamerica's political geography, to march through the obstacles of its physical geography. Like the battle narratives that they often foretell, these crossings construct Mesoamerican space as a domesticated "here" and an unknown "there" to be reached, desired, and eventually, possessed. Our attempts to read Cortés's letter as an itinerary map of New Spain, in effect, falsify its repeated efforts to keep our feet on the ground and our eyes on a prize always beyond the mountains, the river, the causeways crossing Lake Texcoco.

The "here" and "there" of Cortés's itinerary are charged with moral and political freight from the very beginning of the "Second Letter." Having founded a city on the coast of the Gulf of Mexico—the modern-day city of Veracruz—Cortés sets out for the interior, passing through the Amerindian town of Cempoala, which he describes:

> With that purpose I set out from the town of Cempoal, which I renamed Sevilla . . . I left all that province of Cempoal and all the mountains surrounding the town . . . very secure and peaceful; and all of these natives have been and still are faithful vassals of Your Majesty, for they were subjects of Mutezuma and, according to what I was told, had been subdued by force not long previously. When they heard through me of Your Highness and of Your very great Royal power, they said they wished to become vassals of Your Majesty and my allies, and asked me to protect them from that great lord who held them by tyranny and force. (Cortés 2001, 50–51 [1993, 163])

This passage serves a variety of ends, not the least of which is to report the measures that Cortés has taken to secure his rear and, thereby, assure his king that he is a capable conqueror. It also does so by allegorizing the Mexica world. The passage points in two separate directions, toward "all that province of Cempoal" that now constitutes Cortés's rear, and toward the territory of "that great lord," Mutezuma[17], that lies ahead. The here-and-now of the narrative, the farthest point of the small army's advance, constitutes the frontier between these two spaces, a frontier between Christianity and paganism, justice and tyranny, civilization and barbarism. The reader is to believe that Cortés's journey extends the border between the Spanish *civitas*, the city as a "civilized" community, and the barbaric beyond. In the rear of the advance, the domain of law established in Veracruz has been expanded to include Cempoala, which is christened "Sevilla." Its inhabitants have become, we read, vassals of Charles V and allies of his representative Cortés, enjoying security and freedom from tyranny. Beyond the *civitas*, in the land that lies ahead of Cortés's advance, force and terror prevail. Cortés's itinerary, to put it plainly, does not simply move from one place to the next. It moves through an allegorized space, constantly pushing forward the boundary that separates the civilized "here" from the barbarous "there." What reader, persuaded by Cortés's characterization of his own conquest and of the land he marches into, would not want him to press on and succeed?

Cortés allegorizes his itinerary, certainly, in the service of one of his principal rhetorical objectives, justifying his conquistadorial efforts in the light of their dubious legal status. In setting off for the interior, Cortés clearly overstepped the limited authority granted him by his immediate superior, Diego Velázquez, the governor of Cuba. Velázquez had charged Cortés with the task of finding the lost fleet of the explorer Francisco de Garay and had authorized him only to reconnoiter the Mesoamerican coast and to trade with the natives, not to embark upon a march inland. Scholars have long been interested in the various ways that Cortés attempts to persuade his reader of the legitimacy of his actions and have pointed, among other things, to the ways that he draws upon the legal and historiographical traditions of the Castilian past. In short, Cortés tries to paint the conquest of Mexico as a seamless extension, or perhaps a repetition, of Castile's recently completed effort to reconquer Spain from the Muslim powers that had first invaded the Iberian Peninsula in the eighth century.[18] He does this in a variety of ways. He justifies his actions by invoking legal codes that were invented to regulate Castile's military campaign against Islam and a concept of "empire" peculiar to medieval Iberia (Frankl 1962, 1963). He describes Mesoamerican cities as simulacra of the Andalusian cities reconquered from Islam during the Middle Ages, thereby creating the possibility of wealth cloaked in the legitimating auspices of a holy crusade (Boruchoff 1991, 340). He invokes Biblical imagery and medieval forensic rhetoric to concoct a dubious scene of "donation" reminiscent of other such acts of imperial generosity (Elliott 1989b, 36–38). Indigenous myths about the impending return of a culture hero are mobilized to cast Cortés in the role of a returning native, a reconqueror (Gaylord 1992, 133).

Cortés allegorizes his story and its setting in the way I have described, thereby drawing upon a figurative vein common to historical writing about the medieval Reconquest. José Antonio Maravall refers to it in this way:

> Over and again, texts and documents make reference to the "terribilem mortalitatem" of which the Chronicle of San Juan de la Peña speaks. Over and again, life, which consisted fundamentally of the dramatic task of reconquest and repopulation, is seen as surrounded by a frontier of hostility . . . In 1076 . . . from Barcelona, when one gazed upon the utmost limit of the frontier, one saw it as the place of horror and of immense solitude . . . Everywhere in the Peninsula the Saracen was what lay on the other side of Christian existence, what surrounded it with a belt of hostility. (Maravall 1981, 266)

As a characterization of real-life relations between Christians and Muslims in medieval Spain, Maravall's assertion is thoroughly out of date, but as a characterization of how those relations are figured in the documents he examines, it is right to the point.[19] The space of the Reconquest is that of the frontier. It is a frontier, moreover, that is not figured as a line cutting across a map but as an experience of an encounter between a civilized "here" and a barbarous "there." That "here and "there" are figured as contiguous localities, just as we would expect from a culture unaccustomed to imagining territory from on high, as it would through the mediation of a map. Like the point of view adopted by the discursive itinerary, the one here is decidedly earthbound. It differs from the itinerary only in that it is static rather than mobile. When Cortés writes of his advance into the world of the Mexica, he borrows the basic spatial allegory that Maravall outlines, and sets it into motion. The son of a participant in the campaign to retake the kingdom of Granada and thereby complete the Reconquest of Spain, Cortés writes about his own conquest as if it reiterated, in the New World, the old extension of the Christian *civitas* at the expense of the tyrannous heathen.

Cortés's descriptions of the cities of Mesoamerica play an important role in extending and maintaining this political and cultural chiaroscuro. Nowhere is this more evident than in Cortés's treatment of one city in particular, Cholula. The conquest of Cholula is famous—indeed, infamous—for one of the most controversial events in the history of the conquest of Mexico, a bloody encounter in which Cortés and his men killed thousands of the city's residents.[20] The scene for the massacre is set by the crossing of yet another Rubicon. Cortés describes in some detail the urgings of the Cholulans that he come to their city and the repeated warnings of the Tlaxcalans that it is all a trap. Cortés resolves, despite such serious doubts, to march on the city. He arrives at its outskirts, he writes, only to sleep in a ditch the night before he is to meet with its representatives (1993, 191 [2001, 72]). The conqueror's body, so conspicuous in its absence from so much of the "Second Letter," thus makes one of its strategic appearances. The appearance of the body in the story marks one of those boundaries where the difficulties and risks of the journey are most acutely felt, one of those points that deliberately draw the reader into the decisive scene. The paragraphs that follow only reinforce this sense of impending danger, as Cortés and his men see the many signs verifying the Tlaxcalans's warnings. The reader discovers the signs of a trap alongside Cortés as he approaches the city. He waits with the conqueror within, as the smell of a trap grows stronger until the conqueror decides to strike before he is struck (1993, 193 [2001, 73–74]). And so, by drawing the reader into the scene, Cortés hopes to convince him or her that his attack upon the population of Cholula was nothing more than a preemptive strike meant to prevent certain disaster. This qualification is crucial. Without it, his recourse to sudden, explosive violence could completely undermine the allegory he uses to figure his efforts. Without it, the attack might look like the sort of thing that Cortés's detractors later thought it to be, an attempt to intimidate the enemy through a show of strength and brutality. If that were the case, then the colonial *civitas* under construction would prove to be no better than the world of the tyrant Mutezuma. The claim to conquer under the aegis of superior moral authority—justice against tyranny—would utterly crumble as barbarism revealed itself in the heart of civilization.

Recognizing that his own actions threaten to subvert his rhetoric, Cortés struggles to shore up his territorial allegory in the pages following his account of the violence in Cholula. His efforts, however, are so preposterous that they actually reveal its clear fictionality. Remarkably, Cortés insists that the incident has produced a change of heart among the Cholulans, who come to resent their supposed manipulation by Mutezuma and swear their allegiance—in all sincerity—to Charles V. With astonishing boldness, the conqueror plasters the holes in this dubious narrative with narrative and descriptive hyperboles. First, he erases the memory of the massacre. The city, we read, immediately returns to normal: "On the following day the whole city was reoccupied and full of women and children, all unafraid, *as though nothing had happened*" (Cortés 2001, 74 [1993, 194]; emphasis added). Then, Cortés goes so far as to resurrect the dead: "After fifteen or twenty days which I remained there the city and the land were so pacified and full of people *that it seemed as if no one was missing from it*, and their markets and trade were carried on as before" (2001, 74; emphasis added). Before what? The crucial event goes entirely unnamed. Everything is as if nothing had happened, as if there were no bodies whose absence would testify to the massacre that has taken place. The account has simply swept it under the rug of its claim that normalcy returned right away. Having erased the massacre, resurrected the dead, and won over the hearts of his erstwhile enemies, Cortés then converts Mutezuma into the villain, the cause of the disastrous animosity between Cholula and Tlaxcala, and himself, into the solution for Cholula's real problems: "I then restored the friendly relations between this city of Churltecal [sic] and Tascalteca, which had existed in the recent past, before Mutezuma had attracted them to his friendship with gifts and made them enemies of the others" (Cortés 2001, 74 [1993, 194]). Cortés, the reader is to believe, has not inflicted wounds but healed them, restoring old friendships that had been disrupted by the tyrant.[21]

Having healed its wounds, Cortés can now describe the city. Like all the descriptions in the "Second Letter," the description of Cholula is only made once the story of its conquest is completed. As if to compensate for the erasure of the scene of violence, Cortés deploys the civility markers particularly thick and fast: "The city is more beautiful to look at than any in Spain . . . From here to the coast I have seen no city so fit for Spaniards to live in" (Cortés 2001, 75 [1993, 195–96]). The presence of beggars in Cholula serves as occasion for an even more shocking assertion: "And there are many poor people who beg from the rich in the streets as the poor do in Spain and in other civilized places" (Cortés 2001, 75 [1993, 196]). The survivors of the massacre are not only raised to the status of allies, but, for the first time in the discourse on Amerindians, to the status of reasonable people. This account of an incident so out of step with Cortés's rhetoric could, perhaps, only end this way, with an extreme assertion of Amerindian pertinence to a colonial *civitas*. Cortesian rhetoric has become dysfunctional, clumsily moving between a spurious narrative and a counterfeit description in an effort to sustain a political and territorial allegory belied by actual events. The dead must be elided so that the itinerary of conquest can continue its march into the landscape of its own allegory.

But not everything in the "Second Letter" leads us to imagine Mesoamerica from the point of view of an earthbound journey through an allegorized landscape. Like other readers of the "Second Letter" (Checa 1996; Rabasa 1993), I find it difficult to resist the temptation to treat this text as if it were indeed an itinerary map of New Spain and not just a discursive itinerary fleshed out as a story of conquest. I believe this temptation to picture the territory that Cortés does not quite describe responds to Cortés's own writing, or rather, to one of its subtle but influential undertones. Cortés may not explicitly describe New Spain as a whole, but he nonetheless gestures in that direction. He hints at a description—a chorography or a prose cartography—that he does not actually carry out. We have already seen this early in the "Second Letter" when he alludes to the whole of the territory as an "empire" comparable to the Holy Roman Empire and states his desire to describe it all to his monarch. Cortés's conclusion, too, alludes to the whole in provocative ways without actually describing it. It is there that Cortés generalizes about its quality and christens it "New Spain of the Ocean Sea" on the basis of its general similarity with Spain itself (1993, 308 [2001, 158]). But these are not the only places in which Cortés seems to allude to the forest rather than just trace his route among the individual trees. Shortly after the conquest of Cholula, Cortés's itinerary finally reaches Tenochtitlán, the original objective of the expedition and the subject of roughly a third of the "Second Letter." In this portion of the text, narrative and description play off each other, gradually building to a climatic moment which both alludes to that greater, undescribed whole, and patently exposes the arbitrariness of Cortés's attempt to fashion New Spain with a geographical language inherited from medieval Castile.

Once again, the way there is marked by a series of obstacles and boundaries that Cortés must overcome (1993, 198–201 [2001, 77–85]). This time, the series culminates in the conquistador's last and most significant obstacle, the person of Mutezuma himself. Cortés crosses one of the causeways that lead into the Mexica capital, and is met along the way by the *tlatoani* of the Mexica.

This time, it is not Cortés's body, but Mutezuma's, that makes an appearance. For the first time, Cortés has recourse to an extended piece of direct discourse, a speech during which Mutezuma exposes his chest to the conqueror to demonstrate that he is a man made of flesh and blood (1993, 211 [2001, 86]). Eventually, the narrative leads to another speech in which Mutezuma instructs the assembled Mexica nobility to recognize Cortés as a returning culture hero and to swear their allegiance to Charles V. After the speech, all involved do so, in the presence of witnesses—Cortés is sure to point out—and before a notary public, who takes it all down (1993, 227–28 [2001, 98–99]). With the exception, perhaps, of the narrative of the Noche Triste—the night of the conquistadors' narrow escape from the city—nowhere are we as readers more clearly drawn into the here and now of Cortés's story as we are in these episodes. Mutezuma and the other Mexica weep as they sign over their sovereignty to the king of Castile. The leader of the Mexica, supposedly Cortés's final obstacle, has become his instrument. Castile's sovereignty over Mesoamerica—already a reality in the eyes of Spain, thanks to the intervention of the pope—comes to be recognized by the Mexica themselves (1993, 211 [2001, 86]).

Historians have made much of this dramatic and probably fictional scene, the so-called "donation of Mutezuma," through which Cortés cements the legal title of his king over the people that the conquistador has encountered, not to mention his own position as the king's representative in their lands (e.g. Elliott 1989a, 36–38). Without taking away from its importance, however, I would like to emphasize the contribution to Cortés's purpose made by several other, subsequent scenes more strongly marked by Cortés's specifically territorial, and not just legalistic, fantasies. After relating the scene of the donation, Cortés at last describes the city. He has foregone at least one other opportunity to do so, during the narrative of the Spanish approach to Tenochtlán, which could have easily included a description of the city and the Central Valley of Mexico made from one of the heights surrounding them. There we find only partial sketches of the city and its island location (1993, 206–7 [2001, 82–83]). Tenochtitlán, like the other cities of Mesoamerica, is fully described only after it has been legally incorporated into the political space of the new colonial civitas. An extensive description of the city begins with a breathless attempt to describe the treasure that has been won and will be sent home to the king. It then moves on to the larger prize, the city itself, and particularly its rich markets, temples, and palaces. This time, the description makes it possible to picture the layout of the city and its setting on an island in Lake Texcoco (1993, 232–34 [2001, 102–3]).

Not all on these pages, however, is static description. Two brief narratives punctuate the conquistador's repertoire of urban wonders at the edge of the world. Both serve to articulate the description of these wonders with Cortés's emerging image of a new empire to be ruled from Spain. The first of these appears shortly after the narrative of the donation scene, although we do not know whether or not the events it relates took place before or after the speech was made and the oaths taken. It tells of Cortés's attempt to alter the cultural life of the Mexica by tampering with the central symbols of their religious practice. Cortés describes the Templo Mayor, the center of Mexica religious practice, and then tells of his allegedly successful attempt to transform it by destroying its idols and replacing them with Roman Catholic icons. Mutezuma, Cortés writes, collaborates in this act of desecration "with a cheerful visage," and human sacrifice ceases for the duration of the Spanish stay.[22] We are to believe this astonishing claim that the leader of the Mexica collaborated in the desecration of the idols because, as Mutezuma himself explains, he and his people are not natives of the place where they have built their city. Both of his speeches open with the observation that "[n]either I, nor any of those who dwell in this land, are natives of it, but foreigners who came from very distant parts" (Cortés 2001, 85 [1993, 210]).[23] Mutezuma then repeats these misgivings at the Templo Mayor, at the moment of its impending desecration: "All of them, especially Mutezuma, replied that they had already told me how they were not natives of this land, and that as it was many years since their forefathers had come here, they well knew that the might have erred somewhat in what they believed, for they had left their native land so long ago" (2001, 106 [1993, 239]).

The Mexica did indeed have their origins far beyond the Central Valley, and their mythology reflected this history with a foundation myth that told of a primitive migration leading to the founding of a sacred city, Tenochtitlán. The version of this myth that Cortés puts in the mouth of Mutezuma, however, inverts its foundational purpose. Rather than ground Mexica presence in a divine dispensation, it pulls the rug, or the land, out from under their feet. It strips them of the cultural authority that comes with belonging and thus transforms the nature of the encounter between Spaniard and Mexica. Rather than meet as a settled people and an invader, the two encounter each other as wanderers in a land alien, ultimately, to both of them. Mexica pertinence is transformed into a double of Spanish impertinence.[24] With the recognition of Cortés as a returning cultural hero, that encounter becomes one between long-lost kin. Transformed by Cortés's conquistadorial fictions from obstacle into instrument, Mutezuma thus deterritorializes his people, reterritorializes them as a subject kingdom of the Spanish Monarchy, and leads them to embrace the centerpiece of conquest and Hispanization, conversion to Roman

Catholicism. It would seem that the conquest, which began by echoing the Re-conquest in the foundation of a frontier city and in the inscription of a divide between civilization and barbarism, has been completed with the successful assimilation of this once barbarian, now newly Christian, simulacrum of Seville, Córdoba, Granada. At least one of the territories in that vast hemisphere assigned to Castile by the Treaty of Tordesillas has become just as much a part of the crown of Castile as, say, the kingdom of Granada did a generation before.

The transformation of Mutezuma and his empire is brought to its culmination in the second narrative I wish to discuss, one that appears at the end of Cortés's description of the city. The text begins to envision a territory, a kingdom (or empire) not yet entirely consolidated but nonetheless won for the crown. Mutezuma, we read, has instructed Cortés and his men about the routes to various outlying provinces and has even provided the conqueror with a map of the coast.[25] Expeditions set out from the capital in search of mines, gold, and ports, hoping to consolidate the victory and render productive the new territorial acquisition. The conqueror and his men appear to be working entirely in the service of the emperor, and under the once again approving gaze of a happily subject Mutezuma:

> While in this great city I was seeing to the things which I thought were required of the service of Your Sacred Majesty and subduing and persuading to Your service many provinces and lands containing many and very great cities, towns and fortresses. I was discovering mines and finding out many of the secrets of Mutezuma's lands and of those which bordered on them and of those of which he had knowledge . . . All of which was done with such good will and delight on the part of Mutezuma and all the natives of the aforementioned lands that it seemed as if *ab initio* they had known Your Sacred Majesty to be their king and rightful lord; and with no less good will they have done all that I, in Your Royal name, have commanded them. (2001, 112–13 [1993, 248])

Once again, Cortés alludes to the whole territory at once, and even to his efforts to reconnoiter and pacify it as thoroughly as possible. With the trip to the heart of things complete, the heart of darkness won over, the conquistador dissolves the frontier into a unitary image of an emerging "empire," a barely glimpsed map of a "New Spain" about to be brought into being. More important, this protocartographic moment comes accompanied by the climax to Cortés's repeated accounts of Mexica recognition. In this passage, Cortés's authority is not predicated upon Mutezuma's "donation," nor upon the oaths taken by him and the Mexica nobility. Rather, the moment is predicated upon a deeper bond that Cortés projects onto the supposedly cooperative Mexica.

Here, Cortés has Mutezuma spontaneously acknowledge the sovereignty of Charles V in a retrospective, *ab initio* moment of primitive recognition. He speaks of a conquered people that has forgotten that it has been conquered. At the heart of the "Second Letter," at the point where the conqueror's discourse seems almost about to give birth to a description of the whole, lies the fantasy that the conquered might see themselves as something they are not. It is the fantasy that they might think of themselves as always already the vassals of a European sovereign by virtue of their birth in a land now rightfully his. With these episodes, the allegory of the frontier cancels itself out of existence. The journey reaches its destination, where it absorbs into the *civitas* the very city from which tyranny had emanated. The stark division of space into a sphere of justice and one of tyranny disappears.

Like the allegory of the frontier, this fantasy of a territorial whole belonging to the king of Castile by right rather than force also has its roots in the spatial imagination of the Reconquest. Allegorical dichotomies of civilization and barbarism are not the only notions that inform the geographical imagination of Reconquest historiography. The very idea of the Reconquest, Maravall argues, is itself inseparable from another feature of the medieval Castilian territorial imagination, the idea of "Hispania" (Maravall 1981, 249–95). This should not be confused with modern Spain. To begin with, "Hispania" designated, from ancient to early modern times, the whole of the Iberian Peninsula, including Portugal, rather than what we now know as the nation of Spain. Furthermore, modern Spain, like any modern nation-state, is an entity rooted in the abstract, isotropic spatiality of the modern map. The map figures the nation's territory as an isotropic space, thereby suggesting that it is the dwelling place of a culturally and linguistically unified people, and thus supporting political efforts to achieve national unification (Harley and Laxton 2001). Hispania, a territorial ideal that came into existence long before the abstract spatiality of the map was thoroughly deployed in Western culture, represents something different. For the purposes of Reconquest historiography, it names the kingdom that once belonged to the Visigoths, who were the putative ancestors of the kings of the Christian kingdoms of medieval Spain. While Hispania, like the modern nation-state, has clear boundaries, those boundaries are concrete, natural ones, the Pyrenees and the sea. The territory within those boundaries is equally concrete. It is the qualitative dwelling place of its inhabitants, a "place" rather than a "space" (Maravall 1981, 522–23).[26] In order to imagine it, one need not adopt the elevated point of view characteristic of the map: one need only imagine itineraries stretching out over the horizon, toward the natural obstacles that mark its frontiers.[27]

As such a concrete dwelling place, Hispania plays a crucial role in the historiography of the Reconquest. Within the medieval context that produced this historiography, it names the totality that was lost when the Muslims invaded Spain and what is to be recovered when they are finally driven out.[28] It names a totality, furthermore, that rightfully belongs to the kings of Spain's Christian kingdoms, as the putative successors to the Visigoths, and that thus authorizes the identification of their Muslim counterparts as usurpers and tyrants. The "Spain" of any particular moment within the historical process of restoration is not really Hispania, but a tragically fractured work in progress, occupied in part by its rightful sovereigns, the kings of the Christian kingdoms, and in part by tyrannous usurpers, the various Muslim rulers. It is, in a sense, Hispania glimpsed at the local level of the encounter between civilization and barbarism, justice and tyranny. Hispania works in conjunction with the allegory of the frontier outlined above in order to figure Spain as something at once proper and alienated, familiar and exotic, self and other. The myth of Hispania projects a unified entity into both the origins and the projected resolution of a historical narrative. The allegory of the frontier testifies to the experience of historical becoming that lies between those two endpoints, an experience within which that redemptive Hispania is felt only as an absence.

Spanish attempts to legitimate the conquest of the Americas function, in part, by projecting this dual notion of territory onto the New World. Such attempts are predicated upon the papal bull *Inter caetera* (1493) whereby Pope Alexander VI granted Ferdinand and Isabella, as well as their successors, sovereignty over all islands and mainlands discovered or to be discovered to the west of the line of the papal line of demarcation running from pole to pole one hundred leagues west of the Azores, in the expectation that they would use their authority to bring the light of Christianity to the benighted heathen.[29] The document, also known as the "papal donation," assigns the Indies a role in the discourse of the conquest of the Americas similar to that played by Hispania in the historiography of the Reconquest. Like Hispania, the "islands and mainlands" that lie west of the line of demarcation both belong and do not belong to the crown of Castile. Although the pope has granted Castile sovereignty over the Indies, much of them remains undomesticated, even undiscovered. Those undiscovered and undomesticated portions cannot be imagined, for obvious reasons, as kingdoms lost to a tyrannical usurper, but they can be characterized as "occupied territories" of a sort, in that they are inhabited and ruled by pagans that do not yet know they are vassals of a far-off king and that have not yet learned of the true faith. In this way, the papal donation establishes how Spain can "recover" a territory that it had never lost and facilitates the transplantation of the historical ideology of the Reconquest onto the New World. The "Indies," as the lands over which Castile enjoys unrealized sovereignty, become the legitimating origin of conquistadorial discourse, as well as the object to be achieved through continued exploration and conquest.

As Victor Frankl argues, Cortés appropriates the dual notion of territory inherited from the Reconquest for his own conquistadorial project in the so-called "First Letter from Mexico." This document, signed by the members of the newly constituted town council of Veracruz but most likely penned by Cortés himself, tells of the initial exploration of the coast of the Gulf of Mexico by Cortés and his party, as well as of the foundation of Veracruz at the expedition's end. On the one hand, the papal donation authorizes his use of medieval Castilian legal codes, meant to regulate the Reconquest, in the conquest of the New World. On the basis of those codes, he founds a frontier city not unlike the cities founded during Castile's various campaigns against Islam. On the other hand, Cortés mentions that the city is necessary due to the lawlessness of the land. Frankl pinpoints the passage where this happens: the city is necessary "so that this land may enjoy the lordship enjoyed by your other kingdoms and domains" (in Frankl 1962, 38).[30] In other words, Veracruz *can* be founded because the pope's actions have made it possible to apply Castilian law in the Americas, but it *must* be founded because the land is lawless. The "First Letter" thus imagines Mesoamerica as existing at once inside and outside the law: it lies within the sovereignty of Castile but outside the sphere of law and peace that prevails in Veracruz. It appeals, at one and the same time, to the Indies of the papal donation—that ersatz *Hispania* that converts conquest into recovery—and to the allegory of the frontier, that spatial imagination that emphasizes the lived experience of encounter between justice and tyranny (Frankl 1962, 39).

The papal donation, however, was not above suspicion as a pillar of justice in the New World. Jurists and theologians, not to mention monarchs, were often unwilling to accept the "plenitude of papal power" upon which it was predicated, often out of fear for what it could mean to European politics (Pagden 1990, 14–16).[31] So, even in Spain, there were many who were eager to formulate a more secular basis for legitimating Spain's presence in the Americas. Cortés, it would seem, was among these Spaniards, not because he necessarily doubted the legitimacy of the papal donation but because it did nothing to shore up the dubious legitimacy of his own actions. This is why in the "Second Letter" he assigns such a prominent role to the oaths of loyalty to him and to Charles V made by Mesoamerican leaders. Through these oaths, we are to believe, Castilian sovereignty over Mesoamerica would have its basis, not in the papal donation but in the willing and legally binding acceptance of such sovereignty by the duly constituted authorities of the Mesoamerican world.

But it is difficult to believe that Cortés himself was all that convinced of the legitimacy of these legalistic machinations. Or, to put it another way, if he did indeed believe in the legality of what he was doing, the blind spots in his belief are glaring. For one, Cortés does not seem to recognize the cultural divide that separates the political culture of Mesoamerica from his own. His communications with the Mexica depend upon the intervention of two separate translators, yet he writes about his negotiations as if nothing had been lost in the translation.[32] Over and again, as many scholars have noted, he reports that different Mesoamerican peoples have freely become "vassals" of Charles V as if the concept of "vassalage," despite the translation, were clearly understood by all parties involved. Cortés quotes Mutezuma's speech to the Mexica nobility in which the latter urges them to accept Spanish sovereignty and offers no explanation for its allusions to Biblical episodes and Castilian forensic rhetoric (Elliott 1989b, 36–38). It is clear, in other words, that Cortés fictionalizes his account of the conquest by exaggerating the effectiveness of his communication with the Mexica. Certainly, there are moments when these exaggerations read like a Machiavellian effort to place the conqueror and the conquest in the best possible light. Cortés, for example, exaggerates the extent of his control over the world of the Mexica and, particularly, his impact upon their religious practice. There are other moments, however, that speak to Cortés's drastic, inevitable failure to appreciate the havoc that his actions wreak upon the collective psyche of the Mexica. Cortés, for example, notes that Mutezuma was crying as he delivered his speech and that he and the Mexica are in tears as they sign their oaths of allegiance. The conqueror seems puzzled by their tears, but nonetheless characterizes them as tears of joy (1993 228 [2001, 99]).[33]

Just as Cortés swept the massacre of the Cholulans under the rug of rhetorical hyperbole and rapt description, so he leaves the tears of the Mexica for the seductions of treasure and civility. The description of a glittering city is mapped over the wounds of its inhabitants. The description, moreover, includes the narrative of iconoclasm at the Templo Mayor in which Mutezuma is once again made to recognize the impertinence that he and his people share with the Spaniards and to cheerfully accept the changes they bring. It culminates, finally, in Mutezuma's most profound recognition of Charles V as his natural lord. In this piece of rhetorical hyperbole, the tyrant of old sees himself and his people as the papal bull sees them, as always already the vassals and dominions of a European sovereign rather than a recently assimilated "outside." It is this fantasy of recognition—the amnesia of the conquered regarding the conquest—that sits at the heart of the "Second Letter." It is with this fantasy that the text invokes, but does not actually describe, that ersatz Hispania that Cortés has won in the New World and that he is about to lose, when the Mexica turn against him and his allies, forcing them to flee Tenochtitlán for the safety of Tlaxcala.

This fantasy of original recognition, this wishing away of conquest, lasts only a moment. The arrival of ships under the command of Pánfilo de Narváez, a henchman of Diego Velázquez, distracts the conqueror from his task. The result, Cortés argues, is that Spanish authority in Tenochtitlán collapses. His argument, here as elsewhere, relies on the clever use of narrative disposition to fabricate an ersatz rationale for events without causal explanation. Not only does Cortés explicitly blame Narváez for the former's misfortunes, he designs his narrative to make it seem that Narváez is actually to blame for them. No mention is made of the massacre of the Mexica at the Templo Mayor at the hands of Pedro de Alvarado and his men. The narrative of the arrival of the Narváez expedition and of Cortés's response stands in for it, functioning somehow as the implicit cause of the Mexica revolt. Cortés's story has managed to tell exactly the opposite of what must have been going on in the Mexica capital, which, given the events to follow, must have been the scene of increasing resentment and hostility toward the Spaniards. Events prove that Cortés's claim to have established himself as the principal political authority in the Central Valley of Mexico and beyond is just as false as his claim to have quickly and easily put an end to human sacrifice.

Images from the beginning of the narrative reappear to haunt a discourse laden with foreboding. We read that Narváez has established himself in Cempoala, that original acquisition with which the conquest of Mexico began (1993, 256 [2001, 119]). We read how Cortés judges the actions of his fellow Spaniards, accusing Narváez and his men of treason and of being "traitors and perfidious vassals" (2001, 125 [1993, 261]). When Cortés retakes Cempoala from Narváez, he benefits from the misfire of an enemy's gun, just as he had benefited at the outset from the misfire of a weapon wielded by one of Velázquez's men. In each case, Cortés attributes the misfire to Providence (1993, 167, 264 [2001, 53, 126]). But these echoes of earlier episodes only thicken the irony of the impending reversal of fortune. Cortés returns to the capital only to find himself trapped with his men in the now-hostile city and forced to attempt a disastrous escape under cover of darkness. The flight from the city to the safety of Tlaxcala stands in marked contrast to the purposeful march that had brought the Spaniards to Cempoala. Gone is Cortés's command of the territory: "That night, at midnight, thinking that we were unobserved, we quit that house silently, leaving behind many fires; and *we knew no road nor where we were going*" (2001, 139 [1993, 283]; emphasis added). Space is again figured as a series of towns and cities, but this time they appear only as nameless way stations along a desperate itinerary, "a good town," "other villages which were thereabouts," "a plain with some small houses," "a great city with many inhabitants" (2001, 140–41 [1993, 283–84]). That linear spatiality that had served to organize the story of the journey to the capital reappears now, only to find Cortés on the wrong side of the frontier between civilization and barbarism. Loss and powerlessness are the themes of these pages. By stripping the landscape of names and combat of heroic significance, by reducing purposeful agency to the inscrutable action of Providence alone, Cortés brings his narrative to a rhetorical nadir that is structured to stimulate desire to recuperate what has been lost.

And in fact, the end of the "Second Letter" leaves the territorial imagination of the frontier fully in place. Cortés finds himself once again among allies who swear to support him unto death, united both as "vassals of Your Highness" and as victims of the Mexica (1993, 287; 2001, 143). Cortés once again founds a frontier city, Segura de la Frontera, from which he writes to Charles V requesting support.

In the final analysis, what are the accomplishments narrated in the "Second Letter"? Cortés has lost Tenochtitlán, but has converted his loss into symbolic capital. That moment of possession, when the emperor of the Mexica saw himself and his people as the law sees them, has been written into collective memory by Cortés's own text. The rich empire to which that moment alluded has become, like the Hispania of old, a patrimony lost to a tyrant. The contradiction inherent in the Spanish invention of America as both a legal possession and a barbarous New World has been mediated through its inscription into history. Like the Spain of the Visigoths, the Mexico of Mutezuma has become a fondly remembered story about a lost state of innocence. Like the Spain of the Moors, the Mexico of Mutezuma's successor Cauhtemoc has become a territory usurped, ripe for reconquest by an army assembling on the frontier. An impertinent historical ideology has been translated to a New World, where it now grounds a new hope for conquest, a new itinerary to a new city that has been made old.

Empires and Dreams: Images of Tenochtitlán

As I mentioned at the outset, this dramatic tale of conquest and loss soon reached an audience much broader than the royal officials for whom it had originally been written. Apparently at the impetus of individuals close to Cortés, the "Second Letter" appeared in print not long after the final conquest of Tenochtitlán in 1522. Translations into Flemish, Latin, Italian, French, and German followed between 1522 and 1555, as did inclusion of the text in important collections of travel literature, like the *Delle navigationi e viaggi* of Giovanni Battista Ramusio (1554).[34] Two of the early modern print editions are of particular interest to us here because they include editorial paratexts that serve to enhance our understanding of the "Second Letter from Mexico" as a chorography of New Spain in the form of a conquistadorial (or reconquistadorial) itinerary. These are the first edition, for its title page illustration and preface, and the 1524 Nuremburg edition, for its maps of the Gulf of Mexico and of the city of Tenochtitlán. The paratexts of both of these editions reproduce and extend the spatiality of the "Second Letter," with its itinerant structure and its allusion to a totality that it does not describe. Both, in turn, support the notion that this spatiality serves the ideological needs of an expansionist culture by inscribing desire.

The 1522 Seville edition stands out both as the original printed edition of the "Second Letter" and as one of the few pieces of Spanish Americana available in print during the first quarter of the sixteenth century. It was published by Jacobo Comberger, a printer in Seville interested in geographical and travel literature, and particularly in texts relating to the Indies. He published the first Spanish translation of Marco Polo (1503), an unauthorized, partial edition of Pietro Martire's *De orbe novo decades*, entitled *Legatio babylonica* (1511), and the first edition of Fernández de Enciso's *Suma de geographia* (1519). Later, he published the first editions of the "Third Letter from Mexico" (1523), as well as of Fernández de Oviedo's *Historia general de las Indias* (1535). But these titles represented only a small portion of Cromberger's output. Like most sixteenth-century Spanish printers, Cromberger was most interested in publishing devotional books and literature in the vernacular, particularly chivalric romances (Griffin 1988, 145–64). Although he published Oviedo's history, he did so only reluctantly, requiring the author to bear many of the costs of publication himself (Griffin 1988, 159). Even in Seville, then, books about the Indies formed only a small part of the repertoire of books that appeared in print. A reader curious about America—and such readers were few and far between—could turn only to these titles, as well as to the printed editions of the letters of Columbus and Vespucci, as well as to a smattering of cosmographical and geographical works that gave some attention to the New World.[35]

The cartographic resources available to Cortés's readership would have been meager as well. On one level, the problem is an obvious one. Cortés's letter describes fresh discoveries, which have a way of making old maps obsolete. But even those maps that did exist were not likely to have been available. By 1522, there existed any number of maps that depicted what was known of the New World, but these maps either remained in manuscript form, accessible only to those directly involved with the exploration and conquest of the New World, or they appeared in expensive publications intended for the learned, written in Latin, and produced well outside the boundaries of the Iberian world.[36] Barring access to black market charts, the average reader would have been able to turn only to the woodcut map of the Caribbean that accompanied Cromberger's 1511 edition of Pietro Martire's *De orbe novo decades* (fig. 23). We know of no other map, of America or elsewhere, ever printed by Cromberger's press (Griffin 1988, 200). An alternative would have been to turn to the descriptions provided by such texts as those of Enciso or Martire. In any case, the description would not have included the Gulf Coast of Mexico and certainly not the interior of the country.

The readers of the newly published "Second Letter" would thus have had very few materials at hand that could have helped them understand the historical or geographical context of the Cortesian discoveries. They would have understood little more than that Tenochtitlán was "out there," beyond the boundary of the known, within that puzzling landmass to the northwest of what was undoubtedly a New World, the continent we now call South America. Was this landmass an integral part of the New World, or was it the hinterland of the Old? For many years before and after the conquest of Mexico, Europeans speculated that the portion they knew of what we now call North America might represent the southeastern limit of Asia. By marching into it, or by sailing along its western shore, one might eventually discover the world of Marco Polo or the geography of the spice trade. As the century progressed, more and more mapmakers became convinced of the innovation introduced into maps by Martin Waldseemüller in 1507, that the land to the northwest of Panama was also part of the New World, geographically independent from Asia. In the absence of empirical evidence that could decide the matter, a minority of mapmakers asserted the opposite, while yet others remained neutral. In 1522, the question was far from settled. If, then, the "Second Letter" constitutes a chorography of New Spain, it is a chorography that had to be read in the absence of a geography. Its itinerary marches through a territory somewhere out beyond the ocean, beyond the line of demarcation, in the hinterland of the unknown.

It is in this context that we must understand the preface and the image that the Cromberger edition used to package the "Second Letter" for the Castilian reader. The preface reads as follows:

The Second Letter, Sent to His Majesty the Emperor, Our Sovereign, by Don
Fernando [Hernán] Cortés, Captain General of New Spain. In which he gives an
account of the lands and provinces without number that he has newly discovered
in Yucatán in the year 1519 and subjected to His Majesty's Royal Crown. And in
particular he gives an account of a very large and very rich province called Culua,
in which there are large cities and marvelous buildings, much commerce and
great wealth. Among these cities there is one more marvelous and more wealthy
than all the others, called Temixtitan, which has, with extraordinary skill,
been built upon a great lake, of which city and province a powerful lord called
Mutezuma is king: here things terrible to relate befell the captain and the
Spaniards. He tells at length of the great dominion of the said Mutezuma and of
its rites and ceremonies and how they are performed. (2001, 47 [1993, 159])

The text supports some of the generalizations that I have made about Cortés's
letter and the likely horizon of its reception in Spain. It identifies the land discovered by Cortés as lying "in Yucatán," which thereby attests to the general
confusion then reigning with regard to New World geographies and topony-
mies beyond the immediate Caribbean. It also subordinates Cortés's account
of events—"things terrible to relate"—to his description of places—his "account of the lands and provinces without number." However conventional it
is to consider the "Second Letter" as a piece of historiography, we must remember that Cromberger marketed it primarily as a description of an exotic
land, of its fabulous metropolis, and of its splendid king. The "Second Letter,"
in this preface, promises to read, more than anything else, like a chorography
of "Culua."

Strangely, however, the image that appears just above these words—the
only image in the entire book [37]—does not depict even a stylized version of
the city or the land that the letter describes. Instead, it features the image of
a European king, seated on his throne, scepter in hand, looking out attentively
as if granting an audience (fig. 24). Since the "Second Letter" is addressed to
Charles V, we can assume that this stock image is meant here to represent the
young emperor himself. By contrast, the printed editions of Columbus's letter
published a few decades earlier included images of ships and scenes of ar-
mored conquerors encountering naked "savages." One of them, an illustration
that appeared with Giuliano Dati's 1493 verse adaptation of Columbus's letter
provides an illuminating contrast that can help explain Cromberger's apparently strange choice for a title page illustration (fig. 25). It opposes a scene of
discovery in the background to a figure of King Ferdinand in the foreground.[38]
While clearly not a map of the conventional kind, this image is the most
"maplike" of all the woodcuts that accompanied Columbus into print. It includes both the newly discovered colony and the metropolitan center in the

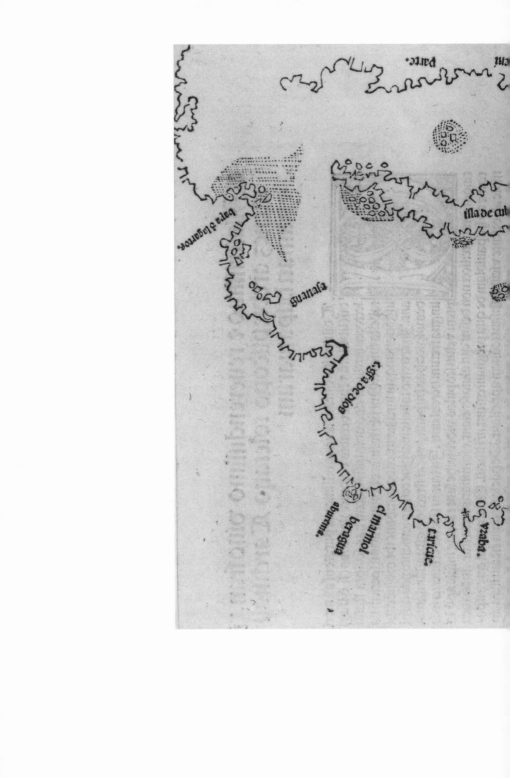

parte.

illa de cub

illa de cub

para ē laganes.

guanaſa

eſtra de oloz

abuzma

el marmol
paragua

caricæ.

vzaba.

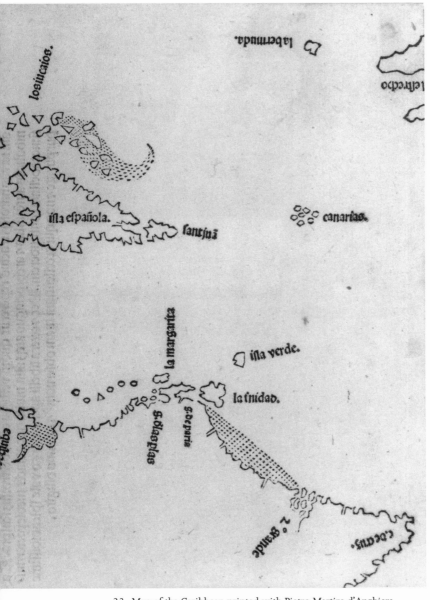

23 Map of the Caribbean printed with Pietro Martire d'Anghiera,
*P. Martyris angli mediolanensis opera. Legatio babylonica Occeani decas Poemata
Epigrammata* (Seville, 1511). The John Carter Brown Library at Brown
University.

Carta de relació ēbiada a su.S.majestad del ēpa-
dor nro señor por el capitā general dela nueua spaña:llamado fernādo cor
tes.Enla ql baze relació dlas tierras y prouicias sin cuēto q bā descubierto
nueuamēte enel pucatā del año de.rir.a esta pte: y ba sometido ala corona
real de su .S.A. En especial baze relació de vna grādissima prouicia muy
rica llamada Culua:ēla ql ay muy grādes ciudades y de marauillosos edi-
ficios:y de grādes tratos y riqzas. Entre las qles ay vna mas marauillosa
y rica q todas llamada Timiritā:q esta por marauillosa arte edificada so
bre vna grāde laguna.dela ql ciudad y prouicia es rey vn grādissimo señor
llamado Autecçuma : dōde le acaecierō al capitā y alos españoles espāto-
sas cosas de oyr. Cuenta largamēte del grādissimo señorio del dicho Autecçuma y de sus ritos y cerimonias.y de como se sirue.

24 Title page illustration of the "Second Letter from Mexico" in the 1522 Seville edition of
Jacobo Cromberger. The John Carter Brown Library at Brown University.

25 Title page, Giuliano Dati, *La lettera dell'isole che ha trovato nuovamente il re di Spagna* (1493). The Albert and Shirley Small Special Collections Library, University of Virginia.

same pictorial space, thereby figuring, however fancifully, the Atlantic space that is brought into being by the discovery and colonization of the Caribbean. It also has Ferdinand look across the Atlantic to watch the discovery as it occurs. His transoceanic gaze apprehends the New World intellectually and politically. It reduces the vast ocean sea to the status—in the language of a later age—of nothing but "the pond" that separates Europe from America. Less anachronistically, it announces the conversion of the Atlantic into a new *mare nostrum* of an emerging maritime power. The text, in turn, lauds Ferdinand as a new "Augustus" (Dati 1968, 34, xi).

Cromberger, I imagine, could have easily concocted a woodcut something like the one that adorns the Dati text, perhaps substituting a fanciful view of Tenochtitlán for the island full of natives. Such an image would have worked well with Cortés's own efforts to figure New Spain as part of an emerging Atlantic world. Cortés must have been well aware of the vast distance that separated Segura de la Frontera from the Hapsburg court, a distance not only geographical, but social, political, and cultural. His "Second Letter," like the many *relaciones* arriving in Spain from the Americas during this early phase of the Encounter, attempts to collapse that distance and thereby make "Culua" present to readers back home. It does this, as we already saw, by identifying those distant and exotic lands as an "empire" commensurate with the empire of Germany, and then assigning that empire a name, "New Spain," which identifies it as a simulacrum of the metropolis. It also assimilates those lands and their peoples to the European imagination, as other scholars have noted, by describing them with a familiar vocabulary, one that makes them seem more apprehensible than they probably were in fact (Boruchoff 1991; Clendinnen 1993). As discussed above, Cortés's indigenous allies are described as "vassals" as if their political culture dovetailed nicely with that of Spain. Their cities are compared with those of Andalusia, and their temples are referred to as "mosques." By this account, Cromberger's image looks like a throwback in the ongoing conceptualization of an emerging Atlantic world. What is apprehended in the pictorial space of the Dati woodcut or even in the Cortesian text itself disappears from the pictorial space of Cromberger's image. Imagine an edition of the Columbus letter that depicted no ships, no islands, and no natives, but only the seated figures of Ferdinand and Isabella.

However, Cromberger's combination of word and image is far from a throwback. Instead, it represents a subtle and powerful gesture toward the emerging Atlantic world that the Dati world depicts with naïve directness. Cromberger's king looks out, as I mentioned, as if granting an audience, but to whom does he listen? Not to the reader, certainly, despite the force of his gaze. The answer is provided by the text below, which identifies the "Second Letter" as a communication between Cortés and Charles V. It invites us to imagine the interview in question as the moment when Cortés's letter arrives before the king and is read to him by an attendant. In this way, the image and text together draw our attention to the communicative power of the Cortesian text, to its attempt to cross the distances that separate the conqueror from his king and make New Spain present with all the efficacy and immediacy of an oral report. The space of the letter's imaginative enunciation thus becomes a figure for the Atlantic world itself. While Dati's Ferdinand looks across the ocean, Cortés's voice resonates across the sea. When he hears his words, the seated king "sees" his new kingdom. This figurative strategy suits the text of the "Second Letter" very well. As we saw, Cortés never actually describes New Spain, but he does allude to it as a totality. Likewise, Cromberger's illustration does not figure "Culua." It alludes to it through a combination of text and illustration that marks the absence of both the city and its image.

Although the king of the Cromberger title page stares out at us, commanding our attention, our eyes are drawn to the windows behind him on both his left and his right. Through them, we have a glimpse of a stylized countryside much like the landscapes that can be glimpsed through windows in the backgrounds of countless Renaissance portraits. Trees, hills, even a building of some kind lie in the far background of the image. Our eyes thus move away from the king who listens to the letter out toward the countryside, where they encounter the Spanish analogues of the places the letter promises to describe. Finally, they reach the horizon, the frontier between what we can see and what we cannot. Beyond it, far beyond it, lies the land of Culua, with its fabulous city and its king. We realize that we, too, like the seated king, rely upon Cortés's words to take us there, so that we can know all those things that the image does not figure. In this way, Cromberger's image entices the reader to embark upon the imaginary journey entailed in following Cortés, not only from Veracruz, but from Spain, all the way to the heart of an exotic and unknown land. The newly discovered land that explicitly appears in the Dati edition woodcut has not so much been erased as suppressed beneath a horizon of knowledge and visibility. While the Dati woodcut figures the new Atlantic world as a realized fact, the Cromberger illustration figures it as an enticing possibility, one to be realized through a journey beyond this frontier, into the unknown.

The paratext that accompanies the 1524 edition of the "Second Letter" represents something else altogether. It consists of two maps printed together on a single page, one of the Gulf of Mexcio from Florida all the way around to the coast of present-day Guatemala and Honduras, and another of the city of Tenochtitlán and its environs (fig. 26). The chart of the Gulf coast provides the reader of this edition with something that the reader of the 1522 edition lacked, a geographical context in which to situate Cortés's narrative. Since it includes the tip of Cuba, it is possible to correlate this image with the earlier map of the Caribbean printed with the 1511 edition of Pietro Martire, as well as with his narrative of the discovery of the Indies. Since it includes the city that Cortés renames "Sevilla," it is also possible to identify the place on the Gulf coast that serves as the point of departure for Cortés's expedition inland. The expedition's destination, the city of Tenochtitlán, then appears in the other map, one of the most famous cartographic images of the sixteenth century. Here, at last, is an image of that exotic land beyond the ocean, of that city that so impressed its European conquerors with its size, wealth, civility, and frightening religious cult. There is the topography that Cortés describes, the

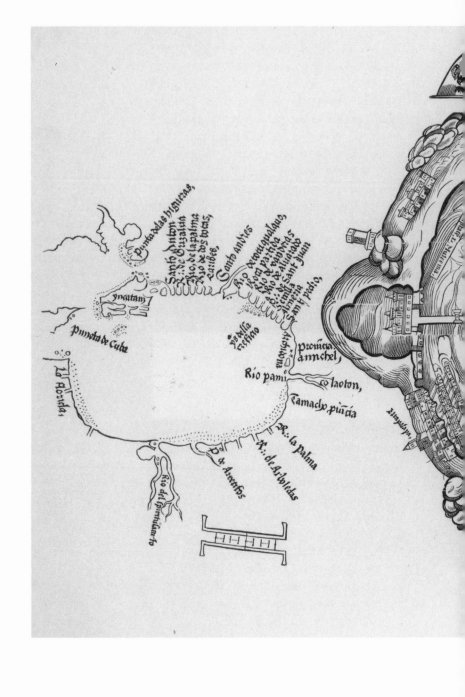

26 Map of Tenochtitlán and the Gulf of Mexico. Published with the text
of the second and third letters in Hernán Cortés, *Praeclara Ferdinandi
Cortesii De Nova Maris Oceani Hyspania Narratio Sacratissimo* . . . (Nuremburg,
1524). The Geography and Map Division of the Library of Congress.

circular province of "Mesyco," with its two lakes and its island metropolis. Depicted are the causeways that link the city to the mainland, the orderly streets and well-built buildings of Tenochtitlán, its great temple, and its market square.[39]

The origins of this image remain somewhat mysterious. It was long thought that the printed version of this map was based upon an original, now lost, that had been drawn by Cortés himself. More recently, this assumption has been brought into question. Some have seen in it the work of a European artist working exclusively from Cortés's verbal description of the city (Apenes 1947). Others, more alert to the discrepancies between the description and the map,[40] insist upon the existence of an original drawn independently of the text, but turn to other conquistadors (Toussaint et al. 1938, 98) and even to an anonymous indigenous artist (Mundy 1998), as the most likely candidates for authorship. In any case, the imprint of the European artist is unmistakable. The houses, palaces, and fortifications are all given a European look. More important, they are set in orderly rows arranged neatly around the city's central ceremonial district. In this way, the map both reflects the geometric rationality of the Mexica city, and makes of that rationality a concrete instantiation of the utopian rationality idealized by Renaissance urbanism. It is with good reason, therefore, that this image has been called "dreamlike" by one of its commentators (Keen 1971, 67). Part of this "dreamlike" effect derives, certainly, from the unusual "fisheye" perspective adopted by the artist, which is visible also in certain views of German cities printed during the 1520s.[41] In the case of the Nuremberg image of Tenochtitlán, this perspective can be described as a series of concentric circles whose scale diminishes as one moves outward from the center (Mundy 1996, xiii). The size of the central square is thereby exaggerated in relation to other features of the city and its setting. As the scale changes, furthermore, so does the angle of the viewer's gaze. At the center, the buildings are rendered in elevation, but the city plan is rendered planimetrically. At the edge of the image, that surface has bent back, so to speak, away from the viewer, slipping underneath the foundations of the structures. There, on the periphery, the map becomes a landscape. To be more specific, it becomes a horizon that envelops both the center of the image and, like the cycloramas of a later age, the viewer.

In order to understand the relationship between the Nuremburg map and the "Second Letter," as I have interpreted it, we must give due attention to the particular way that this image utilizes the fisheye perspective that it shares with other city views. In reference to a 1548 fisheye view of Strasbourg, Juergen Schulz argues that the fisheye perspective has the effect of enhancing the importance of the city center at the expense of the periphery. In this way, it draws the viewer's attention to that part of the city that monumentalizes what is best about it, its piety and civility (Schulz 1990, 11–12). Fisheye views, in other words, sacrifice optical verisimilitude for clarity of message. Like this fisheye view of Strasbourg, or like others of Vienna and of Nuremberg itself, the map of Tenochtitlán also exaggerates the importance of the city's central square. That square, however, does not embody the urbane values of the culture in which the image was meant to circulate. Instead, it embodies those very monstrosities—human sacrifice, idolatry—that characterize the far side of Cortés's frontier. Tyranny and barbarity, not justice and civility, sit at the heart of Tenochtitlán. Their opposites—civility, Christian empire—are marked by the Hapsburg banner that flies on the periphery of the image, on the shores of Lake Texcoco. In this way, the Nuremburg map actually inverts the spatial organization typical of other fisheye views, and imbues its pictorial surface with a creative tension that is absent from the others.

To put it another way, by inverting the usual organization of the fisheye view, by placing what is desirable on the periphery and what is odious at the center, the Nuremburg map gives iconographic form to Cortés's spatial allegory of the frontier. It gives form to the city, not in the timeless present aspired to by most maps, but at that precise historical juncture when dreams of sovereignty rooted in fantasies of mutual recognition have been cheated by the violent reinstauration of the spatiality of the frontier. The image places its readers in the heart of Mexica darkness, but only so that they can appreciate what Cortés wants them to believe, that civilization has barbarism surrounded and is sure to conquer. Interpreted in this way, it becomes a meaningful supplement to Cortés's account of the conquest of the city. His eyewitness narrative cannot take its reader across the frontier it delineates so that we can view the conquest from the perspective of the conquered. When the narrative does this, particularly in its assertions about indigenous loyalty or about Mutezuma's recognitions, it clearly ventures into the ground of rhetorical hyperbole. This map, however, places its reader in the heart of rebel Tenochtitlán, looking out at the horizon for the representatives of Hapsburg might that approach to conquer. It has us imagine the siege of Tenochtitlán from the point of view of the besieged, or rather, the besieged as Cortés has invited us to imagine them, as a group of heathens about to be incorporated into a Christian empire.

An inscription alongside the image announces the conquest of the city as an accomplished fact. It marks the Tenochtitlán of old as a thing of the past, and announces the universal monarchy of Charles V: "This commonwealth had once been powerful and a realm of the greatest glory. [It] has been subjected to the rule of Caesar [Charles V]. He is truly outstanding. The Old

World and the New [now] belong to him, and another [alter; i.e., Tenochtitlán] is laid open to his auspices."[42] The inscription seals the fate of one place, Tenochtitlán, and synecdochically, that of another, the New World. In this way, it closes the rhetorical circle opened by the translator of Cortés's letter into Latin, Pietro Savoragno. Like the introduction to the Seville edition, the translator's preface to the Nuremberg edition treats the Cortesian text as geographical literature, but its rhetorical pitch is even higher. Ferdinand and Isabella, the preface explains, had surpassed the ancients by discovering a land beyond the Pillars of Hercules, of which the classical world was ignorant. Charles V has become the heir to this legacy, pushing the limits of the known world even further. The Cortesian letters, then, are located at the nexus of geographical discovery and imperial ambition, at once outdoing the cosmography of the ancients and celebrating both the knowledge and the power of moderns. Savoragno compares Cortés and his king with the heroes of classical history, Hannibal and Alexander the Great in particular. The inscription on the map announces, in effect, that Enciso's challenge to Charles to outdo Alexander has been met in the discovery and conquest of Mexico (Cortés 1524). As others have noted, the map thus becomes an emblem of this new empire of knowledge and power.

But while the inscription seals the fate of one place, it also refers to another, that ambiguous "alter" that "is laid open to" the "auspices" of Charles V. To what could it refer? I suggest that it directs our attention back to the horizon that bounds the image of the city. Like any horizon, and specifically like that of the Cromberger illustration, it both bounds the field of vision and mediates a relationship with the space beyond. While it marks the limits of vision, it also proffers an invitation to imagine what is beyond. In the interpretation of the image just advanced, that space beyond is all of that territory that has already been brought under the sway of the monarch whose banner now menaces the city. It is the Christian empire, that New Spain that has already been brought into being, that empire whose conquest has only to be completed through the conquest of this last—albeit significant—refuge of tyranny.

Later images of the city, however, allow us to suggest a different identity for this space beyond the horizon. I do not refer to the various images of Tenochtitlán adapted, ultimately, from the Nuremberg map and appearing in various printed venues throughout the rest of the sixteenth century, but rather to those images of the city that graced many maps of the Americas and of the world drawn during subsequent decades.[43] The appearance of Tenochtitlán on maps drawn during the decade after the conquest of Mexico confirms that the discovery of the city by Europeans marked a fundamental change in the way that the New World was perceived.[44] Earlier maps of the Americas were of course replete with toponymy assigned by the Spanish and Portuguese, but rarely, if ever, did they depict the cities founded by the colonists iconographically. With the appearance of Tenochtitlán on the planispheres of Nuño García de Toreno (the "Salviati" planishpere, ca. 1525) and Juan de Vespucci (1526), as well as others, the cities that had for so long populated the Mediterranean world of the portolan chart at last find a worthy American double. A space emerges, one that did not exist before, which ties the urban culture of the near side of the Atlantic to the newly discovered urban culture of the far side. Something else happens as well, something most visible on the planisphere of Nuño García de Toreno (fig. 27). The Toreno (or "Salviati") planisphere is one of the first known maps that incorporates the discoveries of both Cortés's expedition and Magellan's expedition. Not only does the city of Tenochtitlán appear on the map, but so too does the strait bearing Magellan's name and the expansive Pacific crossed by his small fleet. That broad, empty expanse that stretches out over most of the Hispanic hemisphere in Enciso's *Suma de geografía* thus acquires one of its earliest surviving cartographic representations. The eastern edge of that space is clearly marked by the extensive coastline of North and South America. The interior of the Americas, in turn, is decorated by rows of trees in the north and a row of trees and hills in the south. These markings are the successors to similar cartographic decorations, like the one found on the earlier planisphere of Nicola Caverio (1505) and the world map of Waldseemüller (1507). On Waldseemüller's map especially, this line of trees and hills becomes a horizon that bends away from the viewer, not unlike the one that bounds Tenochtitlán as depicted in the Nuremberg edition's map (see figs. 6, 7 above). The decorations on the Toreno planisphere, although less effective technically, are nonetheless equally functional in marking the boundary, the horizon, that separates the known from the unknown. The banner that labels the newfound capital of New Spain—depicted iconographically and thus grossly out of scale—all but joins these lines that reach down to it from the north and up from the south. The banner, which displays the name of the city, becomes itself part of the horizon that marks the limits between the known and the unknown.

If we interpret the Nuremberg image through the lens of the Toreno planisphere, we find that the horizon that bounds the city also beckons the reader. While it speaks of a New Spain all but won, it also speaks of new worlds to conquer, that *alter* that lies beyond the horizon. Certainly, this is what the city of Tenochtitlán meant for Cortés and other conquistadors. It was not long after he completed the conquest of the Mexica capital that Cortés had ships built on the Pacific coast of Mexico to discover where that coast led. Cortés's

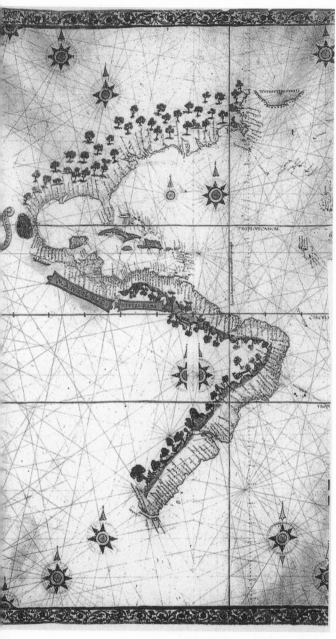

27 Nuño García de Toreno, detail from planisphere (1525). The city of Tenochtitlán is depicted prominently and labeled with a banner. Florence. Biblioteca Medicea Laurenziana, ms. Med. Palat. 249. Used by permission of the Ministry for Cultural Treasures and Activities, Italy. Reproduction by any means is strictly forbidden.

28 Domingo del Castillo, map
of the Pacific Coast of Mexico
(1541). From a copy in *Historia
de la Nueva España* by Fernando
Antonio Lorenzana (1770).
The Rare Books Division of the
Library of Congress.

Domingo del Castillo.
Piloto me Fecit en
Mexico año del Nacimiento
de N.S. Jesu Christo de
M.D.XLI.

La Ciudad de Mexico.

Vanos p.e*
N.ª S.ª
P.ta i S. Pablo.
Boca de la Madalena
P.ta de Peñas.
P.ta de Rosario
El Covido.
Alguna de Caldevas.
Rio de S. Miguel de Culiar.
Rio de la Sal.
P.ta de Chiametla.
Rio del Rain.
P.ta de Xalisco.
P.ta de Escondido
P.ta de la Anegra.
Alguna de Vanderas.

L.º 78' d.L.

P.ta Redonda.
La Isla
P.ta S.
R.ta de Santiago
P.ta de Colima
Cerro de Matin
Rio de Sequatan.
P.ta de Acentuan.
Alguna de Acepan.
Puerto de Acepan
P.ta del Marques.
Alguna de Cilla.
P.ta de los Angeles.
Rio Orado
Barra
Puerto de Guaduaca.
Estado
C.e Berry
Copalica
Playa de Masatlan.
Barra de Tiguantepeque
Provincia de Tiguantepeque
P.ta de Marquilou.
El despoblado.

SUR

en el Estado de el Marques de el Valle. En lo alto pone una
i la llamaron Quivira. En la desembocadura del Rio Colorado en el
uena Gua, i puede ser el Colorado el otro de Miraflores, i puede ser
bre entran en el Seno de Californias.   Navarro Sc. Mex. año 1769.

interest in the South Sea, as he explains to the emperor, clearly reproduces Columbus's dreams of rich Eastern islands:

> All those who have some learning and experience in the navigation of the Indies are quite certain that once the route to the Southern Sea has been discovered we shall find many islands rich in gold, pearls, precious stones and spices, and many wonderful and unknown things will be disclosed to us. (2001, 267 [1993, 432])

Far from frustrating Columbian desires to reach Marco Polo's East by proving, somehow, that a North American continent lay astride the sea route from west to east, the discovery of Tenochtitlán only served to stimulate them. The city was a sign that other wonders must lay beyond, that the exotic, urban world of the East lay just around the next bend in the coast, just over the next range of mountains (White 1971, 288).[45] And so, much of Spanish exploration directed itself northwest from the capital of New Spain, hoping to find in the empty reaches of the cosmographers's maps another city just as worthy of such prominent treatment. One chart emerging from the exploration of Baja California paired Tenochtitlán with the fabled Seven Cities of Cíbola (fig. 28). Others placed Marco Polo's Cathay immediately northwest of the capital of New Spain. One edition of the "Third Letter" consigned the conquest of the city to "perpetual memory" and then alluded to Cortés's new discoveries along the South Sea and to the "many more great provinces, very rich in gold and pearls and precious stones" soon to be discovered there (Cortés 2001, 160 [1993, 310]). Even as the European reading public learned of Cortés's victory in Tenochtitlán, it found the city inscribed as a new point of departure for a new conquistadorial itinerary. That itinerary pressed ever onward, across the edge of a map of empire whose best parts were always those that had yet to be drawn.

4

Francisco López de Gómara (1511–ca. 1564) is best known for his *Historia de la conquista de México*, an early modern bestseller largely responsible for cementing Cortés's reputation among European readers as an audacious hero, a capable military man, and a master of communication. First published in 1552, the *Conquista de México* soon appeared in new editions and was translated into numerous languages. Although it was promptly banned in Spain—for reasons that remain unclear—it found a place on bookshelves throughout Europe and continued to be well known even among Spaniards who were supposedly unable to purchase it. Less popular, but no less significant, was the companion volume to the *Conquista de México*, the *Historia general de las Indias*, which covers the natural and moral history of the whole of the Americas, from Columbus's first voyage in 1492 through the 1540s.[1] In this chapter, I concentrate on this first volume, Gómara's effort to squeeze a discussion of all of the Indies into a single, relatively compact work, written in clear and elegant Castilian prose. Its oft-quoted opening line—in which Gómara claims that the discovery and conquest of the Americas is the most important event in human history since the death and resurrection of Jesus Christ—leaves little room for doubt about the importance that the text assigns to the events it relates. Moreover, the title given to one edition of the two-volume work, *Hispania victrix* (1553), leaves little doubt about how this monumental event is to be interpreted. Clearly this is history struck in registers both nationalistic and imperialistic, meant to monumentalize Spanish achievements and thereby to flatter the monarch to whom it is addressed, the emperor Charles V. It is also a kind of historical writing with clear and specific cartographical dimensions that were essential to the important role it played in the ongoing early modern invention of America.

As we saw in chapter 1, O'Gorman argues quite forcefully that Christopher Columbus is mistakenly regarded as the "discoverer of America." "America" is by its very nature something that is not amenable to discovery. It is, rather, something that has been invented out of the interplay of empirical observations and creative intellectual efforts to make sense of those observations in the light of received ideas. And so the initial wave of news about the Columbian discoveries, as Cristián Roa-de-la-Carrera argues, had been understood entirely through reference to other, purely European events, including the accomplishments of Ferdinand and the struggle against Islam. At the conclusion of Giuliano Dati's verse adaptation of Columbus's letter announcing the discovery, for example, we read, "Here ends the story of the discovery of the new Canary islands of the Indies" (Dati 1968, 40. 68).

Later, with the conquests of Mexico and Peru, the Indies began to acquire greater political and economic importance. As we saw at the end of the previous chapter, the discovery of Mexico challenged the prevailing notion that the Indies were nothing more than another stepping stone in Castile's island-hopping adventure into the Atlantic. It became possible to speak of an "empire" in the New World and thereby to reinterpret the events that had led up to its discovery, as well as the nature of the area in which this empire had been found. This work of retrospective synthesis—the work that made Columbus into the discoverer of something he had never imagined—was done by mapmakers, certainly, but it was also done by historians (Roa-de-la-Carrera 1998, 155–232). These historians drew upon, reproduced, and fleshed out the ideas of Spain's cartographic avant-garde, the cosmographers of the Casa de la Contratación, making of their blank territorial outlines a "place" in the geographical and historiographical imagination of Europe. One of these historians was Gómara.

Gómara was not the first to retrospectively synthesize what had happened and what had been discovered in the western Atlantic as a "history of the Indies." [2] Gonzalo Fernández de Oviedo had beaten him to the punch, first with his *Sumario de la natural historia de las Indias* (1526) and then with the first part of his *Historia general y natural de las Indias* (1535). The former, a slim volume written during an Andalusian intermission to Oviedo's American adventures, represents a miscellany of the natural and cultural history of the Caribbean, while the latter represents an ambitious encyclopedia of Americana.[3] The years intervening between the appearances of these two titles witnessed the publication, in its final form, of Pietro Martire d'Anghiera's *De orbe novo decades* (1530).[4] All of them, crucially, offer something that readers of the letters of Columbus,

Vespucci, and Cortés did not have: maps of the Indies as a whole. These maps provide the reader with a broad geographical context in which to locate the places and events that the texts relate, as well as to appreciate their location relative to his or her own in Europe. The edition of *De orbe novo* published in Venice in 1534, entitled *Libro primo della historia de l'Indie Occidentali*, included a map based upon Spanish sources significantly more extensive than the one that had been printed with the earlier, partial edition of the work in 1511, the *Lyber babylonica* (fig. 29 and fig. 23 above). The texts of Oviedo and Gómara, meanwhile, depend upon prose cartographies much like those of Enciso. It is the function of prose cartographies like these that constitutes the primary focus of this chapter.

The map printed with the 1534 edition of Martire is not the first cartographic image of America ever made, but as a map printed in a widely reproduced book, it is likely to have been one of the best known. Its utility should be readily apparent. There, laid out in plain view, is the complete circuit of the Gulf of Mexico and the location of Tenochtitlán. The Atlantic coastline of the mainland northward to Labrador and southward to the Strait of Magellan is located. The Pacific coast of Central America and northwestern South America as far as Tumbez, the northernmost outpost of the Inca world, is identified, as is also the Atlantic Ocean, including the westernmost portions of Europe and Africa. In this map, the reader could find what the Cortesian text so lacked, a visual "reader's aid" that would help immeasurably in understanding the way that the historical narrative unfolded in space. Such a reader's aid was crucial to the finished version of Martire's text. The individual sections of the *De orbe novo decades* were written over the span of many years, as the events themselves unfolded and news of them reached Martire in Seville. The book as a whole thus has an irreducibly episodic quality. The map then militates against the fragmentary nature of the text itself, providing it with a sort of coherence that the text itself lacks. In the place of a master narrative of discovery and conquest, the reader has a map that can help him or her assemble the parts into some kind of whole. In this way, the map accomplishes the purpose that many sixteenth-century Europeans believed to lie at the heart of geography. History, the argument went, was better understood and more easily remembered when one could visualize its movements on a map.[5] This map, certainly, was one such instrument, which facilitated mastery of the past by helping place people and events in their proper places.

The role of the prose cartographies in the histories of Oviedo and Gómara is not so easily explained. To begin with, we have reason to believe that the notion of the map as mere "reader's aid" is in itself insufficient to understanding the role of any map included in any book. It has been argued, for

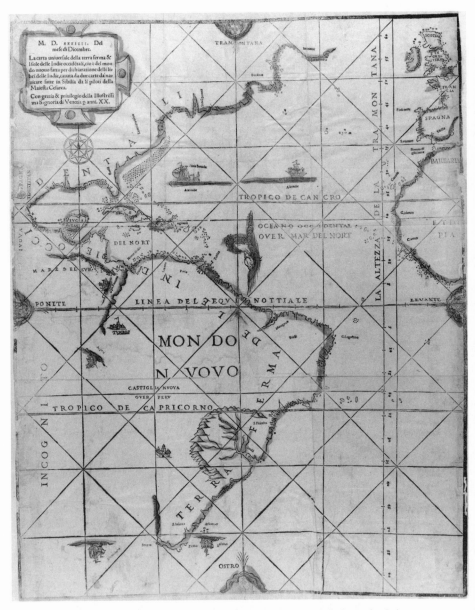

29 America. From Pietro Martire d'Anghiera, *Libro primo della historia de l'Indie Occidentali* (Venice, 1534). A simplified plane chart most likely derived from the cartographic resources of the Casa de la Contratación. The John Carter Brown Library at Brown University.

example, that maps in sixteenth-century Bibles served ends both more subtle and more complex than that of merely illustrating the text they accompanied. In various ways, the inclusion of different kinds of maps in different editions of the Bible served to advance particular theological and hermeneutical agendas (Delano Smith 1990). Could the maps included in the editions of Martire, Oviedo, and Gómara be any more innocent? With regards to Oviedo and Gómara, at least, it appears that the answer is no for the simple reason that neither of their prose cartographies serves the minimal purpose of such a reader's aid, which is to portray the places mentioned in the text.[6] Both histories venture inland in the footsteps of the conquistadors and even sail around the world in the wake of Magellan's *Victoria*, but the maps themselves hug the coastlines of the Americas, hardly ever venturing out of sight of the shore. In this way, rather than figure the topography in which their historical narratives unfold, they mark its spatial threshold, its boundary. Cortés, as we saw, mapped Mexico in and through the linear structure of his narrative. Oviedo and Gómara, by contrast, invent a geographical space as a prelude to their narratives and then convert that space into a stage that they then invest with various meanings. This chapter is concerned with identifying these meanings and the way in which the preliminary cartography makes them possible. It concentrates on Gómara's *Historia general de las Indias* but has some things to say about Oviedo as well, and also about another cartographer-historian, Fray Bartolomé de las Casas.

The comparisons I make between Gómara, on the one hand, and Oviedo and las Casas, on the other, do not pretend to exhaust the problems related to cartography, historiography, and ideology in any of their texts, and particularly not in those of Oviedo and las Casas. Oviedo's *Historia general y natural de las Indias*, like the historical writing of las Casas, represents a massive, rambling, often contradictory corpus that defies summary treatment.[7] Nevertheless, it is still possible to compare Gómara's text with certain aspects of the work of each of them. The three historians knew and reacted to each other's work. Although only a part of Oviedo's *Historia general y natural* was published during the sixteenth century, much of it circulated in manuscript form and seems to have been familiar to Gómara.[8] It is even possible to identify passages in Gómara's history that seem to have been derived directly from the unpublished portions of Oviedo's work (Iglesia 1942, 91). Indeed, Gómara's project can be understood as an attempt to pare and shape the work of his predecessor. Las Casas, meanwhile, reacted with hostility against the historiography of both men. As the self-appointed "apostle of the Indians" one of the most energetic defenders of their rights at court, and as Europe's most outspoken critic of the violent nature of Spain's conquest, las Casas had reason to loathe both of them.

Their work often celebrates empire and often portrays Native Americans in a negative light, even while it admits to the abuses committed by individual conquistadors. When many of Oviedo's manuscripts were lost in a mysterious fire that consumed a publishing house in the city of Córdoba, it was rumored that las Casas was somehow responsible for the blaze. Gómara himself was the one to point the finger (Gerbi 1985, 129), only to then suffer the friar's wrath when las Casas purportedly used his influence at court to ban the publication of Gómara's *Historia general*. It should come as no surprise, then, that while Gómara builds and refines upon the precedent established by Oviedo, las Casas searches for a different vein of geographical writing that would undo the ideological effects of his predecessor's prose cartographies.

The comparisons I make in this chapter among Oviedo, Gómara, and las Casas are thus both possible and justified. They are also necessary if we are to understand how prose cartography contributes to the historical ideology of mid-sixteenth-century Spanish writing about the Americas. This is not an easy task. Theorists like Hayden White, Paul Veyne, Michel de Certeau, and Paul Ricoeur have taught us to think of historical texts as literary artifacts produced in a particular place for particular purposes. We now readily distinguish between "history"—the study of the past or the past itself—and "historiography"—the writing of history, which gives meaning to the past by "emplotting" it, by giving it discursive, often narrative, form. But despite the contributions of other theorists like Edward Said and Paul Carter, who have taught us that geographical writing does something similar, we do not yet adopt a similarly critical attitude toward geographical description, at least not as a matter of habit. Suffice it to say that when we refer to "geography" we have no convenient language by which to distinguish the thing, the Earth, from "the writing of the Earth." Unlike historiography, then, "geography," or "the writing of the Earth" continues to look positively—even positivistically—innocent. For this reason, when we are confronted with pages of prose cartography, pages that do little more than delineate distances and directions from one point to another, we find we have little to say about them. It becomes all too easy to see in them nothing more than a collection of empirical data organized into a tedious discursive form whose role in shaping geography has none of the meaning-making power associated with historical "emplotment."

The antidote to this theoretical blind spot, I believe, is a comparative approach, one that seeks to discover the subtle differences among various prose cartographies that make all the difference. These differences, as we shall see, are there, and they allow us to track the slow, problematic emergence of abstract space in Spanish discourse about the Americas, and with it, the ways that this spatiality could be put to historiographical and ideological use. If nothing else, we discover that the prose cartographies that any modern reader, I am sure, skips altogether when perusing Oviedo and Gómara, constitute nothing less than the indispensable foundations of their historical projects. In Oviedo, we find a prose cartography that clings to the past despite its strident commitment to tackling novel geographical issues. Gómara takes Oviedo's discursive strategies a step further, turning the corner on the hybrid spatiality of early modern Spain, inflecting the planar at the expense of the linear. Las Casas, finally, allows us to perceive the imperialistic purpose in all of this endless mapping through his anxious recoil from the very practice of prose cartography that lies as the root of American historiography.

Oviedo: Maps and Memories

Gonzalo Fernández de Oviedo (1478–1557) was nothing if not a person deeply impressed with the wonder of the New World. As a man of both the pen and the sword, Oviedo was, like Enciso and Cortés, a notable exception to the illiterate or marginally literate adventurers who set off for the Indies in search of their fortunes. He was also well ahead of most of his contemporaries, whether fellow conquistadors or stay-at-homes, in his recognition that the natural and moral history of the Americas needed their own Pliny. For this reason, he devoted a great deal of his adult life to the composition of his massive *Historia general y natural de las Indias,* a work whose true importance became clear only after its author's death. Despite Oviedo's status, since 1532, as the king's official "chronicler of the Indies," the historian experienced enormous difficulty in getting his work into print. Only the first of the three major parts of the *Historia general y natural* was published during his own lifetime, in 1535 and apparently at Oviedo's own expense. A small portion of part 2 saw publication as part of a second edition of part 1 published shortly after the author's death, but the bulk of part 2, as well as all of part 3, appeared only during the nineteenth century. Since then, it has come to be recognized as one of the most important pieces of historical literature in the attempt of sixteenth-century Europe to apprehend the New World.

Such dedication in the face of public indifference tells us something else about Oviedo. Not only was he impressed with the Americas, but he was also impressed with himself as its first historian. Throughout the *Historia general y natural* Oviedo positions himself as the intellectual filter through which authoritative knowledge of the Americas passes. This begins in the prefatory material. One might expect Oviedo to identify his subject matter in a clear and consistent manner, particularly by stating his position on the still-debated geographical relationship between the West Indies and the East Indies. Oviedo, however, does almost nothing to clarify what he means by "the Indies." He simply asserts that he does not write of "*those* Indies . . . but of *these* Indies, islands and Tierra Firme of the Ocean Sea which today are in fact subject to the royal crown of Castile" (Fernández de Oviedo 1959, 1. 1. 1; emphasis added).[9] The point of the distinction is not so much to identify which Indies he is writing about but to impress the reader with their importance. These Indies, Oviedo elaborates, are "a place where innumerable and very great kingdoms and provinces are found, of such admiration and wealth as the books of this *Historia general* of these your Indies will declare" (1. 1. dedicatory epistle).

The distinction also goes a long way toward impressing the reader with the importance of the writer. By "these Indies" Oviedo clearly means "my Indies," or "Oviedo's Indies." Eager to underwrite his historiography with the authority of experience, Oviedo emphasizes his own, American location and alludes to the far-away European location of both readers and of other historians as deficient for understanding the Americas. His location is different, he argues, and that makes all the difference. Having suffered the many troubles that come with long-distance travel, Oviedo can now save his readers from going to the same trouble by communicating all that he has seen through a text "poor in style but rich in truths":

> Let the reader be content with what I have seen and experienced with many dangers to myself—he may enjoy and know without exposing himself to any—and that which he can read without suffering so much hunger and thirst, heat and cold, and other, innumerable troubles, from his own country, without venturing the storms of the sea, or the misfortunes which one suffers over here in this land, as if it were for his own enjoyment and rest that I had been born, and, traveling, had seen these works of nature, or, better said, of the master of nature. (1. 1. preface)

This prefatory rhetoric smacks of equal measures of humility and generosity, as was appropriate for this kind of *captatio benevolentiae*. But as in many such prefaces the humble tone simply provides a smokescreen for powerful assertions. Oviedo uses it to inscribe his own authority as a traveler who has seen it all over the distant, stay-at-home reader who has seen nothing. He inscribes himself as nothing less than a witness—*the* witness—who will communicate to the reader the very work of God. Rather than provide the reader with an image of the Indies, Oviedo, at the opening of part 1, withholds descriptive discourse in order to underscore the reader's reliance upon his efforts to mediate, through his text, knowledge gained through travel, through habitation. These facets of Oviedo's introduction—the marked presence of his voice, the repeated inscription of his American location, the importance of his experience as a traveler—has an impact on every major geographical passage throughout all three parts of the *Historia general y natural.*

It is not until the sixteenth of the nineteen books that constitute part 1 that Oviedo finally turns to broad geographical matters that we might have expected to have encountered much earlier. First, he finally admits that the distinction between "these Indies" and "those Indies" may not be that readily apparent, that European exploration has not penetrated the northwest of the New World, and that therefore European geography cannot know whether or not "these" Indies are physically linked to Asia. Oviedo nonetheless restates his belief that the Indies constitute a geographically separate landmass and offers some specious arguments in support of his contention (1. 16. preface). The historian then turns to his first attempt to map the Indies, to depict them in a way that lends itself to visualization by the reader. The description is worth citing in full, particularly because of the way it uses the image of a hunter's lure to help the reader with this process of visualization. Tierra Firme, Oviedo explains,

> [i]s open, like the figure of a mouth in profile, or like a hunter's lure, and its southern point is at eight degrees, on the other side of the equinoctial line, and this point is called the Cape of Saint Augustine. And departing from this point toward the other, from one land to the next, it would be necessary to sail along that coast more than three thousand leagues along the inside circumference, or within the two points of the hunter's lure. But if we want to trace it around the outside, from point to point, around the side where the sea surrounds this great land, having to enter through the strait that was discovered by the captain Ferdinand Magellan (if, as I said above, it does not meet up with Asia, for it is my opinion that this way is all water, and embraced by the Ocean Sea), more than six thousand leagues one would have to travel. Whomsoever such a route would take would find himself along the circumference of Tierra Firme, according to what we see in the new cosmography. For from the said point to the Cape of Saint Augustine, running toward the Austral part, Tierra Firma stretches down toward the said Strait of Magellan, which lies at fifty-two-and-a-half degrees. And so, enter cosmographers, through the strait that I speak of, and go on to search, from one land to the next, the Cape of Labrador on the northern end, and you will see if the route that runs along the outside of these points is twice as long as that which, as I said, runs along the inside of this land. (1. 16. preface)

Although we cannot know with any certainty what chart may have inspired this description, one can assume that it is no longer extant. The image that Oviedo paints, nonetheless, corresponds to the shape of the coastline as it appears on the charts of the Seville school and, naturally, on printed charts believed to have issued from them. These include Pedro Medina's chart of the

Atlantic World (fig. 5 above), and the chart of America that accompanied the 1534 edition of Pietro Martire (fig. 29 above). In both, we find that the coastline of North America from Florida to Labrador bends dramatically to the east, as it does on almost all the planispheres of the Seville school (figs. 17 and 18 above). When we pair it with the coast of South America from the Yucatán to Brazil, we find the "open mouth" that Oviedo describes.

Does this passage represent a piece of cartographic writing? It certainly does, insofar as it allows its reader to form an image, however crude, of what the Americas look like from the commanding, bird's-eye perspective of a map. More important, this passage speaks of the cultural context that gave birth to part 1 of the *Historia general y natural* and intimates the ideological importance of geography to Oviedo's writing. The recourse to simile, and specifically to similes drawn from a semantic field that has nothing to do with geography or cartography, reminds us that in the 1530s it readers were not assumed to have ready access to maps or even a reasonable degree of cartographic literacy. Other aspects of the passage speak of the ways in which the narrator himself may be only partially acclimated to the world of stasis and abstraction instituted by the new cartography. Oviedo inscribes the Indies as an island by alluding to the possibility of their circumnavigation, but he divides this possible journey in two, one along an "inner" coastline, the Atlantic littoral from Labrador to Brazil, and the other along an "outer" coastline, the route connects these places going around the other way, along the Pacific coast. Oviedo admits quite frankly that much of that outer coastline remains unknown and invites cosmographers to enter and discover the truth of it. With this, the cartographic perspective offered by the original simile, that view from on high implied by the attempt made here to describe what the Indies look like from above, comes back down to Earth.

By handling the two coastlines of the Americas in such an asymmetrical manner, Oviedo begins the work of distinguishing between a "here" and a "there" within the geography of the Indies themselves. The Pacific littoral, as a separate coastline still to be charted, works to render the Indies into a space that bodies move through rather than an island that the eye can apprehend from on high. The far western shore of the Americas becomes the receding horizon of a frontier culture conscious of its own movement westward. Oviedo's call for continued exploration beyond the Strait of Magellan seals this effect, for it converts the strait into a passageway between the known and the unknown, the vanishing point of a space that opens up into what lies beyond. The command to enter it, furthermore, situates both narrator and reader on this side of the passageway, the side of the "inner" coast. The outer coastline becomes a series of future stopping places that still lie ahead in the shared movement of the culture westward, beyond the boundaries that separate a domesticated here from an unknown there. Oviedo's challenge calls upon his compatriots, in other words, to press *plus ultra*.

The inner coastline, meanwhile, becomes the western littoral of a nearly enclosed Spanish *mare nostrum*, one that finds in the Strait of Magellan a new barrier that, like the old Pillars of Hercules, was there to transgress. That *mare nostrum* has been domesticated, Oviedo writes elsewhere, by maritime routes that tie the Atlantic littoral to Spain, and that constitute "the safest of navigations among all those known upon the Ocean Sea" (1. 2. 9).[10] The islands of the Caribbean, meanwhile, the scene of the text's writing and the "here" of its enunciation, provide a privileged vantage point from which to look out over this Atlantic geography. They are "mediterranean," Oviedo insists, insofar as they are enclosed by the two points of the hunter's lure, Labrador and Cape of Saint Augustine. From Hispaniola, Oviedo can look out at the horizon to the west, into which his culture is moving but also back toward the metropolis in the east from whence it came. An imperial geography is inscribed, but it is also set into perspective and marked by the dynamics of Spain's colonial enterprise. It is a space to be moved through just as much as it is a space to be seen and known. It is, in other words, the space of seasoned travelers like Oviedo, of people who can be trusted to write of the Americas because they have trudged through them on their own two feet.

This interpretation of Oviedo's brief description of the Indies finds support in a crucial passage from the end of part 2, where Oviedo readily abandons the notion of an insular America. By the time he wrote this, his contact with certain Italian and Swedish cosmographers seems to have convinced him that the Old and New Worlds were indeed physically linked as parts of one great landmass. The link, however, was to be found in the extreme North Atlantic rather than in the North Pacific. "The land of Labrador," Oviedo writes, "continues northward, and then turns toward the East, and meets up with and is one and the same land as Europe, and it renders mediterranean the said Iceland and Scotland and England and many other notable islands" (2. 39. preface). Oviedo then makes a crucial rhetorical move: he interprets the resultant single world landmass as a harbinger of the impending universal monarchy of Charles V and prays that this empire may be brought into being (2. 39. preface). With this move, he shows that he was a man of his times. Renaissance cosmography was convinced that the cosmos was the meaningful creation of a benevolent Providence and thus was fond of thinking of the map of the world as the graphic image of a divine plan.[11] As Oviedo himself writes, a map of the world is the most beautiful painting one can gaze upon, since its painter is none other than God himself (2. 39. summary relation). In the unity of the world's geography, Oviedo finds the geographical counterpart of a providentialist historiography, one that saw in Charles V the divinely ordained successor to the emperors of Rome, and in his Monarchy, the new empire that would serve as God's instrument in the spread of Christianity throughout the globe. By linking his geography to this historiography, Oviedo imbues his dynamic, perspectival rendering of the Atlantic world with a glimpse of its future, final, political and religious form. He provides his narrative of emerging empire with a totality to which it can aspire, a totality not unlike the Reconquest idea of Hispania or the New Spain of the "Second Letter from Mexico." He also extends his already established portrayal of the North Atlantic as an inland sea of sorts, a Hispanic *mare nostrum*. In the earlier description, Labrador forms one of the points of the hunter's lure, reaching out toward Europe and partially closing the Atlantic in the North. The land bridge in the North Atlantic simply completes the job of sealing this ocean, and thereby converting it, as Oviedo's language suggests, into a new Mediterranean for the new Rome.

But just as we saw in Cortés's "Second Letter," Oviedo's vision of the geographical and political whole to be realized through blessed conquest does not constitute the dominant register of his geographical discourse, particularly not of the second and third parts of the *Historia general y natural*. The passage about the one world that announces an impending world monarchy provides but a coda to a long historical narrative that begins with a very different sort of geographical writing. There, in part 2, book 21, we find Oviedo's prose cartography of the inner coastline of the Americas, beginning with the Strait of Magellan and continuing northward to Labrador. The description of the Pacific coastline appears at the beginning of part 3, in book 39. It, too, moves northward from Magellan's eponymous passage toward California. Both prose cartographies are derived from the charts of the Seville cosmographical school. Oviedo actually names the people whose maps he describes, including Diego Ribeiro, Alonso de Santa Cruz, Sebastian Cabot, and most often, Alonso de Chaves—all cosmographers at the Casa de la Contratación (2. 21; 3. 39). More prolix and meticulous than those of Enciso—whom Oviedo never cites [12]— these many pages of prose cartography read like the following passage about a stretch of coastline along the Gulf of Mexico:

> From the Hermoso River there are twenty leagues until the Palmas River, going north. This Palmas River lies at twenty-four degrees and a third, on this side of the equinoctial line. And between the Hermoso River and the Palmas are the Saint Benito Rivero and the Montañas Rivers. This is the river where Captain Pánfilo de Narváez went to settle and where he and all his men were lost. For none were left save three *hidalgos* and a black slave who related their evil experience, as will be related later, where most appropriate.

From the Palmas River to Cape Bravo the coast runs fifty leagues to the north-east, more or less, continuously circling around, bearing increasingly toward the pole, and climbing the degrees bit by bit. Cape Bravo lies at twenty-six and a half degrees on this side of the equinoctial line. But along these fifty leagues, before the Palmas River and up the coast, lie Delgada Beach, the Altas Mountains, Palmar, and then the above-mentioned Cape Bravo.

From Cape Bravo to the Pescadores River the coast runs thirty leagues toward the northeast; and along these leagues lie the Magdalena River, the Escondido River, Costa Buena, and the Pescadores River, which lies at twenty-eight degrees, on this side of the equinoctial line.

From the Pescadores River to the Espíritu Sancto River the coast runs seventy-five leagues toward the east-northeast, but along this way we find, first, the river they call the River of Gold . . . (2. 21. 8)

It would seem that these two prose cartographies simply flesh out the geometric figure made to stand for the Indies in part 1. Instead, they depart entirely from its example. Unlike the passage about the Atlantic coastline as a hunter's lure or an open mouth, this one provides few generalizations that could help the reader picture the shape of the coastline. While the passage from part 1 allows the reader to see the forest, this one offers only trees. Here, for example, we follow Oviedo's description of a stretch of coastline along the Gulf of Mexico that curves a full ninety degrees, but Oviedo provides only one remark that helps the reader navigate the turn. That remark, moreover, has none of the accessibility provided by the image of the hunter's lure and instead relies upon the reader's familiarity with the technical language of cartography, mentioning a compass bearing, the pole, and the degree.

While the generalization about American geography from part 1 suggested an implied reader with little access to maps, the language of the prose cartographies in parts 2 and 3 suggest an implied reader with a relatively high degree of cartographic literacy. Although it does not provide "reader-friendly" generalizations about the shape of the coastline, it does provide the technical details necessary to reconstruct a crude version of the chart being described. Like Enciso, Oviedo provides measures of both distance and direction from one point to the next (e.g., that a distance along the coast "runs seventy-five leagues toward the east-northeast"). The would-be cartographer may not be able to render the outline of the coast, but he or she can at least get more or less right the spatial relationships among the itinerary's various stopping places. The rest of the prose cartography, in both parts 2 and 3, reads the same way, as a text aimed at a cartographically literate reader who either has a chart available, or is willing and able to go to the trouble of drawing one.

And so it seems that geographical discourse in the *Historia general y natural de las Indias*, when it deals with the whole of the Indies, operates in one of two registers. The first substitutes the geography of the Indies with a geometric figure set into perspective, one that helps the reader conceptualize the continent as a component of an Atlantic empire on the march, but that does little to impart specific geographical information. The second moves from this metaphorical, macrodescriptive register to its technical, microdescriptive counterpart.

But the cartography at issue in this second mode of geographical writing is not the abstract, geometric one of the Renaissance map, but rather, the cartography of the plane chart, with its deep roots in the linear spatiality of old. This point may already be obvious in the way these prose cartographies abandon the morphologies of the bird's eye view for a description that finds its way from one destination to the next. Oviedo avails himself of these prose cartographies as opportunities not just to describe the coastlines of the Indies, but to inhabit them. Although it eliminates handy similes meant to help the reader picture what the coastline looks like from above, Oviedo's prose cartography is not composed entirely of indications of distance and direction. It also digresses into bits of historical narrative. Upon mentioning the Montañas River in the first paragraph of the passage cited above, for example, Oviedo remarks that this place provided the point of departure for a disastrous expedition into the interior. This brief micronarrative is not alone in the sea of Oviedo's prose cartography, which often digress into such embryonic narratives of memorable people and events. Sometimes these narratives are quite brief, serving only to mark the origin of a name or the place of someone's death. "This river is called the River Joan Serranol," we read, "This was a genteel pilot who found himself with the said Captain Magellan" (2. 21. 1). Sometimes they go on at some length, as in the case of the river Paramá, and Sebastian Cabot's expedition there in 1526 (2. 21. 2). Sometimes the micronarratives refer the reader to the book and chapter where the relevant place and event will be discussed. And, sometimes, they make mention of the native inhabitants: "All of these [eighty leagues of coastline] belong to Carib Indian bowmen, who shoot arrows with a highly poisonous, deadly herb, and all are wicked people and they eat human flesh" (2. 21. 6). These micronarratives are particularly thick along stretches of the coastline that Oviedo knew firsthand, such as the Pacific coast of Nicaragua (3. 39. 2).

Seen in this light, the fact that the prose cartographies do so little to help the reader imagine the shape of the coastline is beside the point. These apparent digressions from the steady course of prose cartography can be understood as sallies in a haphazard struggle against the blankness of the map. Frank Lestringant reminds us that a list of toponyms is not merely an inventory of names but a way of activating a metonymic geography, with its own meanings and associations.[13] This is only true, however, about lists of familiar names: it cannot be true of a list of places in the freshly minted New World. Oviedo's micronarratives thus attempt to provide these names with the associations they so desperately lack in Medina's *Libro de grandezas*. They attempt to imaginatively inhabit American space by associating some of its place names with narratives of memorable people and events. In these micronarratives we find, also, the same gesture that marks many of the planispheres of the Seville school, whose spaces are inhabited by narratives of discovery, conquest, and marvel. This, perhaps, is the reason that Oviedo leaves generalizations about the shapes of the inner and outer coastlines of the Americas for other occasions. In the two prose cartographies, he is not just trying to describe coastlines but to render them memorable, to colonize them for the European imagination by converting individual toponyms into real places charged with historical, geographical, and ethnographical associations. In his or her encounter with them, the reader acquires, or hopes to acquire, some of that rich, thick, firsthand knowledge that Oviedo enjoys. With them, Oviedo's insistence upon his authority as an eyewitness, as someone who has *been there*, reveals its deeper roots in the old spatiality of the voyage. In Oviedo's micronarratives, the reader stands a chance of benefiting from his experience of the territory and thereby becoming a surrogate traveler.

In this way, Oviedo's itineraries recall the mnemotechnics of old. In her famous study of the subject, Frances Yates describes how aspiring public speakers were trained to commit to memory a series of loci, or places that could then be filled with the "content" that one wished to remember. Typically, this series of loci took the form of an itinerary through a spacious and varied building, one with many chambers. The chambers then became places in which to store images that recalled the key points of an argument or the events of a narrative. By storing them in order, along a predetermined route through the structure, the speaker could recall these things in the appropriate sequence (Yates 1966, 3). Oviedo uses cartography in ways that have everything to do with memory, in his case, the collective memory of Castile. He traces a path through a space—in this case, the surface of a maritime chart—and places memories of different kinds in many of its stopping places. Like Cortés, he must struggle with the impertinence of America to Europe and vice versa, and, like Cortés, he must thereby accomplish the paradoxical task of grounding history in geography at the same time that he grounds geography in history. He must mobilize cartography as the container in which to sort the pieces of his historiography, and historiography, as the vehicle that invests cartography with meaning. The result is an assemblage of places, in that rich sense of the word so often lost to us today, each one memorable, linked by an itinerary that gives greater importance to the particularity of these places, than to the task of outlining the larger geography that contains them.

When we turn from the prose cartographies themselves to the larger design of parts 2 and 3, we realize that the connections between cartography and historical memory in Oviedo's writing are both broad and deep. These two parts of the *Historia general y natural* are organized in a way that departs dramatically from the example set in part 1. There, like most historians of the time, Oviedo uses the chronology of the events he wishes to emplot as the organizing principle of his historiography. He begins with Columbus and follows the exploration and conquest of the Caribbean through the establishment of a thriving colony on the island of Hispaniola and the subsequent conquest of the surrounding islands. By the time his discourse has exhausted the story of the colonization of Hispaniola and turns its attention to the conquest of the other Greater Antilles, Oviedo's method begins to unravel. At this point, the story moves in various directions at once, and Oviedo must decide upon the order in which to relate the conquests of Cuba, Jamaica, and Puerto Rico. After considering a variety of alternatives, he dismisses the notion of organizing his material along a geographical itinerary from one island to the next, because such a method, he insists, would lack substance (1. 17. preface).

By the time he writes part 2, Oviedo has changed his mind about this way of organizing historical writing. He abandons his original design for one based upon geography rather than chronology. The itinerary from south to north along the Atlantic littoral established in the prose cartography of part 2 provides the subsequent historical narrative with its textual disposition. That narrative hops from place to place along the Atlantic coast of the Americas from the Strait of Magellan to Labrador, stopping at every significant location to tell of its discovery, its conquest, its conqueror, its indigenous customs, its natural marvels, its conversion to the true faith. Part 3 does the same with the Pacific coastline insofar as it was known, moving again from the Strait of Magellan northward to California. The text thus sacrifices chronological coherence for a sort of geographical coherence. Individual narratives of conquest appear as discrete texts, in the arbitrary order established by the prose cartography rather than in strict chronological sequence. In this, Oviedo's writing comes to resemble other historical geographies and cosmographies from the mid-sixteenth century, including Pedro de Medina's *Libro de grandezas* and Sebastian Münster's landmark *Cosmographia* (1544).

This much is obvious to any reader of Oviedo's *Historia general y natural*. What is at issue is the meaning of this organizational choice, one for which Oviedo provides no satisfactory explanation. Some commentators insist that it speaks to the centrality of natural rather than moral history to Oviedo's project (Al-varez López 1957, 555; Salas 1986, 90).[14] But, as Álvaro Belanos points out, parts 2 and 3 actually dedicate considerably less attention to natural history than does part 1 (1991, 18). Oviedo's extensive prose cartographies, there-fore, appear in those parts of the *Historia general y natural* least involved with the natural history of the Indies and most concerned with the history of their conquest and colonization. It is these parts, the ones most concerned with moral rather than natural history, that he organizes geographically rather than chronologically. Oviedo's cartographic prose and his larger project of "carto-graphic history" are thus not related to his interest in nature but to his inter-est in events. He uses prose cartography to ground and organize his narrative of events, thereby suggesting that it provides the metageography of his entire historical project as developed in parts 2 and 3 of the *Historia general y natural*.

Cartography and collective memory are indeed linked in this text, and not only at those points where the prose cartographies digress into historical micronarratives. The link between the two is at the heart of the entire project. The collective memory in question, however, is not exactly the memory of "the conquest," if by this we mean a unified narrative of a military and colo-nial enterprise to be understood as the heroic endeavor of a single nation. In the preliminaries to part 2, Oviedo does indeed allude to such a master nar-rative as the ultimate meaning of his book. There, he praises the bravery of those who have helped conquer half the world for Spain and compares the na-tion favorably with the empires of antiquity (2, preface). But as prefatory rhet-oric gives way to historiographical practice, it becomes clear that "the con-quest" and "the nation" are nothing more than the sum of their parts. They can only be monumentalized by memorializing the audacious men that took sword in hand and marched into the unknown interior. This becomes clear when Oviedo warns his reader not to mistake the organization of the text for the chronology of the larger historical process:

> And as I have said elsewhere, the reader should not look to the order in which one captain precedes others in the discourse of the narrative, for the cause of this is the continuous coast. And this is in no way inconvenient, for each book and particular history declares the time during which each one served, for that is the more substantial precedence. And the most true and praiseworthy advantage of all is in the works of virtue: a more famous and honorable end will come to those of whom we form memories. (2. 21. 11)

With this warning, the potential master narrative of conquest alluded to in the prefatory rhetoric dissolves into its constituent parts. Those parts, we are told, have not been emplotted into a story of the conquest as a whole. That story has been sacrificed so that the individual episodes of the conquest, with their individual heroes—however brutal, however venal—may be remembered in perpetuity.

It is they whom the *Historia general y natural* means to monumentalize, not some abstraction known as "the Spanish nation."[15] Oviedo's map of the Indies becomes the memory map in which he arranges the stories of those great men—great, apparently, even in their avarice and cruelty—whose deeds, the historian claims, outshine those of Jason, Theseus, and Aeneas (2, preface). This organization is precisely what renders them legible and memorable. In this way, parts 2 and 3 of Oviedo's *Historia general y natural* cannot be understood, as it has been in the past, as either an encyclopedia of Americana, or as a miscellany of the sort that was then popular in Spain. The first suggests a truly arbitrary system for categorizing its subject matter, while the second suggests a lack of any real organization at all. Oviedo's *Historia general y natural*— parts 2 and 3 at least—represents neither of these. It is instead best understood as a "cartographic history," a historiographical work that uses cartographic space as its fundamental organizational principle for the purpose of inventing a new geography as a "place" in the reader's imagination. The cartography in question is of course that of the maritime chart, whose linear dynamics and attention to places as a series of stopping points so resembles the spatial tours at the heart of traditional mnemonics. In this sort of history, knowledge is organized according to its place in the world, and thereby makes of its location a *place*.[16] Discourse becomes the vehicle through which we move through this linear succession of stopping places, making of them places, and knitting the whole into a larger totality that we occasionally glimpse when we step back from the textual itinerary to take in that whole, a whole that is little more than the sum of its individually memorable parts. This is the model for American historiography that Oviedo bequeaths to his successor, Francisco López de Gómara.

Gómara: Insularity and (En)Closure

Like the 1534 edition of Martire, one of the early editions of Gómara's two-volume history also included a printed map. In fact, it included two maps, one of the New World and one of the Old (fig. 30). Neither map has anything to do with the text of the *Historia general de las Indias*. The map of the Americas includes North and South America in their entirety, even unexplored sections of the Pacific coast. As the coastlines move northward, they curve outward, suggesting that the continent eventually meets up—in both the east and the west and perhaps even over the pole—with the northernmost extremes of the Old World. This impression finds some support in a presumably unintentional effect created by the physical layout of the maps. They appear on facing pages, but oriented in opposite directions, and thus reinforce the notion that the geography of the world is made up of one huge landmass. This notion is consistent with the geography eventually adopted by Oviedo, and glimpsed at the end of part 2 of his *Historia general y natural*. It is not in any way consistent with Gómara's own statements about universal geography, which never embrace the notion of a single landmass. In fact, those statements very clearly affirm Gómara's conviction that the Old World and the New constitute two separate "islands," as he puts it. "The land which we call the Indies," Gómara insists, "is also an island like our own" (López de Gómara 1979, 21). Later, he asserts that the Pacific coast of North America "continues northward until it finally encloses the land, making it an island, in the vicinity of Labrador or Greenland" (27).[17] In this way, his vision of American geography is closer to that of Waldseemüller, Sebastian Münster, Juan López de Velasco, and many others than it is to that of the map that accompanied his own text into print (fig. 31; see also figs. 6 and 16 above). It is in the chapters where Gómara makes these assertions, and not on that map, that we can find the metageography of his *Historia general*. That metageography, as we shall see, is inseparable from the notion of American insularity. That insularity, in turn, is central to understanding the way Gómara rewrites Oviedo, redraws his map, and thereby pushes early Spanish Americana in directions that are more clearly "modern" and "imperial."

Nowhere does Gómara offer a symbolic interpretation of his insular American geography that in any way resembles Oviedo's imperialist, universalist reading of the unified *orbis terrarum*. On the face of things, it seems that Gómara might not be interested in adding such flourishes to what should be plain geographical description. After all, his entire historiographical project can be understood as an attempt to abbreviate and simplify what one scholar has called the "elephantine" works of Oviedo (Blake 1975, 541). Unlike Cortés and Oviedo, Francisco López de Gómara never traveled to the Americas. His *Historia general de las Indias* is the work of a stay-at-home intellectual who relied for his data upon the firsthand accounts of others, including Oviedo and Cortés. Gómara took these accounts, synthesized them, and pared them down to produce a history that, in true Renaissance style, claimed to both instruct and entertain the reader by eschewing prolixity and ornament for brevity and clarity (López de Gómara 1979, 3). And so, while Oviedo's *Historia general y natural* ranges over many books, Gómara's *Historia general* encloses the entire

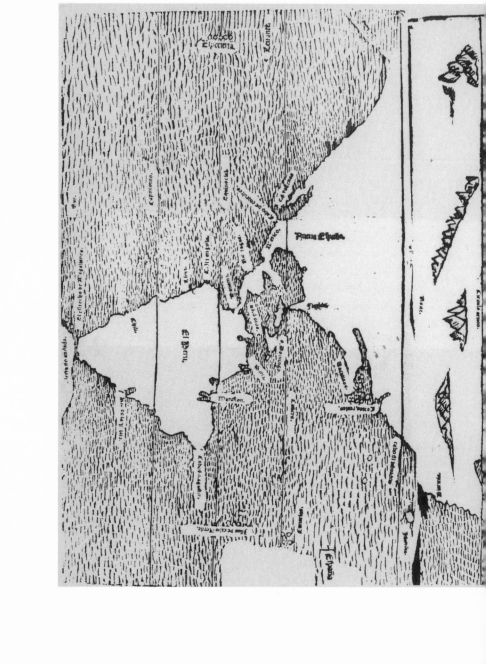

30 Maps of the New World and of the Old printed with López de
Gómara's *Historia general de las Indias* (Zaragoza, 1552). Note how the
Pacific coast of North America curves westward toward Asia rather
than eastward toward Greenland. The two maps are also bound in
such a way as to suggest, informally, that the Old and New Worlds
form one great landmass. The Albert and Shirley Small Special
Collections Library, University of Virginia.

Cathay

INDIA superior

Quinsai

FRA

NO V

Terra

Archipelagus 7448 insularū

Zipangri

Chamaho

Panuco Inf. Tortucar

CVBA

Hispaniol

Temistitan

Sela

Iamica

P ARIA s abundat auro & margaritis

Inf. pdonum

OBIS

Aditicii quam uocant Brasilij & Americam

Catigara

Inf. infortu natæ

Regio Gigantum

Calensuan

Mare pacificum

Fretum Maga

TABVLA·

Hibernia

Corterea

Exteriores

Hifpania

cidentalis

Medera

Fortunatæ inf.

Inf.Hefperidum

AFRICAE
pars

S.Iacobi

Sinus
Atlanticus

bali

nfulę Mar-
gueritarū

31 Sebastian Münster, *Die nüw Welt* (1546). Note how the northwest
coast of North America wraps back to meet Newfoundland, producing an "insular" America consistent with Gómara's geographical
descriptions. The Geography and Map Division of the Library of
Congress.

history of the Indies—save for the conquest of Mexico—within a single elegant volume, composed, as Gómara asserts, of brief chapters, and of terse, clear sentences. It acknowledges that it may err in some particulars, but it asserts that it nonetheless captures the truth of matters in their essence and communicates that truth plainly and openly (3). In keeping with these principles, Gómara's prose cartography of the Americas, which appears in a chapter entitled "El sitio de las Indias," is markedly brief compared to Oviedo's or Enciso's. It is also free of the micronarratives that Gómara must have thought cluttered the plain but informative discourse of prose cartography.

"El sitio de las Indias" appears at the tail end of a multichapter introduction to the *Historia general* that grounds its authority not in the personal experience of its author but in his broad humanistic erudition. These chapters refer received ideas about cosmography and geography to what was then known about the New World. It raises cosmographical questions, only to dismiss them through appeals to various aspects of the Spanish experience with Americas, treated as if they were common knowledge. The tone is graceful, masterful, learned, nationalistic, and self-consciously modern. For example, Gómara surveys the history of opinions regarding the existence of the antipodes, only to conclude with the observation that Spanish ships have settled the question by sailing to the antipodal Indies all the time. Those ships, Gómara adds, have even circumnavigated the Earth, much to the shame of the ancients and the glory, not of moderns in general, but of Spain in particular (López de Gómara 1979, 15–17).[18] This race through the cosmographical problems of the day even leads to an exposition of the form and function of the cartographic grid. Space, in this chapter, is global and rationalized, and the new cartography is the instrument of that rationalization. It would seem that Gómara was not only a good stylist and a capable consumer of cosmographical debate but also a leader in the assimilation of that new spatiality that came with the Renaissance map.

But if we look closely, we discover that the *Historia general* is not at all what Gómara makes it out to be. Words like "clarity" and "brevity," assertions like "I have worked to tell of things as they occurred," immediately associate the text with a Renaissance aesthetic of "natural art," one that expressly avoids ornament and affectation but may in fact only dissimulate its own, very deep, artificiality.[19] In the end, the *Historia general de las Indias* seems very artfully wrought, highly finished, polished, even too much so (Blake 1975, 541). This was not lost upon Gómara's contemporaries. Many of those who had actually been to the New World disapproved of what they understood as his grossly ill-informed attempt to pare the history of the Indies down to its essentials.

One of his most famous detractors is the conquistador Bernal Díaz del Castillo, who formed part of Cortés's company in the conquest of Mexico. Late in life, Bernal Díaz wrote his own *Historia verdadera de la conquista de la Nueva España* purportedly to correct what he took to be the errors and lies disseminated by Gómara and others. The text includes an angry assessment of the *Historia general* in which Bernal Díaz, a man of moderate education, clearly demonstrates that he is ill at ease with Gómara's eloquence and erudition (Díaz del Castillo 1982, chap. 18). Bernal Díaz sensed that Gómara's plain but elegant prose was seductive but untruthful and that this was precisely the danger that the *Historia general* posed to the historical memory of the conquest of Mexico. As we shall see, Gómara's prose cartography of the Americas, like the *Historia general* as a whole, glows with the dim light of an ideological purpose barely perceptible in its prosaic simplicity.

To begin with, that prose cartography depends much more upon the hybrid spatiality of the plane chart than it does on the abstract spatiality of the gridded map with which Gómara explicitly identifies himself. This should not surprise us, if for no other reason than that Gómara's own discussion of the cartographic grid reveals the superficiality of his understanding of its nature and purpose. Gómara makes no reference to the grid as an abstract-positioning system. Instead, he dwells upon the degree as a new standard for measuring distance that replaces older measures like stadia, feet, and paces (López de Gómara 1979, 17). His definition, then, does not take him to a discussion of space in the modern sense, but in that older, linear sense described above. As in Enciso, the discussion of the degree as a measure of distance leads Gómara to an estimate of the circumference of the Earth expressed as a straight-line measure. He asserts that one degree covers seventeen-and-a-half Castilian leagues, and concludes, "And so the orb of the earth measures, in a straight line . . . six thousand leagues. This measure is so certain that all use it and praise it" (17).[20] Gómara's abstract, global space has been both flattened out and, so to speak, collapsed into a single line, a distance, an *espacio* in the unidimensional sense.[21]

Shortly after this brief but revealing exposition of the new cartography, Gómara turns to a brief description of the world's geography and to his more extended prose cartography of the Americas. Like Oviedo, Gómara has derived his description from the maritime charts of the Casa de la Contratación, although, unlike Oviedo, Gómara does not explicitly name the cosmographers whose maps he has used. The following passage about a stretch of the Gulf of Mexico from what present-day Corpus Christi, Texas, to Paraíso, Tabasco, can be made to stand for the whole:

From this bay [i.e., the Bay of Espíritu Sancto], which is at twenty-nine degrees, there lie more than seventy leagues until the Pescadores River. From the Pescadores, which is at 28½ degrees [of latitude], to the Palmas River lies a distance of 100 leagues, near the point where the Tropic of Cancer crosses [the coastline]. From the Palmas River to the Pánuco there are no more than thirty leagues, and from there to Villarica or Veracruz, 70 leagues. Along this stretch lies Almería. From Veracruz, at 19 degrees, there are more than 30 leagues to the Alvarado River, which the Indians call the Papaloapan. From the Alvarado River to Coazucualco we count 50 leagues; from there to the Grijalva River there are more than 40, and both rivers are just below 18 degrees. (López de Gómara 1979, 23)

Like the passage from Oviedo's prose cartography cited above—which traces the exact same stretch of coastline, albeit moving in the opposite direction—Gómara's description immediately reveals its debts to the maritime charts from which it was derived. "El sitio de las Indias" accepts the implicit invitation extended by the chart's dense row of coastal place names to trace a journey along its shores.

It is the differences between this passage and the one from Oviedo, however, that I emphasize. To begin with the obvious one, Gómara's description is markedly shorter than that of Oviedo. Its brevity has been purchased by eliminating many of the places that Oviedo mentions and by silencing the micronarratives upon which his itineraries dawdle. Unlike Oviedo, Gómara sticks to his course along the coastlines of the Indies, never digressing into historical territory. His prose cartography, furthermore, eliminates a kind of detail that Oviedo makes sure to include, compass bearings.[22]

With this final erasure, Gómara's prose cartography undermines one of the central characteristics of this type of writing as it had been practiced by Enciso, Oviedo, and others. Without compass bearings, it becomes impossible for the reader to reproduce, however crudely, the chart that served as the basis for the description. Gómara's reader, however, has no need to do so, because, ironically, the stay-at-home historian has done a much better job than the conquistador-chronicler of helping his reader picture the Indies. He may not be as successful as Oviedo in bringing particular places to life, but he is much more successful in mapping the whole. Although it eliminates the compass bearings, "El sitio de las Indias" punctuates its textual itinerary around the Americas with passages meant to help the reader—in the absence of a map—imagine the shape of the territory being circumscribed. In other words, while Oviedo carries out two different kinds of cartographic writing, descriptive generalization and precise prose cartography, in separate textual locations, Gómara fuses the two. And so, after the passage cited above, we find the following description of the shape of the coastline it traces:

So there are nine hundred leagues of coast from Florida to Yucatan, which is another promontory that juts out northward from the mainland, and the farther it juts out into the water, the more it broadens and turns. It has at sixty leagues to the east the island of Cuba, which almost seals the gulf which lies in between Florida and Yucatan, which some call the Mexican Gulf, others the Floridian, and others the Cortés. (López de Gómara 1979, 23)

That invitation to picture the Indies in the mind's eye, but from a birds-eye perspective, extends from the local to the general. It is not just the individual contours of places like the Gulf of Mexico that Gómara paints for the reader but the Indies as a whole. Gómara takes Oviedo's bifurcated geography and unifies it through the use of a single itinerary around the Indies rather than two separate itineraries dedicated to each of its shores. Gómara's itinerary begins in Labrador and moves southward to the Strait of Magellan along the continent's Atlantic coastline, mentioning the names of important places and the distances from one to the next. It then traces the Pacific coastline northward, to California and beyond. As mentioned above, the itinerary never moves inland to describe the topography of the New World but instead clings to the coast, in effect outlining the continental mass of the Americas. At strategic junctures, it interrupts the forward movement of its geographical and discursive itinerary to make statements that help the reader picture both significant parts and the geography as a whole. It points out, for example, the narrowness of the Isthmus of Panama and the distance across South America at its widest point (26).[23] As Monique Mustapha puts it, these generalizing descriptions permit the reader to "delimit and take in at one glance rather large portions of the American littoral" (Mustapha 1979, 432). But Mustapha fails to mention the most important of these generalizations: At the moment that the itinerary wraps around to where it began, at the place where the figure it inscribes is completed and thus rendered visible, is where Gómara explicitly insists upon the insularity of the Americas. This is where we read, "the coast continues northward until it finally encloses the land, making it an island, in the vicinity of Labrador or Greenland" (27). The moment is crucial in that it both closes the figure being inscribed and characterizes it, suggestively, as an island.

Gómara's use of the term "island" rather than "continent," to refer to this landmass is neither unique nor arbitrary, since the word "continent" was, at the time, only beginning to acquire its now-familiar geographical acceptation. Even half a century after Gómara wrote his *Historia general*, Sebastián de Covarrubias registered no such meaning for it. It should not surprise us, therefore, that Gómara does not use it to refer to the Indies. Neither, however, should it surprise us that he refers to them as an island. In doing so he follows the example—perhaps unwittingly—of a figure no less important than Martin Waldseemüller, arguably the first to confer upon the New World what we would call "continental" status. Ironically, Waldseemüller does so by referring to the newly christened America as an "insula." After asserting that it constitutes the fourth part of what was once thought to be a merely tripartite world, Waldseemüller specifies an important difference between the Old World and the New. "The first three parts [Europe, Asia, and Africa] are continents," we read, "while the fourth [America] is an island, inasmuch as it is found to be surrounded on all sides by the ocean" (Fischer and von Wieser 1907, 173). Thus, in the language that Waldseemüller bequeathed to the century, to insist on American insularity was to establish its geographical independence from the Old World, to confer upon it, in other words, what we would call "continental" status. By contrast, to insist upon the "continental" status of the Americas was to posit that they formed the fourth part of a single great landmass that also included Europe, Asia, and Africa. The French cosmographer André Thevet, for example, rails against those who insist upon the insularity of the Americas, particularly Sebastian Münster. He suggests instead that they are a "continent," *terra firme*, a body of land physically linked with the traditional *orbis terrarum* (cited by Conley 1996, 193). So, while to insist on the insularity of the Americas may look to us like a way of asserting their ontological equality with the other parts of the world insofar as it grants them what we might recognize as continental status, in the language of sixteenth-century geography such insistence in fact marks their difference. Here, then, we begin to identify the significance of Gómara's insistence upon American insularity.

According to O'Gorman, this mark of geographical difference grounds other forms of alterity in ways that are quite useful to a particular ideology of colonial expansion. By physically separating the Indies from the Old World, O'Gorman argues, Waldseemülller and Vespucci divorce the Native Americans from the human family. His argument seems to rely on José de Acosta's systematic, late-sixteenth-century exposition—the first of its kind—of the origins of the Amerindians. As a distinguished editor of Acosta's text, O'Gorman knew the argument extremely well. In the 1590s, Acosta demonstrated that in order to consider the native inhabitants of the New World to be truly human—descendents of Adam and Eve by way of the sons of Noah—it was first necessary to deny the full insularity of the Americas. Quite simply, in the absence of some sort of land bridge linking the Old World to the New, it became impossible to imagine how the progeny of the passengers of the Ark, in particular, the animals, could have made their way from the Ark's final resting place to the New World (Acosta 1986, 100–25). Despite the fact that this argument was not spelled out until late in the century, O'Gorman argues that its general contours were glimpsed much earlier. An insular America was understood to isolate the inhabitants of the New World from those of the Old in geographical, historical, and even genealogical terms, thus making it easier to imagine the Amerindian as a different sort of human being even while explicitly accepting the pope's dogmatic assertion that they were indeed human. In short, the insular América of Vespucci and Waldseemüller, O'Gorman argues, made it possible for Juan Ginés de Sepulveda, that infamous apologist of Spain's colonial efforts, to argue that the Native Americans were natural slaves, fit for conquest by their European betters (O'Gorman 1967, lxxvii).

It may seem that O'Gorman's argument accounts for Gómara's unexplained insistence upon American insularity. Gómara, after all, insists upon the exotic novelty of nature in the Americas, almost in the same breath that he uses to parrot the orthodox dogma of the descent of the Amerindians from Adam (López de Gómara 1979, 5). He rejects the heretical notion of a plurality of worlds, and affirms that various islands that the ancients imagined beyond the Ocean count as "parts of the world" (9). But for at least one of Gómara's twentieth-century readers, his descriptions of the flora, fauna, and, significantly, even the human cultures of the New World, bear out his stated belief in the radical alterity of the Indies. The descriptions emphasize the marvelous, the exotic, and at times even the repulsive and the grotesque (Lewis 1983, 94). The notion of a single "mundo," it seems, does not preclude the notion that its parts may be unequal in nature or value. At the conclusion of the Historia general, furthermore, Gómara explains that he has dealt only with the history of the conquest of the Indies by Spain, not with the justifiability of that conquest. For justifications, the historian refers his reader to the writings of none other than Juan Ginés de Sepúlveda. This conclusion, moreover, comes on the heels of a renewed insistence upon the insularity of the Americas (303). Thus it would seem that Gómara's Historia general is the perfect example of how Europeans made an unacknowledged link between geographical insularity and anthropological difference and thereby figured an America available, in its very nature, for their own imperial designs.

Such an interpretation, however, does not render a full accounting of Gómara's insular America. Quite simply, it stumbles over a single phrase: "The land which we call the Indies," Gómara writes, "is also an island like our own." Although Gómara participates in Waldseemüller's assertion of American "insularity," he abandons the cosmographer's asymmetrical distinction between a continental Old World and an insular New World. Gómara's world, by contrast, is a perfectly symmetrical one, composed of two large landmasses, the Old World and the New, each as insular as the other. His discursive circumnavigation of the Indies is made to correspond to classical assertions of the circumnavigability of the old *orbis terarum*, thus emphasizing this point. The chapter just prior to "El sitio de las Indias" outlines the geography of the Old World in traditional terms, describing its division into three parts and asserting its status as a massive island. As proof of its insularity, it alludes to the Roman geographer Cornelius Nepos, a figure known only through Mela and Pliny, who tells of certain ancient voyages that demonstrated that the *orbis terrarum* could be circumnavigated (López de Gómara 1979, 20–21).[24] Gómara then converts the *orbis terrarum* of the geographical tradition into one half of a symmetrical geography through the simple assertion cited above. At the end of "El sitio de las Indias," finally, he rounds off the pair with an allusion to a third "island or land," the Terra Australis.[25]

The symmetry of this geography does not necessarily change anything in Gómara's stated belief in the radical alterity of people and things American, nor does it change his implicit belief in their inferiority to people and things European. It does suggest, however, that whatever role the thesis of American insularity may have had in enabling Europeans to imagine the Amerindian as a natural slave, here, in Gómara's text, that same insularity performs other, very different functions as well. Certainly, Gómara's insular America performs the task that O'Gorman finds central to such assertions of insularity: it isolates the Amerindian from the human family, which resides in the other parts of the world. That much is inherent in the mere use of the term "island," related etymologically, in Spanish as in English, to "isolated." But because it performs this function within the context of a symmetrical geography, Gómara's insularity only suggests a difference in *kind*, not a difference in *value*. It establishes the Indies as another place but also as a place like *ours*, an island like the one "we" inhabit. I point out this subtle but crucial difference, not in order to argue that Gómara attempts to make the Indies coeval with Europe, but in order to get at the ways in which his imperial metageography functions, ways that are quite different from those that O'Gorman suggests.

Gómara does not just insist on the insularity of the Americas as a geographical truth: he inscribes an insular America at a crucial juncture in his text, between its cosmographical introduction and its historical narrative. Unlike Oviedo's itineraries, Gómara's verbal map does nothing to remind us of the historical procedures by which these places came to be known and named. Very few of the names that Gómara mentions are of indigenous origins, and even those that are go unmentioned as such. All of them, whether coined from European sources of inspiration or borrowed from Amerindian languages, appear on European charts because of the various efforts to discover, explore, conquer, and settle carried out by different European actors, working at different times for different European monarchs. Gómara erases all of this, substituting the singular voyage of his solitary pen for the myriad voyages of the many. This presents a stark contrast to Oviedo's prose cartography, with its peppering of micronarratives of discovery. While Oviedo's itineraries draw a verbal map peopled, at least in part, by the historical memories of the European side of the Encounter, Gómara simply inscribes an irregular geometric figure as bereft of historical associations as it is stridently closed and insular.

In this way as well as others, Gómara's prose cartography is much more effective than that of Oviedo's at inventing an America amenable to an imperialistic historiography. Like the lines that a chartmaker traces on his page, Gómara's discursive itinerary serves to construct a singular geography out of a disparate collection of places either variously discovered or entirely imagined. It fuses a series of places that—from other perspectives, such as indigenous ones—have little to do with each other (Newfoundland and the Strait of Magellan, for example) into parts of a meaningful and coherent geographical whole called "the Indies." It also takes that whole and inserts it in a universal geography by mentioning its spatial relationship with parts of the Old World. In so doing, it works to naturalize the territory it describes in the eyes of the reader. By traveling around the whole before so much as mentioning a single historical journey of discovery, the text prepares its reader to believe in "America" as something coherent, something observable, something amenable to discovery. It renders the continent as something natural, something that can be found rather than something that has been invented. It renders it, moreover, as something amenable to possession. Just as Oviedo's unified geography could be imagined as the possession of a single monarch, so too can Gómara's united, coherent Indies be imagined as a jewel in an imperial crown. As a single, masterful circumnavigation of the continent, Gómara's prose cartography not only echoes the stories of circumnavigation in Pliny and Mela but also reproduces their ideological effects. Just as those tales took pains to make the farthest limits of the earth available for the Roman imperial imaginary, so Gómara's epic voyage of the pen figures the Indies as an apprehensible, even an apprehended, object, made available to the gaze of the imperial eye through cartographic discourse.[26]

In so doing, Gómara's prose cartography makes its most significant departure from the example provided by Oviedo. Ironically, while Oviedo struggles against the blankness of the map, Gómara deliberately inscribes a "blank" geography, an America bereft of meaning. That blankness, that emptiness, is, of course, only apparent, an ideologically determined gesture of erasure. It figures an empty territory meant to stand in for a territory on the ground that is anything but empty, that is in fact inhabited and settled, that has been territorialized by the practices and representations of indigenous peoples. All of this goes unacknowledged by Gómara's island, that abstraction that the discourse has worked hard to camouflage as a work of nature and to make visible to the eye of the imaginative reader. In this way, it tips the balance inherent in the plane chart between linear and planar spatiality, between diachronicity and synchronicity, between the itinerary through space and the spectacularized territory. As we have seen, Oviedo has trouble making the two sides of this Janus-like spatiality work together. Although he is perfectly capable of producing discursive figures that help his reader picture what the Indies look like on a map, his prose cartography works against this gesture, bringing the reader back down to the nitty-gritty of travel and places. Gómara's prose cartography, by contrast, is more fully cartographic. It is more effective than Oviedo's prose cartography at allowing the reader to imagine the Indies from a god's-eye perspective, the perspective of the map. It is much less inclined to draw the reader into the messy particularities of places, their discovery, their exploration, and their conquest. It purposefully inscribes blankness, empty space, rather than struggle against it. It erases the conditions of its own production and thus works better to naturalize the geography it figures. In all these ways, Gómara's prose cartography is more reflective of the emerging spatiality of modernity than are Oviedo's rambling itineraries.

All of this converts Gómara's prose cartography into a crucial instrument for one of his central historiographical gestures, the assertion that Columbus discovered America. As soon as the Historia general completes its journey around the Indies, it immediately turns to the tale of the anonymous pilot who, after having been blown off course by a fierce tempest, purportedly told Columbus of the existence of uncharted lands in the western Atlantic (López de Gómara 1979, 28). Following Oviedo, Gómara takes the legend for truth and tells of how Columbus heard this pilot's deathbed account of his adventure and even acquired his written tale of it, along with "the mark and altitude [that is, latitude] of the lands newly seen and found" (28). So far, Gómara's references to the places discovered by the pilot have maintained an appropriate air of imprecision. The reader knows only what the pilot and Columbus would have known—had he, in fact, existed—that there were uncharted lands of some kind in the western Atlantic. In the next chapter, however, after filling in some of the details of Columbus's biography, Gómara returns to the story of his encounter with the anonymous pilot and assigns those uncharted lands a name: "and thus Christopher Columbus first learned of the Indies" (29). In this way, the text casually identifies those uncharted lands with the continent described a few pages before.[27] The vagaries of the narrative discourse, furthermore, allow this identification to drift from the voice of the narrator to the intentions of the admiral. The text completely abandons the vague geographical language it had used in reference to the anonymous pilot. We do not read that Columbus wants to go to those "uncharted lands in the West." Instead, we read of how hard Columbus worked to travel to the Indies and of how he eventually discovered them (29–32).

Clearly, Gómara's commitment to brevity has produced an anachronism. From his own, mid-sixteenth-century point of view, Gómara knows much more about the geography of the New World than Columbus and the anonymous pilot—again, had he existed—could have ever known. By identifying Columbus's objective as "the Indies," a term already assigned to the whole of the New World, Gómara colors his narrative with a geographical synecdoche that plants the seed of a historical teleology. Surely, the anonymous pilot would have seen the shores of only a few islands, or perhaps a short stretch of the mainland. This, in turn, is all that Columbus could have learned from him. Gómara anachronistically refers this unspecified territory to the whole of which it would be recognized, years later, to form a part. His Columbus does not sail to an island or a mainland but to a synecdoche, one whose figurative structure is inseparable from a specific historical projection. By having Columbus sail to "the Indies," Gómara has him journey to a whole figured physically through one of its parts.

Gómara's account of the first landfall reinforces this implication. The land Columbus reaches, Gómara writes, "was Guanahaní, one of the Lucayo Islands, which lie between Florida and Cuba, upon which he disembarked, and took possession of the Indies and New World which Columbus was discovering for the kings of Castile" (López de Gómara 1979, 32). The gesture is a familiar one. The historian locates Columbus's first landfall on a modern map of the Americas, a map of which Columbus himself had no inkling. This thereby makes the illogical assertion that Columbus has arrived not at a mysterious Atlantic archipelago but in the larger whole, America. To put it simply, all that had yet to be invented in 1492 is projected backward in time as a natural object awaiting discovery. Gómara then mentions the fortress that the admiral leaves behind and calls it "the first house or town that the Spaniards made in the Indies" (32). The first of a series: the Columbian foundation is associated with other foundations to be made elsewhere over the course of the next half century. Just as the geography of the first voyage becomes a synecdoche of what was, in 1492, yet to be discovered, so this component of its history becomes the seed of an empire that was yet to be imagined.

The operation of naturalizing America as an object just waiting to be discovered and claimed is sealed through an appeal to Pope Alexander VI's 1493 bull Inter caetera, the so-called "papal donation" described in chapter 3.[28]

Gómara's Historia general represents the historiographical analogue of this charter, contributing powerfully to the invention of America while all the while operating as if what it invents is in fact its object. Here, Gómara recruits the pope's charter to his own discursive work by attaching the bull's ambiguous geographical language—"all islands and mainlands found and to be found"—to the continent he has already described and which he has converted into the object of Columbus's first voyage. Although the bull never uses the word "Indies" to refer to the lands it donates to Castile, this is precisely the word that Gómara uses to refer to the lands covered by the bull (López de Gómara 1979, 35). Once again, the narrative's brevity allows for a sloppy treatment of chronology that ties past actions to present realities through the insinuation of an intentionality that could never have existed. The Indies—America—becomes that thing that was always there, was discovered by Columbus, and was given to Castile by the Vicar of Christ on Earth.

But while the success of "El sitio de las Indias" in allowing us to picture a continent that we take as a natural entity is crucial to the subsequent story of its encounter, we must remember that Gómara's prose cartography is not all synchronicity, wholeness, and visibility. Returning now to "El sitio de las Indias," we find that it does not entirely divorce itself from old habits of mind. Although it erases the voyages that made it possible, Gómara's prose cartography nonetheless takes the form of a voyage, albeit a fictional one, an epic voyage of the pen around the perimeter of the Americas. It is perhaps inevitable that a discursive cartography should cling to the linearity of the journey, even a counterfeit one, but it is also inevitable that this particular kind of voyage around a large landmass should recall the geographies of old, particularly those of Strabo and Mela. It reminds us that even a counterfeit voyage is enough to draw us into the space being described and to have us move through it rather than just gaze at it from above. The synchronicity of Gómara's prose cartography can still be understood, therefore, as a synchronicity in process, so to speak, much like that of the maritime chart. Although it erases the historical operations that produced it and even denies that the object is in any way "produced," it does so, surprisingly, by substituting them with an idealized version of those very processes. That epic voyage of the pen reveals the Indies to the reader bit by bit, part by part, and thereby attests to the importance of travel, of exploration, to the new knowledge of the moderns and of Spain. But by substituting myriad real journeys with this ersatz double, it also obscures the messy process of invention. The Indies appear stripped of any evidence of the give and take between the ideas and experiences of various explorers and the synthetic efforts of stay-at-home cosmographers. Like a vision, they are made known, not produced.

This element of movement, of diachronicity, in a text that struggles to inscribe a synchronous appreciation of American geography is therefore no discursive appendix. Neither is it a subversive subtext to its opposing element of stasis and synchronicity. In fact, the two function together as the twin components of the metageography of the *Historia general de las Indias* as a whole. Like Oviedo's work, Gómara's history derives its narrative disposition from the course taken by its prose cartography. After telling the tale of Columbus's discovery, the *Historia general* turns to Labrador, the point of departure for "El sitio de las Indias" and tells its history. It then moves down the Atlantic coast and up the Pacific, relating the moral and natural history of each significant place in the order in which they appear along the coast, irrespective of chronological considerations. When the historical discourse reaches the Strait of Magellan, it leaves the Americas behind to tell of the voyage of the *Victoria* around the world, as well as the related efforts by the Castilian crown to lay claim to the Spice Islands. What we discover, then, is that the itinerary that has served to inscribe the Indies as an empty island available for European apprehension does not cancel itself out in the production of this mental image. Instead, it reinscribes itself on a larger scale, revisiting the places along its route and, finally, assigning to each a historical memory in which Europeans play a prominent role.

In one volume, Gómara's history wraps around the whole of the continent, constantly penetrating inward from the coast, filling the emptiness of the interior with names, descriptions, stories, memories. Certainly, there are many place names in the prose cartography that never appear in the historical text, and there are certain junctures where Gómara deviates from his stated plan to stick to his route.[29] These exceptions to the architectonics of the work, however, only bring the careful design of the whole into further relief. The text assigns a discoverer, a conqueror, a narrative of conquest, a series of natural marvels and/or savage customs to each place.[30] Like Oviedo, Gómara insists that by organizing the material in this way he means only to lend clarity to his exposition, but once again we find that the author's choice has implications that he himself may not have recognized. For one, Gómara avoids some of the ideological embarrassments that a strictly chronological exposition may have presented. By the 1550s, the history of Spain's conquest of the Americas had passed through at least three distinct phases: an initial one centered on the Caribbean; a triumphant phase involving the spectacular conquests of Mexico and Peru; and a third, more disappointing, phase that included such regrettable episodes as the civil wars in Peru and the expedition of Coronado. These episodes do indeed appear toward the end of the *Historia general*, but not as the pitiful *denouement* to an internally coherent history of the conquest of the

Americas. Instead, they appear as a collection of tragic episodes associated with a particular place, what is now the southwestern United States and northwestern Mexico. In other words, by avoiding a chronological arrangement of his material, Gómara avoids inscribing the problematic frontier of Spain's conquest and thus robs its most recent phase of its potential to function as an anticlimax.

More important, the use of a geographical itinerary to organize the historical material has the effect of duplicating the doubled spatiality of "El sitio de las Indias" itself. The disposition of the narrative shares with the itinerary of the prose cartography the status of a feigned journey, a counterfeit movement. Not only does it forestall the potential for anticlimax inherent in the metanarrative that it replaces, it also organizes events into an ersatz sequence that acquires its meaning independently of any master plot. It converts the episodes of the conquest into a series of historical tableaux, each one featuring a notable place; a sometimes villainous, sometimes heroic conquistador; and a conquered people.[31] The movement of the discourse from one scene to the next reproduces no historical temporality. Instead, it resembles a tour through a uniform space—a map, a memory theater, a museum—in which the individual tableaux exist simultaneously. Just as "El sitio de las Indias" renders geography visible to imperial eyes, so the *Historia general* as a whole renders history visible as well, as a series of discrete episodes, each centered upon the deeds of a great man, arranged along the surface of a map for all to see and admire. Like parts 2 and 3 of Oviedo's text, Gómara's *Historia general de las Indias* represents cartographic history struck in an imperial register but rendered more effective through the adoption of a smaller cartographic scale, so to speak, of a discursive brevity that reduces the whole of the Indies into a "vision of an ensemble of deeds" (Mustapha 1979, 439).[32]

In the end, Gómara's insular America is no less meaningful than Oviedo's unified *orbis terrarum* and is, perhaps, in that very mute simplicity, more effective ideologically. Having substituted the narrative logic of history with an arbitrary itinerary through space, Gómara is free to provide the text with an overall meaning from without. He does this in the final chapter of the *Historia general*, "Loor de españoles" (In Praise of the Spaniards). There, Gómara forges a conclusion out of the rhetorical excesses Oviedo had used for his introduction and thereby equips his history with something that Oviedo's lacks— a sense of narrative closure. Oviedo died insisting that his history was incomplete, that it lacked the fourth part he had planned for it. Fittingly, his prose cartographies provide the *Historia general y natural* with two open-ended littorals on the frontier between the known and the unknown. These are open geometric forms, open to continued conquest and exploration, the historico-geographical doubles of the cartographical horizons described at the end of chapter 3. Gómara, by contrast, not only completes his historical text but also suggests that the history of the conquest itself has come to a close. He presents in summary fashion the conquest of the Americas, the expurgation of its savage customs, the conversion of its peoples to Christianity, and the establishment there of civil society as faits accomplis. From the beginning, Gómara has had the Indies surrounded. At the end of his history, he goes in for the historical kill. The conclusion represents the historiographical analogue to the assertion, made at the end of "El sitio de las Indias," that the Indies are an island. The geographical enclosure accomplished through the assertion of insularity finds its analogue in narrative closure. Here, the narrator, and with him the reader, steps back to appreciate the whole—both the historiographical and the geographical whole—and find it whole, complete, and enclosed.

Las Casas: Erasing Islands, Questioning Conquests

This interpretation of Gómara's insular America finds some indirect corroboration in an unexpected source—the work of one of his most vociferous enemies, the Dominican friar Bartolomé de las Casas (1484–1566). This is unexpected, among other things, for the simple reason that geographical description of the kind I have been considering does not figure as prominently in the writing of Spain's noted critic of the conquest as it does in either that of Oviedo or Gómara. Geography certainly figures little among the issues that have most often fueled scholarly debate about the apostle of the Indies. Nonetheless, space and territory play a telling role in his writing. The friar's most famous—and certainly infamous—work, the 1542 *Brevíssima relación de la destrucción de las Indias* (Casas 1991; 1992), can easily be understood as an attempt to respond to Oviedo's attempt to populate the map of the Indies with historical memory and to anticipate Gómara's effort to do the same. Where those historians inscribe accounts of the marvelous, tales of native savagery, and memorable stories of European conquest, las Casas inscribes forlorn descriptions of Paradise Lost and gruesome exposés of conquistadorial voracity. More to the point, he does so through a systematic review of American toponymy. Each chapter takes up a major place name for which Oviedo and Gómara fabricate a historical memory—Hispaniola, Cuba, Tierra Firme, New Spain, Peru, among others—and fabricates for each a countermemory. The countermemory works by turning inside out the discourse of the other writers . While others readily admit to scenes of violence on the part of Spaniards, they couch those scenes in broader discursive contexts that mitigate their significance to any assessment of the justifiability of conquest. Las Casas, in effect, zeroes in on such scenes, renders them in hyperbolic terms, and eliminates all else so that violence—brutal, relentless, and gratuitous—is left to stand alone as the essence of conquest. Las Casas admits no exceptions, no isolated corners where cruelty has remained in check, where innocence lives on. Brief as it is, the Brevíssima relación maps the entire Indies as the geography of sadism.

But this approach to the Brevíssima relación is both rather obvious and somewhat beside the point in that it fails to get at the issue we have examined in Oviedo and Gómara, the use of prose cartography for the purposes of colonial historiography. Just as it takes liberty with historiography for rhetorical purpose, so the Brevíssima relación handles geography in a very loose manner, one determined by its rhetorical needs. The arrangement of these scenes of brutality in chapters named for the places where they occurred hardly forms a basis for comparison with the relatively precise geographical writing we have seen in Oviedo and Gómara. Luckily, las Casas wrote other things as well, including his own Historia de las Indias, a clear rival to the earlier efforts of Oviedo. Strangely, however, this extensive and ambitious project eschews detailed, precise descriptions of the Americas. For this kind of writing, we must turn to the first book of his Apologética historia sumaria (ca. 1555). There we find a very flattering description of the island of Hispaniola, one that begins with a prose cartography reminiscent, in precision if not in scope, of the sort of geographical writing we have seen in Oviedo and Gómara. As we shall see, the Apologética historia sumaria constitutes the scene of a problematic engagement with the cartography of empire as embodied in Oviedo and Gómara, one that allows us to glimpse the ideological issues at stake in all of this charting of coastlines with words.

Unpublished in its day and little read now, the Apologética historia sumaria represents las Casas's most sustained attempt to marshal geographical and ethnographical knowledge about the Americas into a reasoned defense of the humanity of the Amerindian. What little attention it has received from las Casas scholarship has tended to concentrate upon the third, and longest, of the text's three major divisions. This third section surveys the cultural achievements of the native inhabitants of the Americas in order to demonstrate that the ways the Amerindians governed their persons, their homes, and their societies demonstrated a high degree of cultural development, one commensurate, at least, with the pagan societies of ancient Greece and Rome. There we find a las Casas capable of portraying Amerindian culture with surprising generosity. Even the practice of human sacrifice, which had so often served Spaniards as evidence of Amerindian savagery, is in Apologética historia sumaria an instance of an admirable religious sensibility, to be respected as the manifestation of profound religious commitment, just as much as it is to be condemned for its misdirected violence (Casas 1967, 1: 242–46). Arguments like this one make it relatively simple for modern-day interpreters to find in the friar a precursor of their own sensibilities. Edmundo O'Gorman, for example, insists that, in this part of the *Apologética historia*, las Casas tells his contemporaries that in the presence of an Amerindian, they are "in the presence of their neighbor, that is to say, of a man just like him, just like he sees himself" (O'Gorman 1967, 63).

For most las Casas scholars, the first two sections hardly seem to exist at all.[33] This should not surprise us, since the argument there appeals to a thoroughly outmoded tradition of geographical determinism that easily steals the wind from any attempt to find in the friar's work the efforts of a forward-looking visionary. There, las Casas attempts to convince the reader that the native constitution of the Amerindian benefits from optimal astrological and environmental determinants. The argument relies on a minute description of the island of Hispaniola that renders the colony an Arcadian paradise, a description that occupies most of the first part of the text. The terms of the description are uniformly superlative. Hispaniola's central plain, "La Vega"—now known as the Cibao Valley—becomes the "true Elysian Fields" and the ideal setting for a new and extraordinary urban culture (1: 51–54). The island is found far superior—in both its inherent attractiveness and its utility for human habitation—to those of the Old World, including England, Sicily, and Crete (1: 103). The second part of the *Apologética historia* then recapitulates traditional notions about the ways that astrological and environmental forces influence human character in order to derive an anthropology from this description. It draws upon a variety of medieval sources, especially Albertus Magnus, in order to convince the reader that none but the most admirable of human beings could arise from such a place.

At the hinge between the descriptive chapters and the theoretical argument, las Casas makes an assertion that, more than anything else in the *Apologética historia*, compels me to identify the text as a foil to Gómara's history. In the twenty-second chapter of the work, las Casas claims that "these Indies" are "part of the true Indies" (Casas 1967, 109). In other words, he identifies himself with those contemporaries who continued to insist that the Americas formed part of Asia. The friar supports this claim through a series of comparisons between natural marvels that he himself has seen in the Americas with others he has read about in Pliny, Strabo, Mela, and others. As we shall see below, however, it is possible to read a more radical possibility into the language las Casas uses and thereby reach more provocative insights into the fortunes of cartography and empire in the sixteenth century. For this, it is necessary to return to the earlier descriptive material and examine the fortunes of prose cartography in the *Apologética historia*.

The description begins by placing Hispaniola on the map, through a reference to its latitude north of the equator, and its distance from Spain. It then
circumnavigates the island, stopping at significant places, in a series of passages similar to this one:

> From that Puerto Real, ten leagues, more or less, if memory serves me right, is
> the port of Monte-Christo, which the admiral thought most unique. Beyond this
> Monte Christi is the port of Isabella, where the admiral established the first town.
> (1: 12)

The passage reads much like Gómara's prose cartography. It traces the coastline from one significant stopping place to another, marking the distances between them but neglecting to mention directions. It reads like Oviedo's prose
cartography in that it does not limit itself to geographical information but
makes various kinds of remarks about the places it mentions. There, however,
the similarities with Gómara and Oviedo cease. Unlike Oviedo and Gómara,
las Casas never mentions that he has used a chart of the island as the source of
his information. Charts of Hispaniola did, indeed, exist, but if las Casas had
access to them, he does not mention them. He does this, moreover, because
he wants to associate his prose cartography as closely as possible with the
experience of travel. At first, the traveler in question is none other than the
"admiral," Christopher Columbus. The route around the island begins at
the point where the admiral made his first landfall on the Hispaniolan coast,
and from there on las Casas makes frequent reference to Columbus's account
of it. As we can see in the passage above, these references to Columbus do not
just serve as citations of source material. They also work to commemorate the
admiral's voyage through reverential citations of his opinions about places and
dutiful mention of his most important actions as discoverer and colonizer.
Through such commemorative allusion, las Casas lends what might otherwise
read like a prosaic outline of the island an air of originary authority. Hispaniola glows in the light of the discoverer and his foundational deeds.

But the passage above also demonstrates the marked presence of las Casas's
own voice in his prose cartography. As the text progresses, references to
Columbus's account gradually disappear, leaving las Casas's own experience as
the sole guarantor of the truth of the description, and his own voice as the sole
mediator between the European reader and the realities of Hispaniola. That
voice thereby attempts to inherit the cultural authority of the admiral's account. As the itinerary moves inland to places that Columbus never visited, the
voice acquires a body, one whose travails serve to underwrite its authority. We
read of las Casas's sufferings as he crosses the island's mountain ranges, of his
joy at discovering a spring of fresh water, of his marvel at seeing an enormous

gold nugget (1: 20, 24, 42, 45). By the time we arrive at the climactic description of the verdant plains of the interior, the most amenable region of an already superlative place, we are to believe what we read because las Casas assures us that, "I myself have covered [every league of the Vega] with my own feet" (1: 47). We are to believe what we read because the author and narrator is a long-suffering traveler whose troubles beg for our trust.

In this way, las Casas's narrative voice continues to resemble that of Oviedo, particularly the one we find in the passages of his prose cartography dedicated to the coast of Nicaragua, which Oviedo knew well, as well as the chapters dedicated to the interior of that country (Fernández de Oviedo 1959, 3. 42.1 and 5). There, like las Casas, Oviedo attempts to authorize his description by appealing to his personal experience of the country and to his sufferings in traversing it.[34] But, as Pagden argues, las Casas is much more insistent than Oviedo upon "the primacy of his eye, the uniqueness of his voice," going so far as to construct his narratives as the enunciations of a pseudo-prophetic visionary (Pagden 1993, 76). Thus while Oviedo cites various charts and distinguishes his opinions from those of others, las Casas would have us believe that he is writing his prose cartography from memory. Although he may acknowledge, as he does in the passage above, that this memory might be dim at times, this acknowledgment only serves to remind us that his memory is behind all this, responsible for everything that we do indeed read.[35]

The friar's attempt to fashion himself as the sole eye, the sole voice, reaches a fever pitch at a moment at once crucial and deeply ironic, when las Casas tells of his ascent of Hispaniola's highest peak and describes the Cibao Valley from the unique vantage point offered by its summit. By this point, the narrative has become intensely embodied, individualized, through repeated references to the friar's own suffering as a mountain climber. Las Casas looks out from the summit and describes the central plain as an unbounded, oceanic expanse:

> From whatever point of this mountain range that men choose to look out . . .
> twenty and thirty and forty leagues stretch out before them, just as if they were
> in the middle of the ocean, at some great height. I believe it to be true that another view as agreeable and delightful . . . in all the world cannot be heard of or
> imagined. (1: 48–49)

Las Casas then does something quite astonishing. Having figured the plain as an oceanic expanse, he asks, "What would the ancients have written about this most fertile island in which there are ten thousand corners, and in this whole orb of the Indies, millions of thousands of places, each one differs . . . from the best of the Canary Islands as does gold from iron and surely even much more?" (1: 50). From atop his perch, las Casas pretends to looks out, not just on Hispaniola, but on all of America. He looks out, moreover, only to find that the whole of the continent is commensurate, in amenity and utility, with the place he has called the "real Elysian fields," the central plain of the island of Hispaniola. That autoptic eye that should logically have remained committed to the local and the particular has become the disembodied onlooker implied by the surface of the map.

This moment is no *mere* hyperbole, no localized rhetorical excess. Nor is it a symptom of the megalomania implicit in las Casas's attempt to make himself the sole authoritative interpreter of the Americas for the European public. The implicit claim made here about both the narrator and the place he surveys—that one is a prophetic visionary and that the other is not just Hispaniola, but the whole of the Indies made available to the prophet's gaze—is, in fact, absolutely crucial to the las Casian defense of the Amerindian on the basis of the environmental determinants of his constitution. In order to defend the full humanity of the inhabitants of all the Americas, las Casas must establish that all of the New World offers circumstances as amenable as those of Hispaniola to the development of rational human beings. Later, he acknowledges as much, when he suggests momentarily that his descriptive discourse is about to reach out from its island base to encompass Tierra Firme as well. Having wrapped up his description of Hispaniola, las Casas writes, "Let us now enter into that most vast mainland" (1: 105). His text, however, immediately cuts off any detailed itinerary through the Americas even before it gets under way. "If we have said much about this island of Hispaniola and its neighbors, then with even greater earnestness," las Casas insists, "can we reasonably affirm the same and even greater excellences and properties of the mainland" (1: 105). No actual description of the mainland appears, since such a description could only be built from the various and certainly partial and varying accounts of numerous explorers. Lascasian authority, if Pagden is right about its prophetic cast, leaves no room for such a crowd. The text acknowledges that there are corners of the Americas that are no tropical paradise, mentioning specifically all of those insalubrious swamps that appear in Spanish accounts, but he does not allow such local particularities to muddy the universal amenity of his Indies. These places are reduced to the status of "monsters," flukes of nature with no power to contradict the truth of las Casas's audacious generalization (1: 108). The reader, then, is to believe what las Casas claims, that Hispaniola constitutes nothing less than a paradise on Earth that represents the Americas as a whole and that it is available to this one narrator who claims to have traversed only its most essential portion.

At this point, it is worth interrupting the discussion of las Casas to return, momentarily, to Gómara. The interpretation offered above of "El sitio de las Indias" and of its foundational role in the historiographical discourse of the text in which it appears makes an important assumption about Gómara's use of the term "isla" to describe the geography of the Americas. In exploring the ways this term serves to figure the Americas not just as a continent independent of Asia but as a coherent, apprehensible entity, as a naked body ready to be tattooed with a Eurocentric historical memory, it assumes that the sheer size of the Americas does not preclude its "insularization." [36] By this I mean the treatment of the Americas, in significant ways, as if it were a true island, defined as a fragmentary geographical entity normally understood through an implicit contrast with a much larger "mainland." [37] This assumption now finds some justification through comparison with las Casas. By generalizing his account of Hispaniola onto the whole of the Americas, las Casas does much the same thing that Gómara does, albeit in a very different way. Both authors, faced with the vast size and variety of the Americas, need to miniaturize the continent in order to domesticate it for historiographical and ideological purposes. In other words, they need to insularize it. Gómara does this by dramatically reducing the scale of Oviedo's cartography and calling the resultant map of America an "island." Las Casas, meanwhile, achieves the same objective by describing an actual island with which he is acquainted and then reducing the whole of the Indies to the status of an extension of that island. Apprehensible precisely because of its (true) insularity, Hispaniola, in effect, becomes nothing but the place where the essence of the New World reveals itself to the friar's prophetic eye.

Now, back to the *Apologética historia*. Las Casas must know that his narrative voice—however authoritative he tries to make it sound—cannot alone support so extravagant a generalization. Therefore, he bolsters his assertion with an argument built upon a selective appeal to the European tradition of geographic writing. Anticipating the theoretical argument that follows in the second section of the text, las Casas turns to the theory of climates, the old habit of supposing that the constitution of human beings was largely determined by the astrological and environmental factors attending to the latitudinal zone that they inhabited. Classical geographical thought had separated the world into five such zones, two frigid ones at the poles, two temperate ones in the middle latitudes, and a torrid zone along the equator. Renaissance cosmology tended to multiply the number of zones and to further distinguish among the characteristics of each. Drawing upon this tradition but moving against the grain of Renaissance cosmography, las Casas defines the Indies as one large zone, extending from the forty-fifth parallel north of the equator (ca. Nova Scotia), down to the forty-fifth parallel south of it (ca. Patagonia), and across 1,800 leagues of longitude (1: 105).³⁸ The zonal language, by definition, homogenizes the area contained within these boundaries and mitigates any differences between las Casas's experience of Hispaniola and anyone else's experience of any other place. It mediates between the limitations of autopsy and the need to generalize about the Indies. Far from inscribing an empty space available to the apprehensive imagination of the imperial apologist, moreover, the zonal language inscribes an America that comes equipped with a ready-made ontology, available to las Casas as eyewitness, and resistant to any characterization as the place of the natural slave.

Of course, in so doing las Casas does not make his case any stronger, since he has done nothing more than replace one baseless assertion (All of the Indies are like this place) with another (They are alike because they are all part of the same climatic zone). It is a move, however, that allows us to better understand the claim that las Casas makes soon afterward, that "these Indies" are part of "the true Indies," as well as to understand what this claim means to the relationship between geography and empire in the *Apologética sumaria*. By defining the boundaries of this zone in geometric terms, las Casas has, in effect, erased the island that he so painstakingly drew. This was already implicit in his description of the Americas from his perch atop what is now called Duarte Peak. There, he extends the oceanic expanse of Hispaniola's central plain beyond the mountains, beyond the coastline that he has so painstakingly traced, to fuse it not only with the ocean beyond that coast but also with the whole of the Indies, the New World in its entirety, itself figured as an oceanic expanse. This oceanic expanse then becomes the massive climatic zone delineated above. The coastline of Hispaniola traced by the prose cartography, in other words, ceases to matter as a significant boundary. It defines a place that is in no way unique but rather is only one portion of a uniformly amenable, uniformly useful, isotropic space.

This gesture, then, allows us to listen to a deafening silence in the chapter in which las Casas assimilates the Americas and Asia. As we have seen, las Casas defends his contention by listing natural marvels he has seen in America and others he has read about in classical sources, and insisting upon the identity of the latter with the former. At no point, however, does he say anything at all about the shapes of large landmasses or the ways in which they might be connected. In other words, he does not mention the central piece of the debate among Renaissance cosmographers in determining the "continental" or "insular" status of the Americas, the possibility that the Old World and the New might be connected in the North Pacific (or the North Atlantic) by a land bridge of some kind. Having erased the coastlines of the island of Hispaniola, las Casas abandons prose cartography altogether and, with it, any apparent interest in the geographical questions that were used to define America's status. Rather than answer Gómara's prose cartography with a counterdescription that would provide a concrete geographic link between, as he puts it, "these Indies" and "the true Indies," las Casas neither confirms nor denies anything about the geography of the continents.

The implication of this move is dramatic. Las Casas suggests that "these Indies" can be understood as a part of "the true Indies" *regardless of how the geography of the continents works out*. The Americas are "Asian," he argues, because they participate in the essence of that which is Asian as defined by classical geography, not because they are physically linked to the old *orbis terrarum*. It becomes possible for a moment to imagine a modality of early modern geographical thought independent of the age-old habit that informs Oviedo and Gómara in which large landmasses are each assigned characteristic human societies in ways that tend to privilege the locus of enunciation at the expense of the other places. Las Casas unwittingly opens a window on the possibility of dissociating human identity from the determinative importance of broad cartographic outlines, of sorting out *otherwise* what counts as a "place" and how that place relates to identity. But he opens this window only to immediately shut it. By describing the Indies as a homogeneous climatic zone, he inscribes them as a counterfeit continent, an alternative island, a space just as well bounded, just as enclosed, as Gómara's America, albeit mapped into a very different rhetoric of empire and its justification.

Conclusion: Posterior Metageographies

As a group, the prose cartographies of Oviedo, Gómara, and las Casas demonstrate both the importance of geographical writing to the early historiography of the Americas, as well as the diversity within that writing. In each case we have seen that writing the history of the Americas is inseparable from a foundational cartography that defines them as a coherent space. In each case, furthermore, we have seen how a shared language of cartographic description allows for subtle but significant variations that allow each historian to map the Americas with contours unique to his own historiographical and ideological objectives. We have also seen how those variations involve diverse deployments of the two spatialities, linear and planar, outlined above, and how neither spatiality can be strictly associated with either the discourse of empire or the discourse of imperial critique. Oviedo and Gómara, the more blatantly colonialist of the three writers examined here, are each much less "geometric" and "abstract" than las Casas, their rival and Spain's greatest critic of empire. If we want to find a space defined in purely abstract, neo-Ptolemaic terms, it is to las Casas that we must turn. Finally, here more than anywhere else in the material I analyze in this book we find that a map is the opposite of an illustration. It is the metageography of a historical discourse that serves to color the Americas with Eurocentric memory, that serves to render the continent available for apprehension by a colonial imagination or that serves to forestall such apprehension by figuring it as the home of our fellow human beings.

Much, however, remains to be said about geography and empire in the work of all three of these authors. Since it is the purpose of this book to open a debate about cartography, literature, and empire rather than to provide a definitive statement on the subject, I close this chapter with a glance at one final topic. Throughout, this chapter has taken Gómara quite seriously, ignoring altogether the many flashes of wit and irony that brighten the *Historia general*. One of those bright spots, however, comes during an episode with a strong cartographic theme related at the end of a series of chapters dedicated to the expedition of Ferdinand Magellan, which extended a Spanish claim to the Spice Islands that rivaled that of the Portuguese. The dispute eventually required cosmographers back home to renegotiate the 1494 Treaty of Tordesillas, which had divided the world between Portugal and Castile by specifying a meridian to be drawn at a certain distance west of the Azores. It did not, however, specify a number of controversial details necessary to determine where that line would fall in the Eastern Hemisphere.[39] Magellan's claim demanded an urgent resolution of the problem, and so cosmographers representing the interests of the Spanish and Portuguese crowns met to resolve the issue in the Castilian frontier city of Badajoz and the nearby Portuguese city of Elvas. One might expect Gómara's account of these negotiations to end with a resounding confirmation of Spanish claims. Instead, they end with an off-color joke. Incapable of determining longitude with any accuracy—like everyone else—the Iberian cosmographers could not resolve the problem of where to locate the crucial meridian. Gómara has the perplexed mapmakers walking through the city of Badajoz and falling upon a boy helping his mother with the laundry. The boy asks them if they are the men who are having so much trouble dividing up the world, and when they say yes, he lifts up his shirttail, bends over, presenting the cosmographers his buttocks, and tells them, "Draw the line right here in the middle" (López de Gómara 1979, 153).[40]

The boy's comment not only makes light of the supposedly serious business of imperial cartography, but it also opens a fissure through the center of Gómara's text. Gómara's decision to circumnavigate the Indies counterclockwise from Labrador, and then to use this route as the organizing principle of his text, places the chapters dedicated to the Strait of Magellan in the center of the composition. The verbal map, in other words, provides the *Historia general* not only with an ideological ground and a narrative disposition, but also with a symmetrical structure. That structure hinges geographically on the Strait of Magellan, and historiographically, on the voyage that discovers that strait. The narrative of that voyage has the effect of tying the Indies themselves to a larger geography. Alone among the stories of exploration and conquest that Gómara relates—save that of Columbus—the tale of the circumnavigation of the Earth by Magellan's flagship the *Victoria* begins and ends in Spain, passing into the Indies from the East and leaving them by way of the West. In this way, it anchors the Indies in a larger imperial geography, one reminiscent of the imperial hemisphere drawn by Fernández de Enciso. Gómara, however, deflates the solemnity that should mark such a narrative through the inclusion of an anecdote that converts imperial cartography, not to mention the *Historia general* that so depends upon it, into the butt of a joke.

A subsequent chapter attempts to recuperate the lofty tone of the narrative by recapitulating the story of the Treaty of Tordesillas. There, Gómara simply assumes that the Spice Islands fall on Spain's side of the line of demarcation, but does not explain the technical details, left unresolved by the cosmographers at Badajoz, that justify such an assumption (López de Gómara 1979, 154–55). In the meantime, why has he included the anecdote about the boy, which so brazenly ridicules the pretensions of cosmographers and monarchs to divide the world on maps? Is this merely an example of Gómara's wit getting the better of him? Or does it somehow erode the text's explicit commitments to mapping and empire? Alternatively, does its attest to the confidence of this text in the power of such things, a confidence so secure that it can afford a joke at its own expense? I will not attempt to answer these questions here. Rather, I offer them as examples of what we still have to learn from the cosmographic pages of the *Historia general*. If these pages seem sterile to a twentieth-century reader, it is only because we have forgotten that space represented for Gómara and perhaps for many of his readers much more than abstraction and the power that it lent.

Chapter 5 treats the last third of the sixteenth century and moves away from strictly historical writing in order to examine the complex historical epic of Alonso de Ercilla y Zúñiga, the *Araucana*. This is considered Spain's most successful attempt to assimilate the Americas within traditional discourse. It is a literary work that would not only become famous for its poetic accomplishments but that would become a centerpiece of Spanish writing about the Americas, spawning continuations, dramatizations, and even parodies. Ironically, we arrive also at the work that most consistently combines the spaces of the line and the plane, not, however, to either reconcile them or successfully hybridize them but to convert the tensions between them into one of the most complex meditations upon empire written during the early modern period. We will also take up the geography I have hinted at in my brief reflection on Gómara's Magellan chapters. In Ercilla, we find not only an American geography, but a global one. Like the episode in the *Historia general*, it relies heavily on the figure of Magellan to attach the Indies to a larger world, but unlike that episode, it corrodes that world with the sort of irony that Gómara only dribbles onto his map.

5

The *Araucana*, an epic poem from the latter half of the sixteenth century written by the soldier and courtier Alonso de Ercilla y Zúñiga (1533–94), represents one of the most important watersheds in the constitution of Spain's identity as an imperial power. In 1492, the Spanish humanist Antonio de Nebrija—writing just as the kingdom of Castile and Leon completed the Reconquest of Granada—challenged Castilian intellectuals to bring about the translatio studii that must follow the kingdom's successful assumption of empire (Nebrija 1992).[1] In effect, Ercilla responded to this challenge by writing in a genre that, during the Renaissance, promised more than any other to establish the authority of a vernacular culture. His epic poem imitates and competes with those of Virgil, Lucan, Ariosto, and eventually, Camões, in a bid for pride of place among the laureates of Spanish and European letters and for the supremacy of Castilian as a cultivated language. Although today, like so many other epic poems, it inspires enthusiasm only among a small group of literary critics, the *Araucana* was something of a sensation in its own time, rapidly assuming the status of a bestseller. On two separate occasions, Cervantes praises Ercilla's text as the finest epic poem ever written in Spanish (1987, 425; 1998, 1 : 86–87).[2] The *Araucana* represents the first European text to successfully import into an authoritative literary genre the peoples, places, and events of the encounter with America. It tells the story of Spain's efforts to quell the rebellion of the Araucanian Indians in the south of Chile, an area that was to become famous—in no small measure due to Ercilla's own portrayal of it—as the site of ferocious resistance to Spain's hegemony over America. For succeeding generations, the *Araucana* would become a literary treasure-trove of things American, providing narrative material and pseudoethnographic data for numerous literary imitations and continuations, both epic and dramatic. What is often lost in this story of the success of the *Araucana*, however, is the very self-conscious manner in which Ercilla's poem addresses the problems of forging a trans-Atlantic, even global, imperial identity. The conventional, laudatory sonnets that open the poem speak of the poet's successful flight from the farthest reaches of the known world to the very summit of Mount Parnassus, but the text they introduce belies such easy transpositions, such triumphant mappings. From the tradition of learned epic, Ercilla inherits a poetic form powerfully embedded in the discourse of travel, movement, and displacement but one that also aspires to a kind of geographical encyclopedism that can, in some ways, be called cartographic. Ercilla's poem develops both of these possibilities inherent in the genre in which he writes and eventually places them in conversation with each other. This inscribes both a triumphant cartography of empire and a critical counter-cartography of imperial desire. Its indisputable importance to early modern Spanish letters, as well as this very innovative treatment of cartographic discourse, earns for the *Araucana* a prominent place in my discussion of imperial cartographic discourse in sixteenth-century Spain. Ercilla's poem represents, I believe, its crowning achievement and serves as a fitting subject for this final chapter.

A single episode from the *Araucana*, its so-called *mappamundi* episode, stands out when we consider the poem as a piece of cartographic literature. Ercilla— who appears in his own poem as one of its principal characters as well as its narrator—has the opportunity to tour the entire world through the mediation of a crystal ball in the possession of the Chilean sorcerer Fitón. The sorcerer names the various places that appear in the crystal ball, calling upon Ercilla, not to mention the imaginative reader, to see them as they materialize. The reader thus encounters them as a series of successive toponyms appearing either in isolation or accompanied by brief epithets or even micronarratives. The following octave serves as an example:

Mira luego a Madrid, que buena suerte
le tiene el alto cielo aparejada;
y a Toledo, fundada en sitio fuerte,
sobre el dorado Tajo levantada;
mira adelante a Córdoba, y la muerte
que airada amenazando está a Granada,
esgrimiendo el cuchillo sobre tantas
principales cabezas y gargantas.

[Look, then, toward Madrid, which the heavens have adorned with good fortune;
and then toward Toledo, founded on a mighty site, above the golden Tagus raised;
Look onward to Córdoba, and death, which, ireful, threatens Granada, brandish-
ing the knife over so many noble heads and throats.] (Ercilla 1993, 27.35)[3]

The forward movement of the itinerary, at once discursive and geographic,
links the successive toponymy into a whole. That itinerary begins at the
Bosporus, and then moves eastward from the Levant to the East Indies. It then
turns back westward, traces through the Middle East and into Africa, and
finally northward into Europe. Spain is the last European country visited before the route crosses the Atlantic to the New World, where it eventually
works its way southward toward Chile. From there, the itinerary crosses the
Pacific to the Spice Islands in the east, thereby encompassing the entire globe.
In this way, the *mappamundi* episode provides a poetic double to the prose cartographies that we saw in the previous chapter. It also recalls one of the maps
I mentioned in chapter 1, the map of the world drawn by Battista Agnese,
which so prominently figures the track of Magellan's *Victoria* (fig. 1 above).

Read from the perspective of this map and of other such maps of mastery,
the *mappamundi* episode seems to sing the praises of Philip's far-flung empire.
In this way, it can be understood as echoing the historical juncture during
which it was composed. Ercilla was a courtier who from a young age dedicated himself to the service of Philip II, that monarch who, as we saw in
chapter 2, keenly appreciated the importance of geography to power. The
mappamundi episode was written most likely during the years after the initial
publication of the *Theatrum orbis terrarum* of Abraham Ortelius (1570), whose famous title page engraving depicts the various parts of the world through an allegory that leaves no room for doubt about which part, according to its maker,
is and should be in charge of the whole. Europa sits triumphantly atop the
assembly of continents, adorned with the trappings of might, knowledge, and
civility. America, by contrast, lies nude beneath her, surrounded by her primitive weapons and her hammock, holding aloft the gory remains of her can-
nibalistic feast. And lest we should forget that the power behind the authority
of Europa is none other than Hapsburg Spain, the atlas comes dedicated to
Philip II himself. The *Araucana*, likewise dedicated to Philip, seems to reiterate
the imperial cartographies of both the Agnese map and the Ortelius illustration.[4] In two episodes leading up to the visionary *mappamundi*, the poem departs
from its Chilean subject matter in order to depict famous Spanish military
victories in Europe and the Mediterranean. The sequence of episodes thus
celebrates Christian right and Spanish might and thereby provides a frankly
imperialistic context in which to read the *mappamundi* episode. In that episode,

in turn, Ercilla's verse cartography circumnavigates the world like the Agnese map, and thereby attests to its intellectual and political apprehensibility by the monarch to whom it is addressed. Like the Ortelius illustration, the three episodes together place a triumphant Hispania at the head of an imperious Europa, the former rightfully commanding the other three parts of the world.[5]

Of course, readers of the *Araucana* and of recent criticism of Ercilla's text know that it can and has been read in other ways as well. Its portrayal of the war in Chile often depicts the Araucanians quite sympathetically, as noble heroes reminiscent of the most admirable figures in European chivalric and epic literature. The poem often depicts the Spaniards, in turn, as venal conquistadors capable of horrendous cruelty. As the text progresses, this suggestive contrast in the depiction of the men is joined by the portrayal of various Araucanian women, who appear to give voice to the suffering of their country. These and other characteristics of the poem have led a number of its readers to conclude that the *Araucana* actually criticizes, rather than celebrates, Spanish imperialism, or at least Spain's imperial project in Chile.[6] But for those who would read the poem in this way, Fitón's map, as I call the itinerary across the Old and New Worlds that takes up so much of the *mappamundi* episode, and the episodes associated with it become a liability. These manifest celebrations of Spanish heroism, Christian right, and Hapsburg majesty stand in stark contrast to the antiheroic, unjust, and even inhumane comportment of the Spanish in Arauco. This contrast would seem to require us to read the *Araucana* in one of two ways: Either the text celebrates Spanish imperialism as a whole but laments the serious shortcomings it suffers in a peripheral colony, or it criticizes Spanish imperialism as a whole by somehow allowing its critical attitude toward the conquest in Chile to contaminate the manifestly imperialistic episodes associated with Fitón's map.[7] Although many influential interpreters of the *Araucana* have favored the first possibility, ultimately, I believe, the second is the more convincing. Whatever other aspects of the text may reveal a spirit critical of Spain's imperial enterprise as a whole, the cartographic discourse of the *Araucana* is the decisive indication.

That cartographic discourse is by no means limited to the *mappamundi* episode, that verse cartography that so resembles the prose cartographies I treated in chapter 4. There, I argued that the prose descriptions of American coastlines found in the histories of Oviedo and Gómara indeed grounded their historiography and ideology. Here, I argue the opposite with regard to Ercilla's itinerary around the world. The *mappamundi* episode should not be understood as the poem's metageography but instead as the imperial cartography that the *Araucana* interrogates. Its true metageography is to be found elsewhere, in another passage from this text that is so intensely cartographic from beginning to end. This passage consists of an apparently irrelevant account of the Strait of Magellan, an account that forms part of the poem's opening verse cartography of Chile. As we shall see, in the first section of this chapter, this account is anything but irrelevant. It inscribes the poem's true metageography, a metageography inseparable from the poem's doubts about Spain's imperial ambitions. In the next section, I examine how this metageography is brought into play against the verse cartography of the *mappamundi* episode as well as against the other episodes that lead up to the vision in the crystal ball. In the third section of the chapter, I turn to a discrete episode from the final cantos of the poem, one which tells of an expedition south of the theater of war in search of the mouth of the strait. This episode provides a coda to the poem's various efforts not to celebrate empire but to question it, as well as to mock the totalizing pretensions of imperial cartographic literature on a global scale. There we see how Ercilla's text finally implodes in self-parody, pessimism, even despair.

A Strait instead of a Shoestring (Part 1 of the *Araucana*)

The *Araucana* was written over the course of roughly three decades and published in successive installments.[8] Each part represents a novel experiment in the composition of heroic narrative in verse. Part 1, which appeared in 1569, is famous for eschewing the fabulations of chivalric romance—and with it, the influential example set earlier in the century by Ludovico Ariosto's *Orlando furioso*—for the dire deeds of contemporary history.[9] It delivers on this promise from the start, it has been argued, by mapping Chile as a real world setting rather than as some far-off literary land (Pierce 1984, 40–42):

> Es Chile norte sur de gran longura,
> costa del nuevo mar, del Sur llamado,
> tendrá del leste a oeste de angostura
> cien millas, por lo más ancho tomado;
> bajo del polo Antártico en altura
> de veinte y siete grados, prolongado
> hasta do el mar Océano y chileno
> mezclan sus aguas por angosto seno.
>
> Y estos dos anchos mares, que pretenden,
> pasando de sus términos, juntarse,
> baten las rocas, y sus olas tienden,
> mas eles impedido allegarse;
> por esta parte al fin la tierra hienden

y pueden por aquí comunicarse.
Magallanes, Señor, fue el primer hombre
que, abriendo este camino, le dio nombre.

[Chile is of great length, along the coast of the new sea called the South Sea. It measures approximately one hundred miles in width from east to west along its broadest part. It is at twenty-seven degrees below the Antarctic pole and extends itself to where the Ocean Sea and the Chilean Sea mingle their waters through a narrow cleavage.

And these two wide seas aspire—overflowing their limits—to come together, beat the rocks, extend their waves, but are impeded from doing so. But here, at last, they pierce the land and can through here communicate. Magellan, My Lord, was the first man who, opening this way, gave it his name.] (1.7–8)

Stanza 7 locates Chile on the map. Chile is no amorphous, distant "elsewhere" but a precisely demarcated portion of the earth's surface, whose location relative to any other point on that surface is readily determinable. In this way, a distant, unknown periphery of Spain's far-flung empire becomes an apprehensible *place*, a location on an isotropic sphere just as available to the ringing cadence of the *octava real* as any familiar setting in the Old World. Such precision is unheard of in epic poems, which usually open with the heat of a battle, the thrill of the chase, or the terrors of a storm, rather than with the calm rationality of geographical description and certainly not with the technical precision of modern cartography.[10] The poem that sings the Chilean war announces its own modernity, its intention to outdo its romance-encumbered Italian precursors not by following their example but by breaking with it.

The passage does all this only to then wander off into an apparent digression. Stanza 8 focuses specifically on the Strait of Magellan, which lies far to the south of the theater of war. Why mention it at all? For starters, Renaissance geography did not think of the Strait of Magellan as an everyday geographical feature. If the primordial act of God's creation consisted in calling up the earth from beneath the sea, then surely those few places where God had allowed the waters to transgress the land that otherwise kept them apart were wondrous indicators of a providential design. For Spain, the strait held particular significance. Its discovery seemed to promise that Spanish commercial interests would finally be able to reach the East by sailing west. And so, the English made plans to seize the Strait of Magellan while the Spanish fretted about its defense. Such enthusiasm for the commercial potential of the strait was not universal, and it waned quickly after the route west through Magellan's passage proved impractical (Gerbi 1985, 102–3, 370). Nonetheless, natural historians like the Jesuit José de Acosta continued to believe that the strait con-

32   Theodor de Bry, after Hans Galle, "The Discovery of the Sea of Magellan," in *America pars*
quarta (1594). Magellan holds an armillary sphere in his hands while he sails through
the strait that bears his name. Above his head is the standard of Charles V. Artillery litters
the deck of his ship. The Albert and Shirley Small Special Collections Library, University
of Virginia.

stituted nothing less than one of the wonders of the world (1986, 179). More
than half a century later, John Milton found it fit to mention only three modern names in *Paradise Lost*: Columbus, Galileo, and Magellan.[11] Theodor de Bry
commemorated its discovery with an engraving in the fourth part of his *America*, based on an earlier illustration by Hans Galle (fig. 32). There, Magellan sits
aboard his ship as it penetrates the passage that would come to bear his name.
He holds an armillary sphere in his hands, testifying to the unity of cosmography and exploration in reducing the cosmos to the status of an apprehensible object. Cannon litter the deck, and the arms of Charles V flutter overhead,
attesting to the will of Europeans to convert apprehension into possession by
force, in the name of Christian empire. They identify Magellan's discovery and
transgression of the southwest passage as a new *plus ultra* for a new geography
and an ever-expanding empire.[12] What better way, then, to begin an epic poem

meant to monumentalize Spain's imperial achievements than by recalling that geographic wonder created by Providence so that Spain could realize its expansionist desires and exceed the limits of the known world not just once, but twice in a single generation?

But then Ercilla's text takes another strange twist when it extends its treatment of the Strait of Magellan into the following stanza:

> Por falta de pilotos, o encubierta
> causa, quizá importante y no sabida,
> esta secreta senda descubierta
> quedó para nosotros escondida;
> ora sea yerro de la altura cierta,
> ora que alguna isleta, removida
> del tempestuoso mar y viento airado
> encallando la boca, la ha cerrado.

> [For lack of pilots or because of a hidden cause, perhaps important and unknown, this discovered secret pathway became hidden to us. Perhaps there was an error in the latitude, or perhaps some islet, moved by the tempestuous sea and ireful wind, shutting up the mouth of the strait, has closed the passage.] (1.9)

José de Acosta and Antonello Gerbi, although separated by centuries, concur that this stanza offers a speculative explanation for the difficulty that Spanish navigators experienced in finding the entrance to Magellan's passage (Acosta 1986, 179; Gerbi 1985, 102 n. 8). In this sense, it has nothing whatsoever to do with the poem's narrative content.

I argue instead that this stanza is crucial to understanding the entire poem. Of particular importance is the suggestion made in the last three verses of the octave, where the poet suggests that the eastern entrance to the strait may have been closed by a natural catastrophe of sorts. An island, he wonders, may have been uprooted by the tempestuous sea and now plugs the entrance to Magellan's wondrous passage. With this bizarre suggestion, the stanzas dedicated to the Strait of Magellan inscribe the counter-cartography of Ercilla's *Araucana*.

In order to understand the function of the stanzas on the strait, we must first remember that much of Ercilla's poetics consists in simultaneously availing himself as much as possible of both the figurative and the referential potential of poetic language. Single passages can remit the reader simultaneously to both a historico-geographical referent as well as to some aspect of the literary tradition.[13] In the case of this particular passage, geographical referentiality comes accompanied by an intertext with a passage from Lucan's *Pharsalia* that loads the geography with historical and ideological freight quite different from that suggested above. The intertext with the passage from Lucan is in itself significant, as others have argued. The first-century Lucan hailed from Cordoba, and like other prominent figures from Roman times born in the Iberian Peninsula, he was considered by early modern Spaniards as one of their countrymen. By turning to Lucan as a source, here as elsewhere, Ercilla inserts himself into a tradition of heroic verse narrative that is at once ancient and national (Nicolopulos 2000, 127).[14] But Ercilla borrows more from this ancient Cordoban than just the prestigious mantle of antiquity. In his description of Chile and the Strait of Magellan, Ercilla emulates a passage taken from early on in the *Pharsalia*. In the years prior to the war, Lucan writes, Marcus Licinius Crassus shared power in the First Triumvirate with Pompey and Caesar. Lucan then casts Crassus as the keeper of the peace between two rivals, an isthmus—the isthmus of Corinth—that preserves the order of the cosmos by keeping the seas separate:

Temporis angusti mansit concordia discors,
Paxque fuit non sponte ducum; nam sola futuri
Crassus erat belli medius mora. Qualiter undas
Qui secat et geminum gracilis mare separat Isthmos
Nec patitur conferre fretum, si terrra recedat,
Ionium Aegaeo frangat mare: sic, ubi saeva
Arma ducum dirimens miserando funere Crassus

[For a brief space the jarring harmony was maintained, and there was peace despite the will of the chiefs; for Crassus, who stood between, was the only check on imminent war. So the Isthmus of Corinth divides the main and parts two seas with its slender line, forbidding them to mingle their waters; but if its soil were withdrawn, it would dash the Ionian Sea against the Aegean. Thus Crassus kept apart the eager combatants.] (Lucan 1928, 1.98–104)

The impending civil war thus becomes nothing less than a cosmographical catastrophe, the rupture of the Isthmus of Corinth and the subsequent mingling of the seas.[15] Ercilla emulates Lucan by transforming Chile into an isthmus, emphasizing how this slender, elongated piece of land that stretches between South America and the Terra Australis keeps apart the "two broad seas."[16] Ercilla, however, inverts the nature of the transformation that, in Lucan, announces the war. In the *Araucana*, the Strait of Magellan is the natural given, so the change invoked by the poem does not consist in the disastrous opening of the "fretum (waters/strait)," but in its closure. An islet, Ercilla writes, has been hurled into the mouth of the Strait of Magellan by a cataclysmic storm. Readers who pick up on the Latin subtext can surmise, by analogy, that this suggestion somehow suggests the revolt of the Araucanians against Spanish rule and the start of the Chilean war.

But in order to understand how this passage figures the coming of war, we must first defamiliarize this description of Chile and then look more closely at Ercilla's subtle invocation of the language of gender and sexuality. If in stanza 7 we find a "shoestring" geography, it is only because we all too readily bring to our reading the exceedingly naturalized cartographies of later generations. Notice that Ercilla at no point resorts to a single mnemonic device, like "shoestring," to describe Chile in a manner that would be easy to visualize and remember. Alonso de Góngora Marmolejo, by contrast, begins his chronicle of the conquest of Chile, written between 1572 and 1575, with just such a device: "The kingdom of Chile is of the manner of the sheath of a sword, narrow and long" (1960, 79). Rather than reduce Chile to a single visual metaphor, Ercilla uses a close succession of figurative strategies to map Chile into both cartographic and ideological space. The first of these three octaves begins in the register of cartographic realism but ends with a peculiar insinuation. Rather than mark Chile's southern limit with a measure of latitude, it alludes to that place where "the Ocean Sea and the Chilean Sea mingle [mezclan] their waters through a narrow cleavage." The poet is referring to the Strait of Magellan, of course, but simple reference is not the only point. The verb mezclar—to mix, to mingle—carries an undertone of iniquity, one that charges this location with particular interest but not of the kind one might expect.

Ercilla develops the transgressive connotations of mezclar into what I call a geographical erotics. The seas, presuming to unite, lap lasciviously at the shores of the continent. Finally, the land parts, revealing a narrow passageway through which the seas can mix, transgress their natural limits. A man appears, penetrating that passageway and giving it his surname. The erotic tension created by the flirtations and transgressions of the seas finds its release in this figure of geographical exploration as the penetrative consummation of a relationship between the explorer and the land. The avoidance of a specific mnemonic device can now be understood as an ideologically productive gesture. The shape of Chile would seem to lend itself more readily to devices with phallic connotations that are inconvenient for figuring colonial desire through images of landscape gendered as female. Góngora Marmolejo's device avoids this problem. He describes Chile not as the masculine sword but as the feminine sheath, or "vaina," a word derived from the Latin root vagina. Ercilla's gesture is more radical. It entirely displaces the potentially masculine geography of Chile with the unambiguously feminine figure of the strait. Magellan arrives to make an honest woman out of the land he penetrates and names.

In this light, it can be no accident that the Araucana introduces both the passage and its discoverer only to then announce that the strait is now closed. At the new strait, Ercilla throws down a new prohibition, a new *non plus ultra*. The poem now closes the strait and thus blocks the imperial itinerary of any future Magellan. The strait becomes an emblem for the will to resist not only Spanish desires to conquer Chile but Spanish desires for an empire that encompasses all the world. The next stanza abandons the strait, zooming out to the image of Chile stretching along a thousand leagues, the thin line that now effectively separates the flirtatious seas and that stands in the way of universal monarchy (1.10). To put this in the gendered and sexualized language that Ercilla himself invokes, the Strait of Magellan recovers its hymen. Chile becomes, like Walter Raleigh's Guyana, a "countrey that hath yet her maydenhead." [17] In this way, Ercilla evokes a piece of the world's geography that had come to represent colonial desire, the impulse to empire, the drive to both apprehend the world and to possess it, but for an unexpected purpose. Ercilla evokes the Strait of Magellan and all that it represents not to celebrate the impending universal monarchy of the Spanish Hapsburgs but to frustrate their desire for domination. In this way, his description of Chile—or, more precisely, his apparently irrelevant description of the Strait of Magellan—becomes a subtle counter-cartography of imperial desire.

But how does this brief description of the Strait of Magellan and its closure become the metageography of the *Araucana* as a whole? Ercilla makes poetic and ideological use of the fact that the conflict in the south of Chile consisted primarily of movements along a north-south axis, along a series of difficult positions ripe for fortification., or easily adapted to the tactics of ambush and raid. Repelled from the south of Chile early in part 1, Ercilla's Spaniards must then fight their way back southward along the ribbon of Chilean geography (fig. 22 above), punching their way through narrow gorges or treacherous mountain passes in order to reach Arauco proper. The spatiality of the *Araucana* thus comes to resemble that of Hernán Cortés's "Segunda carta de relación." It takes the form of a linear itinerary marked by battlegrounds instead of cities and oriented toward an object of desire, the indigenous heartland that takes the place of Tenochtitlán. That heartland is figured in the poem as a *locus amoenus* where the Araucanian Senate meets, where Caupolicán is chosen as their leader, and where the Araucanians celebrate their victories. Unlike other pastoral settings in the poem, this one is never located in the geography of Chile with any precision: the reader knows only that it lies somewhere at the end of the itinerary taken by the Spanish conquerors. The battlegrounds that occupy the nodes of this itinerary are frequently described with language clearly reminiscent of the image of Magellan, his strait, and even the island that has closed it off. The battles that take place at these figurative straits often go badly for the Spaniards, who find themselves—to borrow the expression that Ercilla constantly reiterates—*en estrecho puesto*, in dire straits.[18]

Part 1 of the *Araucana*—indeed, the entire text—lends itself to a lengthy analysis of its many *estrechezas*, its dire straits, which can take the form of mountain passes, treacherous wilderness trails, or secret pathways through the hills into the heart of a fortified position. I will limit myself to only one example from part 1, the first of the *estrechezas* into which the Spanish stumble.[19] The Spanish, poised for their initial counterattack against the rebellion of the Araucanians, must cross the Andalicán River, climb the mountain beyond it, and then penetrate a narrow mountain pass in order to enter the territory controlled by the indigenous rebels. The pass is described in the following terms:

> Un paso peligroso, agrio y estrecho
> de la banda del norte está a la entrada,
> por un monte asperísimo y derecho,
> la cumbre hasta los cielos levantada;
> está tras éste un llano, poco trecho,
> y luego otra menor cuesta tajada
> que divide el distrito andalicano
> del fértil valle y límite Araucaniano.

> [A pass, dangerous, difficult and narrow, through a very rough, upright mountain, its peak raised to the skies, forms the entrance from the north. A short way behind this pass is a field, and then another smaller, upright slope which divides the Andalicanian district from the fertile valley that marks the border of Arauco] (4.90; emphasis added)

Note that in order to get to the Araucanian heartland, the object of desire, the Spaniards must penetrate a treacherous pass between the mountains, described specifically as "estrecho." One of the Chilean heroes, Lautaro, waits in the heights above the pass to ambush the Spaniards, who soon find themselves "en estrecheza," their way blocked by the Araucanian attack (5.44). Not only does this passage represent the first instance of battle topography rendered in the language of *estrecheza*, but it also converts the figurative resistance of Chile encoded by the closure of the strait into a brutal narrative of gendered revenge. Repelled from the pass, many of the Spaniards, including the women who accompany the soldiers, fall into Araucanian hands. These men are butchered, while the women are figuratively raped, literally killed, and their babies aborted:

> Unos vienen al suelo mal heridos,
> de los lomos al vientre atravesados;

por medio de la frente otros hendidos;
otros mueren con honra degollados;
. . . .
Y a las tristes mujeres delicadas
el debido respeto no guardaban,
antes con más rigor por las espadas,
sin escuchar sus ruegos, las pasaban;
no tienen miramiento a las preñadas,
mas los golpes al vientre encaminaban,
y aconteció salir por las heridas
las tiernas pernezuelas no nacidas.

[Some fall to the ground, sorely wounded, pierced through from back to stom-
ach, others have their foreheads cleaved open; others die honorably, beheaded . . .
And toward the sad, delicate women, they did not afford the respect that was
their due: rather, onto their swords they cast them, without heeding their pleas.
They have no regard for the pregnant ones: rather, they direct their blows directly toward their wombs. And so it came to pass that tender, unborn little legs
stuck out of their wounds.] (6.35–36)

That American masculinity, that phallic sword, that had been repressed in the
initial description of Chile so to figure the land as feminine and compliant
rather than masculine and resistant, now returns to take its revenge upon
those who would have penetrated and possessed the land. The bodies of the
purported conquerors are dismembered, while the women who accompany
them—with their unborn children—become of the victims of a sexualized,
violent response to Spanish colonial desire.

This scene—a battle fought in the dire straits of some Chilean *estrecheza*,
figured with language that recalls the initial account of the Strait of Magellan—
repeats itself throughout the *Araucana*. Sometimes, Spanish efforts to penetrate
the land are brutally repelled, as they are here, by the Araucanian enemy. At
other times, the Spanish successfully punch through the strait in question, but
only to despoil the land that lies beyond or to exact revenge upon the Araucanians in ways that rival their brutality here. We thus find ourselves contin-
ually revisiting the same scene of colonial desire, of penetration and possession, of resistance and loss. The metageography of the text, the language of
dire straits, can thus be understood as something of a counter-cartography. It
sets up a spatial figure that inherently and repeatedly resists Spanish efforts
to penetrate the land to conquer Chile. This, however, is not the sum total of
the *Araucana*'s cartographic discourse. In part 2 of the poem, Ercilla brings this
metageography of *estrecheza*, this counter-cartography of empire, into play with
a cartographic discourse of a very different kind, one that maps Chile into a

larger imperial space, both through the juxtaposition of battles in the New World with their counterparts in the Old, and the explicit description of that space in the poem's verse cartography of the world.

Mapping Universal Empire (Part 2 of the *Araucana*)

The cartographic strategies of part 2 of the *Araucana* are a good deal more explicit than the language of *estrechezas* pioneered in part 1. Part 2 of the *Araucana*, which was published in 1578, reverses the stated program of rejecting romance fabulation by introducing magic and prophecy in addition to love.[20] It does so by mixing clearly fictional material derived from the romance tradition with the putatively documentary substance of the *Araucana*. Ironically, part 2 also introduces the eyewitness testimony of its author, who participated in part of the Spanish campaign to subdue this troublesome periphery of its American empire. Part 2 alternates between its account of the Chilean war, narrated in the first person by Ercilla himself, and a series of clearly fictional episodes that together constitute the poem's so-called "web of prophecy."[21] The web of prophecy is absolutely central to my analysis of Ercilla, since it constitutes the most explicit locus of what can be referred to as the poem's imperial cartography. The series of fictional episodes begins with a vision that allows the narrator Ercilla from his vantage point in remote Chile, to witness the capture of the French city of Saint Quentin (1557) by forces under the personal direction of Philip II. The dream also foretells that Ercilla will eventually witness other wonders while under the tutelage of the indigenous sorcerer Fitón (17.38–18). Later, he indeed finds himself in Fitón's underground dwelling, before a crystal ball in which he witnesses the celebrated 1571 Christian victory over the fleet of the Ottoman Turks at the Battle of Lepanto (23.23–24.98). Even later, Ercilla finds himself in Fitón's cave before his crystal ball, dazzled by a vision of the whole world, highlighting the enormous portion that falls under the sway of Philip's crown (26.40–27.58). Together, these episodes dramatically expand the geography of Ercilla's text. They link events on the colonial periphery with renowned military triumphs in the metropolitan center and then refer the whole to a universal geography built out of a verse itinerary.

The web of prophecy constitutes the most intensely self-consciously literary portion of the entire *Araucana*, engaging in ways both obvious and not so obvious any number of poetic precursors. It also represents Ercilla's most elaborate attempt to invest his poem with that encyclopedic "expansiveness" that Thomas Greene considers typical of epic poetry. For Greene, "expansiveness" refers to a number of conventional practices that contribute to the "epicness" of epic, including a particular way of handling space. Whereas tragedy unfolds in a closed and confining space, epic inscribes a totalizing, perfectly visible space which Greene calls the poem's "epic universe":

> Epic answers to man's need to clear away an area he can apprehend, if not dominate, and commonly this area expands to fill the epic universe, to cover the known world and reach heaven and hell. Epic characteristically refuses to be hemmed in, in time as well as space, it raids the unknown and colonizes it . . . We feel as readers that our eye can move easily over the well-lit space before us, that no occasional shadow will forever baffle our gaze. (1963, 10–11)[22]

Epic, in other words, is inherently geographical and colonial. It engages the encounter between here and there, self and other, the domestic and the foreign, not as an accidental theme but as an essential concern. It does so, moreover, for the purpose of achieving symbolic mastery over the whole. Whether Greene is right about the genre in general, his remarks seem tailormade when applied to Iberian verse narrative, which repeatedly constructs an expansive epic universe through deliberate geographical description of the kind that we find in Fitón's map.[23] In the work of Ercilla's Iberian precursors, however, episodes like this work to flatter the potentate to whom the poem is addressed. I contend, however, that Ercilla's text only *appears* to genuflect before the might of the Spanish Hapsburgs. The *Araucana* frames its prophetic visions of monarchical justice, providential triumph, and imperial grandeur with a series of battle narratives whose ideological thrust becomes all the more evident as they come to rely upon the language of *estrecheza* pioneered in part 1. This play of an imperial cartography with the poem's counter-cartography of colonial desire allows us to read Ercilla's text, in the end, as an indictment of Philip's world.

In the *Araucana*, Saint Quentin and Lepanto are not juxtaposed with the Chilean war in some general way: the poem deliberately pairs each of these two metropolitan victories with two particular colonial military encounters. Ercilla casts Saint Quentin as the European mirror of the Chilean battle of Penco, and Lepanto as the Mediterranean double of the Battle of Millarpué. In each case, specific imagery and language serve to pair the American scene with the metropolitan one. In the case of the first pair, for example, Ercilla emphasizes the physical presence of Philip II at Saint Quentin while underscoring his symbolic presence at Penco:

cuanto fue de nosotros *coronada*
de una gruesa muralla la montaña,
de fondo y ancho foso rodeada,
con ocho gruesas piezas de campaña,

siendo a vista de Arauco levantada
bandera por Felipe, Rey de España,
tomando posesión de aquel Estado
con los demás del padre renunciado.

[As we crowned the mountain with a thick wall, surrounded by a deep, wide moat, and armed with eight great field pieces, and within sight of Arauco, raised a standard for Philip, king of Spain, thus taking possession of that state along with the others renounced by his father.] (17.26).[24]

It is not just the flag, but the mountain itself, crowned by the fort as if it were the head of the king, that figures the presence of the monarch. At Lepanto, meanwhile, the Ottoman foe appears in terms derived from classical epic poetry as an assemblage of the many nations of the East arrayed against the valiant but diminutive forces of the West (24.15, 24.34–36). The account of Lepanto, meanwhile, separates the narrative of the Battle of Millarpué from an earlier "gallery of heroes," a description of the combatants typical of epic poetry. Ercilla's description casts the Spaniards and the Araucanians in terms that recall his ancient precursors. The Chilean enemy becomes an enormous and exotic host (21.27–50) reminiscent of the large multinational armies of the East in both the Battle of Actium as narrated by Virgil and the Battle of Pharsalia as narrated by Lucan (Virgil 1909, 8.675–728; Lucan 1928, 3). The Spaniards—New World doubles of the Romans at Actium or the imperialists at Pharsalia—become a small but fearsome power arrayed against all the might the land can muster (21.19–26). Don García Hurtado de Mendoza—commander of the expeditionary force sent from Peru to quell the Araucanian revolt and the king's representative in Chile—calls upon his men to subdue the barbarians and thereby give Spain sway over the whole of the world (21.52). "Set, truly, your strong hearts and tempered souls against these barbarians," he tells them, "for, having conquered this last remnant, you shall clearly have all the world within your grasp" (21.53). Likewise, Don Juan of Austria—Philip's illegitimate half-brother and commander of the Christian forces at Lepanto—urges his men on with a stirring speech that links dominion over the entire world to victory in the impending fight (24.11–18).

The American battles are in this way specifically paired with metropolitan doubles but only for the purpose of drawing a stark contrast between the two scenes. The monarch's presence at Saint Quentin assures that the furor of Mars will not consume the city. Once victory is assured, Philip restrains his men, saving the city from destruction and its women from certain violation. He even gathers all of the virgins and nuns of the city into a safe house to protect them from ravishment by wayward soldiers (18.22–23). The aftermath of the Battle of Penco, by contrast, emphasizes the ravages that war inflicts upon its victims rather than restraint of a just conqueror. Tegualda—the first of three Araucanian women who narrate their stories of love and loss in parts 2 and 3 of the *Araucana*—appears among the corpses that litter the battlefield, searching for the body of her dead husband (20.26–21. 12).[25] She tells the tale of how her husband, a foreigner, had come to her country to compete for her heart and hand rather than to conquer her people, bringing in this way the evidence of conquistadorial slaughter into painful relief. Her tale concluded, she expects Ercilla, who has been listening, to violate and kill her. Instead, he shows her kindness, echoing the restraint and justice of his monarch.[26] Nonetheless, it is Tegualda's expectations, and not Ercilla's actions, that matter most here. They mark the norms of the war in Chile, norms in which brutality is to be expected, and mercy, to be met with the surprise accorded to the rarest of commodities.[27]

In the same way, the battle that ensues in Chile after Ercilla's vision of Lepanto in no way reflects the manifest clarity of the military and moral victory in the Mediterranean. The canto dedicated to Lepanto has been called one of the finest pieces of military poetry of Spain's Golden Age and reads like a clear celebration of the providential triumph of stalwart Christendom over the heathen Turk. The Battle of Millarpué (25.7–26.21), by contrast, represents one of the blackest moments in the account of the Araucanian war. More important, however, it figures this nadir of Spanish action in Chile with language that fully reactivates the imagery of *estrecheza* from part 1.[28] Having staged a surprise attack, the Araucanians are eventually routed and pursued by the Spaniards. The Araucanians attempt to escape the field through a narrow passage, "[t]hrough a densely thicketed, narrow opening which existed between two hills" (26.4) only to find themselves surrounded, trapped by their ferocious enemy. A Virgilian simile compares the conquistadors with hunters who corral their prey in a tight squeeze [término estrecho], and hurl their lances and javelins with "most impatient desire" (26.6). It then condemns "our men who were up to that point Christians" for having passed "all licit boundaries" with their "cruel arms and inhuman acts" (26.7). The echoes of the description of Chile are evident: the "término estrecho," the "desire" of the Spaniards and their deployment of weapons that pierce and penetrate, phallically, rather than cut (6h), the overstepping of "all licit boundaries." This *plus ultra* oversteps not only topographical boundaries but moral ones. Imperial dreams come to fruition in the most un-Christian of atrocities, the king's man is proven to be no substitute for the king. In the wake of the battle, the Araucanian prisoners are forced to hang themselves, transforming the landscape itself into a grotesque parody of the leafy *loci amoeni* that increasingly serve as poetic refuges (26.37–38).²⁹ Spanish desires have yielded monstrous fruit, and in this return to the scene of an original crime the rhetoric of justice, has given way to the brutalities of wartime atrocities. Ercilla's most exultant celebration of Spain's imperialism in the Old World—his narrative of the Battle of Lepanto—is thereby made to coincide with a narrative of New World warfare that assumes almost las Casian proportions in its characterization of the conquest as unjustifiable brutality.³⁰ While Lepanto ends in the erection of a cross, Millarpué ends in the gruesome spectacle of mass hangings.

How to read these juxtapositions of pathos and justice, victory and savagery? The poet himself offers one explanation. In his preface to part 2, Ercilla claims that the purpose of squeezing "two such great things"—the Battles of Saint Quentin and Lepanto "in so humble a place"—his own poem—is to add luster and variety to his sterile subject matter. His narrative of obscure colonial events, in other words, is supposed to gain authority through its association with these respectable metropolitan ones. We are to suppose, as have a number of Araucana critics, that those metropolitan events remain unsullied by the brutality at the periphery and may even serve to compensate for it, assuring the text's purpose as a tribute to Spanish imperialism.³¹ But Ercilla offers another explanation for his decision to include the narratives of famous metropolitan battles that points in a very different direction. "The Araucanians," he writes, "deserve all this because for more than thirty years they have upheld their reputation without ever letting their arms fall from their hands" (463). By this account, the native luster of the Chilean war needs no supplement. On the contrary, Saint Quentin and Lepanto can be included in the Araucana because the Chilean war itself merits their company. This explanation, moreover, is much more compatible than the first—a red herring, perhaps?—with Ercilla's sympathetic portrayal of the plight of the Araucanians, especially as seen through the eyes of characters like Tegualda. It points to an unstated design in the juxtaposition of center and periphery, metropolitan victory and colonial cruelty.

That design can be glimpsed by first noting that the Lepanto episode does not frame the account of Millarpué, nor does Saint Quentin frame Penco. In each case, it is the other way around: the narrative of the metropolitan battle intrudes into the narrative of Chilean events almost in medias res. It is always on the eve of battle, on the brink of attack, that the Araucana turns away from its American material to attend to events in Europe and the Mediterranean. The text, however, never abandons the American scene altogether. On the contrary, each of the episodes of the web of prophecy is mediated by fictions that, among other things, insist upon the American location from which Saint Quentin, Lepanto, and the mappamundi are viewed. In the first episode of the web of prophecy, Ercilla is taken to a pyramidal mountain in the middle of a verdant pasture, "from which his sight discovered the great roundness of the broad earth, including its unknown, barbarous limits, all the way to the most hidden and remote" (17.51). From there, Bellona, Roman goddess of war, reveals to him not only the Battle of Saint Quentin but, in summary fashion, a whole series of accomplishments that will adorn the reign of Philip II. In this way, Bellona tries to seduce the poet away from his American subject matter and toward the composition of a metropolitan epic. But while this magical character derived from the European tradition tries to lead Ercilla away from his epic of the New World, the poem itself announces its intention to map the world from an American point of view. The peak from which Ercilla sees all these things, we read, dwarfs the Atlas and Apennine Mountains of the Old World (17.43),[32] becoming what one critic calls an "Andean Parnassus" (Nicolopulos 2000, 91). Even as Philip II brings an end to the furor of war in France, we are reminded that the observer of these events watches from an American location. "The sun was going down, bit by bit," we read, "in the fiery *Antarctic hemisphere,* while I most happily watched everything that you have heard in this canto" (18.29; emphasis added). From the perspective afforded by the mountaintop, the world as a whole, including both Chile and Europe, is reduced to a single field of visibility. Nonetheless, we do not forget the Chilean here and now from which that vision is enjoyed. Later, just as Ercilla witnesses Saint Quentin from the heights of a decidedly American, albeit magical, mountain, so he witnesses Lepanto and the cartographic vision of the *mappamundi* episode through the mediation of an Araucanian shaman whose lair is located in the heart, rather than on the peaks, of those same Andes Mountains.

Some comparisons with maps both old and new can help us understand what Ercilla is doing here. I have mentioned before that maps, especially elaborate world maps like those of Battista Agnese, make much of their impression by locating their onlooker in a commanding godlike position. Here, in effect, Ercilla equates that otherworldly position with a particular historical and geographical location, Chile during the Araucanian war. In other words, Ercilla reverses the order of priority between the local and the universal standard in any map of empire. The effect is much like the one produced by certain familiar maplike images from the late twentieth century. The most famous of these Saul Steinberg's *A View of the World from 9th Avenue,* which appeared on the cover of the *New Yorker* magazine on March 29, 1976. It depicts a bird's-eye view of Manhattan above Ninth Avenue, with a straight line of sight westward across the Hudson River, the United States, and the Pacific Ocean all the way to Asia (fig. 33). To compress space in this way is to belittle its value with

33   Saul Steinberg, *A View of the World from 9th Avenue*, 1976. © 2002 The Saul Steinberg
Foundation/Artists Rights Society (ARS), New York. Cover reprinted with permission
of *The New Yorker*. All rights reserved.

respect to the metropolitan foreground, which stands out in lively and colorful detail. Ercilla does something similar, but in reverse, when he juxtaposes Penco with Saint Quentin and Millarpué, with Lepanto. In the *Araucana*, it is Chile and the Araucanian war that occupies center stage, monopolizing the center of its historiography and cartography of empire. Saint Quentin and Lepanto, meanwhile, appear on the margins of the story, off on the horizon of this discursive bird's-eye view as reminders of a distant elsewhere very different in its moral quality from the place in the foreground that commands our attention. It is Chile, that distant land home to an obscure and brutal colonial police action, which provides the point of view from which the empire is viewed.

In this way, the *Araucana* turns the cartographic histories discussed in chapter 4 on their heads. There, Oviedo and Gómara assemble a larger American, and even universal, cartographic history out of the disparate places and events of Spanish expansion into the western Atlantic. Gómara in particular renders his cartographic history as a series of homologous compartments, each containing a variable but predictable set of figures, events, and places, all adding up to a vision of the New World as the place of Spanish endeavor. Las Casas, too, gives coherence to the natural and moral world of the Indies through his own cartographic writing—anticartographic writing—designed for very different ends. Particularly in Gómara and las Casas, a coherent vision of the Indies is rendered at the expense of the particular—those events that Gómara chooses to leave out, those less-than-ideal places that las Casas identifies as aberrations. Ercilla, by contrast, concentrates on the local and the particular, albeit figured through the idealizing register of the European poetic tradition. He does so, however, not to return to the state of affairs that we saw in Cortés—chorography without geography, event without a broader history—but in order to figure the larger whole through the unique perspective offered by the part. The periphery, with all its brutality, becomes the point of view from which we are invited to consider the center.

Are we invited, then, to discover injustice and brutality under the manifestly celebratory tone of the three episodes that make up the core of the *Araucana*'s web of prophecy? It has been argued that the Lepanto episode, at least, does indeed grumble critically about Spanish imperialism, under a literary breath more obviously dedicated to shouts of joyful celebration.[33] It is not necessary, however, to argue that each of the episodes of the web of prophecy reiterates the grim view of military endeavor and imperial ambition inscribed by Penco and, especially, Millarpué in order to find a critique of empire in the *Araucana*. In the pages that follow, the analysis will focus on its climactic scene, the *mappamundi* episode, which is the one most urgently related to my cartographic interpretation of Ercilla. Most interpreters of the *Araucana* who have treated this at all characterize it as a politically orthodox compensation for the atrocities committed outside the sorcerer's lair that either betrays the poem's overtly negative view of conquest or attempts to limit the scope of any potential critique to the Chilean war alone. In the wake of conquistadorial brutality at Millarpué, we are to believe, the poem paints a larger picture of imperial and cosmological harmonies that offers Philip II an image of his world as a mirror of his majesty. More recently, however, at least one critic has been struck by the emptiness, the hollowness of the world as seen through Fitón's crystal ball (Fuchs 2001, 45–46). Here, I intend to follow the lead suggested by Ercilla's strategy of framing imperialistic discourse with scenes of conquistadorial brutality, and expose the way in which the sorcerer's globe inscribes the hollowness rather than the glories of empire.

Fitón's map attempts to produce a static image of the world through the inevitably temporal procedures of narrative. As we saw at the outset of this chapter, it takes the form of an itinerary that travels the Old World before turning to the New. Spain's possessions in the Americas appear in the order of their discovery, with Chile bringing up the rear. In various ways, Fitón's map advertises its own modernity, its superiority to the geographical and cartographical legacy of the past. It marks the island of Taprobana (27.10), which on medieval maps rivaled the Earthly Paradise for a position in the extreme East, as "formerly the end and final boundary of the Orient." It offers an up-to-date treatment of Africa, one that includes Egypt, a country considered Asian by the geography of the ancients (Nicolopulos 2000, 255). Most important, it includes a detailed treatment of the New World that dwells on its extensive wonders. The names of Spanish possessions appear along a toponymic itinerary that also includes mention of the snow-covered peaks of the torrid zone (27.45), the ferocity of savage Indians (27.46), the government of the Incas (27.46), and the emeralds of Ecuador (27.43) and the silver of Potosí (27.47). In Chile, Fitón's poetic itinerary picks up the voyage of Magellan's ships through the strait that bears his name and across the Pacific. The Strait of Magellan appears explicitly for a second time in Ercilla's text, this time at the end of a second description of Chile as a series of toponyms:

> Vees la ciudad de Penco y el pujante
> Arauco, estado libre y poderoso;
> Cañete, la Imperial, y hacia el levante
> la Villa Rica y el volcán fogoso;
> Valdivia, Osorno, el lago y adelante
> las islas y archipiélago famoso

y siguiendo la costa al sur derecho
Chiloé, Coronados el estrecho

por donde Magallanes con su gente
al Mar del Sur salió desembocando,
y tomando la vuelta del poniente
al Maluco guió norduesteando.
Vees las islas de Acaca y Zabú enfrente,
y a Matán, do murió al fin peleando;
Bruney, Bohol, Gilolo, Terrenate,
Machicán, Mutir, Badán, Tidore y Mate.

[See there the city of Penco and vigorous Arauco, that state strong and free;
Cañete, La Imperial, and toward the west, Villa Rica and the fuming volcano;
Valdivia, Osorno, the lake and, onward, the islands and famous archipelago,
and following the coast straight toward the south, Chiloé, Coronados, the strait
through which Magellan and his men came out into the South Sea, and taking
the course of the setting sun, toward Malacca northwestwardly sailed. See the islands of Acaca and Zabú before you, and Matán, where he finally died in battle;
Bruney, Bohol, Gilolo, Terrenate, Machicán, Mutir, Badán, Tidore, and Mate.]
(27.50–51)

No mention is made here of the closure of the strait. Magellan, who was seen
penetrating the strait in part 1, now finally exits on the other side. His successful passage through the strait and subsequent voyage across the Pacific links
Chile to the Spice Islands of the East, a link given poetic form by the enjamb-
ment of these two octaves. No mention is made of Portuguese claims to the
Spice Islands, either. In this itinerary, Columbian desires find no impedi-
ment. They do not encounter the Americas as an obstacle but instead as a
wealthy land that can be subsumed through a journey that finally totalizes the
world and the empire, fulfilling imperial desires. The description of the strait
in part 1 only alluded to a larger imperial geography. This time, that geography is figured at length by the *mappamundi* as a whole.

That *mappamundi*, moreover, calls attention to itself as a visual symbol of
monarchical might. It insists that we find its panegyric of empire in its form,
not just in its geographical content. When Ercilla first visits the cave, the sorcerer calls his magical orb a "poma" (23.72). Covarrubias defines "poma" as
an apple and also as a small round container in the shape of an apple often
used to hold aromatic substances (1994, 828); the most significant definition
is one that Covarrubias leaves unmentioned, however. A "poma" could also be
a terrestrial globe. This is the sense in which the word is used, for example,

by Oviedo in his *Historia general* (3. xxxix.4; 120.349). More importantly, "poma"—or "pome" in English—could refer specifically to the orb of monarchical dominion, that symbol of power often paired with the scepter.[34] Ercilla indirectly associates his own text with Fitón's orb when, in the exordium to canto 27, he converts a conventional apology for the prolixity of his material into a subtle metatextual commentary. The exordium praises brevity as a literary virtue and laments that the canto to follow, even as long as it is, cannot possibly contain all that it should. The text identifies itself specifically as a "chico vaso," a "little cup," barely capable of containing all that the poet would pour into it (27.2).[35] Significantly, "vaso" is one of the specific definitions that Covarrubias provides for "poma" (1994, 828). In this way, "chico vaso" becomes the pivot on which this exordium hangs the canto itself, the crystal ball, and the ambitions of imperial cartography. Through it, canto 27 becomes interchangeable with the crystal ball as doubles of the globe, a model of the Earth used to symbolize the imperial ambitions of the Hapsburg monarch.[36]

The text, in turn, calls upon the reader to *see* this object, this discursive globe. It continuously predicates its toponymy with verbs of vision in the imperative mood, "Look" and "See." In some stanzas, a verb of vision represents one of the very few words used that is not a toponym. For example:

Mira a Livonia, Prusia, Lituania,
Samogocia, Podolia y a Rusía,
a Polonia, Silesia y a Germania
a Moravia, Bohemia, Austria y Ungría,
a Corvacia, Moldavia, Trasilvania,
Valaquia, Vulgaría, Esclavonía,
a Macedonia, Grecia, la Morea,
a Candia, Chipre, Rodas y Iudea. (27.29)

[*Look at* Livonia, Prussia, Lithuania . . .]

Of course, the commands are enunciated by Fitón and directed to Ercilla, who thereby knows to direct his attention to different places, but as the *mappamundi* continues, the reader cannot help but feel apostrophized by the sorcerer's imperatives. It is the reader, and not just the character, who is commanded to look and see. But what is it that the reader is supposed to see? Unlike the prose cartographies of Enciso, Oviedo, and Gómara, this text does not allow for the visualization of the geography that it describes. It provides no indications of distance and direction between locations as in Oviedo, and no morphological descriptions of the kind used by Gómara. The absence of this data highlights the fact that what is presented is a map of *words*, as well a to the possibility that the visual arrangement of these words constitute the key to the map's meaning.[37] On the pages of Fitón's map, geographical data are organized into the boxes established by Ercilla's octaves, which become, in effect, the building blocks of his map's spatial armature. This verse cartography consists of forty-eight octaves. Half of them are devoted to Asia, Africa, and Europe, minus the Iberian Peninsula, and the other half to Spain, the Americas, and the Spice Islands. Fitón's map thus describes the world continent by continent, but like the geography of Enciso, the cartography of López de Velasco and others (fig. 16 above), and the historiography of Oviedo and Gómara, it divides the world into two halves, one hemisphere subject to Castile and one that is not.

But while Fitón's map—in its conspicuous alignment with the geography of the moderns, in its close attention to Spanish possessions in the New World, in its reinscription of a well-established universal geography of empire, in its identification with the globe as a symbol of power—seems to celebrate Philip II's "modern" global empire, so do other aspects of this episode part company with geographical panegyric. Despite its manifest modernity, Fitón's map includes some of the hoary legends of the geographical tradition. It mentions griffons and dragons (27.17), the long-sought source of the Nile (18), and the fantastic kingdoms of Meroe (27.20) and of Prester John (27.16).[38] This last inclusion is particularly telling. By the latter half of the sixteenth century, the kingdom of Prester John was a legend in complete disrepute, the object of humanist ridicule, the emblem of an obsolete and foolish belief in monsters.[39] It is, however, the only place in the entire *mappamundi* to be specifically located through a reference to its latitude. It thus combines patently fantastic material with the very modern methods of cartography. The reference is thus a subtle cartographic joke, a textual wink indicating that Fitón's map is not all it may seem to be. A further indication of subterfuge appears when the geographical itinerary reaches the southern limits of the Americas. At that point, the theater of the Chilean war irrupts into the text as "vigorous Arauco, that state strong and free" (27.50). With these words, Fitón answers the characterization of Arauco in Hurtado de Mendoza's speech on the eve of the Battle of Millarpué. There, Arauco was cast as the final remnant of resistance to Spain's drive for universal monarchy. Now, Fitón answers that claim with a patriotic reference to Arauco's successful bid to frustrate Spain's imperial ambitions. We are reminded that, even though the strait may not be blocked in this description of Philip's world, the nucleus of resistance that the closure of the strait has symbolized remains vital and defiant. The totalizing, globalizing, imperialistic impetus of the map's discursive itinerary does not so much include Arauco as bump past it. In Fitón's map, Arauco becomes the rock over which the march of empire stumbles.

This joke, this patriotic jibe, belongs to the enchanter who recites the verses that together make up the *Araucana*'s cartography in verse, but neither the enchanter nor his crystal ball exhibit the gravitas that we would expect from a mouthpiece of imperial panegyric. Fitón's initial appearance in canto 23 draws upon the characterization of two witches in earlier Iberian verse narratives, namely, Juan de Mena's fifteenth-century *Laberinto de fortuna* and, once again, Lucan's *Pharsalia*.[40] But while Lucan and Mena teach us to dread these witches and their art, Ercilla does nothing to suggest that we should fear Fitón. In fact, he even parodies some of the techniques that his predecessors use to make their readers squirm in the presence of black magic and its practitioners.[41] Instead of a terrifying witch, we get Fitón, who, we read, seemed "docile and agreeable" and who "stood looking at me, with urbanity and an affable expression" (23.57). Fitón's crystal ball likewise cheats the expectations generated by its sources, the mantic globe that appears in the tenth canto of Camões's *Lusíadas* and the crystalline urn of the "Second Eclogue" of Garcilaso de la Vega.[42] Both are wondrous objects, divine revelations, steeped in Neo-Platonic dreams of totality. Fitón's crystal ball, meanwhile, represents nothing more than a clever optical device fabricated by the sorcerer himself, he brags, over forty years of study and hard work (23.71). However tough things may have been for Fitón, his claim can do nothing to compete with Camões's mantic globe or Garcilaso's crystalline urn, both given by the gods for the purpose of foretelling great deeds. Like any map, Fitón's orb is a manmade object, an artificial mirror of the world. Moreover, it is one made by a rather quirky, ideologically suspect man.

These details—a wry cartographic joke, a defiant reference to Arauco, an off-beat enchanter, and a decidedly secular orb—are not alone in their efforts to subvert the imperialistic thrust of this verse cartography. If we ignore Fitón's directions to look and see and instead we listen to Fitón's map as an oral performance, we will discover a map that sings. The *mappamundi* episode is one of the most carefully composed pieces of the entire *Araucana*.[43] There, geographic knowledge combines with poetry to produce a majestic performance, one perhaps capable of inspiring in the reader an *admiratio* commensurable with the one experienced by Ercilla before the crystal ball. But if, again, we allow ourselves to be implicated in the sorcerer's shifters and return to the order of the visual, a different possibility emerges. As we saw above, Fitón's map strains to enumerate as many places as possible, at times producing stanzas that, to the eye, resemble little more than lists. It seems that in stanzas such as these, epic discourse reaches, or almost reaches, a breaking point. The mass of geographic knowledge in the early modern period has led the narrator to resort to enumeration in a frenzied attempt to include everything even at the risk of inscribing nothing but what one critic calls a "desiccated list" (Royer 1879, 190). The meter corrals the toponyms into a series of stanzas, but it can reflect no internal coherence within its own boundaries other than what it arbitrarily imposes upon the toponyms through the exigencies of rhyme and meter. Is the music we hear, then, an echo of the music of the spheres, or is it the siren call of a poetic form that can reveal nothing about the world as form? Imperialistic interpretations of the *mappamundi* episode may insist on the first possibility, but we must remember that the second one is no less viable. When we allow ourselves to abandon sonority and temporality for visuality and spatiality, we remember that our experience as readers of this episode is decidedly unlike that of the characters we are reading about. We may remember then that this *poma* is a poem and that the poem is but a "chico vaso." "Chico" is a colloquialism out of step with the sententious tone of the exordium in which it appears, and thus is capable, potentially, of deflating its grave pretensions. A "chico vaso" like Fitón's manmade orb cannot aspire to hold all that an imperial vision demands. The potential for parodic deflation latent in the word *chico* is finally activated not just with respect to the exordium but to the canto as a whole. What looked like a bold attempt to celebrate Philip's world through verse cartography becomes a parody of any attempt to inscribe the world in words.

As we saw in the previous chapter, a list of place names can function as a metonymic geography once the reader activates the meanings associated with the names.[44] Thus cartography and historiography become two sides of the same linguistic coin in both Oviedo and Gómara. But in Ercilla, in the absence of an extensive historiography that can flesh out place names with stories and descriptions, the words on the page can only accomplish their ekphrastic magic and function as a metonymic geography if we as readers bring to them our own knowledge of the New World. That knowledge, in turn, can only be garnered from the corpus of geographical and historical literature, a literature that, in turn, makes repeated claims to describe the world effectively, to accomplish the sort of ekphrasis that seems to fall apart in the *mappamundi* episode of the *Araucana*. The discovery of the Strait of Magellan, as we saw, confirmed for some that the world in fact resembled the cosmographies that purported to reproduce its meaningful form. Now this coincidence of world and text seems to unravel as the shrill insistence of this odd enchanter that we look and see reminds us that his map is a map of words. His *poma/poema* only contains a world insofar as we understand that the world is nothing but the other texts that we bring to our reading. If a poetics of cartography and empire only succeeds by making its objects present to the reader through poetic enargeia, then it would seem that such a poetics stumbles here over the problems of geographic representation.

Turning again to the spatial form of this "chico vaso," this poma/poema, we find that even it betrays misgivings about empire just as it attempts to inscribe its imperial geography. Fitón's map alludes to the existence of an omphalos, a significant center around which the meaning of the whole composition revolves. It mentions the usual suspects for cartographic centrality but constantly defers the identification of a true center. Babylon and Carthage both appear as shattered memories (27.15, 27.23). Jerusalem is not even named, appearing on Fitón's map only as the ruins left by the Romans (27.7). Rome, the Eternal City, in turn, appears as a has-been (27.24). As we come across these ruins, we might suspect that the map is setting up the world up for the accession of Spain to imperial status, that its itinerary will give graphic form to the translatio imperii, but "Spain," "Castile," and "Madrid" do not emerge as convincing candidates for the role of cartographic navel. The toponym "España" appears in the first verse of the Hispanic half of the world and introduces nine stanzas dedicated to the Iberian Peninsula. The three stanzas at the center of this set are dedicated to the Escorial and thus assign to Philip's monastery palace a position analogous to the one occupied by the real Escorial located at the center of Spain. It is not, however, at the center of the map. Fitón's map is composed of an even number of octaves, and thus no single toponym, not even "España," can occupy its mathematical center. The center of the map is empty; it is the space between the octaves about the Spanish Monarchy and those about the rest of the world. It would seem that poetry is at the service of empire here, dividing the world into Hispanic and non-Hispanic hemispheres, but the cost of this strategy is that the centers of monarchical power appear slightly decentered, leaving vacant the map's most privileged position. The axis mundi, in other words, is an empty space on the page. "España," furthermore, appears in the verse, "Mira al poniente España," "Look to the west, to Spain." The here and now of this enunciation is somewhere to the east of Spain, looking westward to the setting sun, the "poniente," and perhaps even a "setting Spain."[45]

It is perhaps no wonder that Fitón follows Magellan to the Spice Islands only to mark the place of Magellan's death. Fitón's American point of view has become a parody of the idealized perspective common to imperial cartography. From that vantage point, the view of the world it offers can only mock the celebration of empire. The poma/poema, as a container, as a text readily accessible to a metropolitan reader, may be apprehensible, but the universe it figures may apprehend neither a world nor an empire. A container and an apple, a *poma*, finally, is also the hilt of a sword, a pommel. The pommel within this tale of the sword, however, does not seem to offer what Don García promises his men, "all the world within their grasp." Its music, like the sweet fragrances held by pomes of another kind, may intoxicate, may enchant, but its imperial dreams seem no more substantial than the whiffs of perfume that arise from the bottle and are lost.

When Ercilla returns to his tale of the sword, he makes no explicit mention, either as narrator or character, of the significance of Fitón's map. The poem nonetheless responds to its fractured dreams of universal monarchy by returning to its images of *estrecheza*, desire, geography, and gender. Ercilla joins an advance party sent to reconnoiter a passage through the mountains of Purén (27.59). In this no man's land between relatively secure Spanish and Araucanian positions, Ercilla and his companions encounter Glaura. Like Tegualda before her, Glaura is caught in a liminal space between opposing bands of male warriors desperately trying to grapple with the unsettling effects of the war upon her personal life. Also like Tegualda, Glaura appears not only to recover her husband but to tell her tale, in which she heroically preserves her virginity and her life through a series of novelistic surprises and reversals and in so doing capturing the sympathy of her captors, not to mention that of the reader (27.61–28.52). Once again, the incident serves to figure counterfeit participants in an idealized encounter. Glaura appears as the quintessential feminine object of desire, while her husband Cariolano serves Ercilla as his trusted manservant (28.4; 28.42). When the two discover each other, Ercilla lets them go their merry way. While the Tegualda episode offered Ercilla an opportunity to provide solace for wounds inflicted by Spanish arms, this episode offers him the opportunity to orchestrate the happy ending that Tegualda's story (or the story of the conquest of Chile) can never have. He also has an opportunity to advertise himself, as Toribio Medina reminds us, as an ideal gentlemanly knight (Medina 1928, 11).[46] The event that immediately follows the happy reunion of Cariolano and Glaura, however, reveals that this attempt to construct the colonialist self and the colonial other as a benevolent master and his young beneficiaries represents nothing other than a misrecognition of colonialist realities, a counterfactual colonial utopia. Husband and wife disappear into the landscape only to make room for a skirmish that, more than in any other passage in the *Araucana*, recalls the description of the Strait of Magellan and its closure. After the interlude, in other words, it is back to the business of desire, penetration, conquest, and violence.

When the narrative finally returns to the story of the war, we find the Spanish troops at a geographic bottleneck. The description of this bottleneck recapitulates the spatial figures of the description of the strait:

> Es el camino de Purén derecho
> hacia la entrada y paso del Estado;
> después va en forma oblica largo trecho
> de dos ásperos cerros *apretado,*
> y vienen a ceñirle en tanto *estrecho*
> que apenas pueden ir dos lado a lado,
> haciendo aun más *angosta* aquella vía
> un *arroyo* que lleva en compañía.

[The Purén route goes directly to the pass that marks the entrance to the state of Arauco; afterward, it bends obliquely for a long stretch, hemmed in by two rough mountains that squeeze it into such a strait that hardly two men can go abreast. The way is made even narrower by a stream that it carries along with it.] (28.54; emphasis added)

Note the elements of this description: the gorge is a narrow passageway surrounded by rocks with a stream flowing through it. The space beyond is the Araucanian heartland, the military objective of the whole war. The Araucanian warriors are in the hills above, throwing rocks at the Spaniards in the gorge, threatening to block the way (28.56–57). A Virgilian simile compares them to a storm that, just like the storm that has blocked the Strait of Magellan, threatens the land below with "rays, stone, and tempest" from above (28.58).

The Spaniards win the battle in the gorge and pass through, but the conquest of Arauco is left incomplete. We might expect to find that ever-elusive *locus amoenus* that serves to figure the Araucanian heartland somewhere on the other side of this gorge, the last of the *estrechezas* through which the Spaniards pass. But although that *locus amoenus* appears once again after the battle in the gorge in the final canto of part 2, it once again goes unlocated, and we do not witness the arrival there of the Spaniards. Nor do we see them capture the place in part 3, in which the Spaniards fight a guerrilla war in a sterile and hostile landscape. The Spaniards thus manage to pass through this one last strait into the space beyond, but their passage does not in any meaningful way realize the totalization of imperial space or the satisfaction of imperial dreams. The figuration of the locus, furthermore, suggests that the poem will never provide a sincere imperial cartography, a sincere testimony to Spanish accomplishment as an expansionist power. Not only is the Araucanian *locus amoenus* never specifically located, but it serves as the setting for scenes that no European could have witnessed, even had they occurred. This ostensive fictionality marks it not as a representation of Araucanian identity but rather as a poetic stand-in for what Ercilla cannot know about the Araucanians and what the Spaniards can never possess. Arauco, in the end, lies outside the *mappamundi*, outside the *poma/poema*. It lies in some idealized and unpossessable elsewhere that cannot be reduced to Iberian wills no matter how many straits they penetrate or how many spaces they come to possess. Thus, in the wake of a verse cartography whose panegyric possibilities seem thoroughly corroded by its own parodic acid, the counter-cartography of *estrechezas* makes a decisive appearance. It dashes any lingering hopes of global mastery by reinscribing a conquistadorial itinerary that does not, will not, reach its Tenochtitlán, that finds itself always on the verge of conquest, its object of desire always on the other side of the next mountain pass.

The True Story of a Trip to Magellanica (Part 3 of the *Araucana*)

Part 3 of the *Araucana* (1589–90) continues in the vein of part 2, interweaving eyewitness accounts of the Chilean war with additional romance episodes, but it also develops the cruelty of part 2 into gruesome brutality, and the plaintiveness of its romance episodes, into pathos. It does not, however, relate the end of the war, for the simple reason that at the time of Ercilla's death the war in Chile was far from over. Throughout Chile's history as a kingdom of the Spanish Monarchy, the indigenous peoples in the south of the country fiercely resisted Spanish rule. When Chile won its independence from Spain in the nineteenth century, they directed their resistance against the territorial ambitions of the new nation. For this reason, the *Aracauna* cannot truly conclude its tale: it can only bring it to an end. It does this through two successive culminating episodes. The first complete edition of the poem (published in 1590) ended shortly after the capture and execution of Caupolicán and the election of his equally fearsome replacement. The final edition of the poem (1596), produced under the direction of Ercilla's widow, adds a second conclusion, an intercalated narrative of a voyage south of the theater of war that foretells the despoliation of whatever unspoilt corner remains of a once-paradisiacal America.[47] In this episode, we encounter the poem's final explicit reference to the Strait of Magellan, as well as its final *estrecheza* and its final metapoetic commentary upon the very possibility of cartographic literature in an imperial vein.

First, however, a few words about the way part 3 prepares us for this culminating episode. The reader follows the Spaniards into Arauco only to find a desert in the place of the coveted Araucanian *locus amoenus*. Battles yield to massacres as the military stalemate leads both sides to adopt increasingly desperate military measures. The narrator becomes increasingly frank in his condemnation of the Spanish fighters, who "in an inhuman manner have exceeded the laws and limits of war, committing in their explorations and conquests, enormous and unheard of cruelties" (32.4). He concatenates episodes that build upon the text's growing sense of pathos and outrage. Once again, an Araucanian woman appears to tell her tale of love and loss, and this time the reader is left to wonder whether she, like the land, will ever produce children or even live another day (32.31–42). Afterward, the reader, along with some of Ercilla's companions, hear the poet retell the story of Dido from Virgil's *Aeneid* as an exemplary tale of enlightened overseas colonialism, one that offers a clear contrast to the benighted struggle that surrounds them in Chile (32.43–33.54). Finally, the text arrives at the first of its two conclusions, the story of the capture and execution of Caupolicán, a gruesome incident that brings a grotesque climax to the poem's dynamic counter-cartography of *estrechezas*.

Up until this point, the language of *estrechezas* is conspicuous in its absence. With the arrival in Arauco proper, the purposeful linearity of parts 1 and 2 is lost. Rather than push onward through one "strait" after another, the Spanish force disperses to scour the land in search of Caupolicán. Eventually, however, the search stumbles upon success, and the language of *estrecheza* snaps back into place. An Araucanian informant takes a group of Spaniards, Ercilla among them, to Caupolicán's hiding place, "[b]y a narrow, unused route" along "a narrow, intricate trail" carved in the mountains by "a stream and a rocky spring" (33.60–62). Unaware of their approach, the general suffers the dishonor of capture, only to have his own wife compound his ignominy through word and deed. Frisia angrily thrusts their infant child into the arms of her disgraced husband, proclaiming that he has become its mother rather than its father (33.81). This figurative transgendering of Caupolicán makes of him a counterfeit version of the land itself, that feminine entity that has for so long been the object of attempted Spanish penetration and possession. Finally, Spanish colonial desire has in its grasp a suitable double of the object of its desire, an unexpected "woman" whose body provides the colonialist subject with temporary satisfaction. The Spaniards impale the general, who does not even wince at the pain. The text compares his stoicism with that of a bride on her marriage bed who suffers the pain of deflowerment with ladylike decorum. But this grotesque allusion to colonial husbandry, to a loving and productive marriage of conqueror and conquered, quickly gives way to other images, ones that identify the execution as an act of brutal, punitive sodomy. The body of Caupolicán, in effect, becomes the final *estrecheza* of the war in Chile, one that reveals the conquistadorial effort as an act of homosexual rape. The

execution scene thereby inscribes Spanish colonial desire—within the preju-
dices of the time—as the degenerate perversion of that most contemptible of
deviants, the sodomite.[48]

The second counterfeit conclusion to this necessarily inconclusive historical verse narrative involves an expedition that supposedly left Arauco right in
the aftermath of Caupolicán's execution. In February 1558, under the leadership of Don García Hurtado de Mendoza, a small expeditionary force that included Ercilla set out overland in search of the Strait of Magellan. The party
eventually reached the Island of Chiloé, at a latitude of roughly 42°S, many
hundreds of miles north of their ultimate objective. This apparently extraneous episode provides the focus for this final part of my analysis of the *Araucana*.
Historians have long treated it as a *carta de relación* in verse, and have mined it
for what it can tell us of the historical expedition to the south of Chile. At least
one literary critic, Beatriz Pastor, has read it very differently, as an allegory of
the conquest of the Americas as a whole and even of conquest in general. Far
from extraneous, this episode is, for Pastor, the principal vehicle of the *Araucana*'s highly critical ideological posture (1992, 257–62). I will build upon her
interpretation of the search for the strait in ways that highlight its relevance to
the cartographic strategies of the *Araucana* and that provide a fitting denouement to my general argument.

In the wake of Caupolicán's death, the land trembles once again with the
fury of Araucanian war preparations, as the leadership, gathered in the *locus
amoenus*, elects Tucapel as successor to their martyred general. In this way, the
Araucana returns to the scenes and figures of the beginning of the war, as well
as to the beginning of its own discursive trajectory. A new beginning, in other
words, takes the place of what should be an ending (34.33–41). But rather
than go on with its tale of a brutal, stalemated police action, the *Araucana* abandons its principal narrative altogether and sets its sights on new horizons to
the south. The Spaniards cross the treacherous Ancud pass—figured as a new
estrecheza, needless to say (34.61)—only to get lost in the wilderness beyond.
In a moment reminiscent of a host of colonial narratives that tell the stories of
conquistadorial failures—including those of Alvar Nuñez Cabeza de Vaca and
Francisco Vázquez—the conquistadorial longing for rich kingdoms to conquer erodes in the realization that the land is sterile and uninhabited (35.30).[49]
Hope for wealth gives way to fear of death. Once again in dire straits, the
Spaniards discover renewed vigor and apply their swords to the thickets. This
time, however, their efforts grant them something more than a brief reprieve
before the next struggle. The woods "unweave" themselves, revealing, on the
other side of the wilderness, an unspoilt land of milk and honey (35.38–40).
In the Caribbean, Columbus believed that he had found the terrestrial paradise.

Now that discovery repeats itself at the southernmost limit of the Indies. For the first time, the Spaniards in the *Araucana* have broken through the geography of *estrechezas* to find a *locus amoenus*—"the spacious and fertile fields of Ancud" (35.40)—like the one that had so thoroughly eluded them in Arauco.

Finally, it seems, colonial desires will find some fulfillment in the possession of this Chilean Arcadia and Spanish imperialism will incorporate one of those final, unassimilated remnants of the world that stand between it and its dream of worldwide dominion. But, as we might expect, possession brings with it only destruction. When the Spaniards find a fruit sweeter than the manna that fed the Israelites, they fall upon it like a plague of locusts, ravaging the land to satisfy their hunger and thirst (35.45). The rapacious conquistadors then encounter the inhabitants of this Arcadia. Like the innocents of the Golden Age, they live in perfect harmony with the natural law, knowing nothing of greed, injustice, or evil, (36.13–14). The scene of the encounter, however, gradually reproduces the standard tropology of the conquest literature. The Amerindians confuse the Spaniards with gods (36.4); they are fascinated by blond hair and beards; and they are frightened by horses and firearms (35.15). Here as elsewhere, the arrival of the conquistadors tolls the final days of Paradise. The standard that arrives in Arcadia, the text laments, is not that of the pious Philip II but that of avarice, one of the seven deadly sins (36.14). In this way, Ercilla's travel tale becomes an allegory of the conquest as a whole rather than the account of a specific journey to a specific place. It traces a conquistadorial itinerary into terra incognita only to reach the same end as that reached by Columbus, Cortés, and Pizarro—the destruction of their objects of desire. Just as Tenochitlán was destroyed by the conquerors who hoped to possess it, so too this Arcadia, an emblem of a whole, once virgin continent, is doomed to despoliation.

Pastor's argument concerning this final scene goes even further. According to her, the imminent ruin of this Chilean Arcadia does not merely allegorize the conquest of the Americas, it "questions all conquests, challenges imperialism itself as an ideological model rather than a particular application, rejects all forms of brutality . . . as being inseparable from any war" (1992, 262). But even more is going on here. First, Pastor's interpretation assumes that the expedition sets out for an "illusory third world" (1992, 258; emphasis added). This loses sight of the expedition's actual objective as stated in Ercilla's text. By looking more closely at that objective, we can discover ways in which the episode addresses itself to more specific historical circumstances. Second, and more importantly, this episode does not just interrogate conquest and imperialism, generally or specifically: it also extends the metapoetic reflection begun in the parodic gestures of the *mappamundi* episode in ways that question the very possibility of inventing America for European consumption. It does so, moreover, by turning the tables on the counter-cartographic discourse that, up until this point, has served to interrogate the totalizing fantasies of imperialism but not necessarily the impulse to empire itself.

In a speech made at the outset of the journey, Don García tells his men that they are about to embark on the conquest of "another new world," a third one. There, Spanish spirits will be able to expand beyond the limits of the "two worlds" that they already know. This "new new world" is Magellanica, more commonly known as the Terra Australis or the Great Southern Land. This was a massive, unknown continent believed to occupy most of the Southern Hemisphere. It established itself on European maps during the course of the sixteenth century and remained there until the eighteenth, when the Pacific voyages of Captain Cook finally dispelled it (fig. 34).[50] Although belief in its existence and even if some of its cartographic contours may have had roots in early Portuguese voyages along the coast of Australia, its place in Renaissance geography was cemented by cosmographical necessity.[51] The Terra Australis fills the otherwise watery Southern Hemisphere with land rather than sea and thus responds to Biblical statements about the proportion of land to sea in the world at large.[52] Alonso de Santa Cruz believes in its existence (Cuesta Domingo 1983, 1: 289). So does Gómara, who calls for continued exploration to effect its discovery (López de Gómara 1979, 19). Abraham Ortelius not only included it in his map of the world but also assigned it a place in the title page allegory of the *Theatrum orbis terrarum*. There, it appears as a bust beside a supine America, a partial figure for a part of the world as yet only partially known (see fig. 8 above).[53] Ercilla, moreover, has mentioned the Terra Australis in earlier episodes of the *Araucana*. The Great Southern Land is present implicitly in the treatment of Chile as an isthmus between two landmasses (1.7–9). It also makes an appearance on Fitón's map:

Vees las manchas de tierras, tan cubiertas
que pueden ser apenas divisadas:
son las que nunca han sido descubiertas
ni de estranjeros pies jamás pisadas,
las cuales estarán siempre encubiertas
y de aquellos celajes ocupadas
hasta que Dios permita que parezcan
porque más sus secretos se engrandezcan. (27.52)

[See the stains of lands, so thoroughly veiled that they can barely be devised: those are the ones that have never been discovered nor trod upon by foreign feet. They will remain forever concealed and by those clouds occupied until God allows them to appear so that their secrets may be ever more aggrandized.]

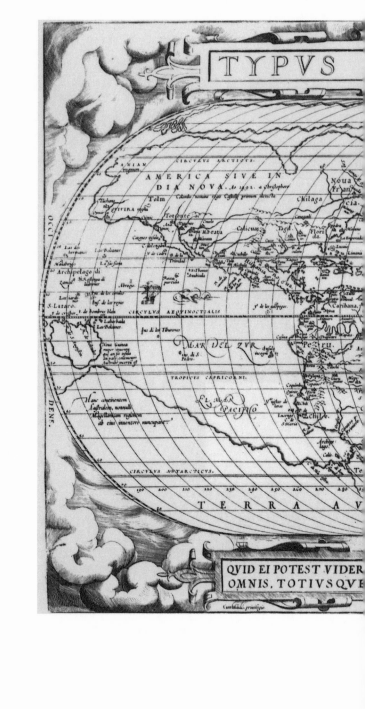

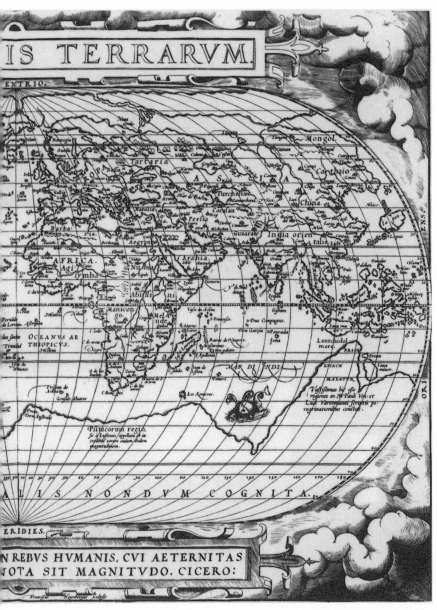

34 Abraham Ortelius, *Typus orbis terrarum*, from the *Theatrum orbis terrarum* (Antwerp, 1570). Note the "Terra Australis nondum cognita" that occupies so much of the Southern Hemisphere. This is the hypothetical southern land represented by the bust in Ortelius's title page engraving (see fig. 8 above). The Albert and Shirley Small Special Collections Library, University of Virginia Library.

Don García's speech and the narrator's remarks that introduce it respond to specific images from this octave. There, we see that foreign footsteps have never marked this land, that its eventual exploration has been reserved by God for a given historical moment, and that it is the home of marvelous secrets. Ercilla thus marks the moment at which Don García's feet cross the boundary separating America from the hinterland of the third world (35.4). Ercilla has Don García tell his men that since two worlds are not enough to accommodate them, they must conquer a third, where they will have power without limit. There, in a new world that the heavens have kept concealed, they will rule over countless provinces of inestimable wealth (35.5–8). The aristocrat's speech recalls Alexander at the easternmost limits of India, lamenting that he has no more worlds to conquer, as well as Julius Caesar on the shores of the English Channel, ready to embark upon the conquest of what he believes is a vast and undiscovered land.[54] Having given up on the conquest of Arauco, Don García Hurtado de Mendoza sets out to find the Strait of Magellan and to conquer the land of Magellanica beyond it. In this way, he echoes the fantasies of other sixteenth- and seventeenth-century Europeans, for whom the undiscovered Terra Australis had become the place where cities and riches much like those in Marco Polo's writing would assuredly be found, and where the conquests of Cortés and Pizarro would most assuredly be repeated (Broc 1986, 169; Fausett 1993).

By recognizing that the objective of the expedition as it is figured in Ercilla's text is not just the rediscovery of the Strait of Magellan but the conquest of the Terra Australis that lies beyond it, we add a layer of historical referentiality to Ercilla's allegory. The 1581 annexation of Portugal and its Indias orientales to the already vast Monarchy of the Spanish Hapsburgs, Geoffrey Parker argues, only intensified the global ambitions of Philip II, not to mention the imperialistic rhetoric surrounding his reign. A medal struck in 1583 featured Philip's image on one side, and on the other, an image of a terrestrial globe surrounded by the inscription "Non sufficit orbis" (The world is not enough). In the years that followed, various officials proposed grandiose designs, including the conquest of southeast Asia and the annexation of China (Parker 2002, 24–25). But by the mid-1590s, when this episode was added to part 3 of the Araucana, the promise of global empire that arose from the Portuguese annexation had given way to the disgrace of the defeat of the Armada. The war with England was dragging on, as were the troubles in the Netherlands. The kingdom of Aragon had become a problem, and economic crises had set in. In this context, the Araucana is fitted with a tale of a disastrous attempt to overstep the boundaries of what Spain already knew and possessed, as if its already vast empire were not enough for its valiant spirit. Ercilla's critical discourse is not directed, then, at war, conquest, and imperialism in general but at the specific schemes and the very self-image of the Hapsburg Monarchy in its headiest days. Don García's hopes to conquer Magellanica with his small expeditionary force come to mock Philip's hopes to achieve dominion over the entire world with the limited resources available even to a Monarchy as vast as his own. The Hapsburg aspiration to lord over the world becomes the object of conquista-dorial satire.

This satirical allegory of imperial designs and imperial dreams comes accompanied by a literary parody that turns the table on the historical and ge-ographical discourse that has so far served to subvert dreams of spatial total-ization. So far, Magellan and his strait have explicitly appeared in two highly determined registers, a chorography and a mantic vision. As we saw, in each case, Ercilla shows himself quite capable of manipulating and treating ironi-cally the language of geographic description and the tradition of epic prophecy to advance his own highly critical poetics of cartography and empire. With the story of the expedition, another apparent "digression," Ercilla's poetics of car-tography and empire dresses itself in yet another discursive costume, that of testimonial narrative. In so doing, it finally evokes Magellan's strait in the lan-guage of the *Araucana*'s own self-acknowledged origins, that of the eyewitness account that travels from the farthest reaches of Philip's domains back to its center. It also returns to one of the roots of Hispanic cartographic writing about the Americas, the *carta de relación* with its linear metageography. Like the poem as a whole, however, this episode combines claims to eyewitness au-thority with a series of literary allusions and poetic fabrications that convert it into a parody of the genre into which it inserts itself.

As the *Araucana* progresses, it exhibits an increasingly explicit preoccupa-tion with its own writing. Canto 34, for example, ends with the following octave:

Ya el español con la presteza usada
al último confín había venido,
dando remate a la postrer jornada
del límite hasta allí constituido;
y puesto el pie en la raya señalada,
el presuroso paso suspendido,
dijo (si ya escucharlo no os enoja)
lo que el canto dirá, vuelta la oja. (34.66)

[Now the Spaniard, with his customary diligence, had arrived at the utmost end
of the world as then known—putting an end, during the final stretch of his
march, to the limit of the world as then constituted—and, his foot upon the

crucial line, his urgent pace suspended, he said (if listening to him does not annoy us) what the canto will say once the page is turned.]

The explicit referent of "el español" in the first verse is García Hurtado de Mendoza, the Spaniard whose foot is poised on the frontier between Arauco and terra incognita, but there are other, more interesting, implicit referents. Ercilla's references to his own poetic activity, from the preface to part 2 onward, often conflate the levels of story and discourse, assuming as their own the spatiality of the poem itself. Often, these references take the form of peculiar endings to cantos, endings that replace the conventional practice of referring to the text as a song and to the poet as its singer with references to the poet as writer and the poem as his written text. The remark cited here represents the most "bookish" of these peculiar canto endings, the one that most strongly draws our attention to, not the act of writing, but our own experience as readers of a book. Here, in a canto ending that more than any other calls attention to the textuality of this text, it is difficult to resist an interpretation of the entire stanza as a remark about the narrative discourse. At this moment, "el español" refers not just to the captain-general but to the language of the poem, and perhaps to the Spanish language in general. All three, the commander, the poem, and the culture, arrive here at a boundary, the end of a canto, and stand poised to enter what has never entered into the language before, the undiscovered country beyond. That country, moreover, is not precisely the Terra Australis believed to cover much of the Southern Hemisphere, but a suspect territory of words.

When the narrative finally reaches its Chilean Arcadia, it once again warns us that we are traveling along a merely discursive itinerary to a land at least as literary as it is real. The *Araucana*'s description of the lands and peoples reached by the expedition is introduced by what seems to be a conventional assurance of the veracity of the travel tale in the face of presumed refutation by stay-at-homes:

Quien muchas tierras vee, vee muchas cosas
que las juzga por fábulas la gente;
y tanto cuanto son maravillosas,
el que menos las cuenta es más prudente;
y aunque es bien que se callen las dudosas
y no ponerme en riesgo así evidente,
digo que la verdad hallé en el suelo
por más que afirmen que es subida al cielo. (36.1)

[He who sees many lands, sees many things that people then determine to be fables. And inasmuch as those things are wonders, he who tells less is the most prudent. And although it is good that doubtful things be silenced and that it is therefore clear that I should not risk my reputation, I say that I found the truth here on earth, for all it's said that it had risen to the heavens.]

This gesture constructs the account to follow as a testimonial, referring to a "truth" that is "found" on "the ground" and which the narrator heroically shares at some risk to his own reputation.[55] But, once again, a claim to referentiality reveals its intertextual soul. The passage imitates the exordium to canto 7 of *Orlando furioso*:

> He who has left his native country sees
> —As further off he goes—things far removed
> From what he thought to find; and when he is
> Recounting them at home, may be reproved
> For telling lies, since ignoramuses,
> Unless with touch and sight they've plainly proved
> A thing, will not believe it; thus it comes,
> This canto will seem strange to stay-at-homes. (Ariosto 1975, 7.1)

This canto of Ariosto's chivalric romance relates the journey of the knight Ruggiero to the island of the sorceress Alcina, the fictional antipodes of the world of *Orlando furioso*. He arrives there on the back of a hippogriff, a magical being thought by some to represent an allegory of the poem itself. The *Araucana* thus introduces its account of Ercilla's "real" ends of the earth and of Spanish travels there by imitating the language of chivalric romance, and particularly, by alluding to Ariosto's fictionalized stand-in for the New World. Rather than assure the reader of the facticity of what is to follow, then, the passage from Ercilla confuses matters. It plays with the reader's expectations by blurring the boundary between truth and fiction, history and romance, eyewitness testimonial and tall tale. It signals that the description of Arcadia that follows has been built from the stuff of literature just as much, if not more, as it has been cut from the cloth of life.

In light of these considerations, we must interpret a crucial episode from the narrative of the expedition. Ercilla and a small group of companions set out on their own, cross an unidentified body of water, and visit several of the distant islands. The autoptic claims of the narrative discourse are reaffirmed by an ethnographic stanza authorized by its initial word, "Vi" (I saw) (37.20). The group finally comes up against a strait whose swift current does not allow them to cross with any safety. Most historians believe this to be the Chacao Channel, the passage that separates the island of Chiloé from the mainland of Chile. Ercilla and ten of his men make the dangerous crossing, briefly reconnoiter the land beyond, and return to the main camp. The crossing echoes, albeit only in a general way, the story of Hero and Leander, a commonplace topos of Spanish Golden Age poetry.[56] Leander, the reader will recall, braved the treacherous waters of the Hellespont every night in order to visit his lover Hero on the other side, only to have one of his visits end with his own tragic drowning. Ercilla's description of the canal mentions how the current makes it impossible for a man to arrive on the opposite shore alive (36.24). It also emphasizes the heroism of the original crossing, as well as the danger of the return trip across the "furious waters" (36.27).[57] The background presence of the trope of Leander crossing the Hellespont gives this Chilean crossing its literary resonance, its sense of danger, its character as heroic activity. It suggests, even, that this crossing of a New World Hellespont is meant to be understood—despite the failure of the historical expedition to get that far south— as the crossing of the Strait of Magellan itself. If so, what happens next would take place on the shores of Magellanica. In any case, it represents the poem's final push beyond the boundaries of what is unknown and other, its final attempt to incorporate into its discursive empire a terra incognita.

Ercilla tells us that he proceeded, on his own, some distance into the land on the other side of the canal and inscribed some verses on a tree. He would have the reader believe in the literal truth of the event and understand that his inscription certifies his discovery of the land to the south of the canal he has crossed. It is the mark of his passing through the hinterland of Magellanica. The inscription appears as a canto in the text of the *Araucana*:

> Aquí llegó, donde otro no ha llegado,
> don Alonso de Ercilla, que el primero
> en un pequeño barca deslastrado,
> con solos diez pasó el desaguadero
> el año y ciencuenta y ocho entrado
> sobre mil y quinientos, por hebrero,
> a las dos de la tarde, el postrer día,
> volviendo a la dejada compañía. (36.29)

> [Here, where no other has ever been, arrived Don Alonso de Ercilla, who with only ten companions passed the mouth of the channel in a small ballastless boat in the year 1558, during February, at two in the afternoon, to return the next day to his party.]

With the reading of this octave strikes the vertigo of encountering poetic audacity. We are to believe that what we have before our eyes on the printed page is identical to an inscription carved on a tree in the farthest reaches of the earth, on the shore of a promised land as yet to be fully explored. In the space of a single octave, the *Araucana* makes its boldest cartographic move, attempting, through it, to utterly collapse the distance, the *espacio*, that separates the metropolitan reader from the Terra Australis. What Cortés attempts through domesticating description, Ercilla here attempts through inscription and citation.

A savvy reader like Mary Gaylord would recognize the incident as an imitation of Lucian's "True Story." In this hilarious parody of "truthful" travel writing by the satirist Lucian of Samosata (ca. 115–200 C.E.), a mock Odysseus recounts his voyage beyond the Pillars of Hercules to a series of ludicrous imaginary lands, including the Island of the Blest. There, he encounters Homer and asks him to pen a couple of lines suitable for inscription on a tablet of beryl, which he plans to put up near the harbor as testament to his passage. Lucian reproduces the text for his reader: "Lucian came here, saw all there was to see, / Then sailed back home across the wine-dark sea" (Lucian 1990, 285). The passage from Lucian pokes fun at the travel writer's efforts to authorize outlandish claims about far-off places through the production of specious documents. The readers are to believe that the inscription is actually where it is said to be, and that, therefore, the narrator has actually been where he or she claims to have been, because they have a copy of it right there in front of them. What more could a reader need? Ercilla's version of this episode, like the *Araucana* as a whole, conflates the role of the epic poet and the epic traveler, managing at once to poke fun at the two genres, learned narrative poetry and travel writing, into which both the episode and the whole poem insert themselves. Rather than find textual communion with terra incognita, metropolitan readers find themselves once again in contact with their own readings. The *Araucana*'s claims to authority on the grounds that "Ercilla was there" dissolve under the corrosive influence of this joke that Ercilla, the poet, has at the expense of Ercilla the explorer, Ercilla the soldier, and Ercilla the would-be historian. The only voyage the readers take on the wings of this parodic *carta de relación* is to the contents of their own libraries stocked with European classics.

Ercilla returns from the ends of the earth not only to Arauco, but shortly afterward to Europe. His narrative returns to military matters but not to the Araucanian war, which he finally renounces as "wars of unknown, hidden Indians" (36.44). His heroic crossing and act of discovery thus function as a substitute conclusion to a story that has not ended but *has* lost the will to go on. The final digression into the narrative of the expedition has taken over from the principal military narrative, providing a conclusion that that story could not deliver. And that conclusion, as we saw, represented a final, ironic, spatial gesture. With the dissolution of the testimonial travel story into the repeated tropes and jokes of the literary tradition, the real Magellanica remains as elusive as ever. Its essence and its promise are revealed to be what they always were, the textual fantasies of a cartography informed by a tradition, one that needs Magellanica in order to keep alive its own cartographic and imperial desires. In unmasking Magellanica, the *Araucana* also unmasks the pretensions of its own imperial cartographic writing, revealing that the only empire it can celebrate is the one that it can apprehend, and that its apprehensive powers are limited to the words it can mine from other texts. Most important, the text admits to these limitations even when it sings in the counter-cartographic register of itineraries, eyewitness accounts, and their many *estrechezas*. It thereby renounces not only the fantasies of totalization inscribed in its imperial cartography but also the colonial desire inscribed, although never satisfied, in its language of *estrecheza*. Renouncing not only its subject matter but its very power to map a world empire, the *Araucana* concludes with a new beginning, a new story of a new war in Portugal in which the anxieties of producing a totality out of separate pieces are imported from the Americas and restaged on the Iberian scene.[58]

Weeping for Magellan

This cartographic interpretation provides fresh fuel to the fires that have raged around the ideology of the *Araucana*. Those debates have often fastened on particular facets of the poem that have gone all but unexamined here. Time and again, critics have treated the web of prophecy as an unassailable locus of transparent imperialist discourse. They have placed great emphasis upon the poem's often sympathetic treatment of Araucanian culture and specific Araucanian characters. They have done much the same with the poem's treatment of Europeans, particularly its increasing disgust with conquistadorial brutality. Attention has fallen upon the ways that these and other components of this complex poem engage sixteenth-century controversies surrounding the justifiability of Spain's military and political enterprise in America, as well as the closely related question of the nature and origins of the Amerindian.[59] Rarely, however, has the *Araucana* been interpreted as a text that engages these issues, as well as others, by inventing its own discourse about empire, conquest, violence, the Americas, and the Amerindian. This, I hope, is what my cartographic interpretation of the poem has achieved. It has tried to read the poem closely in order to uncover its own, quite unique poetics of cartography and empire, a poetics engaged with, but irreducible to, the debates over the nature of the New World and of its conquest.

I have argued that there are portions of the *Araucana* that are obviously related to the new spatiality of the new maps insofar as they provide broad surveys of territory from commanding points of view and suggest that distant places coexist on a single surface that is at once imperial and cartographic. On the face of things, these portions include the cartographically precise description of Chile with which the poem opens, the spectacular *mappamundi* episode, and the story of the journey to Magellanica, with its grand imperial designs. In each case, the poem calls upon the reader to visualize territories mediated by the cartography of the Renaissance, its techniques, its point of view, its geographical fantasies. In each case, poetry and cartography collude, or seem to collude, in celebrating Hapsburg pretensions to universal monarchy.

The ideological power of these portions, however, is undermined by the counter-cartographic—that is to say, counter-ideological—thrust of other episodes built upon a different, linear spatiality, upon *espacio* in the most common early modern sense. The alternate spatiality manifests itself in the counter-cartography of *estrechezas* that emerges surreptitiously from the description of the Strait of Magellan and that then provides a constant topographical counterpoint to the manifestly cartographic and imperial designs of the rest of the poem. It, and not those manifestly cartographical episodes, provides the *Araucana* with its basic spatial and topographical language. We can easily imagine an edition of Ercilla's poem that excises the description of Chile, the *mappamundi* episode (not to mention the web of prophecy), and the narrative of exploration. After all, such an edition would not be very different from various versions of the poem that have indeed appeared in print. But we cannot imagine the *Araucana* without its linear succession of *estrechezas*, its general movement of retreats and advances along the thin line of Chilean geography, through the bottlenecks that isolate one region from the next. It is this geography of the straits that constitutes the metageography of the poem. It may have never formed a conscious part of Alonso de Ercilla's design for his heroic poem, but it is nonetheless consistently identifiable in all three of its parts, providing it with an imagistic and ideological unity that compensates for its alleged aesthetic shortcomings. From the perspective provided by this metageography of *estrechezas*, what seemed like a panegyric of empire begins to look like a parody of cartographic writing in an imperialistic vein. Finally, the *Araucana* does all this only to then turn the tables on its own language of *estrechezas*. In the story of the trip to Magellanica, the text acknowledges that the colonial desires contained in the language of *estrechezas* are themselves venal and destructive even when they do not find satisfaction in the totalization of imperial space. The opposition it has created between imperial cartography and the counter-cartography of colonial desire thus becomes the Scylla and Charybdis of Ercilla's own poetics. The poem escapes this pinch by submitting its own counter-cartographic discourse to the corrosive influence of parody, a parody that, in effect, renounces the possibility of using discourse to invent America for the European reader.

Looking back at my earlier chapters from the perspective offered by this interpretation of the *Araucana*, we find that Ercilla's poem in effect recapitulates and rewrites much of what we have seen before. Like the plane chart, the *Araucana* combines a two-dimensional, fully cartographic vision of territory with a unidimensional, protocartographic movement through it. To put it another way, Ercilla's text combines the linear movement of Cortés's "Second Letter from Mexico" with the cartographic survey of Gómara's "El sitio de las Indias." It combines these two spatialities, moreover, in order to do something that we have not seen before: it sets these two spatialities against each other, using unidimensional *espacio* to undermine cartographic space. Then, it rejects both, allowing its narrator to fall silent, and break into tears. In this way, it demonstrates a sophisticated grasp of the various discursive opportunities offered by Hispanic early modernity and recognizes in all of them, linear and planar spatialities alike, the discursive cartography of empire.

CONCLUSION

The death of Alonso de Ercilla in 1594 preceded by only four years the death of Philip II, that monarch so keenly aware of the importance of maps to the exercise, both practical and symbolic, of power. What followed was a century usually thought of as that of Spain's decline. By the middle of the seventeenth century, Spain was no longer a credible power, despite its continued hold over much of Italy, the Low Countries, and the Americas. Although its literary and artistic life flourished, its economy was in disarray and its political and military fortunes gradually waned. So, too, did its cartographic enterprises. Iberia, which had once led Europe in the arts of oceanic navigation and maritime cartography, had decisively lost its lead, as early as 1570, to the emerging powers of northern Europe. The seventeenth century widened the gap between north and south. Although the Hapsburg crown continued to produce maps and Spain certainly imported maps and atlases from northern Europe, neither effort seems to have made maps as commonplace in Spain as they became north of the Pyrenees.[1] This was true even in the conduct of warfare. Geoffrey Parker relates that in 1642, in the wake of Catalonian and Portuguese revolts against the rule of the Spanish Hapsburgs, the cosmographer-royal of Spain desperately solicited a counterpart in the Netherlands for maps of Portugal and Catalonia but to little avail. Even in the Netherlands, where the Hapsburg Monarchy faced persistent military opposition, the availability of accurate maps depended upon the private efforts of whatever aristocrat was in charge of Spain's affairs (Parker 2002, 117–21).

In recent years, the commonplace notion that seventeenth-century Spain should be understood as a nation in decline has come under fire, as various scholars have pointed out the surprising resilience of a complex and cumbersome state system in the face of the many adversities posed by the period.[2] The Hispanic Monarchy may not have prospered, but neither did many other European states, and it certainly cannot be said to have collapsed. Apparently, as Kagan (2002) has argued, the crown even continued to produce maps. The recent discovery of a maritime atlas dating from the 1630s suggests that the court of Philip IV, at least, continued to recognize the importance of cartography to power and continued to sponsor the production of maps. As in earlier times, however, the crown seems to have kept its maps in manuscript form (Kagan 2002). This, in turn, may have inhibited their popularization in the culture at large. But whatever may have been the reality of decline or decadence, cartographic or otherwise, it is clear that as the century rolled on, Spanish intellectuals came to believe that their country had fallen behind the rest of Europe in the production and use of maps (Hernando 1999, 113). One lamented that Spain had long lost its leadership in the art of navigation and did not even have at its disposal respectable navigation manuals written in Castilian (Gaztañeta 1692). Another complained that, outside of Spain, "Princes, subjects, political and military men are always poring over charts" while Spain itself remained ignorant of their use (Fernández de Medrano 1686, 4–5).

Complaints like these, along with advent of the Bourbons as the new kings of Spain, brought about a thorough reform of Spanish cartography during the eighteenth century. The Spanish Bourbons imported cartographic techniques and institutions from their French cousins that would map Spain and its empire with a degree of precision and a level of ambition that would have thrilled Philip II and Juan López de Velasco. The creation of those institutions and the development of those maps coincided, as we saw, with the popularization of the word *espacio* in its modern sense as the name of an area rather than as a distance or an interval of time. It coincided, too, if our dictionaries do not lie, with the final establishment of the modern scale map as the hegemonic form of geographical representation in the West. It coincided, finally, with the decisive reorientation of Spain's imperial imaginary out toward the Atlantic and the Pacific rather than toward Europe. By 1761, it had become possible to picture the Spanish Monarchy as it stretched from Madrid to Manila in a way that the sixteenth century had only barely approximated. In that year, a Jesuit priest in the Philippines known as Vicente de Memije fashioned an allegorical map of Spain's Atlantic and Pacific empire (fig. 35). On it, the Monarchy appears as a unified body politic crowned with the kingdoms of Spain itself, draped with the Indies and the Pacific, and shod with the islands that Memije called home. It is a body immaculately conceived, enlightened by the Spirit, armed to defend the faith embodied in the Roman Catholic Eucharist. Possessed by the

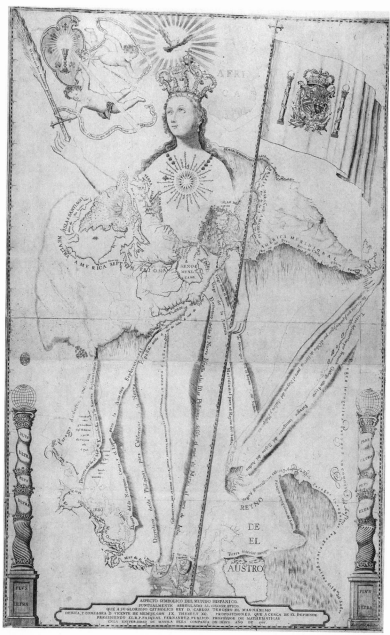

35 Vicente de Memije, *Aspecto Symbólico del Mundo Hispánico: puntualmente arreglado al Geográfico* (Manila, 1761). The Hispanic Monarchy as a virgin queen. The image is derived from a map of the Monarchy from Spain to the Philippines, also drawn by Memije. Courtesy of the British Library.

fervor of militant religious orthodoxy, this body is also in possession of those secular practicalities indispensable to a global, maritime empire. A compass rose provides this imperial virgin with her radiant heart. Maritime routes become the folds in the garment that link the West Indies to the East. The graduated line of the equator bears the arms of the Bourbon kings and promises, perhaps, to extend their sway round the full girth of the globe. Even the garments themselves—derived from a map of Spain's overseas territories—rustle with the sounds of empire.

Memije's image provides a striking contrast to the allegorical map of "Europa Regina" that we saw at the outset of this study (see fig. 4 above). There, Spain appears as the head of a European body politic: its newly won American possessions have not yet made it onto the map. Memije in effect pivots the earlier image one hundred eighty degrees. The War of the Spanish Succession has cut the Spanish head off what was left of its old, European body, but the twin processes of the invention of America—and indeed, of the Atlantic and the Pacific worlds, of "the Indies" broadly conceived—and of the invention of the map, with its power to render visible spaces and territories of vast expanse, have come to its rescue. They have made it possible to reattach that head to a different body, one that was not quite visible two centuries before. Memije's image thus brings a dramatic climax to a story that began in Tordesillas in 1494 and that can be traced through the history of Spanish cartography of the Americas, across the maps of Ribeiro (fig. 17 above), García de Toreno (fig. 27 above), Medina (fig. 5 above), Gutiérrez (fig. 18 above), and López de Velasco (fig. 16 above), as well as many others. In this series of maps and mappings, we glimpse first the delineation of a space and a frontier (everything beyond the line of demarcation), then the delineation of a landmass, a possession, and finally the coherent expression of both at once, a map that spectacularizes both the original line of demarcation and its eastern extension, as well as all the territories known to lie between. Memije's image brings this story to its culmination by taking the territories in this space and making them an integral part of a Hispanic body politic. With his image, that new Hispanic metageography, that "Greater Spain" that lurked in the margins of Medina's *Libro de grandezas y cosas memorables de España*, an imperial Spain whose body was not European, finally comes into view. With it, too, we come upon a dazzling example of the modern collusion between empire and cartography that had been gestating since Iberian ships began to sail to both the East and West Indies.

This book has traced a series of episodes in this process, as well as in one of its most significant counterpoints. We have seen how the geometrically rationalized spatiality so in evidence in Memije's image and in the map that accompanies it only gradually emerged out of the expansionist culture of early modern Europe as represented by Spain. As we have seen, the culture that first sent caravels across the Atlantic (and down the African littoral) was a culture rooted in the linear spatiality of the Middle Ages, that sense of space as distance rather than area, that habit of imagining territory in and through the body's journey from one place to the next. That spatiality, as we saw, served well the initial efforts of Spaniards eager to reach out over the horizon and apprehend the distant New World, maintaining a surprising lease on life despite the increasing dissemination of modern maps with their abstract spatiality. In Cortés, we saw how the linear spatiality of Marco Polo and the itinerary map worked well to invent a New Spain caught between justice and tyranny in the process of becoming an American empire. In Gómara and Oviedo, the hybrid spatiality of the plane chart and Enciso's *Suma de geographia*—its combination of line and plane, movement and stasis, tour and map—could be developed into various cartographic histories that served to forge an America populated by the European imagination. In las Casas, we found a counterexample to the imperialistic cartographic histories, one that struggled against the strategies of containment inherent in Gómara's insularizing prose cartography. Finally, in Ercilla, we found that the new cartographic sensibility developed into a visionary experience that appears to celebrate empire only to draw upon the dynamic linearity typical of Cortés to bring its pretensions of mastery into question.

These various essays into the cartographic literature of early modern Spain lead to one principal conclusion. It has been said that "the mapping of the world opened up a way to look upon space as open to appropriation for private uses" (Harvey 1990, 228), and that the cartographic rationalization of space made possible the idea of a world "over which systematic dominance was possible" (Woodward 1991, 87). These remarks and others like them are surely true in many ways, but not as statements about the relationship between colonialism and cartography at their origins. As we have seen, the new culture of abstract space introduced during the fifteenth century remained the province of a small group of technical specialists throughout the sixteenth. The thousands of other historical agents involved in the discovery, conquest, and colonization of the Americas did not need to imagine the world through the medium of geometric abstraction in order to take an interest in controlling and possessing it. Nor did the authors we have seen need a fully developed cartographic culture to imagine empire, to celebrate it, or to question it. If anything, we have seen how the culture of abstraction grew significantly only well after Europeans ventured beyond the Pillars of Hercules. Far from fueling the origins of colonialism, the culture of abstraction begins to look like a rationalization after the fact, an attempt to grapple with the challenges posed by a wider world, a world built by the travels of a culture who thought about space primarily in terms of distance.

Naturally, this conclusion cannot be the final word about spatiality, mapping, empire, and discourse in the early modern Hispanic world. For one, the approach I have adopted in this book does not allow it. I have intended to strike a middle register, somewhere in between close specialization and broad generalization. I have not limited myself to a single text, author, genre, historical moment, or geographical location. Nor have I attempted to synthesize everything that could be said about cartography, literature, and empire in the early modern Hispanic world. Instead, I have ventured into a variety of texts written at different moments in the history of Spain's encounter with America, dealing with different places in the Spanish Indies, in different modes of historical writing, and addressed to different audiences for different purposes. Within my series of readings I have thus traded comprehensive coverage for strategies of close reading, and various potential forms of coherence, for generic and historical diversity. I hope that these two choices have made it possible to achieve a variety of objectives. By paying close attention to a limited number of cartographic texts, both iconographic and discursive, I hope to have discovered certain historical particularities in the analysis of cartography, literature, and empire that would have gone unnoticed by a more generalized treatment of this subject. By introducing some diversity into the texts I have analyzed, my goal was to provide a glimpse of the wider history of space and mapping, iconographic and verbal, toward which this book points but which it does not pretend to provide.

That wider history has yet to be written: the vast undiscovered country of Hispanic cartographic literature has yet to be explored. That literature includes many and various attempts to figure in words both the New World and the Old, for a multitude of purposes. These attempts include selections from the corpus of Spanish Americana and early colonial writing, such as the work of Pietro Martire d'Anghiera, the Peruvian chronicles of Pedro Cieza de León, the Inca Garcilaso de la Vega, and Guamán Poma de Ayala. They include the massive *Décadas* of Antonio de Herrera, an ambitious attempt by an officially sponsored historian to synthesize the natural and moral history of the Indies that included a number of printed maps. Don Quixote's ride on Clavileño reminds us, too, that there are territories to be explored in the literature of the Spanish Golden Age. Ercilla's poem provides an obvious point of departure for the study of Cervantes's masterwork as well as his lesser-known works, such as the highly geographical *Los trabajos de Persiles y Segismunda* (1617). Another critical itinerary might turn to Góngora's *Soledad primera* (1613), where we encounter an elderly man who recites a diatribe against Spanish imperialism in the form of a narrative of westward movement reminiscent of the itinerary taken by Fitón's map. Yet another course could lead to the theater of Lope de Vega, Tirso de Molina, and Calderón de la Barca, and in particular, to that handful of plays that figure American events. And yet another takes us to Baltasar Gracián's Criticón (1651–57), whose protagonist, born on an island halfway between Europe and America, embarks on a journey through an allegorical map of Gracián's world.[3] All of these texts have been read, analyzed, and studied over the course of many years. What have we to learn, either about the texts themselves or about the history of spatiality in Spain, by examining them specifically as cartographic literature, as attempts to map a new metageography for an emerging imperial power? A great deal, I am sure, about the complex process by which a central aspect of modernity came into existence.

This work need not be limited to the Hispanic context. A quick glance at the Oxford English Dictionary will demonstrate that "space" had many of the same meanings in early modern English that it had in early modern Spanish, including that of a chronological or topographical distance between two points of reference. A cursory exploration of the history of topographical and nautical cartography, moreover, will reveal that itinerary maps were used everywhere, not just in Iberia and the Iberian New World, as were both portolan and plane charts. What we have in Spain, then, is not a singular phenomenon but a particularly interesting case study in an aspect of the larger European passage to modernity. The relatively high degree of bureaucratic organization attained early on by Spanish colonialism has preserved a body of "amateur" maps that may not be as easily found in other countries but that are nonetheless essential for perceiving the alternatives to modern space at play in the culture. It is interesting, too, because, with the passage of time, this spatiality that, in all probability, was once common to all of Europe became something "Spanish" as the cartographic revolution began to flourish in northern Europe, leaving Spain behind. But, again, it is not entirely unique. Elsewhere in early modern Europe and America space was figured—as it is still figured today—by touring through it discursively rather than picturing it. Elsewhere people drew maps that clung to the tour or combined it with the static image. How important was this tendency before the hegemony of the map reduced the tour and the way-finding map to the margins of real cartography? This is but one of the questions to be addressed by a cultural history of spatiality rooted in the plurality and mutability of the notion of space itself.

Ultimately, I hope to have sparked interest in cartography and literature that will continue to press into the many textual territories that this book leaves unexplored. I hope also to have provided some useful parameters for continued investigation. Future investigation—if there is any—would be attentive to issues of how language figures geographies and of how its figures reflect, perpetuate, utilize, and sometimes even transform various notions of "space" or of what it means to map. It would be cognizant that, in different places and at different times, "space" changes, and so does the spatial capacity of language. Certainly, some kinds of space—such as distance—may harmonize more easily than other kinds with the linear flow of language. This is not to say, however, that discursive communities cannot reach implicit agreements about the ways in which language can, indeed, come to figure spaces that do not conform with its linearity. It would be cognizant, moreover, of cartography—whether verbal or iconographic—as a practice embedded in the assumptions and needs of the people who do the mapping. In the case of my own field, this would mean recognizing the place of Spanish Americana in early modern Hispanic cultural studies. It would mean questioning the ways in which our field has been territorialized, and thereby realizing what new worlds of investigation can be constructed when the boundaries of the field are redrawn. It would also be alive to the ideological obfuscations that attend to mapping—any kind of mapping—that pretends to reduce distant places into figures that have meaning for us here.

I arrive, at last, to the final consideration of these concluding pages. Over the course of the past twenty years, at least, the study of the Columbian encounter and the events that ensued has been cast in tones of melancholy, regret, guilt, and outrage. For very good reason, too, given the tremendous human and natural destruction wrought by the expansion of Europe into the non-European world. In this light, what does it matter how Europeans conceptualized space? Did it make a difference to the Amerindian suffering from the destruction and change wrought by colonialism that the colonial powers-that-be were not fully "modern" in some sense? Did the difference I have outlined in the spatiality of European culture in any way blunt the edges of European swords? Probably not. But as we come to grips with our own emergence from the modernity that began, more or less, when Martin Waldseemüller christened the New World "America" or when Cortés scuttled his ships on the Mexican shore, we would do well to think long about the political valence we assign to whatever, in our own culture, preceded that modernity and now exists only at the margins of that modernity, silent and stripped of its authoritative crown. We tend to imagine such alternatives to the modern as inherently liberating, yet we would do well to remember that they, too, can be instruments of power. A rectilinear grid is not the only armature upon which one can map an empire.

NOTES

Chapter One

1. The so-called "Charles V Atlas" forms part of the collection of the John Carter Brown Library at Brown University in Providence, RI. A limited-edition facsimile of this atlas is also available. See Agnese (1875).

2. For the role of the winds, personified as cherublike heads, in creating such three-dimensional spaces on Renaissance maps, see Jacob (1992, 150–52).

3. Historians of cartography once downplayed Spain's role in the early modern carto-graphic revolution since the number of sixteenth-century Spanish maps that survive to the present day is quite small in comparison with the number of maps produced in other countries. More recently, this interpretation of Spain as a cartographically backward na-tion has come into question because it is clear that the scarcity of Spanish maps in modern archives has to do with the policy of the Crown to keep its maps out of print, not with a failure to produce or use manuscript maps. Still, this policy may have stunted the devel-opment of cartographic literacy in Hispanic culture, which is an issue that I address in my conclusion. For cartography and the state in the early modern period, see Buisseret (1992). For an overview of state-sponsored cartography under Philip II, see Parker (1992; 2002). For the later Hapsburgs in particular, see Kagan (2002).

4. Thus, Walter Mignolo rightfully identifies a "core period" spanning from roughly 1570 through 1630 as central to his analysis of spatial rationalization in the service of Hispanic empire (1995, xv). For applied science during the period after 1550, see Vicente Maroto and Piñeiro (1991). For cartography and exploration in particular, see Cuesta Do-mingo (1999). For cartography and the state during the reign of Philip II, see Parker (1992).

5. For a problematic but lively discussion that works hard to defamiliarize the map image, see Wood and Fels (1992). For a more recent discussion of maps and power, see Black (1997).

6. Throughout this book, I use "America" in the way that it is used in Spanish, not in the English of the United States. It is meant to refer to the New World as a whole—both

239

"North" and "South" America—and not to either of the two continents exclusively and never to the United States of America. Although this usage may seem strange to some readers, it is consistent with the vast majority of the texts I will be discussing.

7. The problem is compounded by the fact that these maps are scattered in a variety of European and American archives, most of them outside the Spanish-speaking world. Others appear in early modern Spanish books and are therefore more readily available, but these are not as important as the manuscript maps. These difficulties have led some scholars to conclude that Spain simply did not make or use maps, leading to serious distortions in the history of Spanish and even of early modern cartography. Great strides have been made toward rectifying this state of affairs in the last fifty years or so, and particularly in the last fifteen, through the publication of several high-quality secondary sources, some of which reproduce many of the manuscript maps in color. See especially Berwick (1951), Cerezo Martínez (1994), Hernando (1995), Martín-Merás (1992), and Vindel (1955). On the vicissitudes of Spanish cartographic production in the sixteenth and seventeenth centuries, see Hernando (1999) and Kagan (2002).

8. The same, of course, could be said about the collusion of maps and empire in early modern Portugal, which, regrettably, falls outside my expertise.

9. All quotes come from the 1944 edition of Medina's *Libro de grandezas y cosas memorables de España*. All further citations will be made parenthetically in the text. For more on navigation as a sign of Spanish modernity, see Maravall (1966, 561–62).

10. See Elliott (1970, 1992), as well as Chiappelli et al. (1976), Ryan (1981), Grafton and Siraisi (1992), Pagden (1986, 1993), and Kupperman (1995). I have more to say about an important precursor to all of these projects, the work of Edmundo O'Gorman, in the pages that follow.

11. The geographical literature of the ancient world—Strabo's *Geography*, in particular, (1923, 3: 136–76)—described Spain as the "head" of Europe, referring, usually, to its exceedingly temperate climate, its rich farmlands, and its many natural resources. As Charles of Ghent, now the emperor Charles V, became increasingly identified with his Spanish possessions, it became possible to shift such rhetoric about the excellence of Spain from the sphere of the natural to that of the political. This is precisely what Bucius does in this image, which, according to Lewes (2000, 134), spawned a minor genre of "Europa Regina" figures. These images give iconographic form to something long ago recognized by Fernand Braudel. Throughout the reign of Charles V and well into that of his son and successor Philip II, Spain was primarily oriented toward Europe and the Mediterranean rather than toward the Atlantic (Braudel 1973, 2: 1184–85).

12. Also known in English as Peter Martyr d'Anghera and in Spanish as Pedro Mártir de Angléria.

13. Dates in each case refer to the year of the first printed edition. Some of these texts enjoyed various editions and translations and were also included in collections of travel narratives.

14. *The Invention of America* was originally published in 1958, but I cite from the revised and expanded 1986 edition of *La invención de América* first published in 1977 and reissued by the Fondo de Cultura Económica in various later editions. Subsequent references to *La invención de América* will be made parenthetically in the text. *La invención de América* builds upon O'Gorman's 1951 work, *La idea del descubrimiento de América*. More recently, Eviatar Zerubavel

(1992) has made a similar argument. Martin Lewis and Kären Wigen (1997), meanwhile, have synthesized O'Gorman's argument with those of many others into a critique of the whole system of continents, as well as other, similar "metageographies."

15. In a later restatement of an earlier salvo in this argument, J. H. Elliott rejects the notion that the assimilation of America by European culture can be understood as a "linear development from incomprehension to assimilation" (1992, xii).

16. Ryan's words encapsulate the assumptions of many other scholars. See, for example, Franklin (1979), Greenblatt (1991), Hulme (1992), Mignolo (1995), Pagden (1986, 1993), Pastor (1992), Rabasa (1987), and Todorov (1984).

17. The "region," Paul Veyne, remarks, is to geography what the "plot" is to historiography, the product of an encounter between data and expectations, between nature and culture (1984, 295–96). On "emplotment," see the work of Hayden White (1973, 1978, 1988). On the ideology of geography, see also Said (1978, 1993).

18. The Italian cosmographer Giacomo Gastaldi is famous for his 1565 map of the world, which depicted a contiguous coastline extending from what we now know as the Pacific coast of North America, across the Pacific all the way to southeast Asia. Less well known is a slightly earlier map by Caspar Vopel, which advanced the same geographical idea but using the very same cordiform cartographic projection that Waldseemüller had adopted for his famous 1507 map. The toponymy of this 1558 map of the world clearly converts New Spain (modern Mexico and Central America) into a hinterland of Marco Polo's East. The map, entitled *Nova et integra universalisque orbis totius iuxta Germanam neotericorum traditionem descriptio*, was printed in Venice and is in the collection of the Houghton Library, Harvard University. A reproduction of this map is currently unavailable. For further discussion of the fortunes of Waldseemüller's hypothesis in the history of Renaissance cartography, see Zerubavel (1992) and Burden (1996).

19. Oviedo's geography becomes an emblem of the universal monarchy aspired to by Charles V or, at least, by some of the official rhetoric surrounding him. The geography of las Casas, by contrast, contributes to his attempt to defend the humanity and rationality of the native inhabitants of the Indies and thereby to criticize the methods through which that empire had been constructed. Acosta's geography, finally, is meant to forestall some of the threats posed by an insular America to received theological and anthropological notions. In doing so, it also serves to figure an American culture in need of the civilizing and evangelical benefits that only Hispanic imperialism can bring.

20. O'Gorman himself recognizes that Waldseemüller's hypothesis was contested over the next several decades, even by its proponent, and would not be empirically confirmed until the discovery of the Bering Strait some two hundred years later (149–51). See his introductions to Acosta's *Historia natural y moral de las Indias* (1598), and, especially, to Las Casa's *Apologética historia sumaria* (ca. 1555). Both are conveniently reprinted in O'Gorman (1972). Nonetheless, in *La invención de América*, O'Gorman makes little of these instances of backsliding, even when they issue from the pens of the very Spanish historians upon which he so heavily relies. Eager to tell his story of the transformation of one metageography into another, O'Gorman reduced the many instances of geographical "backsliding" to the status of accidental modifications to an innovation—Waldseemüller's—that has been accepted in its essence. The fundamental leap of the imagination contained in the cosmographer's hypothesis must be understood to persist, even in geographies that seem to deny

it by physically linking the New World with the Old. Only in this way can O'Gorman make his larger point, that the invention of America as an independent continent grounded the passage of European culture from medievalism to modernity.

21. For a fuller discussion of medieval *mappaemundi*, see Woodward (1987) and Edson (1997).

22. My use of "spatial structure" or "armature" to refer to the basic geometry of these maps echoes Denis Wood's discussion of "tectonic codes" in cartography. According to Wood, each map "employs a tectonic code . . . a code of construction, which configures graphic space in a particular relation to geodesic space." He is referring explicitly to mathematical projections, but his remark can clearly be extended to include other "codes of construction," like the T-O framework outlined here. According to Wood, "While iconic and linguistic codes access the semantic field of geographic knowledge, the tectonic code provides their syntactical superstructure; this is the code through which we signify not what, but where. In molding the map image, the tectonic code allows it to refer to the space we occupy and experience; and inevitably it is laden with our . . . preconceptions about that space." See Wood and Fels (1992, 124–25).

23. Drawing primarily on early modern maps, J. B. Harley has articulated a theory of the map as a "thick text" or a "socially constructed form of knowledge." See his essays "Maps, Knowledge, and Power" and "Deconstructing the Map," reprinted recently in Harley and Laxton (2001, 51–82, 149–68).

24. It has been argued that this development is intimately connected to the rediscovery of linear perspective, the cultural context favored by Lefebvre. Samuel Edgerton (1987) makes the link between the two, while Svetlana Alpers (1987) identifies cartography with the unique perspective of Dutch landscape painting. David Harvey, building upon Lefebvre's work, finds the story of Renaissance cartography particularly revealing in an attempt to understand the rationalization of space under capitalism (1990, 240–59). Edward Casey sees in the cartography of the Age of Exploration a hinge between medieval speculations about space and the decisive triumph of space over place in seventeenth-century philosophy, one of Lefebvre's culprits in the triumph of abstract space (Casey 1997, 115).

25. For Kagan, the many and varied nonscientific and marginally scientific maps of the period become members of a single class, a "symbolic cartography" that is heir to "another far older, and more widely diffused cartographic tradition that had less to do with observation and careful measurement than with religion and the representation of space in highly symbolic terms" (2000, 55). John Gillies identifies an ancient "poetic geography" that persists in and through the maps of the cartographic revolution despite its many scientific innovations (1994, 4). This poetic geography consists of more or less arbitrary acts of imaginative territorialization, not unlike the invention of America itself. Both Kagan and Gillies make productive use of these concepts but tend to overgeneralize their scope.

26. Michel de Certeau (1984, 120–21) and Frank Lestringant (1993a, 326–27) recognize that the plurality of cartographic forms and mapmaking communities in the early modern period can be interpreted in terms of patterns of resistance to an increasingly hegemonic modernity. While I agree with them that these pluralities are significant, I re-

ject their attempt to read resistant cartographies in utopian or nostalgic terms. For more about the politics of cartographic heterogeneity, see chapter 2.

Chapter Two

1. Bruno Bosteels (1996) offers fascinating insights into the meaning of cartographic metaphors in contemporary Marxism and poststructuralism. Bosteels himself acknowledges that the meanings he explores represent only a small part of what map words have come to mean in the past few decades.

2. For similar definitions, see Bagrow (1985, 22) and Crone (1962, xi). For discussion of this and other definitions, see Harley and Woodward (1987, xv), as well as Jacob (1992, 29–138).

3. All references to the *Diccionario de autoridades* are to the on-line edition of the text. See the list of works cited for details.

4. *Diccionario de autoridades*, s.v. "Espacio," at http://buscon.rae.es/ntlle/SrvltGUI LoginNtlle.

5. *Diccionario de autoridades*, s.v. "Mapa," at http://buscon.rae.es/ntlle/SrvltGUI LoginNtlle.

6. All references to Covarrubias Horozco, *Tesoro de la lengua castellana o española*, are made parenthetically in the text and are taken from the 1994 edition in the list of works cited.

7. The *Oxford English Dictionary* (OED), 2d ed., registers a similar definition for "space" in premodern and early modern English, as a "lapse or extent of time between two definite points, events, etc." and "delay, deferment."

8. For more on the Treaty of Tordesillas, see Albuquerque (1973). On the importance of the 1524 negotiations, see Brotton (1997, chapter 4).

9. These centers represent only those directly sponsored by the crown. The Society of Jesus, for example, established its own geographical and cartographical infrastructure and produced its own maps. Catalonia and Mallorca, meanwhile, continued to produce the traditional nautical charts for which they had become famous in the late Middle Ages. Since the chapters that follow examine texts directed toward the crown, I have decided to omit the work of these alternative centers from my discussion. For more about the contexts of Spanish overseas cartography, see the essay by David Buisseret in Woodward (forthcoming).

10. This summary is primarily drawn from José María López Piñero's introduction to the art of navigation in Spain (1986, 79–150). See also López Piñero (1979, 198–99).

11. For the politics of cosmography in sixteenth-century Spain, see Lamb (1976, 1995) and Sandman (2001).

12. Anthony Pagden's excellent translation of the letters that Cortés wrote Charles V distorts matters by using the English "map" to translate the circumlocutions that Cortés uses to refer to representations of territory. For example, the original Spanish "hicieron una figura en paño" becomes "they drew on a cloth a map" (Cortés 1993, 530; 2001, 340), rather than "they drew a figure on a cloth." The more literal translation captures the novelty of maps and map use in the 1520s.

13. Harley and Woodward's *Cartography in Prehistoric, Ancient, and Medieval Europe and the Mediterranean* dedicates substantial attention to medieval *mappaemundi* (286–370), portolan charts (371–483), and local and regional cartography (484–501).

14. Some of them may very well represent relics from a Roman past that was much more familiar with the surveying techniques necessary to produce such images that was the European Middle Ages. Although the learned were familiar with the techniques used by the Romans and in their own time by Muslims, there is no evidence that this learning was ever applied. It is not clear that any of it informed the production of the few topographical maps that have survived (Harvey 1987a, 494–95).

15. Dilke (1987, 238–42) provides a very useful introduction to the Peutinger Tabula, as does Harvey (1980, 133–47; 1987a, 495–98), who also examines several medieval English itinerary maps.

16. The Diccionario de autoridades does not register this word. The Real Academia Española's Diccionario de la lengua española, 2st ed., defines "croquis" as a "A quick drawing of a territory, landscape or military position, which is done by sight and without recourse to geometrical instruments."

17. Later, in reference to the nautical charts of Alonso de Santa Cruz in particular, Mignolo (1995) argues, "The maps attached to his Islario general, together with the written discourse . . . focus on the coastline and wind directions rather than on the possessions of the Spanish empire, as is the case of . . . López de Velasco" (287).

18. Not everyone sets aside way-finding maps the way Mignolo does. Michel de Certeau provides a telling contrast, one that can help us discover how the circulation of way-finding maps signifies much more than the personal experiences of their makers. In The Practice of Everyday Life, Certeau explores the ways in which space is figured by modernity and its institutions, as well as the ways in which these figures of space run into the resistance of individuals who use space in alternate ways. At one juncture, he assigns pride of place to precisely the sort of map that Mignolo ignores, the nautical chart, as a site of resistance to the modern. Unlike the map, which erases from its face the historical operations that brought it into being, the nautical chart acknowledges them. The images of ships that decorate so many of these charts serve to recall the journeys that first traced the geographies they figure (Certeau 1984, 120). Charts thus become emblems of resistance to modernity and its power. While way-finding maps are disqualified by the cartography of the Renaissance as "real" maps, their commitment to the journey persists to our own day in the various ways we use space against the grain of modernity's spatial fix. Frank Lestringant follows in Certeau's wake as he notes that the cartography of the humanists never established a complete monopoly over early modern mapmaking. Sailors continued to make and use the same sort of nautical charts that they had been using since the late Middle Ages, which thus marked a site of resistance to the increasing hegemony of the modern map (Lestringant 1993a, 326–27). Notice, however, that while both Certeau and Lestringant authorize us to turn to nautical charts as a site where we might be able to explore this alternative spatiality of the early modern period, neither fully outlines the spatial imagination of the nautical chart itself. The chart is a site of resistance, it is "not that," rather than a figure of a spatiality in its own right. Anthony Grafton, meanwhile, maps out the different cartographic traditions that informed humanists and practical people but does not try to reach conclusions about the politics inherent in the difference (Grafton and Siraisi 1992, 11–94).

19. Mignolo, in his own attempts to free historical discourse from the hegemony of the gridded map, tries to undermine this bias by proposing that we speak not of "maps"

but of "territorial representations." Like Harley's definition, this category is open to different determinations of what constitutes a "territory" and how it can be rendered in graphic form. It is meant to be inclusive and to place such artifacts as Mexica *pinturas* on a level playing field with European maps. In this way, the story of territorialization so central to the history of the 1492 Encounter comes to be understood as a confrontation between different, incommensurable territorial imaginations, each one expressed in its own graphic idiom rather than as the substitution of primitive mapping with scientific cartography (Mignolo 1991).

20. For more on the history of place, see Casey (1997) and Tuan (1977).

21. In this, Polo's book resembles other texts that circulated in late medieval and early modern Spain. They include the *Itinerario* of Ludovico Varthema (1510), the *Itinerarium* of John Mandeville (1496), the *Andanças e viajes* of Pero Tafur (ca. 1436–39), and the anonymous *Libro del conoscimiento* (ca. 1450). Together, these and other travel narratives constitute discursive analogues to the itinerary map. The exigencies of travel provide the logic used to rationalize space.

22. This is the title of the early-fourteenth century, Franco-Italian text that most scholars believe to be the earliest and the closest to the original. It is in the Bibliothèque Nationale, Paris, ms. Fr. 1116 (Larner 184).

23. Greco-Roman geographical discourse is essential to what we know—or think we know—about cartography in the ancient Mediterranean world. Very few ancient maps have survived to our day, requiring us to infer what they must have been like from other texts of other kinds, such as discursive geographies and historiography. In *La mappa e il periplo*, Janni argues that the inferences usually made by classical scholarship have been fundamentally misguided. That scholarship tends, for example, to infer that lengthy geographical descriptions, like those of Strabo or Pomponius Mela, would have come accompanied by maps, or at least that they demonstrate a certain amount of cartographic literacy in the culture that produced and consumed them. It also tends to translate words that refer to different kinds of geographical descriptions as "map" or "chart" and thereby reach generous conclusions about map use in antiquity. Janni argues that these inferences ignore the many crucial stumbling blocks presented by geographical language itself and thereby mistakenly project onto antiquity a sort of cartographic culture that it did not have. Strabo, for example, uses language of movement and orientation in a manner that resists translation into cartographic form. Janni thus advocates a more conservative treatment of classical geographical discourse, one that leads to a very different assessment of "ancient cartography." Map use, he argues, was not widespread in antiquity, and neither was the tendency to imagine the world through the two-dimensional spatiality of the map. The predominant spatial imagination of the Greco-Roman world was actually quite different from that of the modern West in that it tended to imagine the world through the unidimensional spatiality of the itinerary or periplus, rather than the two-dimensional one of the map. It constructed its world as a network of possible itineraries radiating out from a concrete, grounded center of enunciation toward the horizon rather than as a surface that could be pictured and surveyed from an imaginary height. The ancients, in this sense, can be considered a precartographic, or noncartographic culture (Janni 1985, 17–47). The Russian scholar Alexander Podossinov has reached the same conclusion, independently of Janni. Readers of English can appreciate his argument through his review

of the first volume of Harley and Woodward's *History of Cartography* (Podossinov and Checkin 1991). Their position is that of a small minority. For the majority view, see Dilke (1985, 1987).

24. For further discussion of early modern navigational techniques, see Cerezo Martínez (1994), E. G. R. Taylor (1971), and Waters (1958).

25. For expediency's sake, I will not delve into the many debates surrounding the origins and use of the charts. For an up-to-date discussion of these issues, including an ample bibliography, see Campbell (1987, 371–483).

26. Harvey calls this map "impressively accurate" and attributes that accuracy to Cusa's crucial innovation, the use of a compass to measure the angles of itineraries (Harvey 1980, 146–47).

27. For more details about Esquivel's project, as well as references, see Parker (2002, 103–7). Parker also devotes attention to Spanish efforts to map the theater of war in the Low Countries.

28. Santa Cruz outlines his methods in his treatise on longitude, which remained in manuscript form throughout the early modern period. There are at least two twentieth-century editions of the work, including the one included in Cuesta Domingo's anthology of Santa Cruz's writings. See Cuesta Domingo (1983, 1: 139–202)

29. For more on López de Velasco's projects, see Parker (1998, 62–65), Vicente Maroto and Esteban Piñeiro (1991, 399–406), and Edwards (1969). The technical aspects of this project are discussed by Ursula Lamb (1969, 51). Clinton Edwards reproduces the simplified directions for making astronomical observations as they were printed in 1582 (1969, 19–21).

30. Standard works on the history of navigation and nautical charts in sixteenth-century Spain, include Puente y Olea (1900) and Pulido Rubio (1950). For more recent contributions, see Cerezo Martínez (1994), Martín-Merás (1992), and Sandman (2001). For an accessible introduction to navigation, geography, and cartography in early modern Spain, see López Piñero (1986).

31. "Navigazione d'altura significa un nuovo senso della bidimensionalità della super-ficie terrestre: essa sta alla carta come la navigazione costiera sta al periplo. Per navigare lungo costa bastava l'elenco dei porti, delle distanze, con qualche indicazione di direzione qua e là, come un di più; ora, por attraversare i mari e per arrivare non troppo lontano dal punto giusto, occorre una rotta, un azimuth, cose che si collocano non più lungo una *linea*, ma su una *superficie*" (Janni 1985, 59).

32. In this way, David Turnbull argues, institutions like the Casa de la Contratación can be thought of as distinctively modern. They functioned as "knowledge spaces" in which local information could be assembled for cosmopolitan consumption, in which knowledge was standardized, and in which state control was exerted over territorial ex-pansion (1996, 7–9). His remark can easily be extended to the office of the chronicler-cosmographer.

33. I refer to the cartographic projection developed in 1569 by Gerhard Mercator, and later, in 1599, made practicable by the publication of a set of mathematical tables by the Englishman Edward Wright. Mercator, like many other early moderns, tended to mingle cosmography and religion. Since he was a Protestant, his publications ended up on the Inquisitorial Indices of Prohibited Books of 1612 and 1632 (López Piñero 1979, 253).

Although, like other banned books, his works may very well have been widely read and studied, it would have been dangerous to publicly acknowledge familiarity with them by producing a map based upon his ideas.

34. For a concise and highly readable introduction to the problem of the longitude, see Sobel (1995, 1998).

35. Barbara Mundy (1996) carries out one of the finest, recent discussions of maps of this kind. Her first chapter, moreover, paints an eloquent picture of the expectations of the cosmographers and of their frustrations with the results of their projects.

36. When, during the 1520s, Colón was appointed pilot major and placed in charge of supervising the education of pilots and the production of charts, he worked to enhance the control of the cosmographers over the training of pilots and, thereby, the practice of navigation. On the importance of disciplined field agents for the exercise of long-distance control, see Law (1986, 246–51) and Sandman (2001, 160–211). For more on Colón's attempts to assert such control at the Casa de la Contratación, see Sandman (2001, 108–14).

37. The most recent English translation of Don Quixote translates the same line less literally: "Who was waiting a good distance away"(Cervantes Saavedra 2001, 1: 8).

38. One of them is the chart of the Coatzalcualco River drawn by Francisco Stroza Gali that accompanied the Relación geográfica de la Provincia de Coatzacualco (1580). It includes a wind rose, a scale in leagues, and even provides both the latitude and the longitude of the river's mouth (Acuña 1982, 2: 126). The text of the report, in turn, provides the elevation of the Villa del Espíritu Santo, the province's major center of population, as "seventeen degrees, more or less," and specifies that Mexico City lies thirty leagues to the west-northwest (Acuña 1982, 2: 117). When it turns to questions about nearby coastlines and bodies of water, the report demonstrates a mariner's experience with shoals, storms and the like (Acuña 1982, 2: 124–25).

39. Barbara Mundy suggests that the cosmographers expected their respondents to return geometrically-rationalized maps of their localities (1996, 34), but one of the printed versions of the questionnaire they sent out suggests that, on the contrary, the cosmographers had much lower expectations. It asks for the "height or elevation of the pole [i.e., the latitude] at which lie the said towns," but only "if it had been taken and was known, or if there were someone available who knew how to take it." It asks for the distance between the province and the seat of its audiencia, as well as the distances among the towns of the province, but it does not ask the respondents to map out these routes segment by segment, complete with compass bearings. The respondents are asked only to relate how far one town is from another, "in which direction it lies," and whether or not the routes present rough going (Acuña 1982, 2: 21).

40. Barbara Mundy examines the latter three (1996, 35–38). For the texts of all four of these relaciones, as well as the maps that accompanied them, see volumes two and three of Acuña (1982).

41. Luis Fernando Restrepo has reached similar conclusions about the persistence of linear spatiality in early modern Hispanic culture. Restrepo, however, locates the source of this linear spatiality in the Christian theological vision of life as pilgrimage (2002, 85-86; see also Restrepo 1999). Ahern (1989) makes brief mention of the linear spatiality of conquest narrative as well.

42. As Alison Sandman argues, "Just as the modern subway traveler might know the train connections necessary to get between two stations without knowing their relative locations above ground, pilots in the sixteenth century relied on a series of routes and compass bearings, attaching little importance to latitude and less to longitude" (2001, 4). Later, she explains that the appearance of latitude scales on charts should not lead us to conclude that the measure of latitude assumed a large role in the practice of the pilots who used them. "Even in 1545," Sandman writes, "a group of pilots argued that latitude measurements were too uncertain to rely on, especially given the possibility of cloudy weather, so that compass bearings were the key to successful navigation. With information about latitude but not longitude, the best that pilots could do was to estimate their position, just as they did using compass bearings . . . [M]ost relied on compass bearings and estimated distances, using the latitude, if at all, as a correction to their estimated position" (100–1).

43. Some examples of Santa Cruz's use of *espacio* in its unidimensional sense: "but knowing how much space there is between two places"; "saying that the space that stretches between east and west is reasonably called longitude"; "a large rock that is off the southern coast of the island, separated from it by a short space." See Cuesta Domingo (1983, 1: 208, 24, 339). Santa Cruz was not alone in thinking of latitude and longitude in this sense. For Gerónimo Girava, a Spanish resident of Milan and author of various, mostly derivative works on cosmography, *espacio* is more often synonymous with *distance* rather than *area*. He explains, for example, how the Ancients traveled the distance between two places of known latitude and longitude and then "measured the space of the earth that they had covered" (1556, 258).

44. Some of these *derroteros* find their way into writing through the curious *Itinerario de navegación* of Juan de Escalante de Mendoza (1575). There, a dialogue between a master pilot and a novice takes the reader down the Guadalquivir from Seville to Sanlucar, and then to the Canaries, to the Americas, and even around the Cape of Good Hope to the East Indies. Along the way, the novice learns not only the itineraries of travel, but also the science of cosmography and related disciplines. See Escalante de Mendoza (1985, 19–20). The Council of Indies refused to license the printing of the work for fear that its detailed presentation of maritime itineraries would fall into the wrong hands (13).

45. "All those things have vanished / like a shadow, / and like a rumor that passes by; / like a ship that sails through the water, / and when it has passed no trace can be found, / nor track of its keel in the waves" (Wis 5.9–10).

46. I cite from a modern edition, published in 1948. A digitized version of the first edition is also available, but the numbered pages of the 1948 present a decided advantage over the unnumbered folios of the *princeps*. An early modern English adaptation of Enciso's text is also available (Fernández de Enciso 1932). Since the translator, Roger Barlow, edits Enciso just as much as he translates him, and even adds original material of his own, I have chosen to provide my own translations of Enciso's text rather than cite from Barlow.

47. Since no better method for locating a line of longitude was available, it defined the location of this line in terms of distance, placing it three-hundred-seventy leagues west of Cape Verde (Albuquerque 1973; Cerezo Martínez 1994, 176). This method was far from accurate or reliable, creating ample room for debate as to where, precisely, the line fell in the New World. Enciso takes a stand on this issue, placing it somewhere be-

tween the mouths of the Marañon and Orinoco Rivers (Fernández de Enciso 1948, 25; see also Cerezo Martínez 1994, 177–78).

48. This attempt to blend the language of quantitative cosmography and descriptive geography is, in fact, one of Enciso's central innovations in the *Suma de geografía* (Broc 1986, 71–73; Melón 1950).

49. Although classical scholars have speculated that Mela's text, in antiquity, would have come accompanied by a map, and have even tried to reconstruct what that map might have looked like, we could join Pietro Janni in rejecting such notions as anachronisms and instead identify in this passage that linear, noncartographic spatiality that he believes was common to the classical world (1985, 30–47).

50. "There is an enormous contrast between the descriptive geography of the Orient," writes Amando Melón, "full of fantasy, historical memory and ancestral names, and the terse, realistic geography dedicated to the Western world. The only historical digression is the inclusion of the picturesque *Requerimiento*" (Melón 1950, 42). The *requerimiento* was the name given to the official document that conquistadors were required to read to native populations before conquering them. It called upon them to submit peacefully to Hispanic rule and Catholic conversion, or to face military action.

Chapter Three

1. Throughout this chapter, I cite from a 2001 reprint of Anthony Pagden's 1971 translation of Hernán Cortés's *Letters from Mexico*, but also include the corresponding page numbers from Angel Delgado-Gómez's 1993 critical edition of the same text, entitled *Cartas de relación*.

2. I thus must quibble with the use of "map" to translate words like these in Anthony Pagden's otherwise excellent translation of the Cortesian correspondence with Charles V, which I cite in this chapter.

3. For the legal circumstances surrounding Cortés's departure, see Elliott (2001).

4. According to Pagden, Cortés wrote his letters to Charles V with an eye toward their eventual publication (2001, 50).

5. For a bibliography of early modern literary works celebrating Hernán Cortés, see Martínez (1990). As some of the most important documents to emerge from Spain's encounter with the Americas, Cortés's letters to Charles V have attracted the attention of countless historians and literary critics. For some of the richest accounts of Cortés's enterprise, and of his version of it, see Elliott (1989a, 2001), Clendinnen (1993), Frankl (1962; 1963), and Loesberg (1983). Clendinnen is particularly good at demonstrating how Cortés's persuasive powers have misled one of the most well-known contemporary students of the "Second Letter," Tzvetan Todorov (1984).

6. Arthur H. Robinson and Barbara Petchenik distinguish rigorously between maps and language, insisting that images have no language and that language is irreducibly temporal, that is, nonspatial (1976, 43). J. Brian Harley is among those that contest this argument, (Harley and Laxton 2001, 158–64).

7. OED, 2d ed., s.v. "discourse."

8. I single out Krieger's work from the vast bibliography on the topic of ekphrasis because of the exceptionally broad definition he gives to the term. By contrast, Jean Hagstrum, in her early and influential work on the subject, defines ekphrasis as "giving

voice to a mute art object" and "a rhetorical description of a work of art" (1958, 18). Krieger, in turn, reflects upon and "ekphrastic impulse" or an "ekphrastic principle" meant to embrace any attempt to figure objects in space through the medium of language or to give spatial form to literature (1992, 9). His book-length study of the subject builds upon the insights of his earlier essay, which W. J. T. Mitchell has called "the single most influential statement on ekphrasis in American criticism" (1994, 153n8). For the scholarship on ekphrasis, see Grant Scott (1991). For ekphrasis in the Hispanic context, see Emilie Bergmann (1979).

9. The same could be said of a seminal piece of writingcriticism on cartography and literature, Huggan (1994).

10. Here I am oversimplifying Conley's position for brevity's sake. His argument does indeed attend to the itinerary as a form of cartographic writing, but it emphasizes how the itinerary serves to inscribe a surface. Rabelais's books, Conley argues, "strive to become a verbal projection of a mythic world that contains the French nation and all the surfaces of the globe as it was then known" (1996, 137).

11. It should come as no surprise, perhaps, that the sixteenth century gave the same name to discursive and iconographic figures of territory. Both constituted "descriptions."

12. It is for this reason that my discussion of Spanish cartographic literature does not begin with Columbus. Although Columbus's writings initiate European discourse on the New World, the transformation produced by Cortés's writing is so radical as to constitute a new beginning.

13. The anonymous author of the brief history of the conquest of New Spain that appeared in 1606 as part of Giovanni Battista Ramusio's *Navigationi e viaggi* by contrast, begins with a general description of New Spain that sets forth its boundaries and characterizes its climate, topography, and vegetation (Díaz Cardenas 1941, 19–21).

14. One of these exceptions is Cortés's description of the volcano Mount Popocateptl (1993, 199 [2001, 77–78]). The paucity of similar passages leads J. H. Elliott to conclude that Cortés enjoyed limited powers of observation (1992, 19). I argue instead that they manifest a set of priorities that Cortés shares with the culture of his time. As Peter Dunn argues, "Narrative discourse in the Golden Age does not describe. It has a narrow range of stylized epithets for natural phenomena: 'cópudos árboles,' . . . 'ásperas montañas,' . . . 'caudalosos ríos'" (Dunn 1993, 118).

15. For Juana Gil Bermejo, the letter's descriptive discourse is one of the things that makes it a piece of geographical, as well as historical, writing (1963, 135). One of the other things Gil Berjemo mentions is the fact that the "Second Letter" localizes the peoples and places of Mesoamerica. The issue of localization is crucial and is taken up below.

16. For further discussion of linear spatiality in conquest narrative discourse, see Restrepo (1999, 2002) on narratives about Colombia, and Ahern (1989, 1994) on narratives about what is now the southwestern United States.

17. The name of the leader of the Mexica has been spelled a variety of ways, perhaps most commonly *Montezuma*. I have adopted this spelling for the simple reason that it is the one used by the translation of Cortés that I cite.

18. Cortés is not the only one to do so, nor is his or any attempt to emplot the conquest as a continuation of the Reconquest a purely ideological move without historical basis. In the New World, Spaniards naturally drew upon their practical experience in war-

fare against Islam as well as upon their ideas about the meaning of such warfare. For more on the subject, see Chaunu (1979, 85–197), Elliott (1998, 140–44), Fernández-Armesto (1987, 85–197), McAlister (1984, 3–72), and Sánchez Albornoz (1983). See also Fuchs (2001). Felipe Fernández-Armesto reminds us that even though the historical experience of warfare against the Moors may have equipped Castile with practices and institutions that were readily shipped across the Atlantic, the historical ideology of the Reconquest could not make the journey as easily. How could such an idea be used as a model to write the history of a place, America, "where Christ and Muhammad had never been heard of" (1987, 213)?

19. Since Maravall wrote *El concepto de España en la Edad Media*, historians have come to recognize the Reconquest and many of its attendant notions as fabrications of medieval historiography. This includes the claim made by the kings of Castile and Leon to be direct successors of the Visigoths. On this point, see Messmer (1982). It is nonetheless useful to talk about the Reconquest as a powerful historical ideology, particularly since it was mobilized practically on the eve of Columbus's first journey to the New World by Ferdinand and Isabella and was, thus, very much a part of the culture of late-fifteenth and early-sixteenth-century Castile.

20. Contemporary accounts differ as to the reason for the killing. For a comparison of the accounts found in sixteenth-century sources, see Marcus (1977).

21. Cortés's strange remarks have not gone unnoticed by his commentators. Ramón Iglesia, for one, finds in them astonishing examples of how the conqueror recreates realities to suit his account of the conquest as a primarily peaceable process (Iglesia 1942, 131). He does not see these statements as part of an attempt to allegorize territory.

22. The phrase "con alegre semblante" appears in Cortés (1993, 239), but not in the Pagden translation (Cortés 2001).

23. This text is from the first speech. In the second speech, the language is slightly different, but the point is the same: "[W]e are not natives of this land, but came from another far away" (2001, 98 [1993, 227]). The formula is repeated in a later scene in which Cortés recruits Mutezuma's help in destroying the idols of the Templo Mayor. Mutezuma is willing to accept Cortés's religious innovations because he and his people are not "natives of this land" [naturales desta tierra] (2001, 106; 1993, 239).

24. I use "impertinence" here and in the pages that follow, somewhat idiosyncratically, to refer to the quality of "not belonging," of "being out of bounds" characteristic of the European presence in America.

25. Once again, Cortés does not refer to the image he is provided with as a "mapa" but as a "figura," a drawing (1993, 223 [2001, 94]). Although he recognizes the usefulness of such drawings and seems to avail himself of them when Mutezuma makes them available, his writing suggests that he does not possess a fully modern conception of map and space.

26. Diego Catalán quite usefully refers to "Hispania," in this sense, as a *solar*, or "dwelling place" (1982, 34–49).

27. Even if we shift our definition of the cartographic away from modern obsessions with geometric rationalization and instead adopt the much looser definition of any figure of territory that assumes a bird's-eye point of view, "Hispania" does not necessarily become a cartographic entity, a territory visible only through the mediation of some kind of map. Certainly, the word names a totality that can only be made *visible* to the earthbound

eye of human beings through the imaginary flight of cartographic perspective, but this does not mean that it cannot be rendered *intelligible* without such flight. Medieval descriptions of Spain ultimately have their roots in Greco-Roman literature, specifically the work of Strabo and Pomponius Mela. Strabo's description of Iberia provides us with a well-known image: "Iberia is like an ox-hide extending in length from west to east, its foreparts toward the east, and in breadth from north to south" (Strabo 1923, 3.1.3). Is Strabo's imaginary ox-hide a map of sorts, inviting the reader to assume that bird's-eye perspective? Perhaps, but it can also be read as a metaphorical flight into the concrete meant for a reader unaccustomed to such abstraction. Note that when Strabo delineates the boundaries of the Iberian Peninsula, he makes one of his most famous "errors." He describes the Pyrenees as the "eastern side" of the peninsula, "stretching from north to south" when, in fact, they run predominantly from east to west (Strabo 1923, 3.1.3). Pietro Janni interprets this "mistake" as a manifestation of Strabo's spatial imagination. Since the predominant direction of travel from Spain to France is west to east, the Pyrenees are experienced as a boundary perpendicular to that vector. Strabo's description reflects this experience of travel, not a geometrically rationalized reality, and thus exemplifies the itinerant spatiality that dominates his *Geography* (Janni 1985, 21).

28. This, at least, is the notion of Hispania that is deployed in Castilian historiography when the medieval historian Rodrigo Jiménez de la Rada and his many successors pair traditional praise for Spain with a new topic, the lament for the loss of Spain (Maravall 1981, 289). The "descriptions" of Spain that appear in these histories do not really describe Spain in any sense that can be considered "cartographic." They do not trace frontiers, delineate parts, or identify spatial relationships among places. Instead, they enumerate the excellences of the Spanish climate, of its agriculture, of its cities, of its natural resources, etc., without locating any of these things with any precision. They then lament the ruin of all these things supposedly caused by the Muslim invasion.

29. Djelal Kadir includes this text among those "charters of empire" that "engender a world that they then convert into their goal and take as their object" (Kadir 1992, 92). The papal donation, Kadir specifies, generates a world that can be given by a pope to a king on the basis of broad legal and historical principles—entirely European, of course—that imagine the pope as a universal monarch invested by God with the authority to do this sort of thing (76–78).

30. Frankl cites the Spanish, "para que en esta tierra tuviesen señorío como en sus reinos y señoríos lo tienen." The translation here is my own.

31. As the unity of Latin Christendom disintegrated, the authority of the papal donation only dwindled. Eventually, Protestants would be able to scoff at the notion that Spain was granted sovereignty over the whole of the New World, noting that not even the Catholic king of France accepted its legitimacy. See, for example, John Milton's writings on the subject (1851, 466).

32. Jerónimo de Aguilar, a Spaniard who had been a captive of the Maya in the Yucatán, translated between Spanish and Maya, while an Amerindian woman known as Doña Marina translated between Maya and Nahua, the language of the Mexica. As time went on, Doña Marina, who was Cortés's lover as well as his translator, learned to speak Spanish, and thus made it possible to eliminate one of the layers of translation involved.

33. Historians, both then and now, have expressed reservations about Cortés's account

of his actions in Tenochtitlán and of his claim to have gained quick and easy control over the life of the city. The narrative of iconoclasm and evangelization in the Templo Mayor is particularly suspect. Gonzalo Fernández de Oviedo doubts that Mutezuma could ever have assisted so eagerly in the desecration of the idols and expresses bewilderment at the tears of the Mexica on what, presumably, should have been joyous occasion (Iglesia 1942, 86). For further discussion, see Wagner (1944, 255–63) and especially Clendinnen (1993, 21).

34. For a list of the principal editions of the Cortesian correspondence, see the introduction by Ángel Delgado Gómez to his edition of the *Cartas de relación* (Cortés 1993, 73–89). See also Medina (1952, 1–61).

35. That is, of course, assuming that these titles were available in local bookshops or in accessible private collections. The available inventories of Spanish book collections from the sixteenth and seventeenth centuries indicate that books about the Americas may have been hard to come by before midcentury (Dadson 1998, 71–94).

36. Official attempts to preserve emerging geographical knowledge as state secrets tended to keep maps out of print in both Spain and Portugal. For the importance of state secrecy to the cartography of the Age of Discovery, see Harley and Laxton (2001, 91–94). The very nature of print itself may very well have contributed to keeping Iberian maps in manuscript form. Manuscript charts could easily be revised, redrawn, and discarded as new discoveries were mapped. Print maps, more expensive to produce and therefore more permanent, were not so easily transformed or tossed out. I thank John Hebert, director of the Geography and Map Division of the Library of Congress, for this observation.

37. The extant copies of the 1522 Seville edition do not contain any maps. Despite this fact, some scholars insist that this edition must have come accompanied by one and have even suggested that it was an earlier version of the map that accompanied the 1524 Nuremburg edition. Nonetheless, it has been argued that the originals of both the letter and the Mesoamerican map could have arrived in Germany, where Charles V found himself at the time, without passing through Seville. The makers of the Nuremburg map could then have had access to an image that was unavailable to Cromberger (Toussaint, Orozco, and Fernández 1938, 120).

38. Giuliano Dati, *La lettera dell'isole che ha trovato nuovamente il re di Spagna*, is available in an edition that combines a facsimile of the 1493 Italian edition with an English translation. See Dati (1991).

39. For help in identifying these features of the map, see the diagram in Cortés (2001, 25).

40. The two contradict each other on some points, it has been demonstrated, and each includes geographical information that the other leaves out (Mundy 1998, 29). Nonetheless, the map was included in the Nuremburg edition without comment, allowing us to conclude that the person responsible for its inclusion in the 1524 edition did not consider these discrepancies to be important, or was not even aware of them.

41. Richard Kagan places the Nuremberg map in the context of these fisheye views, provides bibliography on the subject, and reproduces some examples (2000, 65–66). For a fisheye view of the siege of Vienna printed in Nuremberg in 1529, see Landau and Parshall (1994, 227–28).

42. This is Richard Kagan's transcription of the epigram. He also provides the follow-

ing transcription: "Res fuerat praestans & Gloria fumma / Orbis fubiectus Caesaris Imperio, / Hic longe praeftat, cuius nunc Orbs Eous, / Et Nouius \, atque alter panditur
Asupitijs" (2000, 212).

43. For the legacy of the Cortés image in other early modern depictions of Mexico-
Tenochtitlán, see Toussaint (1938, 117–26) and Apenes (Apenes 1947, 20–21).

44. On this point, see Rabasa (1993), 96–98.

45. Various historians have written of Cortés's interest in the northwest of Mexico
as part of the crown's effort to find a maritime route through Mesoamerica that could be
used in lieu of the impractical one discovered by Magellan. Abel Martínez-Loza has argued that, whatever orders Cortés may have received from above, his own interest in
exploring the area northwest of New Spain was motivated by different geographical hy-
potheses. Drawing on evidence from the Cortesian correspondence itself, Martínez-Loza
insists that Cortés, like other early modern Europeans, believed that Mesoamerica was
actually a peninsula of Asia. Thus, rather than sail along the coasts of the Gulf of Mexico
in search of a strait, Cortés sailed up the Pacific Coast in search of the East (Martínez-Loza
1990).

Chapter Four

1. *Historia general de las Indias* is actually the title to the two-volume set. For the sake of
clarity and economy, I reserve it for the first volume alone. For a contemporary English
translation of the *Conquista de México*, see López de Gómara (1964). Although the *Historia general* was translated into English during the sixteenth century, I am unaware of the existence
of any more modern translation.

2. For an overview of Hispanic historiography of the New World during the first half
of the sixteenth century, see Merrim (1996).

3. For this characterization of Oviedo's *Historia general y natural*, see Turner (1964).

4. For an English translation of this text, see Martyr d'Anghera (1970).

5. See, for example, the account that Abraham Ortelius gives of the utility of his atlas
in the preface to his *Theatrum orbis terrarum* (Ortelius 1964). An earlier, Spanish-language
example of this topos can be found in Gerónimo de Girava's translation of Peter Apian's
1524 *Cosmographia* (Girava 1556, 255–56).

6. I take this definition of a map that functions as a reader's aid from Ingram (1993, 30).

7. This chapter does not touch upon the issue of the hand-drawn maps that accompany certain manuscripts of *Historia general y natural de las Indias*. Although these images certainly have a bearing upon the cartographic discourse of Oviedo's text, they have little to
do with that text as a model for Gómara. For more on Oviedo's illustrations, including
a reproduction of one of the maps, see Turner (1985). Other maps associated with the
Historia can be found among the plates in volume 121 of the *Biblioteca de Autores Españoles*, the
fifth and final volume dedicated to the *Historia general y natural de las Indias*.

8. Part 1 of the *Historia general y natural de las Indias* was published in 1535 in Seville by
Jacobo Cromberger, and once again in Salamanca in 1547 by Juan de Junta. Part 2,
book 20 was printed separately by Francisco Fernández de Córdoba in Valladolid. The rest
of the *Historia general y natural de las Indias* remained unpublished until the nineteenth century,
when the first complete edition was published by J. Amador de los Ríos of the Academia
de la Historia (1851–55). Most contemporary scholarly work refers to the edition pub-

lished as part of the *Biblioteca de Autores Españoles*, volumes 117–21, under the direction of Juan Pérez de Tudela Bueso, in 1959. This edition follows the text established by Amador de los Ríos, and it is the one to which I refer. For details about the dissemination of Oviedo's text, both in print and in manuscript, see Gerbi (1985, 129–32).

9. Following the conventions established by Oviedo scholarship, I cite the *Historia general y natural* according to its divisions into part, book, and chapter. In some cases, I cite prefaces or other unnumbered sections of Oviedo's text by the brief title the author provides.

10. Oviedo explains that he shares the opinion of "all those who have sailed it so many times . . . that it is the most secure sailing route among all those that we know of on the Ocean Sea" (1. 2. 9).

11. See, for example, the "Diálogo de la tierra," in Mexía and Mulroney (1930, 126–33).

12. Antonello Gerbi mentions this strange exception in Oviedo's otherwise conscientious treatment of sources. He argues that it is highly unlikely for Oviedo to have been unfamiliar with Enciso's popular *Suma de geografía*, but that the historian may have avoided mentioning the book as a way of snubbing its author, whom Oviedo probably thought of as a rival (Gerbi 1985, 88–91).

13. See both "Rabelais et le récit toponymique" and "Fortunes de la singularité," reprinted in Lestringant (1993a).

14. It is often said that Oviedo's *Historia general y natural de las Indias* is primarily a work of natural history, one that indulges in the history of the conquest as a secondary concern. See, for example, Enrique Alvarez López (1957), Gerbi (1985), and Merrim (1989). For an interpretation that sees natural and "general" history as a unified whole, see Merrim (1984).

15. Compare Oviedo's approach to the one adopted, centuries later, by J. H. Elliott. Elliott introduces the history of Spain's conquistadorial enterprise by referring to two great "arcs of conquest," one that moves from the Caribbean northwestwards into Cuba, and then into Mesoamerica and North America, and another that moves from the Caribbean into Panama, and from there into South America (Elliott 1984, 171–72). In this way, Elliott provides the history of the conquest with what Mikhail Bakhtin calls a "chronotope," a distinctive configuration of both space and time that lies at the heart of a narrative structure. Oviedo, by contrast, sets his treatment of space *against* the chronology of the conquest. The result is that the chronotope of the big picture—an essential building block of that missing master narrative—disappears from view.

16. Merrim makes a similar point, but believes more strongly in Oviedo's attempt to have the reader picture the whole: "Spatial or iconic (in the semiotic sense), too, is the shape of knowledge in the work of Oviedo, geographer. His history, as I have suggested, aspires to the condition of a cosmography . . . Exhaustiveness, precision, and the attempt at plastic representation through verbal means all converge in the general history of a writer, who, as so many of his statements attest, understood the primacy of the image over the word" (Merrim 1988, 242). While Oviedo did indeed appreciate the power of images, I believe that Merrim's assessment undervalues the ways in which his discourse actually undermines the visible totalities it inscribes—the hunter's lure—just as it undermines the master narrative to which it alludes.

17. It seems reasonable to suppose that the maps were probably added to the text by

the printer, who may have been aware of the increasing importance of maps to historical texts and therefore of the importance of including maps in Gómara's book, but who probably lacked the resources necessary to fabricate a more appropriate image. In this way, the maps included in the Hispania victrix attest to the ways that the arts of mapmaking and book illustration in Spain lagged behind advances made in other parts of Europe.

18. These opening chapters of the Historia general de las Indias have been cited as examples of Gómara's humanist erudition or of his identification with the experience of moderns over the received wisdom of the ancients (Iglesia 1942, 110–13; Lewis 1983, 138–43). Nothing, it seems, has been said about how they exemplify the close relationship between geographic knowledge, Renaissance cartography, and the emergence of a culture at once nationalistic and colonial.

19. Blake makes a similar point, characterizing Gómara's style as "sober" and associating it with Renaissance admiration for the natural (1975, 540).

20. Gómara conveniently fails to mention that the Portuguese do not agree with the Castilians about the number of leagues to be assigned to each degree of longitude at the equator, and that the disagreement about this detail was central to the determination of territorial rights in the western Pacific.

21. In this, Gómara's texts are not exceptional in any way. See the brief discussion in chapter 2 of the way Alonso de Santa Cruz handles latitude and longitude.

22. Gómara's prose cartography has been called "exhaustive" and "precise" by one of the few scholars to pay it much attention, Mustapha (1979, 432). By comparison with the prose cartographies of Oviedo, it is neither.

23. Gómara makes other such generalizing descriptions about Golfo Cuadrado, Florida, the Yucatán Peninsula, Nombre de Dios, the Orellana River, the Plate River, the isthmus of Tehuantépec, and Punta de Ballenas (22–27). See also Mustapha (1979, 432).

24. For the texts to which Gómara refers, see Romer (1998, 3. 45) and Pliny (1938, 5. 4).

25. In this way, Gómara's universal geography coincides perfectly with that of the cosmographer-royal, Alonso de Santa Cruz. The world, Santa Cruz claims, is made up of three immense "islands," the Old World, the New World, and the hypothetical Terra Australis (Cuesta Domingo 1983, 1: 289). The Terra Australis was a massive continent believed to occupy most of the Southern Hemisphere. More will be said about it in chapter 5.

26. For the connection between the stories of circumnavigation in Pliny and Mela and the imperial imaginary of ancient Rome, see Romm (1992, 122).

27. During the whole episode, Mustapha argues, Gómara refers to the Indies as if it was a perfectly well-known territory, which appeared from the outset as it would come to be known in 1550 (1994, 206).

28. For Roa-de-la-Carrera, the papal bulls granting Castile sovereignty over the New World held much greater importance as foundational documents than did the letters of Columbus. Part of his evidence is drawn from Gómara's history itself, which cites the full text of Inter caetera but demonstrates no knowledge of the Columbian letters that had circulated in print shortly after his first voyage (Roa-de-la-Carrera 1998, 65–80). One of Gómara's historiographical and ideological accomplishments, he adds, was to link this crucial foundational document to the Columbus narrative, thereby fusing the historical

and juridical foundations of Spain's empire in America into a single history guided by a providential design (148).

29. For more details, see Mustapha (1979, 434–36).

30. Mustapha mentions the monotony of this form of organization. The pattern that Gómara uses to tell the story of each place is established early on, in the Columbus episode, and is repeated throughout the whole of the *Historia general* (Mustapha 1979, 436).

31. For Mustapha, Gómara's use of geography to organize history produces a spatial juxtaposition of discrete, unified episodes that together constitute a gallery of great men and their deeds (Mustapha 1979, 437–38). My argument builds upon Mustapha's point by emphasizing the continued importance of movement in this otherwise highly spatialized—in other words, static—presentation of American history, not to mention the central importance of American insularity to the ways that the Indies are here figured as an apprehensible whole. Mustapha, I believe, is correct in many of her judgments of Gómara's text but fails to specify how Gómara produces the vision of empire that he does indeed inscribe.

32. I have no doubts about the long-lived influence of this historiographical model. Reflecting upon my initial encounter with the history of Spain's experience in the Americas in elementary and secondary school, I remember being impressed by the need to associate individual places with the men who discovered them (Columbus discovered America, Cortés discovered Mexico, Pizarro discovered Peru, Coronado discovered the Southwest, De Soto discovered the Mississippi River, and so forth) but not with the order in which these discoveries occurred.

33. In a brief characterization of this text, the noted historian Lewis Hanke describes the third section, as if it represented the whole of the text's argument, as "a tremendous accumulation of information on the customs and life of the Indians." (Hanke 1952, 7). See also Hanke (1959, 54–55). Marcel Bataillon, likewise, makes only brief mention of the earlier material in his various essays on las Casas (1966). Elliott's summary of the *Apologética historia* mentions its division into two distinct arguments but only elaborates upon the second (1992, 48). Likewise, Pagden makes only the briefest mention of the argument presented in the first two parts (1986, 138–39).

34. See Pagden (1993, 51–88) for an extended comparison of the narrative voices of Oviedo and las Casas.

35. The narrative voice in las Casas merits comparison with that of the French cosmographer André Thevet. At one point, Thevet contradicts the ancient and medieval belief that the ocean served as a boundary for the *orbis terrarum* with the assertion that it is earth which encloses the world's waters. In support of this statement, he makes a similarly grandiose claim about the purview of his own gaze, asserting simply that he has *seen* this to be the case. For more, see Lestringant (1991, 43–51).

36. The term "insularisation" has been defined in the following manner: "The setting of a group of representations and scenarios in an island, or some analogous space, demands, it is clear, an interpretation. To be brief, I call this phenomenon 'insularization.'" The neologism underscores that the operation consists in displacement somewhere else, in localization at a distance and in imaginary enclosure" (Dubost 1995, 48).

37. For the mutual implication of "continent" and "island," see Racault (1995, 9–10).

38. Las Casas deviates from contemporary example both in his insistence upon one

massive temperate zone framed by two frigid ones rather than upon multiple zones, as well as in the purpose to which he puts the resultant geography. Lestringant tells us that the theory of climates had traditionally been used to privilege the locus of enunciation over other locations (Lestringant 1993b). Here, as we can see, las Casas has turned that language against the sort of geopolitical hierarchies that it has traditionally supported.

39. For more details about this issue, see the discussion of Enciso in chapter 2.

40. The story is reminiscent of a famous Renaissance map by the French cosmographer Oronce Finé, or at least of the interpretation given it by Tom Conley. This map depicts the world in what is known as a "cordiform projection," but Conley suggests that the heart is not the only body part that it models. In one of its printed versions, bare-bottomed cherubs and a bare-breasted female figure surround the doubled globes of the map, reinforcing the impression that the image constitutes an erotically charged, Rabelaisian joke (Conley 1996, 124).

Chapter Five

1. Curtius explains that "The Bible furnished medieval historical thought with yet another theological substantiation for the replacement of one empire by another . . . The word *transfertur* ('is transferred') gives rise to the concept of *translatio* (transference) which is basic for medieval historical theory. The renewal of the Empire by Charlemagne could be regarded as a transferal of the Roman *imperium* to another people. This is implied in the formula *translatio imperii*, with which the *translatio studii* (transferal of learning from Athens or Rome to Paris) was later co-ordinated" (Curtius 1973, 28–29). Nebrija extends this process of transference so that it culminates in the Spain of his day.

2. Ercilla's is not the first Renaissance epic written in Spanish, only the first to be widely read and celebrated. For an overview of the epic poem in Spain, see Pierce (1968). For the Spanish colonial epic in particular, see Avalle-Arce (2000). For a discussion of the genre that emphasizes questions of national self-fashioning, see Davis (2000).

3. Following the conventions established by Ercilla scholarship, I cite the *Araucana* by canto and stanza.

4. The poem is addressed to Philip II through the repeated use of apostrophe, a device that has been interpreted as a way of collapsing the distance separating the Chilean periphery from the Spanish metropolis and rendering empire visible to the person of the monarch (Albarracín Sarmiento 1986; Davis 2000, 31–39). For alternative interpretations of these devices, see Avalle-Arce (1971; 2000, 53–66), Pastor (1992, 263–72), and Pierce (1984, 62–69).

5. For interpretations that find in the *Araucana* a celebration of Hispanic imperialism, see Concha (1969, 38–49), Lerner (1991), Nicolopulos (2000, xiv), and Pierce (1984, 436).

6. Beatriz Pastor underscores the ways that Ercilla supposedly humanizes and ennobles the native inhabitants of Chile (1992, 207–75) For an antidote to this interpretation, see Cevallos (1989). Elizabeth Davis builds upon Cevallos's argument (2000, 39–60). Recently, David Quint has interpreted the *Araucana* as an "epic of the vanquished" (1994).

7. Agustín Cueva dispatches Fitón's map as an ideologically inauthentic imperial delirium, inconsistent with the poem's increasing bitterness towards colonial atrocities (1978, 37). Ramona Lagos argues that the clearly heroic tone of the metropolitan episodes serves

to underscore the antiheroic brutality of the Chilean war (1981, 178–79). Quint, almost alone among the critics of the *Araucana*, questions the extent to which the European battle scenes can be said to celebrate empire, but he ignores the *mappamundi* episode altogether (1994, 178–85).

8. Part 1 of the poem was printed for the first time in 1569, part 2 in 1578, and part 3 in 1589. The three parts appeared together for the first time in 1590. An expanded edition incorporating material that Ercilla wrote but never inserted into the piece appeared in 1596. My interpretation addresses itself to this full, final edition (Ercilla 1993).

9. This gesture has been interpreted as a manifestation of the poem's *verismo*, that tendency supposedly characteristic of the Spanish spirit to favor the representation of the real over the inverisimilitude typical of epic poetry in other literary traditions. The notion of *verismo* is derived from the work of Ramón Menéndez Pidal, who opposed the innate historicism of Castilian epic, as he saw it, to the practice of epic poetry in the rest of Europe. His arguments included Ercilla, and have had a durable effect on criticism of *La Araucana* (Menéndez Pidal 1949, 127; 1951, 203–5).

10. Thomas Greene notes that epic poetry usually subordinates the inscription of space to the presentation of incidents and condemns Lucan's *Pharsalia* for its excessive indulgence in what he calls panoramic description (1963, 19–21).

11. My thanks to James Nohrenberg of the University of Virginia for this observation.

12. For a fitting literary comparison, see the sonnet by Ercilla's contemporary, Fernando de Herrera, which begins "Éstos qu'al imperio turco, en cruda guerra" (1985, 818). In it, Herrera refers to both the Strait of Gibraltar and the Strait of Magellan, and praises daring Spain for transgressing both. The tendency to identify Magellan's passageway, as well as its hypothetical counterpart to the north, the Strait of Anian, as the modern-day analogue to the old Pillars of Hercules was not unique to Herrera. See Gillies (1994, 167–68).

13. According to Isaías Lerner, the language of love-as-battlefield so common to lyric poetry in Ercilla's day becomes uncannily literal in the *Araucana*. The figurative swords that slay amorous speaking subjects become real ones that slay Spanish soldiers. Lerner notes, however, that the return of these metaphorical vehicles to their literal ground does not divorce them from the literary tradition. Rather, it seems to intensify the effectiveness of these poetic topoi (Lerner 1991). A similar fusion of reference and imitation is taking place here.

14. According to Quint, he also inserts himself into a particular vein of the tradition of Western epic poetry that takes the side of the losers against the victors. For Quint, Lucan's poem represents the source of a counter-tradition of anti-imperial epic poetry opposed to the imperial tradition that has its source in Virgil's *Aeneid*. He traces certain formal resemblances between the *Pharsalia* and the *Araucana* in order to present Ercilla's poem as the Renaissance installment in this counter-tradition and to make a case for a vigorously anti-imperial program in Ercilla's text. The argument, however, ignores too much in both Lucan and Ercilla to be fully convincing. When Quint's argument turns to the *Araucana*, it seems to forget about the *imperial* commitments of the *Pharsalia*. The *Pharsalia*, of course, vehemently rejects the Caesarian imperialism that the *Aeneid* supports. Julius Caesar is its villain and the defeated leaders of the Republic, Pompey and Cato, its heroes. But despite this opposition to Virgil and the caesars, Lucan's poem remains both Virgilian and

imperialistic in a crucial way. As Quint himself observes, Lucan rejects the emperors without rejecting the empire: "He takes as a given the history of Rome's unswerving rise to imperial greatness even as the *Pharsalia* portrays the Caesarian emperor *not* as the culmination but rather as the fall or disruption of that history" (1994, 157). Ercilla's imitation of the Republican Lucan, therefore, is in itself insufficient to suggest an analogous, unambiguous anti-imperialism in the *Araucana*. The source is anti-Caesarian, not anti-imperial. If we are to identify an anti-imperial discourse in Ercilla's poetics, we must look elsewhere.

15. This is not an isolated metaphor in Lucan. According to Lapidge (1979), the *Pharsalia* often figures social and political chaos through images of cosmic dissolution.

16. Despite the 1578 voyage of Sir Francis Drake, which proved that Tierra del Fuego was an island and not the headland of some vast, undiscovered southern continent, European cartography continued, well into the eighteenth century, to portray the Strait of Magellan as a passageway between two continents, South America to the north and Magellanica, or the Terra Australis to the south. Ercilla participates in this misconception, as does José de Acosta. See Acosta (1986, 179–82). This misconception has important consequences for part 3 of the *Araucana*, as I shall argue below.

17. In *The Discoverie of Guiana* (1596), as quoted in Montrose (1993, 188). It is important to note that early modern English used "countrey" as a euphemism for the vagina. Images like these will seem all too familiar to those readers acquainted with the ways in which colonial discourse genders the land as female and its conqueror as male. The gendering of the land and its conqueror allows this discourse to encode its stories of exploration, conquest, despoliation, and settlement in the language of love, desire, seduction, rape, and marriage. For fundamental contributions to our understanding of how and why geography is gendered by colonial texts, see Certeau (1988), Kolodny (1975), and Montrose (1993). For a discussion that ranges over many aspects of cartographic history, see Lewes (2000). For a recent discussion of the role of specifically Petrarchan structures of gender and desire in the discourse of early modern colonialism, see Greene (1999). For a discussion of colonialism as rape in Spanish Golden Age poetry, see Mary Gaylord Randel (1978).

18. In this and other instances, Ercilla's editor Isaías Lerner notes that "estrecho" is used to refer to the peril of the situation, and thereby limits the implications of the word to "danger" or "risk." There is no need, however, to foreclose the spatial connotations of this word, signifying a danger associated with perilous enclosure, particularly in light of the fact that its first appearance in the poem comes so soon after the description of the Strait of Magellan. By availing ourselves of the spatiality suggested by "estrecho," furthermore, we recover the origins of the usage that Lerner insists upon, the notion of being caught between Scylla and Charybdis, of being caught in dire straits. Note also that "peligro" could have been substituted for "estrecho" without affecting the poetic meter. The word choice may have been quite intentional.

19. For a more detailed discussion of images of *estrecheza* in part 1, see Padrón (1997, chapter 3).

20. The reasons for this change of plan do not need concern us here. For more, see Nicolopulos (2000, 42).

21. Recent critical attention to the web of prophecy has identified it as a vital part of

Ercilla's project, thereby rescuing it from the neglect and even the vituperation it had long received. These efforts began with the work of Concha (1969) and have recently borne considerable fruit in the monographic study of the web of prophecy carried out by Nicolopulos (2000).

22. For remarks similar to those of Greene, see Bowra (1973) and Frye (1973). Greene elaborates upon Aristotle's brief discussion of epic poetry in the *Poetics*, where epic is distinguished from tragedy through a comparison of the length and shape of their plots (Greene 1963, 10–11).

23. For earlier Iberian verse cartographies, see the anonymous, thirteenth-century *Libro de Alexandre* (*Libro de Alexandre* 1988, 276–94, 1792–98, 2508–13, 76–87), Juan de Mena's fifteenth-century *Laberinto de fortuna* (1994, 34–53), and Luis de Camões's sixteenth-century *Os Lusíadas* (1973, 3.6–20, 10.90–140). For commentary on the description of the world in the *Libro de Alexandre*, see Rico (1970, 50–59); on *Laberinto de fortuna*, see Lida de Malkiel (1950, 30–32). For an interpretation of Ercilla's *mappamundi* episode in the light of these precursors, see Nicolopulos (2000).

24. The opening of part 2 narrates events from the winter (Southern Hemisphere) of 1557. Charles V abdicated in January 1556.

25. Her voice breaks into the poem despite the poet's unconvincing reassurance, in the exordium that precedes her appearance, that he will stick to his chosen subject, not matter how dry, and avoid the allure of love (20. 1–5). However transparent this rhetorical move may be—Ercilla promises one thing and delivers another, as if he were not the hand behind both the promise and its breach—it goes a long way toward marking these female voices as "independent" ones. The protracted tendency of Ercilla critics to look for historical Araucanians behind these obviously literary figures attests to the effectiveness of the gesture. This tendency was dealt its death blow only thirty years ago. See Lía Schwartz Lerner (1972).

26. Amid the devastation of the battlefield, the poet becomes the source of Tegualda's solace rather than of her grief and thus figures himself, in the words of one critic, "as perhaps the most perfect example of the ideal soldier. In his actions he is always noble, generous, compassionate, a defender of helpless women and magnanimous toward a defeated foe" (Aquila 1977, 74).

27. For the story of Tegualda as a utopian counter-discourse to the history of the Chilean war, see Vila (1992, 219–23).

28. That language is by no means absent from the narratives of Penco and Saint Quentin. For more details, see Padrón (1997, 189–95).

29. Pedro de Valdivia was the original conqueror and governor of Chile. His death at the hands of the Araucanians forms one of the initial incidents of the rebellion (3: 63–70).

30. For las Casian discourse in the *Araucana*, see Ciriaco Pérez Bustamante (1952).

31. This, in fact, is what many of the critics of the *Araucana* have done. For imperialistic and anti-imperialistic accounts of the *Araucana*, see notes 5 and 7.

32. Readers of Latin American literature will recognize in this comparison between an Andean peak and European mountains an early version of a commonplace tendency to magnify the grandeur of the Andes at the expense of Old World mountain ranges.

33. See Quint (1994, 157–59). Quint's reasons for finding an anti-imperial discourse

in Ercilla's portrayal of Lepanto concern the poem's simultaneous imitation of both the imperialist Virgil and the anti-imperialist Lucan.

34. After Philip II was crowned king of Portugal in 1581, which thus added Portugal's possessions in Africa and Asia to his already vast inheritance, the globe came to symbolize his imperial reach (Parker 2002, 19–27). It should be noted that part 2 of the *Araucana* appeared in 1578, the same year that witnessed the death of the childless King Sebastian of Portugal, making it possible for Philip to aspire to the Portuguese crown.

35. Hispanists will note that the colloquial quality of *chico* is out of keeping with the grave sententiousness of an epic exordium. I will further discuss the use of this adjective below.

36. The title of the canto reinforces this notion of the interchangeability of the poem and the crystal ball: "In this canto is placed the description of many provinces, mountains, cities famous by nature or because of wars" (735). Few of the canto titles begin with the demonstrative "En este canto," and most of those continue with the passive verb phrase "se contiene." The title of canto 27 is the only one to replace "se contiene" with an impersonal form of *poner*, a verb that even in this passive construction suggests an agent who is doing the "putting." The title thus functions to objectify the canto as a container into which the geographic content is placed.

37. In this way, Fitón's map resembles the cartographic writing analyzed by Conley. See especially his discussion of the poetry of Jean Molinet (Conley 1996, 48–61).

38. Meroe lies on the Nile between the kingdom of Prester John and Cairo, below a point where the river reaches "a narrow rocky passage that is made continuously more narrow by the converging walls, and from which a waterfalls flow out with a furious din" (27. 20). With the way blocked by the waterfall to the south, and the Ottomans to the north, Meroe is effectively inaccessible to Europeans.

39. Accounts of the fantastic African kingdom of Monomotapa soon took the place of Prester John, showing a fascination with its wealth and elaborate court life very reminiscent of the old tales (Broc 1986, 146).

40. Nicolopolus argues that Fitón draws upon not Lucan and Mena but the figure of Severo in the "Second Eclogue" of Garcilaso de la Vega. He cites, among other things, the same passage from Garcilaso's poem cited here, which describes Fitón as "severo." See Nicolopulos (2000, 106–17). Unlike the witches in the Latin poems, Severo inspires not fear but awe. Nonetheless, the difference has no impact upon my argument. For Severo, see the "Second Eclogue" (Vega and Morros 1995, 1059–128).

41. I refer to the inventory of magic substances that Ercilla constructs by imitating Mena and Lucan. For more details, see Padrón (1997, 219–20).

42. For the identification of this subtext, see Nicolopulos (2000, 206).

43. Nicolopulos mentions that when Ercilla rewrote part 2 of the poem for the 1589–90 edition, canto 27 received extensive attention (2000, 258).

44. See both "Rabelais et le récit toponymique" and "Fortunes de la singularité," reprinted in Lestringant (1993a).

45. Ercilla thus seems to anticipate what Gaylord Randel calls the heliotropic geography of the diatribe against navigation in the *Soledad primera*, in which the itinerary of Spanish imperial destiny is also the route of the setting sun (1978, 105–6).

46. In a similar vein, Charles Aubrun compares Ercilla's gallant treatment of his

Amerindian captives with the generosity of Rodrigo, the ideal Christian knight in *La historia del Abencerraje y la hermosa Jarifa*, who shows a similar courtesy to his Moorish captives. He also points out that this idealized self-fashioning is supported by the role assigned to Africans in Glaura's story. It is the unruly slaves and not their Spanish masters who have posed the greatest threat to Glaura's virginity. Their infamy, it has been argued, serves to absolve the Spaniards of any possible guilt, to bring Spanish virtue and heroism into even greater relief (Aubrun 1956, 270–72).

47. The narrative of this journey appears in cantos 34. 44 through 36. 43.

48. This discussion of the incidents in part 3 of the *Araucana* that lead up to the narrative of the voyage south of Arauco abbreviates a more nuanced account published elsewhere. See Padrón (2000).

49. In this way, the journey narrative from part 3 of the *Araucana* joins other colonial narratives among what Pastor calls "the narrative discourse of failure" characterized by a recalcitrant natural world, the physical suffering of the conquistador, and the degeneration of exploration into wandering (1992, 116–29). Pastor notes the difference between this narrative and earlier accounts. In Chile, the conquistadors actually find the paradise they sought. See Pastor (1992, 259–60).

50. Numa Broc argues that successive influence of the cordiform world map of Oronce Finé (1531), the double cordiform world map of Gerhard Mercator (1538), and the world map of Abraham Ortelius (1570) established the Terra Australis as a fixture of sixteenth-century geography. By the second half of the sixteenth century, its existence was accepted as a matter of fact (Broc 1986, 168–72). For reproductions of the Finé and Mercator maps, see Shirley (1983). For the Ortelius map, see figure 34 above. Ironically, this development represents a step backward from the Iberian planispheres of the first quarter of the sixteenth century. See figures 17 and 27 above.

51. James Enterline has recently argued that knowledge about the southern continent has its origins in Portuguese knowledge of the existence of Australia. He admits, however, that "[o]nce introduced, nevertheless, this polar continent was in truth seized upon by all geographers, in the absence of any further real information from Australia, as a cosmographical necessity on the grounds of symmetry to balance the northern lands, and was retained in most later maps" (1972, 53–54). Belief in the existence of the Terra Australis marks one of the limits of the "modernity" of early modern geography. It speaks of the period's willingness to shape its image of the world according to the ideological needs of its cosmography rather than the empirical determinations of exploration. For the relationship between empiricism and speculation in early modern maps, see Jacob (1992, 192–93) and Lestringant (1993a, 262).

52. Roger Bacon and Pierre d'Ailly cite the Book of Esdras on this point (O'Gorman 1986, 63).

53. John Gillies discusses this famous image at some length, remarking on the instability in Ortelius's account of the continents. His predecessor Mercator uses the word "continent" in a consistent manner and thus comes up with three of them, the Old World, the New, and the Terra Australis, or "Magellanica." Ortelius, on the other hand, hopes to preserve the classical number four and for this reason creates an allegory that counts the three classical continents, Europe, Africa, and Asia, separately, and adds America as a fourth. "The status of Magellanica," Gillies tells us, "is left vague" (Gillies 1994, 162).

The southern continent is included in the allegory but as a bust rather than as a human figure (Gillies 1994, 225 n. 13).

54. James Romm text cites Florus, author of the second-century *Epitome of Roman History*, who figures Caesar's passage into Britain as an Alexander-style search for new worlds to conquer: "Having traversed all lands and seas Caesar faced Ocean and, as if the Roman world were no longer enough, contemplated another" (*Epitome* 1.45.16) (1992, 141).

55. Like other such gestures in early modern Spanish writing, it may have actually done very little to reassure a savvy sixteenth-century reader about the facticity of the material it introduces, and may even have suggested the opposite. See Gaylord (1996).

56. In his copious sixteenth-century annotations to the poetry of Garcilaso de la Vega, Fernando de Herrera tells us that the myth of Hero and Leander, the basis for Garcilaso's sonnet 29, is so well known that there is no point in recounting it (2001, 451). Herrera reproduces Hero and Leander poems by Martial, Virgil, Diego de Mendoza, Juan de Cetina, and himself, among others.

57. "Furia" and "embravecimiento" are common terms in the Leander poems cited by Herrera, as well as in those of Garcilaso and Hernando de Acuña. See Rivers (1991, 105).

58. Space will not allow me to consider this final canto, which reads like a defense of Philip II's annexation of Portugal that draws upon just war theory. I suspect, however, that this canto should be read, like the rest of the *Araucana*, for a critical discourse contained within its manifest effort to toe the imperialist line. Some of Ercilla's contemporaries, such as Saint Teresa of Avila, Fray Luis de León, Miguel de Cervantes, and the dramatist Juan de la Cueva, were critical of the Portuguese annexation in ways sometimes explicit and sometimes implicit. On Cervantes, see King (1979), and on Cueva, see Watson (1971). My thanks to one of the anonymous readers at the University of Chicago Press for this observation.

59. For Ercilla and the discourse of Bartolomé de las Casas, see Durand (1964) and Pérez Bustamante (1952). Elizabeth Davis mentions similarities between Ercilla's treatment of the Araucanians and the position articulated by Franciso de Vitoria and the School of Salamanca (Davis 2000, 40).

Conclusion

1. For the decline of Spanish cartography during the seventeenth century, see Agustín Hernando (1999). Hernando argues that the paucity of seventeenth-century maps suggests a significant decline in map production.

2. See, for example, Dandelet (2001) and Mackay (1999).

3. Pedro Ruíz Pérez has made an important step toward examining the spatiality of this literature by identifying the spatio-temporal figure of the pilgrimage as the privileged space of Spanish Baroque writing (1996).

WORKS CITED

Acosta, José de. 1986. *Historia natural y moral de las Indias*. Edited by J. A. Franch. Madrid: Historia 16.

Acuña, Rene. 1982. *Relaciones geográficas del siglo XVI*. 8 vols. Etnohistoria: Serie Antropológica, 58. Mexico City: UNAM, Instituto de Investigaciones Antropológicas.

Agnese, Battista. 1875. *Portulan de Charles Quint donné à Philippe II*. Edited by F. Spitzer and C. Wierner. Collection Frédéric Spitzer. Paris: J. Claye.

Aguilar, Fray Francisco de. 1977. *Relación breve de la conquista de la Nueva España*. Edited by J. G. Lacroix. Serie de historiadores y cronistas de Indias, 7. Mexico City: UNAM, Instituto de Investigaciones Históricas.

Ahern, Maureen. 1989. The Certification of Cibola: Discursive Strategies in *La relacion del descubrimiento de las Siete Ciudades* by Fray Marcos de Niza (1539). *Dispositio* 14, nos. 36–38: 303–13.

———. 1994. *La relacion de la jornada de Cibola*: Los espacios orales y culturales. In *Conquista y contraconquista: La escritura del Nuevo Mundo*. Mexico City: Colegio de México.

Alba, Jacobo Stuart Fitz-James y Falcó, duque de, ed. 1951. *Mapas españoles de América: Siglos XV–XVII*. Madrid.

Albarracín Sarmiento, Carlos. 1986. El poeta y su rey en *La Araucana*. *Filología* 21 (1): 99–116.

Albuquerque, Luis de. 1973. O Tratado de Tordesilhas e as dificuldades técnicas da sua aplicação rigorosa. In *El Tratado de Tordesillas y su proyección*. Colóquio Luso-Español de História Ultramarina, 1. Valladolid: University of Valladolid, Seminario de Historia de América.

Alpers, Svetlana. 1987. The Mapping Impulse in Dutch Art. In *Art and Cartography*, edited by D. Woodward. Chicago: University of Chicago Press.

Alvarez López, Enrique. 1957. La historia natural en Fernández de Oviedo. *Revista de Indias* 17 (69–70): 541–602.

Anderson, Benedict. 1991. *Imagined Communities: Reflections of the Origins and Spread of Nationalism.* Revised edition. New York: Verso.

Apenes, Ola. 1947. *Mapas antiguos del Valle de Mexico.* Mexico City: UNAM, Instituto de Historia.

Aquila, August J. 1977. Ercilla's Concept of the Ideal Soldier. *Hispania* 60 (1): 68–75.

Ariosto, Ludovico. 1975. *Orlando Furioso: A Romantic Epic.* 2 vols. Translated by B. Reynolds. New York: Penguin.

Aubrun, Charles. 1956. Poesía épica y novela: El episodio de Glaura en *La Araucana* de Ercilla. *Revista Iberoamericana* 21: 261–73.

Avalle-Arce, Juan Bautista. 1971. El poeta en su poema: El caso de Ercilla. *Revista de Occidente.* 2d. ser., 32 (95): 152–71.

———. 2000. *La épica colonial.* 1st ed. Anejos de RILCE, 35. Pamplona: Ediciones Universidad de Navarra.

Bagrow, Leo. 1985. *History of Cartography.* Edited by R. A. Skelton. 2d. ed. Chicago: Precedent Publishing.

Bataillon, Marcel. 1966. *Études sur Bartolomé de las Casas, réunies avec la collaboration de Raymond Marcus.* Thèses, mémoires et travaux, 5. Paris: Université de Paris IV, Centre de recherches de l'Institut d'études hispaniques.

Bergmann, Emilie. 1979. *Art Inscribed: Essays on Ekphrasis in the Spanish Golden Age.* Cambridge: Harvard University Press.

Black, Jeremy. 1997. *Maps and Politics: Picturing History.* London: Reaktion Books.

Blake, Jon Vincent. 1975. Fernández de Oviedo ante López de Gómara. *Romance Notes* 16: 536–42.

Bolanos, Alvaro Felix. 1991. La crónica de Indias de Fernández de Oviedo. ¿Historia de lo general y natural, u obra didáctica? *Revista de Estudios Hispánicos* 25 (3): 15–33.

Boruchoff, David A. 1991. Beyond Utopia and Paradise: Cortés, Bernal Díaz and the Rhetoric of Consecration. *Modern Language Notes* 106: 330–69.

Bosteels, Bruno. 1996. A Misreading of Maps: The Politics of Cartography in Marxism and Poststructuralism. In *Signs of Change: Premodern, Modern, Postmodern,* edited by Stephen Barker. Albany: SUNY Press.

Bowra, C. M. 1973. Virgil and the Idea of Rome. In *Parnassus Revisited: Modern Critical Essays on the Epic Tradition,* edited by Anthony Yu. Chicago: American Library Association.

Braudel, Fernand. 1973. *The Mediterranean and the Mediterranean World in the Age of Philip II.* 2 vols. Translated by S. Reynolds. New York: Harper Colophon.

Broc, Numa. 1986. *La geographie de la Renaissance, 1420–1620.* Paris: Éditions du C.T.H.S.

Brotton, Jerry. 1997. *Trading Territories: Mapping the Early Modern World.* London: Reaktion Books.

Buisseret, David, ed. 1992. *Monarchs, Ministers and Maps.* Chicago: University of Chicago Press.

Burden, Philip D. 1996. *The Mapping of North America: A List of Printed Maps, 1511–1670.* Stamford, CT: Raleigh Publications.

Calderón de la Barca, Pedro. 1987. *El gran teatro del mundo.* Edited by E. F. Cortés. Madrid: Cátedra.

Camões, Luís de. 1973. *Os Lusíadas.* Edited by Frank Pierce. Oxford: Clarendon Press.

Campbell, Tony. 1987. Portolan Charts from the Late Thirteenth Century to 1500. In *The

History of Cartography, edited by J. B. Harley and David Woodward. Chicago: University of Chicago Press.

Carter, Paul. 1988. *The Road to Botany Bay: An Exploration of Landscape and History*. New York: Knopf.

Casas, Bartolomé de las. 1967. *Apologética historia sumaria*. 2 vols. Edited by E. O'Gorman. Mexico City: UNAM, Instituto de Investigaciones Históricas.

———. 1991. *Brevísima relación de la destruyción de las Indias*. Edited by A. Moreno Mengíbar. Seville: Er Revista de Filosofía; Naples: Istituto italiano per gli studi filosofici.

———. 1992. *A Short Account of the Destruction of the Indies*. Edited and translated by Nigel Griffin. London: Penguin.

Casey, Edward S. 1997. *The Fate of Place: A Philosophical History*. Berkeley: University of California Press.

Catalán, Diego. 1982. España en su historiografía: De objeto a sujeto de la historia. In *Los españoles en la historia*, by R. Menéndez Pidal. Madrid: Espasa-Calpe.

Cerezo Martínez, Ricardo. 1994. *La cartografía náutica española en los siglos XIV, XV, y XVI*. Madrid: Consejo Superior de Investigaciones Científicas.

Certeau, Michel de. 1984. *The Practice of Everyday Life*. Translated by S. Rendall. Berkeley: University of California Press.

———. 1988. *The Writing of History*. Translated by T. Conley. New York: Columbia University Press.

Cervantes de Salazar, Francisco. 1971. *Crónica de Nueva España*. 2 vols. Edited by A. M. Carlo. Biblioteca de Autores Españoles (Continuación), 244–245. Madrid: Ediciones Atlas.

Cervantes Saavedra, Miguel de. 1987. *La Galatea*. Edited by J. B. Avalle-Arce. Clásicos Castellanos. Madrid: Espasa-Calpe.

———. 1998. *Don Quijote de la Mancha*. 2 vols. Edited by F. Rico and J. Forradellas. Biblioteca Clásica, 50. Barcelona: Instituto Cervantes: Crítica.

———. 2001. *The Ingenious Hidalgo Don Quixote de la Mancha*. Translated by J. Rutherford. New York: Penguin Books.

Cevallos, Francisco Javier. 1989. Don Alonso de Ercilla and the American Indian: History and Myth. *Revista de Estudios Hispánicos* 23 (3): 1–20.

Chaunu, Pierre. 1979. *European Expansionism in the Later Middle Ages*. Translated by K. Bertram. Amsterdam: North Holland Publishing Co.

Chaves, Jerónimo de. 1545. *Tractado de la sphera que compuso el Doctor Ioannes de Sacrobusto con muchas additioes. Agora nuevamente traduzido de Latin en lengua Castellana por el Bachiller Hieronymo de Chaves: el qual añidio muchas figuras tablas, y claras demonstrationes: junctamente con unos breves Scholios, necessarios a mayor illucidation, ornato y perfection del dicho tractado*. Seville.

Checa, Jorge. 1996. Cortes y el espacio de la Conquista: La Segunda carta de relacion. *Modern Language Notes* 111: 187–217.

Chiappelli, Fredi, Michael J. B. Allen, and Robert L. Benson, eds. 1976. *First Images of America: The Impact of the New World on the Old*. 2 vols. Berkeley: University of California Press.

Clendinnen, Inga. 1993. "Fierce and Unnatural Cruelty": Cortés and the Conquest of Mexico. In *New World Encounters*, edited by S. Greenblatt. Berkeley: University of California Press.

Colón, Fernando. 1988. *Descripción y cosmografía de España*. 3 vols. Seville: Padilla Libros.

Concha, Jaime. 1969. El otro Nuevo Mundo. In *Homenaje a Ercilla*, edited by Luis Muñoz
García. Concepción, Chile: University of Concepción, Instituto Central de Lenguas.

Conley, Tom. 1996. *The Self-Made Map: Cartographic Writing in Early Modern France*. Minneapolis:
University of Minnesota Press.

Cortés, Hernán. 1524. *Praeclara Ferdinandi Cortesii de Nova maris Oceani Hyspania Narratio Sacratissimo. ac Invictissimo Carolo Romanorum Imperatori semper Augusto, Hyspaniarum Regi Anno Domini.
M.D.XX. transmissa . . .* Nuremburg.

———. 1993. *Cartas de relación*. Edited by Á. Delgado Gómez. Madrid: Castalia.

———. 2001. *Letters from Mexico*. Translated and edited by A. Pagden. New Haven: Yale
Nota Bene.

Covarrubias Horozco, Sebastián de. 1994. *Tesoro de la lengua castellana o española*. Edited by
F. C. R. Maldonado. Madrid: Castalia.

Crone, G. R. 1962. *Maps and Their Makers. An Introduction to the History of Cartography*. London:
Hutchinson's University Library.

Cuesta Domingo, Mariano. 1983. *Alonso de Santa Cruz y su obra cosmográfica*. Madrid: Consejo
Superior de Investigaciones Científicas.

———. 1992. La cartografía en 'prosa' durante la época de los grandes descubrimientos
americanos. In *Actas del Congreso de Historia del Descubrimiento, 1492–1556*. Madrid: Real
Academia de la Historia.

———. 1998. *La obra cosmográfica y náutica de Pedro de Medina*. Madrid: BCH.

———, ed. 1999. *Descubrimientos y cartografía en la época de Felipe II*. Valladolid: Seminario
Iberoamericano de Descubrimientos y Cartografía.

Cueva, Agustín. 1978. El espejismo heróico de la Conquista (Ensayo de interpretación
de *La Araucana*). *Casa de las Américas* 19 (110): 29–40.

Curtius, Ernst Robert. 1973 [1953]. *European Literature and the Latin Middle Ages*. Translated
by Willard R. Trask. Princeton: Princeton University Press.

Dadson, Trevor J. 1998. *Libros, lectores y lecturas: Estudios sobre bibliotecas particulares españolas del
Siglo de Oro. Instrumenta bibliológica*. Madrid: Arco/Libros.

Dandelet, Thomas James. 2001. *Spanish Rome, 1500–1700*. New Haven: Yale University
Press.

Dati, Giuliano. 1968. *La lettera dell'isole che ha trovato nuovamente il re di Spagna: Poemetto in ottava
rima, Scelta di curiosità letterarie inedite o rare dal secolo XIII al XIX ; disp. 136*. Edited by Gustavo
Uzielli. Reprint of 1873 edition. Bologna: Commissione per i Testi di Lingua.

———. 1991. *Columbus in Italy: An Italian Versification of the Letter on the Discovery of the New World,
with Facsimiles of the Italian and Latin Editions of 1493*. Translated by Martin Davies. London:
British Library.

Davis, Elizabeth B. 2000. *Myth and Identity in the Epic of Imperial Spain*. Columbia: University
of Missouri Press.

Delano Smith, Catherine. 1990. Maps as Art and Science: Maps in Sixteenth-Century
Bibles. *Imago Mundi* 42 : 65–83.

Díaz Cardenas, Luis. 1941. *El conquistador anónimo: Relación de algunas cosas de la Nueva España*.
Mexico City: Editorial America.

Díaz del Castillo, Bernal. 1982. *Historia verdadera de la conquista de la Nueva España*. Edited by
Carmelo Sáenz de Santa María. Madrid: Instituto "Gonzalo Fernández de Oviedo,"
Consejo Superior de Investigaciones Científicas.

Diccionario de Autoridades. 2001. Real Academia Española 1726–1739 [cited September 10, 2001 2001]. Available from http://buscon.rae.es/ntlle/SrvltGUILoginNtlle.

Dilke, Oswald Ashton Wentworth. 1985. *Greek and Roman Maps: Aspects of Greek and Roman Life.* Ithaca, NY: Cornell University Press.

———. 1987. Itineraries and Geographical Maps in the Early and Late Roman Empires. In *Cartography in Prehistoric, Ancient, and Medieval Europe and the Mediterranean,* edited by J. Brian Harley and David Woodward. Chicago: University of Chicago Press.

Dubost, Francis. 1995. Insularités imaginaires et récit médiéval. In *L'insularité thématique et représentations: Actes du colloque international de Saint-Denis de La Réunion, avril 1992,* edited by Carpanin Marimoutou and Jean-Michel Racault. Paris: L'Harmattan.

Dunn, Peter. 1993. *Spanish Picaresque Fiction: A New Literary History.* Ithaca: Cornell University Press.

Durand, José. 1964. El chapetón de Ercilla y la honra Araucana. *Filología* 10: 116–35.

Edgerton, Samuel Y. 1987. From Mental Matrix to Mappamundi to Christian Empire: The Heritage of Ptolemaic Cartography in the Renaissance. In *Art and Cartography: Six Historical Essays,* edited by D. Woodward. Chicago: University of Chicago Press.

Edson, Evelyn. 1997. *Mapping Time and Space: How Medieval Mapmakers Viewed their World.* The British Library Studies in Map History, 1. London: British Library.

Edwards, Clinton R. 1969. Mapping by Questionnaire: An Early Spanish Attempt to Determine New World Geographical Positions. *Imago Mundi* 23 : 17–28.

Elliott, John Huxtable. 1970. *The Old World and the New, 1492–1650.* The Wiles Lectures, 1969. Cambridge: Cambridge University Press.

———. 1984. The Spanish Conquest and Settlement of America. In *The Cambridge History of Latin America,* edited by L. Bethell. Cambridge and New York: Cambridge University Press.

———. 1989a. The Mental World of Hernán Cortés. In *Spain and Its World, 1500–1700.* New Haven: Yale University Press.

———. 1989b. *Spain and Its World, 1500–1700.* New Haven: Yale University Press.

———. 1992. *The Old World and the New, 1492–1650.* New York: Cambridge University Press.

———. 1998. The Seizure of Overseas Territories by the European Powers. In *Theories of Empire, 1450–1800,* edited by D. Armitage. Expanding World, 20. Brookfield, VT: Ashgate.

———. 2001. Cortés, Velásquez and Charles V. In *Letters from Mexico,* edited by A. Pagden. New Haven: Yale Nota Bene.

Enterline, James. 1972. The Southern Continent and the False Strait of Magellan. *Imago Mundi* 26 : 48–59.

Ercilla y Zúñiga, Alonso de. 1993. *La Araucana.* Edited by I. Lerner. Madrid: Cátedra.

Escalante de Mendoza, Juan de. 1985. *Itinerario de navegación de los mares y tierras occidentales 1575.* Madrid: Museo Naval.

Fausett, David. 1993. *Writing the new New World: Imaginary Voyages and Utopias of the Great Southern Land, Utopianism and Communitarianism.* Syracuse, NY: Syracuse University Press.

Fernández de Enciso, Martín. 1948. *Suma de geografía.* Madrid: [n.p.].

———. 1932. *A Brief Summe of Geographie.* Translated by Roger Barlow. Edited by E. G. R. Taylor. London: Hakluyt Society.

Fernández de Medrano, Sebastian. 1686. *Breve descripción del mundo y sus partes ó guia geographica y hidrographica: Dividida en tres libros . . . por el capitán D. Sebastián Fernández de Medrano. . . .* Bruselas: Herederos de Francisco Foppens.

Fernández de Oviedo, Gonzalo. 1959. *Historia general y natural de las Indias.* Biblioteca de autores españoles (Continuación), 117–20. Madrid: Ediciones Atlas.

Fernández-Armesto, Felipe. 1987. *Before Columbus: Exploration and Colonization from the Mediterranean to the Atlantic, 1229–1492.* Philadelphia: University of Pennsylvania Press.

Ferrer Maldonado, Lorenzo. 1626. *Imagen del mundo sobre la esfera, cosmografía, y geografía, teórica de planetas, y arte de navegar. . . .* Alcalá: Juan García y Antonio Duplastre.

Frankl, Victor. 1962. Hernán Cortés y la tradición de las Siete Partidas. *Revista de Historia de América* 53–54:9–74.

———. 1963. Imperio particular e imperio universal en las Cartas de Relación de Hernán Cortés. *Cuadernos Hispanoamericanos* 165:443–82.

Franklin, Wayne. 1979. *Discoverers, Explorers, Settlers: The Diligent Writers of Early America.* Chicago: University of Chicago Press.

Frye, Northrop. 1973. The Encyclopedic Form of the Epic. In *Parnassus Revisited: Modern Critical Essays on the Epic Tradition,* edited by A. Yu. Chicago: American Library Association.

Fuchs, Barbara. 2001. *Mimesis and Empire: The New World, Islam, and European Identities.* Cambridge Studies in Renaissance Literature and Culture, 40. New York: Cambridge University Press.

García de Céspedes, Andrés. 1606. *Regimiento de navegacion mando haser el rei nvestro señor por orden de sv conseio real de las Indias a Andres Garcia de Cespedes sv cosmografo maior, siendo presidente en el dicho consejo el conde de Lemos.* Madrid: Juan de la Cuesta.

Gaylord, Mary Malcolm. 1992. Spain's Renaissance Conquests and the Retroping of Identity. *Journal of Hispanic Philology* 16:125–36.

———. 1996. The True History of Early Modern Writing in Spanish: Some American Reflections. *Modern Language Quarterly* 57 (2):213–25.

Gaylord Randel, Mary. 1978. Metaphor and Fable in Góngora's *Soledad Primera. Revista Hispánica Moderna* 40:97–112.

Gaztañeta, Antonio de. 1692. *Norte de la Navegación hallado por el quadrante de reduccion. . . .* Seville.

Gerbi, Antonello. 1985. *Nature in the New World: From Christopher Columbus to Gonzalo Fernández de Oviedo.* Translated by J. Moyle. Pittsburgh: University of Pittsburgh Press.

Gil Bermejo, Juana. 1963. La geografía de Méjico en las cartas de Cortés. *Revista de Indias* 23 (91–92):123–203.

Gillies, John. 1994. *Shakespeare and the Geography of Difference.* New York: Cambridge University Press.

Girava, Gerónimo. 1556. *Dos libros de cosmographia, compuestos nuevamente por Hieronymo Girava tarraganes.* Milan.

Góngora Marmolejo, Alonso de. 1960. Historia de Chile. In *Crónicas del reino de Chile,* edited by F. E. Barba. Biblioteca de Autores Españoles (Continuación), 131. Madrid: Ediciones Atlas.

Grafton, Anthony, and Nancy Siraisi. 1992. *New Worlds, Ancient Texts: The Power of Tradition and the Shock of Discovery.* Cambridge, MA: Belknap Press.

Greenblatt, Stephen. 1991. *Marvelous Possessions: The Wonder of the World.* Chicago: University of Chicago Press.

Greene, Roland. 1999. *Unrequited Conquests: Love and Empire in the Colonial Americas.* Chicago: University of Chicago Press.

Greene, Thomas. 1963. *The Descent from Heaven: A Study in Epic Continuity.* New Haven: Yale University Press.

Griffin, Clive. 1988. *The Crombergers of Seville: The History of a Printing and Merchant Dynasty.* Oxford: Clarendon Press.

Hagstrum, Jean H. 1958. *The Sister Arts: The Tradition of Literary Pictorialism and English Poetry from Dryden to Gray.* Chicago: University of Chicago Press.

Hanke, Lewis. 1952. *Bartolome de las Casas, Historian: An Essay in Spanish Historiography.* Gainesville: University of Florida Press.

———. 1959. *Aristotle and the American Indians: A Study of Race and Prejudice in the Modern World.* Bloomington: University of Indiana Press.

Harley, J. B., and Paul Laxton. 2001. *The New Nature of Maps: Essays in the History of Cartography.* Baltimore: Johns Hopkins University Press.

Harley, J. Brian, and David Woodward, eds. 1987. *Cartography in Prehistoric, Ancient, and Medieval Europe and the Mediterranean.* Preface by J. Brian Harley. The History of Cartography, 1. Chicago: University of Chicago Press.

Harvey, David. 1990. *The Condition of Postmodernity: An Enquiry into the Origins of Cultural Change.* Cambridge: Blackwell.

Harvey, P. D. A. 1980. *The History of Topographical Maps: Symbols, Pictures and Surveys.* London and New York: Thames and Hudson.

———. 1987a. Local and Regional Cartography in Medieval Europe. In *Cartography in Prehistoric, Ancient, and Medieval Europe and the Mediterranean,* edited by J. Brian Harley and David Woodward. Chicago: University of Chicago Press.

———. 1987b. Medieval Maps: An Introduction. In *Cartography in Prehistoric, Ancient, and Medieval Europe and the Mediterranean,* edited by J. Brian Harley and David Woodward. Chicago: University of Chicago Press.

Hernando, Agustín. 1995. *El mapa de España. Siglos XV–XVIII.* Madrid: Centro Nacional de Información Geográfica.

———. 1999. The Spanish Contribution to the History of Cartography. *Cartographic Journal* 36 (2):111–23.

Herrera, Fernando de. 1985. *Poesía castellana original completa.* Edited by Cristóbal Cuevas. Madrid: Cátedra.

———. 2001. *Anotaciones a la poesía de Garcilaso.* Edited by Inoria Pepe y José María Reyes. Letras Hispánicas, 516 Madrid: Cátedra.

Hillis, Ken. 1994. The Power of Disembodied Imagination: Perspective's Role in Cartography. *Cartographica* 31 (3):1–17.

Huggan, Graham. 1994. *Territorial Disputes: Maps and Mapping Strategies in Contemporary Canadian and Australian Fiction.* Toronto: University of Toronto Press.

Hulme, Peter. 1992. *Colonial Encounters: Europe and the Native Caribbean, 1492–1797.* London and New York: Routledge.

Iglesia, Ramón. 1942. *Cronistas e historiadores de la conquista de México: El ciclo de Hernán Cortés.* Centro de Estudios Históricos Nueva Serie, 31. Mexico City: Colegio de México.

Ingram, Elizabeth M. 1993. Maps as Readers' Aids: Maps and Plans in Geneva Bibles. *Imago Mundi* 45:29–44.

Jacob, Christian. 1992. *L'empire des cartes: Approche théorique de la cartographie à travers l'histoire*. Paris: Albin Michel.

Janni, Pietro. 1985. *La mappa i el periplo: Cartografia antica e spazio odologico*. Rome: Giorgio Bretschneider.

Joseph Fischer, SJ, and Franz von Wieser, SJ, eds. 1907. *The Cosmographiae Introductio of Martin Waldseemüller in facsimile*. New York: U.S. Catholic Historical Society.

Kadir, Djelal. 1992. *Columbus and the Ends of the Earth: Europe's Prophetic Rhetoric as Conquering Ideology*. Berkeley: University of California Press.

Kagan, Richard. 2000. *Urban Images of the Hispanic World, 1493–1793*. New Haven: Yale University Press.

———. 2002. *Arcana Imperii: Maps, Knowledge, and Power at the Court of Philip IV*. In *El atlas del rey planeta: la descripción de España y de las costas y puertos de sus reinos*, by Pedro Texeira Albernaz. Madrid: Nerea Editorial.

Keen, Benjamin. 1971. *The Aztec Image in Western Thought*. New Brunswick, NJ: Rutgers University Press.

King, Willard. 1979. Numancia and Imperial Spain. *Modern Language Notes* 94 : 207–14.

Kolodny, Annette. 1975. *The Lay of the Land: Metaphor as Experience and History in American Life and Letters*. Chapel Hill: University of North Carolina Press.

Krieger, Murray. 1967. The Ekphrastic Principle and the Still Moment of Poetry; or Laokoön Revisited. In *The Play and Place of Criticism*. Baltimore: Johns Hopkins University Press.

———. 1992. *Ekphrasis: The Illusion of the Natural Sign*. Baltimore: Johns Hopkins University Press.

Kupperman, Karen Ordahl, ed. 1995. *America in the European Consciousness, 1493–1750*. Chapel Hill: University of North Carolina Press for the Institute of Early American History and Culture, Williamsburg, VA.

Lagos, Ramona. 1981. El incumplimiento de la programación épica en *La Araucana*. *Cuadernos Americanos* 40 (238): 157–91.

Lamb, Ursula. 1969. Science by Litigation: A Cosmographic Feud. *Terrae Incognitae* 1 : 40–57.

———. 1976. Cosmographers of Seville: Nautical Science and Social Experience. In *First Images of America: The Impact of the New World on the Old*, edited by Fredi Chiappelli, Michael J. B. Allen, and Robert L. Benson. Berkeley: University of California Press.

———. 1995. *Cosmographers and Pilots of the Spanish Maritime Empire*. Collected Studies Series, CS499. London and Brookfield, VT: Variorum.

Landau, David, and Peter Parshall. 1994. *The Renaissance Print, 1470–1550*. New Haven: Yale University Press.

Lapidge, Michael. 1979. Lucan's Imagery of Cosmic Dissolution. *Hermes* 107 : 344–70.

Larner, John. 1999. *Marco Polo and the Discovery of the World*. New Haven: Yale University Press.

Law, John. 1986. On the Methods of Long-Distance Control: Vessels, Navigation, and the Portuguese Route to India. In *Power, Action, and Belief: A New Sociology of Knowledge?* edited by J. Law. Sociological Review Monograph, 32. London and Boston: Routledge & Kegan Paul.

Lefebvre, Henri. 1991. *The Production of Space*. Translated by D. Nicholson-Smith. Cambridge: Blackwell.

Lerner, Isaías. 1991. America en la poesía épica aurea: La versión de Ercilla. *Edad de Oro* 10 : 125–40.

Lestringant, Frank. 1991. *L'atelier du cosmographe; ou, L'image du monde à la Renaissance*. Paris: Albin Michel.

———. 1993a. *Écrire le monde à la Renaissance: Quinze études sur Rabelais, Postel, Bodin et la littérature géographique*. Caen: Éditions du Paradigme.

———. 1993b. Europe et théorie des climats dans la second moitié du XVIe siècle. In *Écrire le monde à la Renaissance: Quinze études sur Rabelais, Postel, Bodin et la littérature géographique*. Caen: Éditions du Paradigme.

———. 1994. *Mapping the Renaissance World: The Geographical Imagination in the Age of Discovery*. Translated by D. Fausett. Oxford: Polity Press.

Lewes, Darby. 2000. *Nudes from Nowhere: Utopian Sexual Landscapes*. Lanham, MD: Rowman & Littlefield.

Lewis, Martin W., and Kären E. Wigen. 1997. *The Myth of the Continents: A Critique of Metageography*. Berkeley: University of California Press.

Lewis, Robert Earl. 1983. The Humanistic Historiography of Francisco López de Gómara (1511–1559). Ph.D. diss., University of Texas at Austin.

Libro de Alexandre. 1988. Edited by Jesús Cañas Murillo. Letras Hispánicas, 280. Madrid: Cátedra.

Lida de Malkiel, María Rosa. 1950. *Juan de Mena, poeta del prerrenacimiento español*. Publications of the *Nueva Revista de Filología Hispánica*, 1. Mexico City: El Colegio de México.

Loesberg, Jonathan. 1983. Narratives of Authority: Cortés, Gómara, Díaz. *Prose Studies* 6: 239–63.

López de Gómara, Francisco. 1964. *Cortés: The Life of the Conqueror by His Secretary*. Translated and edited by Lesley Byrd Simpson. Berkeley: University of California Press.

———. 1979. *Historia general de las Indias y vida de Hernán Cortés*. Edited by J. G. Lacroix. Caracas: Biblioteca Ayacucho.

———. 1987. *La conquista de México*. Edited by José Luis de Rojas. 1st ed. Crónicas de América, 36. Madrid: Historia 16.

López Piñero, José María. 1979. *Ciencia y técnica en la sociedad española de los siglos XVI y XVII*. Barcelona: Labor.

———. 1986. *El arte de navegar en la España del Renacimiento*. 2d ed. Barcelona: Editorial Labor.

Lucan. 1928. *The Civil War*. Translated by J. D. Duff. Loeb Classical Library. New York: G. P. Putnam's Sons.

Lucian of Samosata. 1990. *Satirical Sketches*. 1st Midland Book edition. Translated by Paul Turner. Bloomington: Indiana University Press.

Mackay, Ruth. 1999. *The Limits of Royal Authority: Resistance and Obedience in Seventeenth-Century Castile*. Cambridge Studies in Early Modern History. New York: Cambridge University Press.

Maravall, José Antonio. 1966. *Antiguos y modernos*. Madrid: Sociedad de Estudios y Publicaciones.

———. 1972. *Estado moderno y mentalidad social (siglos XV a XVII)*. 2 vols. Madrid: Ediciones de la Revista de Occidente.

———. 1981. *El concepto de España en la Edad Media*. 3d ed. Madrid: Centro de Estudios Constitucionales.

Marcus, Raymond. 1977. La conquete de Cholula: Conflit d'interpretations. *Ibero-Amerikanisches Archiv* 3: 193–213.

Martín-Merás, Luisa. 1992. *Cartografía marítima hispánica: La imagen de América.* Madrid: Lunwerg for Ministerio de Obras Públicas, Transportes y Medio Ambiente.

Martínez, Jose L. 1990. *Hernán Cortés.* Mexico City: UNAM, Fondo de Cultura Económica.

Martínez-Loza, Abel. 1990. Las ideas geográficas de Hernán Cortes. *Anuario de Estudios Americanos* 47 : 3–26.

McAlister, Lyle N. 1984. *Spain and Portugal in the New World, 1492–1700.* 10 vols. Edited by B. C. Shafer. Vol. 3 of *Europe and the World in the Age of Expansion.* Minneapolis: University of Minnesota Press.

Martyr d'Anghera, Peter. 1970. *De Orbe Novo: The Eight Decades.* 2 vols. Edited and translated by Francis Augustus MacNutt. New York: Burt Franklin.

Medina, José Toribio. 1928. Las mujeres de *La Araucana* de Ercilla. *Hispania* 11 (1): 1–12.

———. 1952. *Ensayo bio-bibliográfico sobre Hernán Cortés. Obra póstuma.* 1st ed. Santiago de Chile: Fondo Histórico y Bibliográfico José Toribio Medina.

Medina, Pedro de. 1944. *Libro de grandezas y cosas memorables de España,* Clásicos Españoles I. Obras de Pedro de Medina. Madrid: Consejo Superior de Investigaciones Científicas.

Melón, Amando. 1950. La geografía de M. Fernández Enciso (1519). *Estudios Geográficos* 11 (38): 29–43.

Mena, Juan de. 1994. *Laberinto de fortuna y otros poemas.* Edited by C. d. Nigris. Biblioteca Clásica, 14. Barcelona: Crítica.

Menéndez Pidal, Ramón. 1949. Poesia e historia en el *Mio Cid:* El problema de la épica española. *Nueva Revisita de Filología Hispánica* 3 (2): 113–29.

———. 1951. *Los españoles en la historia y en la literatura.* Buenos Aires: Espasa-Calpe Argentina.

Merrim, Stephanie. 1984. 'Un mare magno e oculto': Anatomy of Fernández de Oviedo's *Historia general y natural de las Indias. Revista de Estudios Hispánicos* [Puerto Rico] 11 : 101–20.

———. 1988. Writing a Book of the World: Fernández de Oviedo and Guimarães Rosa. In *Selected Proceedings of the Thirty-Fifth Annual Mountain Interstate Foreign Language Conference.* Johnson City: Research Council of East Tennessee State University.

———. 1989. The Apprehension of the New in Nature and Culture: Fernández de Oviedo's *Sumario. Hispanic Issues* 4 : 165–99.

———. 1996. The First Fifty Years of Hispanic New World Historiography: The Caribbean, Mexico, and Central America. In *The Cambridge History of Latin American Literature,* edited by R. González Echevarría and E. Pupo-Walker. Cambridge and New York: Cambridge University Press.

Messmer, Hans. 1982. Menéndez Pidal y la Reconquista, su ideología y realidad. In *Actas del coloquio hispano-alemán Ramón Menéndez Pidal,* edited by Wido Hempel y Dietrich Briesemeister. Tübingen: Max Niemeyer Verlag.

Mexía, Pedro, and Margaret Lois Mulroney. 1930. *Diálogos o coloquios of Pedro Mejía,* Studies in Spanish Languages and Literature, 1. Iowa City: University of Iowa.

Mignolo, Walter. 1991. Colonial Situations, Geographical Discourses and Territorial Representations: Toward a Diatopical Understanding of Colonial Semiosis. *Dispositio* 14 (36–38): 93–140.

———. 1995. *The Darker Side of the Renaissance: Literacy, Territoriality and Colonization.* Ann Arbor: University of Michigan Press.

Milton, John. 1851. A Manifesto of the Lord Protector of the Commonwealth of England, Scotland, Ireland, &c. Published by Consent and Advice of His Council. Wherein is shown the Reasonableness of the Cause of this Republic Against the Depredations of the Spaniards. In *The Prose Works of John Milton*, edited by R. W. Griswold. Philadelphia: J. W. Moore.

Mitchell, W. J. T. 1994. *Picture Theory*. Chicago: University of Chicago Press.

Montrose, Louis. 1993. The Work of Gender in the Discourse of Discovery. In *New World Encounters*, edited by S. Greenblatt. Berkeley: University of California.

Mundy, Barbara. 1996. *The Mapping of New Spain: Indigenous Cartography and the Maps of the Relaciones Geográficas*. Chicago: University of Chicago Press.

———. 1998. Mapping the Aztec Capital: The 1524 Nuremburg Map of Tenochtitlan, Its Sources and Meanings. *Imago Mundi* 50 : 11–33.

Mustapha, Monique. 1979. Geographie et humanisme: Note sur la structure de la *Historia general de las Indias* de Francisco Lopez de Gomara. In *Les Cultures ibériques en devenir: Essais publiés en hommage à la mémoire de Marcel Bataillon (1895–1977)*, edited by C. A. Georges Duby, Jacques Lafaye, and Jorge Guillen. Paris: Fondation Singer-Polignac.

———. 1994. Le Statut de l'episode colombien dans la *Historia General de las Indias* de Francisco López de Gómara. In *Christophe Colomb et la découverte de l'Amerique: Réalités, imaginaire et réinterprétations*, edited by José Guidi and Monica Mustapha. Aix-en-Provence: Publications de l'Université de Provence.

Nebrija, Antonio de. 1992. *Gramática de la lengua castellana*. Edited by Antonio Quilis and Manuel Alvar. Madrid: Ediciones de Cultura Hispánica.

Nicolopulos, James R. 2000. *The Poetics of Empire in the Indies: Prophecy and Imitation in "La Araucana" and "Os Lusíadas."* University Park: Pennsylvania State University Press.

O'Gorman, Edmundo. 1951. *La idea del descubrimiento de América*. Mexico City: Centro de Estudios Filosóficos.

———. 1967. Preliminary Study. In *Apologética historia sumaria*, by Bartolomé de las Casas. Mexico City: UNAM, Instituto de Investigaciones Históricas.

———. 1972. *Cuatro historiadores de Indias, siglo XVI*. 1st ed. SepSetentas, 51. Mexico City: Secretaría de Educación Pública.

———. 1986. *La invención de América*. Mexico City: Fondo de Cultura Económica.

Ong, Walter. 1988. *Orality and Literacy*. New York: Routledge.

Ortelius, Abraham. 1964. *Theatrum orbis terrarum* . Edited by R. A. Skelton, Facsimile edition. Amsterdam: N. Israel.

Padrón, Ricardo. 1997. Travels without a Hippogriff: Empire, Cartography, and Literature in Early Modern Spain. Ph.D. diss., Harvard University.

———. 2000. Love American Style: The Virgin Land and the Sodomitic Body in Ercilla's *Araucana*. *Revista de Estudios Hispánicos* 34 : 563–86.

Pagden, Anthony. 1986. *The Fall of Natural Man: The American Indian and the Origins of Comparative Ethnology*. 1st pbk. edition with corrections and additions. Cambridge and New York: Cambridge University Press.

———. 1990. *Spanish Imperialism and the Political Imagination: Studies in European and Spanish-American Social and Political Theory, 1513–1830*. New Haven: Yale University Press.

———. 1993. *European Encounters with the New World from Renaissance to Romanticism*. New Haven: Yale University Press.

———, ed. 2001. Introduction to *Letters from Mexico*, edited by A. Pagden. New Haven: Yale Nota Bene.

Parker, Geoffrey. 1992. Maps and Ministers: The Spanish Hapsburgs. In *Monarchs, Ministers and Maps*, edited by D. Buisseret. Chicago: University of Chicago Press.

———. 1998. *The Grand Strategy of Philip II*. New Haven: Yale University Press.

———. 2002. *Success Is Never Final: Empire, War, and Faith in Early Modern Europe*. New York: Basic Books.

Pastor, Beatriz. 1992. *The Armature of Conquest: Spanish Accounts of the Discovery of America, 1492–1589*. Translated by L. L. Hunt. Stanford: Stanford University Press.

Pérez Bustamante, Ciriaco. 1952. El lascasismo en *La Araucana*. *Revista de Estudios Políticos* 46 : 157–68.

Pérez de Moya, Juan. 1573. *Tratado de cosas de Astronomía y Cosmographia y Philosophia Natural ordenado por Iuan Perez de Moya*. Alcalá: Iuan Gracián.

Pierce, Frank. 1968. *La poesía épica española del Siglo de Oro*. Translated by J. C. C. d. Bethencourt. 2d. ed. Madrid: Gredos.

———. 1984. *Alonso de Ercilla y Zuniga*. Biblioteca Hispanoamericana y Española de Amsterdam, 4. Amsterdam: Rodopi.

Pliny. 1938. *Natural History*. The Loeb Classical Library. Trans. Harris Rackham, W. H. S. Jones, and D. E. Eichholz Cambridge, MA: Harvard University Press.

Podossinov, Alexander V., and Leonid S. Checkin. 1991. Extended review of *The History of Cartography* edited by J. Brian Harley and David Woodward. *Imago Mundi* 43 : 112–23.

Polo, Marco. 1993. *The Travels of Marco Polo: The Complete Yule-Cordier Edition*. 2 vols. New York: Dover.

Puente y Olea, Manuel de la. 1900. *Los trabajos geográficos de la Casa de la Contratación*. Seville: Escuela Tipográfica y Librería Salesianas.

Pulido Rubio, José. 1950. *El piloto mayor de la Casa de la Contratación de Sevilla*. Seville: Escuela de Estudios Hispano-Americanos.

Quint, David. 1994. *Epic and Empire: Politics and Generic Form from Virgil to Milton*. Princeton: Princeton University Press.

Rabasa, Jose. 1987. Dialogue as Conquest: Mapping Spaces for Counter-Discourse. *Cultural Critique* 6 : 131–59.

———. 1993. *Inventing America: Spanish Historiography and the Formation of Eurocentrism*. Norman and London: University of Oklahoma Press.

Racault, Jean-Michel. 1995. Avant-Propos: De la définition de l'île à la thématique insulaire. In *L'insularité thématique et représentations: Actes du colloque international de Saint-Denis de La Réunion, avril 1992*, edited by Carpanin Marimoutou and Jean-Michel Racault. Paris: L'Harmattan.

Restrepo, Luis Fernando. 1999. *Un nuevo reino imaginado: Las Elegías de varones ilustres de Indias de Juan de Castellanos*. Bogotá: Instituto de Cultura Hispánica.

———. 2002. Sacred and Imperial Topographies in Juan de Castellano's *Elegías de varones ilustres de Indias*. In *Mapping Colonial Spanish America: Places and Commonplaces of Identity, Culture, and Experience*. Edited by Santa Arias and Mariselle Meléndez. Lewisburg: Bucknell University Press and London: Associated University Presses.

Rico, Francisco. 1970. *El pequeño mundo del hombre: Varia fortuna de una idea en las letras españolas*. Madrid: Editorial Castalia.

Rivers, Elias L., ed. 1991. *Poesía lírica del siglo de oro*. Madrid: Cátedra.

Roa-de-la-Carrera, Cristián Andrés. 1998. La historiografía del descubrimiento en *La Histo-ria de las Indias* de Francisco López de Gómara. Ph.D. diss., Princeton University.

Robinson, Arthur Howard, and Barbara Bartz Petchenik. 1976. *The Nature of Maps: Essays toward Understanding Maps and Mapping.* Chicago: University of Chicago Press.

Rojas, Fernando de. 1989. *La Celestina.* Edited by D. Severin. Madrid: Cátedra.

Romer, Frank E. 1998. *Pomponius Mela's Description of the World.* Ann Arbor: University of Michigan Press.

Romm, James S. 1992. *The Edges of the Earth in Ancient Thought: Geography, Exploration, and Fiction.* Princeton: Princeton University Press.

Royer, Alphonse. 1879. *Étude Littéraire sur "L'Araucana" d'Ercilla.* Dijon.

Ruiz Pérez, Pedro. 1996. *El espacio de la escritura: En torno a una poética del espacio del texto barroco.* Perspectivas Hispánicas. Bern: Lang.

Ryan, Michael T. 1981. Assimilating New Worlds in the Sixteenth and Seventeenth Centuries. *Comparative Studies in Society and History* 23 (4): 519–38.

Said, Edward. 1978. *Orientalism.* New York: Random House.

———. 1993. *Culture and Imperialism.* 1st ed. New York: Knopf.

Salas, Alberto M. 1986. *Tres cronistas de Indias: Pedro Mártir de Anglería; Gonzalo Fernández de Oviedo; Fray Bartolomé de las Casas.* Mexico City: Fondo de Cultura Económica.

Sánchez Albornoz, Claudio. 1983. *La Edad Media española y la empresa de América.* Madrid: Ediciones Cultura Hispánica.

Sandman, Alison. 2001. Cosmographers versus Pilots: Navigation, Cosmography, and the State in Early Modern Spain. Ph.D. diss., University of Wisconsin at Madison.

Schulz, Juergen. 1990. *La cartografia tra scienza et arte: Carti e cartografi nel Renascimiento italiano.* Modena: F.C. Panini.

Schwartz Lerner, Lía. 1972. Tradición literaria y heroinas indias en *La Araucana. Revista Iberoamericana* 38 (81): 615–26.

Scott, Grant F. 1991. The Rhetoric of Dilation: Ekphrasis and Ideology. *Word and Image: A Journal of Verbal / Visual Enquiry* 7 (4): 301–10.

Shirley, Rodney W. 1983. *The Mapping of the World: Early Printed Maps, 1472–1700.* Holland Press Cartographica Series, 9. London: Holland Press.

Sobel, Dava. 1995. *Longitude: The True Story of a Lone Genius Who Solved the Greatest Scientific Problem of His Time.* New York: Walker.

Sobel, Dava, and William J. H. Andrewes. 1998. *The Illustrated Longitude.* New York: Walker.

Strabo. 1923. *The Geography of Strabo.* 8 vols. Loeb Classical Library, 2. New York: G.P. Putnam's Sons.

Taylor, Eva G. R. 1932. Introduction to *A Brief Summe of Geographie,* translated by Roger Barlow and edited by E. G. R. Taylor. London: Hakluyt Society.

———. 1971. *The Haven-Finding Art: A History of Navigation from Odysseus to Captain Cook.* New augmented edition. London: Hollis and Carter for the Institute of Navigation.

Thongchai, Winichakul. 1994. *Siam Mapped: A History of the Geo-Body of a Nation.* Honolulu: University of Hawaii Press.

Thrower, Norman J. W. 1996. *Maps and Civilization: Cartography in Culture and Society.* Chicago: University of Chicago Press.

Todorov, Tzvetan. 1984. *The Conquest of America: The Question of the Other.* Translated by R. Howard. New York: Harper Perennial.

Toussaint, Manuel, Federico Goméz de Orozco, and Justino Fernández 1938. *Planos de la Ciudad de México: Siglos XVI y XVII. Estudio histórico, urbanístico y bibliográfico.* Mexico City: "Cvltvra."

Tuan, Yi-Fu. 1977. *Space and Place: The Perspective of Experience.* Minneapolis: University of Minnesota Press.

Turnbull, David. 1996. Cartography and Science in Early Modern Europe: Mapping the Construction of Knowledge Spaces. *Imago Mundi* 48 : 5–24.

Turner, Daymond. 1964. Gonzalo Fernández de Oviedo's *Historia general y natural de las Indias: The First American Encyclopedia. Journal of Inter-American Studies* 6 : 267–74.

————. 1985. Forgotten Treasure from the Indies: The Illustrations and Drawings of Fernández de Oviedo. *Huntington Library Quarterly* 48 : 1–46.

Vega, Garcilaso de la, and Bienvenido Morros. 1995. *Obra poética y textos en prosa.* Biblioteca clásica, 27. Barcelona: Crítica.

Vergil. 1909. *The Aeneid.* Translated by J. Dryden. Edited by C. W. Eliot. Harvard Classics, 13. New York: P. F. Collier and Son.

Veyne, Paul. 1984. *The Writing of History.* Translated by M. Moore-Rinvolucri. Middletown, CT: Wesleyan University Press.

Vicente Maroto, M. I., and Mariano Esteban Piñeiro. 1991. *Aspectos de la ciencia aplicada en la España del Siglo de Oro.* Estudios de Histoira de la Ciencia y de la Técnica 5. Madrid: Junta de Castilla y León.

Vila, Juan Diego. 1992. El personaje de Tegualda y su doble iniciación (histórica y poética) en *La Araucana* de Ercilla. *Signos* 25 (31–32):213–25.

Vindel, Francisco. 1955. *Mapas de América en los libros españoles de los siglos XVI al XVIII* (1503–1798). Madrid: [Gongora].

Wagner, Henry A. 1944. *The Rise of Fernando Cortés.* Documents and Narratives Concerning the Discovery and Conquest of Latin America, n.s., 3. Berkeley: University of California Press.

Waters, David Watkin. 1958. *The Art of Navigation in England in Elizabethan and Early Stuart Times.* New Haven: Yale University Press.

Watson, Anthony. 1971. *Juan de la Cueva and the Portuguese Succession.* London: Tamesis.

White, Hayden. 1973. *Metahistory: The Historical Imagination in Nineteenth-Century Europe.* Baltimore: Johns Hopkins University Press.

————. 1978. *Tropics of Discourse: Essays in Cultural Criticism.* Baltimore: Johns Hopkins University Press.

————. 1988. *The Content of the Form.* Baltimore: Johns Hopkins University Press.

White, John Manchip. 1971. *Cortés and the Downfall of the Aztec Empire.* New York: Carroll and Graf.

Wood, Denis, and John Fels. 1992. *The Power of Maps.* London: Guilford Press.

Woodward, David. 1987. Medieval *Mappaemundi.* In *Cartography in Prehistoric, Ancient, and Medieval Europe and the Mediterranean,* edited by J. Brian Harley and David Woodward. Chicago: University of Chicago Press.

————. 1991. Maps and the Rationalization of Geographic Space. In *Circa 1492: Art in the Age of Exploration,* edited by J. A. Levenson. New Haven: Yale University Press.

————, ed. Forthcoming. *Cartography in the European Renaissance*. The History of Cartography, 3. Chicago: University of Chicago Press.

Yates, Frances. 1966. *The Art of Memory*. Chicago: University of Chicago Press.

Zerubavel, Eviatar. 1992. *Terra Cognita: The Mental Discovery of America*. New Brunswick, NJ: Rutgers University Press.

Zumthor, Paul. 1993. *La mesure du monde: Représentation de l'espace au moyen âge*. Paris: Éditions du Seuil.

————. 1994. *La medida del mundo: Representación del espacio en la Edad Media*. Translated by A. Martorell. Madrid: Cátedra.

INDEX

abstract space, 35, 36, 82–84; emergence of, 142, 143
Acosta, José de, 21, 164, 190, 192
Actium, battle of, 200
Agnese, Battista, 3; Charles V portolan atlas, 2–7
Agnese map of the world, 1–7, 9, 187, 203
Aguilar, Fray Francisco de, 102
Altatlauca-Malinaltepec, *Relación geográfica de*, 76–78
Alvarado, Pedro de, 115
America: continental status of, 27–29, 163–168; discovery of, 168, 169; geography of, 26–29, 145, 147, 155, 163, 164, 179, 183, 184; insularity of, 26, 27, 155, 163–173, 179, 180; invention of, 12–32, 116, 124, 138, 167, 169, 170, 186, 219, 222, 230, 235; maps of, 118, 125–131, 136, 138–140, 145, 146, 154, 155; named, 20; as paradise, 175, 178, 217, 218; as political entity, 98
Amerindians, 164–168, 188
Antonelli, Giovanni Battista, 63, 64, 73
Apologética historia sumaria, 21; America as paradise, 175, 178; American insularity in, 179, 180; Amerindian culture in, 174–179; cartographic history in, 205; climatic zones in, 179–181; Columbus in, 176;

compared with *Historia general de las Indias*, 175, 176, 179; compared with *Historia general y natural de las Indias*, 175; geographical description in, 180, 181; Hispaniola in, 175–180; imperialism in, 178, 180; itinerary in, 176, 178; narrative voice in, 176, 177; prose cartography in, 174–183; structure of, 175
La Araucana, 3, 44, 75, 183–231; America as literary genre in, 185, 186; Araucanians, depiction of, 188, 200, 202; Arauco, 215–218, 222; *axis mundi*, 212; Battle of Lepanto, 198–205; Battle of Millarpue, 199–201, 206, 209; Battle of Penco, 199–201; Battle of San Quentin, 203, 205; battle topography in, 196, 197; brutality in, 196, 197, 201–202, 215–217; Cariolano, 213; as *carta de relación*, 217; cartographic history in, 205; cartographic strategies of, 198; Caupolicán, 195, 215–217; Chacao Channel episode, 225, 226; chorography, 223; circumnavigation in, 187; colonial desire in, 194–202, 207, 213–218, 228, 229; compression of space in, 203, 205; conception of space in, 97; conquest allegories, 218; counter-cartography in, 192, 195, 197, 199, 219, 229; Don Juan of Austria, 200;

281